CW00344227

SIGHTLINES
A Stadium Odyssey

By the same author

Villa Park – 100 Years
The Football Grounds of Britain
The Football Grounds of Europe
League Football and the Men Who Made It – the Official Centenary History of the Football League
Soccer in the Dock – a History of British Soccer Scandals
Soccer Skills, Tricks and Tactics
Guide to Safety at Sports Grounds (editor)

Anthologies:
Saturday's Boys
Perfect Pitch

SIGHTLINES
A Stadium Odyssey

SIMON INGLIS

YELLOW JERSEY PRESS
LONDON

Published by Yellow Jersey 2000

2 4 6 8 10 9 7 5 3 1

First published in Great Britain in 2000 by
Yellow Jersey
Random House, 20 Vauxhall Bridge Road,
London SW1V 2SA

Random House Australia (Pty) Limited
20 Alfred Street, Milsons Point, Sydney,
New South Wales 2061, Australia

Random House New Zealand Limited
18 Poland Road, Glenfield,
Auckland 10, New Zealand

Random House (Pty) Limited
Endulini, 5A Jubilee Road, Parktown, 2193, South Africa

The Random House Group Limited Reg. No. 954009
www.randomhouse.co.uk

A CIP catalogue record for this book
is available from the British Library

ISBN 0 224 059688

Papers used by Random House are natural,
recyclable products made from wood grown in sustainable forests.
The manufacturing processes conform to the environmental
regulations of the country of origin

Printed and bound in Great Britain by
Biddles Ltd, Guildford and King's Lynn

CONTENTS

ACKNOWLEDGEMENTS

As well as to those named within the text, sincere thanks for support, succour, hospitality and advice go to the Bresnik and Chiswick families, Mark Corby, all the Elevators, Nick Hanna, Andy Hansen, Gerald Jacobs, Camilla Jerrard, Katie Kollisias, the Krasnov family, Bassan Mahfouz, Marcela Mora y Araujo, Judi Miles, Ivan and Mary Moseley, the Platt family, Julian Radley at Panstadia, Dr Tony Spawforth, John Williams and Martin and Claudia Tasker.

Special thanks also go to staff at the Beirut *Daily Star*, to Tracy Johnston at the New Zealand Media Resource Unit and to everyone at HOK+Lobb.

I must also add extra special thanks to Justine for her life-saving e-missives; to my agent Robert Kirby, for taking me seriously, and to my ever patient and wise editor at Yellow Jersey, Rachel Cugnoni.

Finally, to my best pal and beloved Jackie, thanks for everything and more.

To Wendy, Harold and Judith,
and in memory of Jonathan

PROLOGUE: PANEM ET CIRCENSES

In the consulship of Priscus and Commodus [AD 78].
Vicarius of Rome to his friend Anorakos of Elis.
Greetings!

To you, my fond Greekling and your household, I offer a Roman's belated gratitude for the shelter proffered during the Olympic festival of last year. You were too kind.

We talked often during the games of the traditions of the stadium and of the trials we spectators must endure. I now bring news of developments in Rome. Since the fire, there are so many new edifices, so many wonders to behold; fountains, streets, baths, arcades; and yet – I know not how to write it in Greek – *e pluribus unum.*

Truly, a new wonder is here in the making.

Anorakos, I shall be frank. For all you pederasts who quiver at the sight of naked youths cavorting in the dust of those shallow pits you Greeks call stadiums, understand that this new marvel in Rome promises to be the acme of popular entertainment and, by Jupiter, I declare it shall be the death of athletics, and of many a gladiator and felon too! Though it is not yet completed, I have been spying on its construction, and can scarcely contain my admiration.

The building can be called neither a stadium nor a circus, for it shall be fully enclosed and oval in shape, and its arena will be too small for chariots. Instead the bills are calling it the 'amphitheatre' because it is like two theatres cojoined, face to face. Such buildings exist elsewhere in the Empire, though all on a lesser scale. I have seen two on my travels, in Arelate, which is in Gallia, and in Pompeii, that beauteous Italian city watched over by the magnificent Vesuvius.

But some old fellows I met around the construction site have since told me many interesting stories of earlier 'amphitheatres' in Rome, and since I know you Greeks cannot resist a historical treatise, I thought to write some of them here and now for your edification.

Over a century ago, before our imperial masters put the Senate in its proper place and delivered us all from cursed politics, our theatres were primitive, wooden affairs, built for a season of performances and then dismantled (if fire did not destroy them first).

Imagine this, Anorakos. In bygone days members of the audience often had to stand up throughout entire performances, for it was argued by the self-appointed arbiters of the public good that if seats were provided citizens would fall into idle ways and never leave the theatre. Spartans and catamites, the lot of them! They just hated to see a man's rump put to its proper use.

An ostentatious senator, Marcus Aemilius Scaurus, stepson of Sulla, apparently sponsored the first permanent theatre in Rome. This was said to have been a lavish structure of marble, glass and wood, able to accommodate 80,000 people. If so, I suspect the majority must have been tourists, for there have surely never been that many true Romans willing to patronise mere drama.

A few years after Scaurus, another foolish fellow, called Gaius Scribonius Curio, embarked upon a scheme remembered even today for its, shall I say, 'curiosity'. Lacking great wealth, but anxious to further his political career at a time of unrest in the Republic, Curio built not one wooden theatre, but two. If that were not unusual enough, he sited the theatres back to back. In the morning, each one offered its own entertainments, undisturbed by the other. Then, and here is the wonder, a signal was given and the two structures, each a half-circle with 20,000 spectators still in their seats, swivelled round on a series of pivots, so that stage met stage, corners met corners, and a single, round amphitheatre was thus formed, ready for Curio's gladiators to enter the fray. *Sui generis*, Anorakos, you must surely concede.

Sceptics at the time marvelled that any sensible citizen, not least a Roman, Conqueror of the Earth, should risk himself in such a rickety contraption. But the wits declared Curio's political intentions to be quite obvious: he wished to impress the swaying voters!

Alas, after a few performances the pivots failed, leaving the two theatres joined for ever at the hip like man and wife, and, *ergo*, devoid of all novelty to the world or to each other. (I know not if this tale of Curio's contraption be true, though it has been written as such. But then who can trust the contents of a book?)

Years after Curio, there was an amphitheatrical catastrophe during the time of Tiberius. Death in the arena is normally a sight to be welcomed and, more, celebrated. It is how we Romans learn fortitude in battle. But in a town call Fidenae, hardly a day's ride from Rome, there appeared one of many itinerant gladiators intent upon profit, who erected a wooden amphitheatre on ground too marshy to bear the weight. It is said that more than 4,000 spectators perished in the subsequent collapse. Some say as many as 20,000, while others bid higher still at 50,000, although this I cannot believe.

In response to the calamity, the Senate decreed that no man with less than 400,000 sesterces to his name be permitted to stage shows. But in any case this was over sixty years ago, and our great builders have learnt much in the interim, both about construction in stone and the arrangement in general of buildings for public entertainment. Further accidents of this type are thus most unlikely in future years. You may have my word on that as a Roman.

Since then, for many a year our major spectacles have been staged in other quarters. Do you remember I described to you the venerable Circus Maximus in Rome? Whatever the wonders of the new amphitheatre, I shall never entirely desert the Circus, for, apart from being the bastion of the mighty Greens (charioteers supreme!) it is the one public place in Rome where a man and woman need no excuse to squeeze up close. Such intimacies to be had! I confess I have let my own hand stray, especially at the climax of a race when, accompanied by the pounding of hoofs and the hurrahs of the multitude, many a polite and well-bred girl's thoughts have turned, blissfully, to love.

Alas, however, the old Circus Maximus remains quite ill-suited for the spectacle of combat. Gladiators and beasts often appear tiny in the distance, forcing one up and down from one's seat like a whore's garments; and because the length of the track would allow an errant beast or timid swordsman plenty of scope for turning tail, the shows have to be confined to a pen formed by iron railings. Most unsatisfactory.

Hence – and here, you will note, I return triumphant to my starting point with whips flashing and wheels running true – our glorious Flavian Caesar, Vespasian, has been moved to sponsor a more fitting home for our manly pursuits: the greatest amphitheatre the world has known, no less, and surely the greatest it ever will know. What is more, the building is being financed in part by a tax upon the city's latrines. Thus every drunk in the city may claim to have emptied his purse for this wondrous erection! As a true Green, I am honoured to be among them.

In Year One of the 215th Olympiad [AD 81].
Anorakos of Elis to his honourable friend, Vicarius the Roman.
Warm greetings!

Oh Olympia, Queen of Truth, servant of Zeus and champion of peace! I declare, Vicarius, such a festival you missed this year. Or were you there in the stadium? I looked all over for you.

After a pleasant ride from Elis my party stayed at Olympia the full six nights, in our usual spot overlooking the west wall of the *palaestra* (where I have many dear friends among the trainers). As you remarked when you kindly accepted my offer of hospitality at the previous festival, few enough spots are free from the throng, but as a true Olympian I may be relied upon to find one.

Such is the renewed popularity of the festival that we heard rumours that a system of reserved places may be introduced for the stadium. I will fight such an abomination, I will, for this would run contrary to the sacred principles. Whether outside or inside the stadium, a freeman must be exactly that: free to attend and free to take his chances. Spectatorship is a sport in itself, is it not?

But a tainted one too, I regret. I have never seen so many pedlars as there were around the Altis this year, offering their nasty little terracotta statuettes of Nike as if Olympia were some common bazaar. If he were alive today the great Phidias would fall on his chisel to behold the coarse miniatures of his Zeus being hawked around for a few quarters a time. Send the pedlars to account before the brother of Zeus, say I, and see how their vulgar business fares in H*d*s! Flogging is too good for them, really.

Not that they lack for gullible customers. As you saw, thousands of victors are honoured at the Altis in bronze and stone. (There would have been more on display but for the visit of the light-fingered Nero of late, unlamented memory.) Yet how the boorish riff-raff gawp and snigger as they pass by the victor's memorials, barely heeding the stirring tales of athletic valour told so eloquently by our excellent guides. The exception as always remains the statue of the great Polites of Keramos, whom I myself saw as a young man win the Stadion, Diaulos and Dolichos all in one day – by fair means too, rather than the foul methods used by the odious six-time victor Nero only four years before. You may say it was the followers of Christos who put Rome to the flame, but I believe those who point to the late Emperor. Any man, be he Emperor or road mender, who dares fiddle a race in front of Olympia's Priestess is surely capable of any misdeed.

I near forgot this year's worthy victors. Hermogenes of Xanthos easily won the Stadion and was a narrow winner of the Diaulos. He shall certainly wear the olive wreath again, if I am any judge of a runner (and at the gymnasium in Elis I am often acknowledged as such). Tiberius Claudius Rufus of Smyrna took the Pankration. His boxing skills were too clumsy for my taste but he wrestled well, considering the heat. The cousin of a friend who has entry to the oiling room revealed in our tent one night that this Tiberius was promised 30,000 sesterces for taking the olive crown back to Smyrna. I think these payments quite contrary to the Olympian spirit, but fear my voice goes unheeded, even among the gymnasiarchs.

My present quandary is whether to visit the Nemean games at Argos or the Isthmian festival at Corinth next year, or whether to wait until Delphi two years hence for the Pythian games. These Sacred Games – with Olympia, forming our quartet of treasured *agones* – seem more popular than ever. Delphi, especially, is overrun by traders and religious touts these days. Apollo taught us to 'know thyself'. Now it would seem only 'thy price' matters.

Yet, I concede, we live in blessed times when a freeman may indulge his sporting fancies once a year, or even more often if in possession of a steady horse. Hardly a city in the Empire does not seek to mimic our ancient rites by luring the athletic guilds to compete in honour of this or that idiot potentate, mindless that, when a purse of gold is in the offing, unsavoury characters are drawn to the games like ants to a honeypot. The result? Our finely honed athletes are too often tempted, while spectators grow tired of sport. Too much, too often, is a poor recipe for any of life's dishes, say I.

Your tale of Curio and his performing theatres reads like fanciful nonsense. I shall take it, how do you say in Rome, *cum grano salis*?

Nor do I comprehend how your Circus Maximus and this wondrous new amphitheatre can possibly merit their place in the midst of a crowded metropolis. It could never be thus with a stadium, for how, in a city, could athletes possibly find sufficient repose and fresh air to train before their events? As for spectators, sport is no casual offering to be sampled a few paces from one's threshold like a loaf of bread. There must first be pilgrimage, sacrifice, ritual and rural calm to honour its sacred tradition. A stadium is a sanctuary, not a corner tavern.

I also cannot fathom why, instead of constructing this new amphitheatre of which you speak, your finest carpenters did not simply construct a wooden platform over the track of the Circus, to bring the spectacle (the abomination, I call it) closer to the stands. Added to this, a temporary arrangement of seats across the track could create, as it were, an amphitheatre within the Circus. The usual 250,000 seats for the Circus would, I estimate from your descriptions, have to be reduced to perhaps 100,000 for the *ad hoc* amphitheatre within its midst – shall we call it our Circus Minimus! – yet surely this compromise would be acceptable.

But foolish me to think of compromise. You Romans have the world's quarries at your disposal, slaves to keep occupied and time to fill, so of course you must build a separate amphitheatre. I must also suppose that it has not even entered your noble heads to think of building a stadium.

In the consulship of Domitian for the eighth time and of Flavius Sabinus [AD 82].
Vicarius of Rome to his friend Anorakos of Elis.
Greetings!

No, I was not in your stadium last year, nor will be for some time. After five days squatting on the slopes of Olympia I marvel you can sit down to write at all. If your all-powerful Olympic Councillors would afford a few marble benches for those other than the élite, then maybe I would risk my buttocks at your quaint little festival. But on reflection, no, still I would not. When I was there, you informed me there were 50,000 men and boys gathered. I'll wager flies outnumbered us all. I still flinch at the memory and threaten my slave that, should he fail to please me, then we shall be off to Olympia again, forthwith! Note: he has been dutiful ever since.

As to your suggestion of a wooden platform over the track of the Circus, my friends in Rome's architectural fraternity tell me that apparently such a contrivance was once considered and dismissed many years ago, on two counts. It would have taken a week or more to erect such a platform, and the stable owners and their followers were not willing for races to be suspended for such a length of time. (As a Green I applaud their impatience.) Also, they tell me that for all the ingenuity of a wooden platform, we spectators would not have been able to see the gladiators as well as we might in a dedicated amphitheatre. Thus it was realised some time ago that the two beasts – the horses and the fighters – simply could not be happy bedfellows.

The result of that conclusion is now before you, or at least should be if one of your light-fingered countrymen has not untied this scroll. Sealed to the papyrus is an interesting coin for your study. It was struck by our new and most esteemed Emperor Titus, son of the deified Vespasian. See the edifice it depicts? This is the amphitheatre of which I wrote some time ago, a gift from the Flavian Emperors not merely to Rome but also to the world.

As can be seen, the structure is three storeys high. Its circumference measures over 1,100 cubits, and is decorated harmoniously in the Greek orders. There are eighty arched entrances uniformly spaced around the street-level arcade. Near 50,000 spectators can be accommodated in the galleries; a trifle compared with the Circus Maximus, it is true, but in such luxury as can hardly be imagined.

This is what I can tell you from my several visits to the amphitheatre, each of which has left me trembling with almost indescribable joy.

The opening ceremonies dedicated by the excellent Titus, two years ago, lasted for some hundred days, I tell not a lie, and were wilder than Saturnalia. Princes and paupers came from all corners of the Empire to pay their respects to our beneficent new Emperor and to feast upon the ever-changing daily *miracula*: elephants, lions, dancers, nymphs, sacrifices to Mars and Diana, Neptune and Minerva. Whenever Titus entered his podium, the roar of the crowd echoed as if Jupiter himself had crashed down from the heavens.

In the morning the arena belongs to the *venationes*, the animal shows. I could not gain entry to the inaugural spectacle (though I would willingly have strangled an ox for the chance), but it is said 5,000 animals were slaughtered on that one blessed day alone. What better way for us Romans to show our utter contempt for death. Let the Empire quake before our steely resolve!

After the *bestiarii* have blunted their swords, or succumbed to their fate, the sand is cleared while pipers keep us breathless onlookers amused. Then enter the gladiators, to a herald of tubas and horns. Magnificent, and despite the awesome scale of the amphitheatre every combatant is perfectly visible from every vantage point, thanks to what I believe are called the 'lines of sight' from the seated galleries.

Thus we may see quite clearly every agonised visage, every throat given up to the sword, and know that even the lowliest of murderers or thieves can find dignity in their final moments. No running race in a stadium could ever teach such a lesson.

Another advantage: to find one's seat in the amphitheatre is simplicity itself. We who are assiduous enough to have friends and patrons in the right places are given counters, like small coins, in advance. Though *gratis*, they are worth a king's ransom on the day of a spectacle, being the sole means of entry and – hear this, Anorakos – ensuring the bearer a marble seat on which one can, if of the correct rank, place a cushion. Picture the luxury, my raw-rumped Greekling, and then tell me your stadium is superior. Better still, tell this to your womenfolk, for in the amphitheatre, women have the top-most gallery entirely to themselves; wives and mistresses together, draped in their fineries. The necks of some I spied last week were festooned with live snakes. Imagine, they say the creatures cool them down.

I know you would rather die on the Altis than admit women to the stadium. But better, surely, to have them where you can see them, rather than cavorting with who knows whom while you are at the games. And that's another fine thing. While the fillies sit inside the amphitheatre, we lusty colts may trot downstairs to find a mount or two beckoning in a shady archway. (Titus's Hundred

Day revelries attracted to Rome some of the finest beauties in the Empire, and, glory be, most have stayed on, such is the surge in trade.) From one entrance of pleasure to another, one then idles to a neighbouring arch, where all kinds of comestibles can be purchased before returning to one's seat, which awaits one's return like a faithful dog tied to a post. Luxury, Anorakos, luxury!

Another invention of which I think you know little in the east is a device first tried in the amphitheatre at Pompeii (alas, they say the amphitheatre is all that survives from the catastrophic eruption). When the games' sponsor is sufficiently generous a canvas awning is stretched over the top of the amphitheatre like a giant sail, to protect our feverish brows from the sun. And when unfortunate odours rise from the bloodied arena, as they must on warmer days, perfume is sprayed beneath the canvas to bring sweet relief to the more delicate noses in the upper galleries.

But, Anorakos, there is more! For thanks to the divine powers of our Emperor, our amphitheatre defies nature. Can you believe this? I could not, until seeing it with my own eyes. One minute there are gladiators and beasts scurrying about on the sand, on *terra firma*. Then they are all gone, replaced by a flurry of slaves working with timbers and doors and gates, and the next minute the amphitheatre is awash with water – plentiful enough to drown a man – for the most pleasing of nautical displays.

I have seen midget triremes, each with oarsmen, re-enact stirring sea battles as fought by Corcyra against Corinth. Or it may have been Athens fighting Rhodes, or perhaps Syracuse, but who cares! So overwhelmed am I by the spectacle that they are all Greeks to me.

Also on the water, but under torchlight after sunset, we have seen the story of the beautiful priestess Hero and her lovelorn Leander. As with all the legends there are tedious soliloquies to endure before the action starts, but this gives us landlubbers plenty of time to place wagers on the outcome. Will tonight's Leander manage to swim to his Hero on the far shore and therefore earn his freedom? Can the felon avoid the jaw-snapping crocodiles gathered with menace around the man-made islands? Or will a sudden wave – which arrives from nowhere, we know not how this is done – overwhelm him just as he nears his goal?

My friends and I have taken to calling this magical intervention 'Caesar's Wave', and in its honour and for our amusement in each section of the amphitheatre we spectators rise and fall like frenzied worshippers, affecting to mimic the sweep of water over Leander's body.

For certain these nautical interludes confirm the powers of the Emperor, who cannot but be hailed as a brother to Triton, creator of waves and mentor to Thetis, goddess of the sea. But another reason for their popularity, to be blunt, is that the shows are accompanied by shoals of frolicking beauties, scantily attired and swimming in delightful harmony under the twinkling torches. Some say that these Nereids are but common whores, though their tails look fine enough to me.

So I ask you, Anorakos, how can your tame races and primitive stadiums compete against these brilliant entertainments? Answer: they cannot. Indeed, I envisage amphitheatres such as this one rising up across the Empire, bringing pleasure to thousands of loyal subjects and work opportunities for thousands more; that is, a living for some, a dying for others!

One final morsel I know you shall feast upon. I should mention that the amphitheatre is built upon the very spot where, within our own lifetimes, the unlamented Nero laid out the grounds of his monstrous palace, and where all that remains of his evil shadow is the towering statue of himself ordered from your countryman Zenodorus. This stone giant remains, as tall as the amphitheatre and hard by its outer wall. Yet Nero's visage has now been remodelled to that of the sun-god Helios, a loss of face for the departed Emperor if ever there was. Seeing the two structures together, the giant statue and the amphitheatre, I fancy I know which one is now the true colossus!

In Year Three of the 215th Olympiad [AD 83].
Anorakos of Elis to his friend Vicarius the Roman.
Greetings!

So, your triumphs are shrunk upon a coin. Most apt, say I. This new amphitheatre shadows not only half of Rome but all my waking thoughts too. Man must feast on dishes other than meat if he is not to constipate his spirit. You write of spectacles. I read only of murder and extravagance. Marble seats for thousands of *hoi polloi*, regardless of whether they have ever been victors, regardless of whether they have even been competitors? Such needless comfort, and so ill-earned!

Tell me, Vicarius: what happens if an enemy or uncouth Stentor sits next to you in this new amphitheatre of yours? Surely you are forced to endure his wild ejaculations all day without being able to slip away, as one can so easily on the slopes of Olympia. And you are wrong to suggest that our slopes are undeveloped through neglect. They remain so by tradition. We shift and make space for fellow spectators, and thereby honour both them and ourselves. I cite a perfect example of this during the last festival. An old gentleman came tottering amongst us on the slopes, just as the Stadion was to be run. 'Sit down, sit down!' shouted a few impatients, until a group of Spartans rose as one to make space for the aged one. Applause for their gesture broke out, and I saw the old man smile and say this: 'All Greeks know what is proper, but only Spartans do it.'

No, Vicarius, the sacred simplicity of our stadium is, in itself, a gift, and one that has served us well – as you may note from the date of my missive – throughout 215 Olympiads, spread over eight hundred years. Till before the rise of Rome, even.

Purity and tranquillity are noble lights to guide our paths. We need no sunshades nor perfumes in our stadium. The mystic essence of our beauteous land suffices. At Olympia, all earthly discomforts and differences are forgotten. Hatred and war bow down before Kronos, father of Zeus. For sport, the gift of the gods, we Greeks lay down our arms, and give ourselves up to nature's gifts. Her barbs too.

I grant that our athletes today are hardened performers with little knowledge of the ancient spirits that bless their efforts. As long as there is a gymnasium in Elis I shall fight to ensure that the old traditions are not forgotten. But, if I fail, at least in their pursuit of victory and honour these fine youths are harming no one, save the slothful and irreligious, who must stand ashamed by such damning comparison.

I am to Delphi for the games next month and perhaps to consult the oracle on a personal matter. I don't recall if your travels took you there, but the stadium is truly charming. Cut into the rocks of Mount Parnassus, it is not quite as large as Olympia but allows splendid vistas of the valleys beyond. A stadium should, I believe, celebrate its landscape as well as its athletes, whereas, from your description, your amphitheatre quite excludes its surrounds; a blessing, perhaps, in fetid Rome but a cruel denial of nature in our blessed arcadia.

If you cannot return to our shores to discover this for yourself, good health be with you, if it may.

In the consulship of Domitian for the tenth time and of Oppius Sabinus [AD 84].
Vicarius of Rome to Anorakos of Elis.

Greetings!

Still hanging on to your old customs and beliefs, I see. But the *vox populi* is against you, Anorakos. The gladiator's sword is mightier than the pentathlon. The amphitheatre is here to stay. It is 'thumbs down' for your Greek sports. There can be no reprieve. Athletics is like poor buried Pompeii: consigned to history.

Still, I must refute your accusations. You write of murder in the amphitheatre. I say, justice. Those who die are doomed to die whatever. It is their deserved fate as felons, zealots and enemies of the Empire. Remember that your own festivals began as funeral rites, and for there to be a funeral there must be a corpse. So we Romans simply perform the whole process in one: sentence, death, despatch. Efficiency, education and entertainment, all at once. That clarity of thought, Anorakos, is why we Romans, not you fawning Greeks, rule the world.

If only you could hear the eloquent, howling cries of zealots torched to death in the amphitheatre, you would not doubt my word. They are clothed in jackets of tar, by the by, this method a quite ingenious progression from other more summary forms of execution, though one's eyes smart dreadfully from the smoke when there are a score or more alight. Maybe you should try this at Olympia to keep away the flies, instead of sacrificing all those bulls.

(Talking of which, one splendid show I saw recently at the amphitheatre re-enacted the legend of Queen Pasiphae and the bull, bedevilled by Poseidon into unnatural acts. Need I say more, save, ouch! Of course the girl will never walk again.)

You complain of athletes becoming ever more mercenary. (Ill-fed swine who flail naked in dust and oil, I call them, but that is not the issue.) Yet you know that the very word athlete means in your language 'one who competes for a price'. So, pray, what price for victory would you value most? A crown of olive branches, or life itself? I know which I would prefer. Your athletes are corrupt fools, as is well acknowledged by the numbers of bronzes to Zeus at the very entrance to your stadium, financed, as you told me yourself, from the fines imposed on those who were caught cheating, or who pulled out of races they knew they could not win. No such weaknesses corrupt the pure spirit of gladiatorial combat, for, tell me, what man would ever sell his life for a purse of gold?

Look also in your own hallowed Temple of Zeus at Olympia. Is it not depicted there that your precious Pelops, besotted with Hippodameia, cheated in the famed chariot race against her royal father, by sabotaging his chariot? Did he then not kill his accomplice, Myrtilos? Are these the lessons for your cherished athletes to follow?

Your story of the geriatric and the Spartans is quaint. I counter with a tale from the time of the deified Augustus. The Emperor was at the circus and spotted a knight drinking in the crowd. The wise Augustus – who well understood how the races pacify our grumbling hearts just as bread settles our stomachs – sent a herald to tick off the transgressor. If the knight wanted to imbibe, he was told, he should go home to do so. 'Ah yes,' the knight was said to have replied, 'I have done wrong, but it is all very well for the Emperor. He has a reserved seat, whereas if I leave the circus I shall lose my place and not regain it.' A brave but honest man, and justly reprieved for his wit, for there was another time, I know not when but it is oft talked about, when such was the clamour to find a place in the Circus Maximus that in the riotous confusion a hundred or more desperate souls perished, including twenty knights and twenty women.

Such anarchy cannot be the mark of a civilised society, and I thank Jupiter that such calamities could never occur inside our new amphitheatre. There, we spectators flow like columns of ants, in and out through numbered arches (the numbers are written on our counters), up and down stairways, along sweeping arcades, from where we are guided to our seats by place finders. You may call this prescriptive, turning us pleasure-seekers into military units. I call it discipline.

You remind me there have been festivals at Olympia for 800

years. How come, then, that there is still no aqueduct to bring plentiful fresh water to the stadium? Eight hundred years and still waiting.

No, Anorakos, it is clear what today's men of leisure thirst for, and through Rome they shall have it. Indeed, I shall concede only one annoyance arising from the popularity of the amphitheatre. The current mania for the spectacles is turning every buffoon in Rome to poetry. One in particular, a newly arrived Hispanic called Martial, has quite made his name with a set of oily little epigrams, purely on the spectacle.

How I despise this new-found obsession with our popular pursuits. For every dull poem extolling this gladiator or that, there are a hundred ordinary men whose honest cries of 'Die now!' or 'Slit his throat!' impart far more eloquence. Yet I hardly dare dine in respectable company these days for fear that some old equestrian will regale me with his newly gained and always imperfect knowledge of the gladiator's art.

Better that you should see for yourself the pleasures of which I write rather than read of them in some silly ode.

In Year One of the 216th Olympiad [AD 85].
Anorakos of Elis to Vicarius the Roman.
Greetings!

From your letters, I think it unlikely we shall see you this summer at Olympia. Your heart has abandoned true sport. Your eyes see victory only in the blood of innocents. But if you do come, look for me and we shall talk more and drink fine wine from Samos. Hermogenes of Xanthos is favourite for the Stadion, should you wish to spice your visit with a wager.

Rumours in the gymnasium suggest that the esteemed Domitian is to build a stadium in Rome. Is this true, Vicarius? Is it possible that you may yet be persuaded of the ecstasies to be had from our Greek pursuits?

Be in good health, and pardon my brevity. My presence at the gymnasium before the games leaves little time for correspondence.

In the eleventh consulship of Domitian [AD 85].
Vicarius to Anorakos.

My philosopher friend and gloomy Cassandra, it would appear that we Romans are not lost yet. Our very best of Emperors, Domitian, has indeed ordered work to start on a veritable 'stadium' in Rome, of all places.

Where he expects to find 30,000 idiots to feast upon your beloved athletics I cannot guess, for what use is athletics to a Roman? I ask, why throw a javelin a great distance if not to kill? Why run fast other than to chase an enemy? Why wrestle if not to conquer?

Thus I have no doubt that this new stadium will, in time, be forced to show beasts and gladiators in order to draw a crowd. But Domitian cannot help himself and if there is a building to be built, he will build it. Next to the stadium will be a large new theatre, the Odeum. I doubt that the city needs any more outlets for pleasure, but who knows what future distractions mankind will invent in order to while away the hours of leisure.

Still, Domitian has not been negligent towards his family's amphitheatre. A fourth storey has been completed, to provide an extra gallery, and so that we may see better after darkness he has introduced a cunning chandelier, suspended on ropes and bathing the arena below in light. Is there no end to our people's invention?

Feeling himself to be reviled, none the less – which he is in certain quarters; though, I make clear, not mine – Domitian has also resorted to beneficence beyond even that of his late brother, the deified Titus. Did I ever describe to you how one of the former Emperor's favourite ploys was to have small, hollow wooden balls thrown into the crowds? Some were empty. Some contained promissory notes for money, horses or chickens. One lucky fellow won himself a new villa (I swear this on my life, for the bastard was sitting only a few steps from myself). Well, Domitian does not bother with the wooden balls. He has gold coins, exotic delicacies, Numidian partridges even, tossed shamelessly into the crowds, who then fight amongst themselves like washerwomen. Truly, it is at times as raucous as any combat on the sand.

So you see, Anorakos, the public will not be persuaded against the amphitheatre. Give people what they want and they will surely never desert you, as Julius Caesar so wisely declared in past times. Those who entertain also wield power. To which I humbly add, why should spectators not win prizes too? Olympia must learn these modern ways or fade away.

I fear I am repeating myself in our correspondence. I have only your best interests at heart.

In Year Two of the 216th Olympiad [AD 86].
Anorakos to Vicarius.
Like the simple Scythians your thoughts are muddled. They persuade me that there are no spectators so blind as those who see only the contest and not the context.

The stadium is but a vessel for man's deepest thoughts and sensibilities. It is both the mark of our civilisation and its measure. Perhaps your new stadium in Rome will be scorned, as you predict. But here amongst the Greeks the stadium has survived the humiliations of recent times and, though battered in spirit, it will rise again, fear not. There will be sport in the stadium long after Rome's last spectator has grown weary of blood.

These, however, are the ramblings of an older Anorakos than the one whose tent you chanced upon nine years ago.

The final Sacred Games of the current cycle is over. Olympia now rests. Again Hermogenes of Xanthos took the wreath for the Diaulos, as I foresaw, but was bested in the Stadion by Apollophanes of Tarsos, also known as Papes. I doubt you are interested, but Titus Flavius Metrobius (of Iasos) was the victor in the Dolichos. Titus Flavius Artemidoros of Adana won the Pankration. Diogenes of Ephesos was again victor in the trumpeters' contest, his fifth triumph in five Olympics, for which he will surely be immortal. The equestrian events were shrouded in dust, and took the lives of four horses and one rider. The crowds were mighty as ever.

Death at Olympia is of course a rare tragedy, and has always been for honour. Remember I told you of Diagoras, a previous winner, there to see his two sons Damagitos and Akoussilaos each win his contest? The victorious duo then bore their father proudly around the stadium on their shoulders. Amid the throng a man shouted to Diagoras from the slopes, 'You have reached the summit of happiness and glory. You can die happy!' whereupon the ecstatic Diagoras expired. I still weep to imagine such a blessed fate. For no death is without higher meaning, say I.

Vicarius, as you are cocksure so I shall be candid. You may have the guise of a spectator, but you are actually an accomplice. Your sophisticated amphitheatre is a monument only to your empire's might, not to its moral strength. Spectators who are sheltered from the sun and from the elements are cocooned in a falsehood. If our sporting heroes do sweat and toil, we who celebrate their endeavours must surely share their subjection. To do otherwise would be to become mere observers; dumb children who see but do not learn.

I conclude with a cautionary tale, concerning the victorious athlete Theagenes. Did I tell you this before? My memory fails me so much these days. Anyway, the story is this.

Seeing Theagenes' noble statue at the Altis at Olympia, one of his former rivals, a brute of a man, could scarce restrain his envy. He pummelled and pummelled the statue so vengefully that soon the statue shook and teetered, until finally it toppled and crushed him, dead. *Quod erat demonstrandum.*

You see, Vicarius, one day your cries of vengeance will sound so loud that they will bring down the amphitheatre, with its awnings, perfumes, chandeliers and easy comforts, and all the greedy, idle loungers and profiteers within it shall perish. And as the dust settles, the ghosts of the innocents will claim the hearts of the people. Pure sport, as we know it in the stadium, will triumph from then on.

I may be an old fool, but I need no oracle to tell me of this eventuality, only my heart. Vicarius, I say again, your sumptuous revelries are not for ever.

The stadium will never die.

1 BACK TO THE GARDEN

'Sightlines' is the term architects use to describe the quality of view that a spectator has of the action, either over or between the heads of the spectators sitting in front.

In order to make the detailed calculations required to provide quality sightlines, architects use the following formula:

$$N = \frac{(R + C) \times (D + T) - R}{D}$$

Unfortunately I was never much good at maths, so instead, this is how I would describe my view.

I would say that, on balance, much as I like sport I prefer stadiums.

Now, were I an academic, I might easily be persuaded to conduct some meaningful research into this foible. But I am not, and I have not, while in any case dozens of eager-beaver sociologists, economists, geographers, pyschologists *et al* have muscled their way past me in the queue for the turnstiles over the last decade. Having sampled the stadium experience they emerge, blinking with delight and using such terms as 'perceptual stimulation', 'enhanced gratification' and 'liminal zones'. I rather envy their freedom with words. Poetic licence really only goes so far.

Intellectuals have similarly 'discovered' the stadium. What fun they find it is to attend a football match or a baseball game in pursuit of empirical research and junk food, and then deconstruct it all for the benefit of their clever chums.

There is, however, one fundamental aspect of a stadium's allure, beyond definitions, measurements or formulas, that I would dearly like to understand more fully, for I am certain that few sports fans in the world do not, consciously or subconsciously, share my predilection. Male ones, at least.

What's more, I think we might need help.

Anton Chekhov once wrote, 'What a luxurious thing Nature is! I could just take her and eat her up . . .'

I know just what he means.

Scene One. Chelmsford, Essex, circa 1960.

Every summer my brother, sister and I would leave Birmingham to stay with Uncle Bill and Aunty Freda in their small village just outside Chelmsford. They lived down an unadopted road, in a 1950s bungalow stacked high with seeds and soil samples. Bill, a jovial, ruddy-faced Glaswegian, lectured at the local agricultural college and liked to bring his experiments home. Freda, also Scottish, was a teacher and an all round good egg. They had no children of their own, but were part of a wider, yet close-knit family of card-carrying Communists in the midst of a hostile, Tory heartland. Bill and Freda were also surely the only party members west of Moscow to denounce mayonnaise as a bourgeois affectation, and were definitely the last people in Essex to buy a television.

Despite minor deprivations such as these, we three young suburbanites adored our visits. As the youngest, although I could not yet understand dialectical materialism I was at least better prepared for the Cuban missile crisis than most of my classmates.

One Saturday afternoon, when I was five or six years old, Freda took us to a park in Chelmsford, where, by the by, we saw in the distance some green, corrugated fencing. From our side of this fencing we could hear vague rumblings from a crowd. As we moved nearer, through gaps in the fence I caught glimpses of an expanse of turf. Although in my mind's eye the encounter has no doubt become idealised over the years, I am certain that at that moment something clicked.

This was my first experience of a football ground.

Back in Birmingham a few months later I wrote the word 'stadium' for the first time, in a school composition, together with the words Villa Park, Wembley and 'fludlights'. (I only know this because my old school books turned up a couple of years ago. The unnerving discovery that my interest in stadiums went back so far into my youth almost had me believing in predestination.)

That sensation of standing on the outside of a secret paradise, of wanting desperately to go in, has never left me. Nor has the memory of that Chelmsford ground; turf on the outside, turf on the inside; public space and private space, separated by a humble, green, corrugated fence.

It was around that time too that I began to understand what Uncle Bill did for a living. Apart from going on about the down-trodden workers, Bill also talked about nitrates and soil and the importance of feeding the starving masses. His greenhouse was filled with dozens of tiny pots, each one growing a few blades of grass.

Scene Two. Moseley, Birmingham, circa 1969.
From my bedroom window I enjoyed perfect sightlines into the gardens of both our neighbours' houses. On our left lived Mr Lambie, a retired, taciturn man of whom we children knew little other than the fact that should one of our balls ever land on his side of the fence none of us dared knock on his door to ask for its return.

Mr Lambie did not approve of stray balls. His garden was neat to the point of sterility. One day I saw him, head down, kneeling on a rubber mat in the middle of his impeccable lawn. With a pair of small scissors he was painstakingly trimming the top of each rogue blade of grass that had dared to grow too big for its roots.

As an adolescent with attitude, with shoulder-length hair and Captain Beefheart croaking on my Dansette – 'It's the blimp Frank, it's the blimp!' – I suppose I should have reviled boring old Mr Lambie for his bourgeois obsession. Yet I thought of him as a solitary craftsman. What he was doing, what he was trying to achieve, did not seem to me at all perverse. After all, his lawn often looked better than the pitch at Villa Park.

Scene Three. Lord's Cricket Ground, London, circa 1987.
It was the end of a NatWest Final, I think; a good day's cricket in the late summer having provided a welcome respite from the clamour of football. I have always been far too polite to invade a pitch at the end of a football match. But at cricket grounds, strolling on to the pitch after the final ball is, more or less, an accepted, and acceptable, ritual. For the *cognoscenti* in particular, it offers a chance to inspect the wicket as closely as the ropes will

allow; to gather around the strip of shaven turf as if enjoined in a spiritual pilgrimage.

For those readers who have experienced the sensation of stepping on to a perfectly manicured expanse of turf, be it a bowling green, a green on a golf course, or a first-class cricket ground, no further comment is necessary.

But for those who have not, that first contact between the soles of one's shoes and the turf is a uniquely sensual moment. Indeed it is a hard-hearted individual who does not reach down at that same moment and stroke the finely cut grass, if only to gain proof that it is indeed real, and not some artful substitute. When Martina Navratilova first competed at Wimbledon, in 1973, it was said that she had never seen a grass court before. On being shown the Centre Court for the first time, her immediate response was to kneel down and touch the surface in reverential wonderment. I always liked Martina, but having learnt of her action I now find I like her even more.

To run one's fingers along the tips and crinkly edges of finely meshed blades of grass, to feel their evenness on the palm of one's hand, is to cross the line between distant admiration and intimate appreciation. I go further. I doubt if any spectator can genuinely empathise with a player until he or she has stood on a perfect playing surface and felt its slight give, its subtle spring. To feel this under one's feet, and at the same time to be caressed by the circulating air, to be enwrapped by the all-pervading, aromatic sense of place – the *genius loci*, as it is aptly called – is to be touched to the core by man's inestimable ability to make the very best of this beautiful, fearful, contrary world.

Coming to this discovery for the first time at Lord's, on that late-summer evening, I knew exactly what I had to do. I took off my shoes and socks and felt the short grass caress the soles of my bare feet. A friend who was with me at the time laughed, but I was not alone in doing this. Others were taking off their shoes too. But among them I realised I was the only male.

Some say that to walk barefoot through grass is subconsciously to seek a return to the innocence of the Garden of Eden, before The Fall. If so, it is as well that Adam was joined by Eve rather than Steve, for with no other distractions the two men would probably have pottered about on the grass all day and in the evening built themselves a garden shed.

But Adam was distracted, and, ever since, we men have been trying to get ourselves back to the garden. What is it, I wondered that evening at Lord's, about men (*homo masculinus*) and grass (*poaceae*)?

Scene Four. A groundsman's hut in Melbourne, 1998.
Most people have their own favourite bit of the typical 'behind-the-scenes' stadium tour; maybe the hush of the oak-panelled boardroom, or the clinical sparseness of the linament-scented dressing-rooms. But the tours seldom lead visitors to the best part of a stadium or sports ground, the groundsman's hut. His lair. His hideaway.

If you can manage to track it down, usually at the end of a dark corridor deep within the bowels of a stand, or in some utilitarian outhouse suitably distanced from the VIP car park, and if he will talk – for these guys are not hired for their sociability – you can learn more from a groundsman about the heart and soul, and the light and dark, of a stadium than from anyone else.

Frank, sunburned and dusty in a hut in a suburban Melbourne stadium, was only too happy to natter with an inquisitive 'pom' over a cold drink and a fag, as he sat me down on a fertiliser sack amid all the paraphernalia of his profession. So happy, in fact, that after a fifteen-minute monologue on creeping fescues, perennial rye-grasses and silica sands I had to remind him gently that I was no turf expert, only an interested admirer. 'Yeh,' conceded Frank ruefully, 'the groundsman's lot can be a pretty lonely one at times.'

The groundsman, he explained, spends most of his week out there in the middle as the ruler of his patch, the master of his universe, but then promptly disappears the moment the actors file on to the stage, hoping against hope that the heavy-footed lummocks who pass for sportsmen will not inflict too much harm on his precious plot. I told Frank that some groundsmen I have met cannot bear even to watch a game, so emotionally involved are they in their turf's welfare. Instead they brood in the recesses of the stadium, like anxious parents waiting for their teenage kids and pals to vacate the living room, before emerging to survey the damage.

To catalogue the routine tasks of a groundsman is to be reminded of how rooted are our field sports in the rhythms and vagaries of the natural world. Seeding. Dressing the top soil. Solid tining. Brushing and harrowing. Levelling, fertilising, pricking, spiking and raking. Irrigation and scarification. Mow and roll, roll and mow.

So much planning is needed, so much patience; always waiting for the right moment. Not too wet, not too dry. Tease out the thatch. Get air to the roots. Sand slitting, sand grooving, subsoiling, mole ploughing. Then finally, when no more can be done other than to pray, laying down the white lines, the lines that lend the turf its true definition.

Think of the signs and symbols of the twentieth century; the ones that need no explanation in any part of the world. Which would be most instantly identifiable? The Stars and Stripes perhaps? The Coca-Cola logo? The McDonald's arches? My contender would be the markings of a football pitch. Evolved in Britain between 1863 and 1902, with a flourish – the penalty arc – added in 1937, the football pitch is so classic a piece of design that it remains almost invisible. One has to be reminded that it is an invention and not some ancient pictogram, handed down through the ages. It is man's most familiar signature upon the pure green canvas of turf.

It is men, in particular, making their mark. First they tame the land, then they codify, or tame, the game – be it soccer, tennis, rugby, cricket, whatever – and, finally, they mark out the territory.

The groundsman's work is always on the line too. Every inch of his work is out there, on display, for all to see. And that does mean all, for in my experience one of the surest means of persuading a groundsman to talk freely is to introduce a favourite topic of conversation: 'the buggers I have to please'.

Frank's two main candidates were as follows.

First, and most obviously, the player, whose 'precious bloody feet' are wrapped in anatomically engineered footwear with flexible out-soles, hand-stitched kangaroo leather and the latest in carbon-fibre studs, blades or spikes; who spends all week working on his game. And then, what do you know, one awkward bump or dip in the pitch and his ankle could turn, his pass could bobble, a single could turn into a four or an easy catch turn into a favourite on the bloopers' Christmas compilation video. 'Oh, he's fluffed it! Would you believe that!' A whole game, a whole season, could turn sour, and Frank knows bloody well who will get the blame.

Second comes the team coach, who may insist on conducting a training session on the pitch shortly after a bloody great downpour. Who, in summer, may demand that the dry turf be saturated before a game (to tire out a technically superior opposition, perhaps), or that the grass be left long or short, or that the touchlines be drawn narrower or wider than usual. Honestly, there's no pleasing some people.

After Frank had calmed down I added a couple of *bêtes noires* from my own sampling of the English groundsman's little black book of awkward buggers.

The most awkward bugger of all, I suggested, is the greedy stadium owner or operator who demands that his architects provide tall, cavernous stands with overhanging roofs, leaving nature few gaps to penetrate. Earth, wind, rain and fiery sun be damned. So what if the typical grass pitch (in England at least) needs, er . . . between 2.5 and 3.0 megajoules per square metre per day of photosynthetically active radiation in the 700–900 nanometre wavelength. (I didn't manage to quote the exact figures at the time, but Frank seemed to catch my drift and kept nodding conspiratorially as if to say, 'Yeh, the bastards.')

Who cares if the groundsman has to allow for reduced evapotranspiration on the shaded side of his pitch? Bums on seats and banqueting suites are what counts.

Which leaves plenty of scope for my next bugger: the turf technologist and his legions of fellow experts and salesmen.

'Try this, try that,' they implore the groundsman. 'Buy this miracle cure. Buy that sexy loam. Fertilisers, new strains of grass, new sand mixes, new synthetic implants. The best root-zone a man can get. Perfect ball-bounce. Excellent resistance to soil compaction. Two- or three-wheel-drive rotary mower with full grooming attachments, deluxe seats and variable speed cutters. High torque.'

Smooth talk. We're talking big business here.

But Frank and I agreed that the biggest bugger of them all, the bugger of all buggers in the buggering universe, has to be television. Or, more precisely, the all-seeing, all-exposing eye of colour television, which cannot help but lay bare all the bare patches and imperfections of the not-so-perfect, and therefore still quite normal, pitch.

Grass, as any groundsman will testify, can be a sensitive, as well as a hardy, plant. It is prey to maladies whose names, like hobgoblins lurking in the forest, disguise their evil intent; red thread, fuserium, snow mould, parsley pint and pearlwort, they are called. Dollar spots, fairy rings and puffball rings are their calling cards for the Franks of this world. Weedkiller and cosmetics can help. Green dye or green sand have been known to save a groundsman's blushes if all else fails before the TV cameras start rolling. But the groundsman knows it's a cover-up, and he has his pride. He knows that other groundsmen will be watching and passing judgement.

Now maybe all these weeds and fungal infestations are the groundsman's fault (though seldom will he admit it). Maybe they are not (whatever anyone else might say). But the groundsman needs to have a thick skin and an equable temperament to cope with the comments. 'You see,' said Frank, 'virtually every bloke in this club has a lawn of his own, so of course they're all bloody experts.' Except, that is, when the star player, club manager or the chairman happens to experience problems with his own precious lawn, in which case Frank is then expected to give up what little free time he has to pop over and sort it out.

'There's a mate, Frankie. Oh, and don't worry, I've told the wife to sort you out with tea and a biscuit.'

No matter how qualified or experienced is the groundsman, he who works on the land expects to be treated as a hired hand. 'Yeh,' added Frank, 'and I'm expected to do all this on a budget of less than one tenth of what they get over at the MCG [the Melbourne Cricket Ground] across town.'

Yet many and varied are the compensations. Surrounded by his mowers, tools, keys, penknives, rods, twines, buckets and shears, his boots and his all-weather gear, his soil samples and seed packets, his old tranny and his even older locker, Frank was patently a contented soul. As I was too, chatting with him in the underbelly of the stadium, breathing in the still, frowzy air of engine oil, sand and grass cuttings. Even Marsha, that month's sultry centrefold, spreadeagled amidst Frank's wall planners and maintenance rotas, seemed to smile benignly down on his cosy quarters. Not that she would have understood a word of what we were going on about.

In fact you could just imagine her complaining, 'Jeez! What is it about you guys and bloody grass?'

Scene Five. A late morning in late summer on the outskirts of Arnhem, in the Netherlands, 1998.

This was my fourth visit to a newly completed stadium in less than six months. Honestly, you wait two or three years for one to open, and then, whoosh, suddenly they're sprouting up all over the place. Still, that was the Nineties for you.

Arnhem's new stadium is shiny, glass and metallic-looking, set in the middle of newly surfaced car parks, surrounded by newly surfaced roads and newly planted grass verges. The location could be pretty well anywhere in western Europe: orderly, innocuous and totally anonymous.

A Dutch journalist and friend, Tijs – pronounced Ties – who is very tall and who shares my interest in stadium architecture, had come along for the visit. In common with so many new stadiums of the so-called post-modern era, this one looked much like any other 'leisure box' put together by representatives of the Euro business community. But at least it had a few tricks up its sleeve. That was why I'd gone there in the first place. Don't imagine I go running off to every new stadium that opens, just for the hell of it.

One of the Arnhem stadium's tricks is a roof with sections which open and close over the pitch, so that games and other events can be staged in all weathers. This sort of engineering wheeze is all the rage in the stadium business these days. But the retractable roof is a mechanical trifle compared with the Arnhem stadium's finest trick of all, its retractable pitch. This lies on a vast slab of concrete which slides in and out of the stadium, on Teflon pads, pushed or pulled by four electric motors through a gap under one of the stands. I was impressed. Very impressed. So impressed that I was actually appalled. Quite literally the earth moved for me. I realised I was looking at the future of grass: boxed, clipped and delivered to your door. The ultimate stadium accessory.

Arnhem's pitch may have been the only one of its kind in the world at that time, but I knew it wouldn't be long before there were others, and then before you knew it everyone would be saying, 'Retractable roofs? Old hat! What we really need is a retractable pitch.' And so on. Remember how we once thrilled to the purr and rumble of the fax machine before the Internet won our hearts?

Anyway, in order that I would be able to write articles about this clever new pitch in Arnhem, there I was with Tijs on that late summer's morning, busily making notes and taking photographs accompanied by the stadium's PR woman – who, judging by her flat delivery and tense expression, would have preferred not to be showing us around at that particular juncture in her busy working week – while at the same time a local reporter and photographer took notes and photographs of me making notes and taking photographs, for an article the Arnhem daily newspaper was planning to publish about me as an author, about my visit to this new stadium and about my reactions to it, when suddenly and quite annoyingly a mobile telephone rang.

I say annoyingly because, in the middle of all this talking and writing and photographing and being photographed, that was all any of us needed, a mobile telephone ringing. Until I realised that it was *my* mobile telephone ringing.

Well, of course, that changed everything. That my cheapo little British mobile telephone should work at all in the Netherlands somehow seemed far more miraculous than a vast, grass-covered slab of concrete moving slowly in and out of a building on Teflon pads.

'Sorry, everyone,' I sighed as I answered the telephone, pretending to be irritated.

So the PR woman stood aside, humphing, and Tijs stood aside, and the local reporter stopped making notes, and the local photographer stopped taking photographs of me, and I found myself listening to the impressively clear voice of a reporter from the BBC back in London, asking me whether I'd be available to do a live radio interview in half an hour about something or other related to the redevelopment of Wembley Stadium.

I looked at the PR woman and at Tijs, then at the local reporter, then at the local photographer, and they all looked back at me, and I could see through the windows behind them that it was now quite sunny outside, and I could smell the new carpets in the corridor of the stadium where we were standing, and then I looked down at my notebook covered in facts about this new stadium and its miracle pitch, and at my camera, full of shots of this new marvel, which was in the Netherlands, where I was then, right at that very moment, and I thought extremely hard in a focused sort of way for a matter of five seconds or so, no more, probably less, and then I said to the reporter back in London, 'Oh what the hell. Why not?'

After all, I am a 'stadium expert'.

All the same, looking out at that retractable pitch, I suddenly felt uneasy.

Uneasy on a late summer morning. Uneasy amid the burgeoning devices and complications of the modern world.

* * *

The book of Genesis tells us that on the third day God created dry land. But what was the first living entity he created on that dry land? Two days before he created a single fish or fowl or any 'living creature that moveth' he created, and I quote: 'grass, the herb yielding seed, and the fruit tree yielding fruit'. Note the order. Grass first.

Only on the sixth day did he get round to creating man. In other words, the garden came first, the gardeners later.

Grass is the most important plant known to mankind. Grass feeds us (in the form of rice, cereals, sugar cane and suchlike). It feeds the animals we like to eat and the animals whose milk we like to drink. Almost a quarter of the earth's vegetation consists of grasslands. There are some 7,500 species of grass, several of which are eminently suitable for playing games upon; species with wonderfully evocative names such as Kentucky bluegrass (*poa pratensis* to those in the know), Bermuda, red fescue and velvet bent grass.

Grass is clever stuff. It dissipates heat. It absorbs sound and carbon dioxide, and, get this, it also produces oxygen. Several years ago I pinned up on my wall a note which reads as follows: 'One football pitch provides enough oxygen for 20,000 people for one half-hour.' I have no idea where this information came from, or even if it is true, but on the same slip of paper I subsequently added, 'One hectare of mowed turf grass has a density ranging from 75 million to 20 billion shoots,' together with the source of this data, an American agronomist called W. M. Lush. His name I see is followed by several childish, but I think in the context perfectly reasonable, exclamation marks.

I have been aching for an excuse to use those two titbits for years.

Although the British claim to have the best groundsmen in the world, the United States is undoubtedly the centre of the lawn universe. There are reckoned to be 30 million acres of lawn in the

USA, requiring billions of gallons of water and 70 million pounds of chemicals to maintain every year. The lawn-care industry alone is hugely influential, not only on the domestic front but in terms of golf-course maintenance. A lot of rich and powerful Americans play golf, and they like things to be just right.

Had grass been an ugly sort of plant none of this could have come about. But patently it is not. 'Nothing is more pleasant to the eye than green grass finely shorn,' said Francis Bacon.

We like the smell of grass too. Rather as supermarkets waft the smell of fresh bread across the aisles from their in-store bakeries, the recreated odours of freshly cut grass are used to 'invigorate' people in public areas, such as airport lounges.

However, when it comes to stadiums, I would argue that the allure of grass goes deeper still. Bear with me on this. Among theorists there is a debate as to the origins of architecture. Did architecture begin the moment a man first erected a structure – say, a wooden framework – with the intention of placing an animal skin across it? Or did architecture predate this, when man first marked out his territory with a few strategically placed stones?

Having trod some of the finest sports pitches in the world I have no doubt where my vote lies. Without the delineation of space there can no architecture. In simple soccer parlance, it is the act of putting down 'jumpers as goal posts'. There lies an open field. Lay down four jumpers, two at each end, and immediately you have a football pitch ('pitch' as in the act of setting up a camp). For greater definition add corner flags. For absolute definition, white lines or a boundary rope.

For sure, no architecture is visible, in the sense of buildings or structures, but any structures that ensue – be they wooden railings or a small stand – have their form dictated by the marked-out pitch.

It is for this reason that when spectators enter a stadium most of us instinctively register the turf first. Before grandstands, before burger bars, before floodlights and scoreboards, we understand that the grass, and the delineation of that grass expanse, came first.

Even if we know the pitch to have been newly laid, or to have been laid on land that was something else before, emotionally we regard that turf as the natural anchor which links us with the past, with the earth, with the natural world from which all sport derives. At a stadium, quite literally, we get in touch with our grass roots.

Even if the turf is finely bred, chemically enhanced and mechanically aided with irrigation pumps, undersoil heating and plastic drainage pipes, the knowledge that one could dig one's hand into the subsoil and pick out a worm or a bug – and thus connect with Mother Earth – is enough.

That, for me, is why a stadium in the midst of a city is such a treasure, such a miracle, and why the groundsman is a true artist. It is why the sight of a perfect pitch stirs all our emotions, whether we realise it or not. Why grass is, indeed, God's own carpet.

It also explains why spectators are so turned off by stadiums that rely on synthetic grass (that devil's spawn of Astroturf, invented in 1965 in circumstances I shall come to in Chapter 12). There can be no emotional attachment to artificial turf. Chekhov would not have wanted to eat it. Nor would sheep. And sheep are surprisingly important in this context.

Sheep. Not creatures one would necessarily think of when talk turns to matters sporting. But think again. Without the nibbling tendencies of sheep, backed up by a few scythe-wielding retainers, it would have been well nigh impossible to keep grass short enough for our forebears to have even considered the likes of cricket or croquet. How else would Sir Francis Drake have been able to play bowls on Plymouth Hoe when news of the Armada emerged? Sheep were keeping the turf at Lord's in trim long before the Marylebone Cricket Club even employed a groundsman. (Percy Peake, their first, was appointed in 1864 and in common with most early groundsmen was a gardener first and foremost.)

Sheep were, and are still, ideal for several reasons. They are tidy and voracious eaters. They have dainty little hoofs that do not trample the grass, and their droppings are too small and firm for players to worry about unduly. Even better, in times past ground owners were able to charge farmers and butchers for grazing rights, thus establishing a perfect symbiosis between sport and animal husbandry.

Although sheep dined and defecated on pitches well into the twentieth century – occasionally joined by other grazers, such as geese at Lord's – the beginning of the end of their role in sporting life actually came some years earlier, with a technological advancement recorded in England in 1830. In horticultural circles this breakthrough has long been celebrated as a watershed, if not as a gardenshed. But who in the world of sport has even heard the name Edwin Beard Budding?

Budding, a none too successful Gloucestershire engineer and carpenter, was to become the unsung patron saint of all groundsmen. Apparently he was working part-time in a mill when he made the inspired connection between a rotary cutting device, used to trim the nap of carpets, and its possible application for the 'heavenly carpet' of turf. (At Versailles the French aristocrats actually called their lawns *tapis vert*, or green carpets.)

With the aid of an engineer, John Ferrabee, Budding soon set about designing the first ever machine for 'cropping or shearing the vegetable surface of lawns, grass plots or pleasure grounds'. So immediately successful was this first mower that the appearance and quality of the world's turf effectively changed beyond all measure from that time onwards. For this alone we spectators (and groundsmen, and players) must for ever be in debt to Budding's genius.

One of the other, equally significant benefits of his invention was that middle-class home owners could now grow and tend their own lawns. Nor did the operator of the mower have to be male. Several advertisements from the Victorian era show women in their stays and bustles, happily pushing the latest model with barely a bead of perspiration to despoil their feminine ease.

Of course the ads were complete tosh. Women had quite enough on their plates inside the home to be bothered with such outdoor vanities as lawns. In any case, once the man of the household got his hands on one of the newfangled mowers, that was it. The lawn has remained the preserve of the male of the species ever since.

When I asked a number of pyschologists why this might be and, more specifically, what is it about men and grass, either they did not understand or, more likely, they found my questions insufficiently interesting for further investigation. Or maybe they just thought that I was bonkers, since one suggested, only half in jest, that I might get clearer answers from a therapist. (Actually I suspect he had a bit of a turf complex himself, judging by the way he kept insisting that since he had only a tiny lawn he wasn't really qualified to comment.)

So instead I turned, as so often I do when seeking a deeper understanding of this 'thing' I have about stadiums, to John Bale, a geographer at Keele University. Bale has written a great deal on stadiums, examining in particular the numerous metaphors we apply to them: stadiums as cathedrals or hallowed places, stadiums as machines or prisons, and, most persuasively in the context of turf, stadiums as parks, gardens or even as havens. As a romantic, the notion of a private paradise in an urban jungle has always been my own personal favourite, conjuring up as it does the image of a walled or secret garden.

Bale was also one of the first academics to introduce British students to the work of an American philosopher and cultural geographer, Yi-Fu Tuan.

Tuan's essays on *Dominance and Affection: The Making of Pets* show man, or, rather, men, in a somewhat unsympathetic light. Adam may not have had time for gardening before he was distracted by Eve, but over the centuries his male progeny have left few stones unturned in trying to reduce women, weaker men, animals, plants and landscapes to what Tuan called a state of 'frozen perfection'.

Dogs, roses, turf; they are all recipients, or victims, of men's dominance in Tuan's searing analysis. But he stresses that this mastery is also ambivalent, for it is equally grounded in affection. Thus men's love is, in a very real sense, a form of dominance.

Moreover, argues Tuan, sport can exist only through 'the mastery of nature', and the only people interested in pursuing such a course for any length of time have been, almost exclusively, men.

This surely explains why, in all my travels, I have yet to meet a single woman working at a senior level on a stadium pitch. Indeed, in the whole world I know of the existence of only one grounds-woman at a stadium: one Heather Nabozny, appointed as 'groundskeeper' for Detroit's Tiger Stadium in April 1999. Britain's Institute of Groundsmanship reports fewer than ten females among its total membership of some 10,000. But none of them works at a stadium. Yet.

Nor do I know of a single household in which the woman, rather than the man, mows the lawn. Maybe there are such homes, but, like barbecues and carving the roast, lawns are generally accepted as 'a man thing'. Men do the lawns. Women do the flower beds.

America's leading lawn guru, Warren Schultz, has likened the lawn to a businessman's dark suit – a symbol of conformity (and therefore of a lack of imagination) – contrasted by the flowers in the surrounding beds, which represent the loud, colourful tie, chosen by the businessman's wife. An unkempt lawn, jokes Schultz, is just plain un-American, the sign of a weak man, a Communist even.

The British take a different view, or at least some do. Only recently a journalist at the *Guardian* newspaper took a dig at the new breed of 'arcane' and 'fractured' degree courses currently on offer in Britain's universities. Stadium Studies has not yet reached the curriculum (though surely it is only a matter of time), but subjects such as Tableware, Golf Management and Saddlery have, and were picked out for predictable scorn. But by far the most laughable course, concluded the *Guardian* journalist, was one on Turfgrass Science. The writer was, of course, a woman. A male writer would have gone for the Tableware. Every time.

So what have I learnt about men and grass, and about my predilection for perfect pitches? For a start, that it really is only men who give a damn. But, worse, that our quest for perfection in turfgrass is in reality a manifestation of our male fear of disorder and of our conscious or subconscious urge to control all things, living or controllable. Not a pleasant bag of tricks to be caught with red-handed, but I have to admit it is a fair cop. Guilty as charged, your honour.

But may I beg that one further charge be taken into consideration? For if there is one thing that I love more than an expanse of immaculate turf – I almost blush to confess this – it is . . . a perfect edge.

There, I've said it. The years of denial and secret passion are over. I can come out of the closet and join my fellow obsessives openly in the tool section of our local garden centre.

A sharply defined edge to a pitch is, I declare, an absolute joy to behold. Even better, a pitch whose turf is bordered by a surface of contrasting colour or texture, such as a terracotta shale track. Ah, happiness indeed.

Yet show me an otherwise luscious pitch which peters out at the touchlines in a ragged, straggly sort of fashion, or abuts an unkempt track of grey mush, and I am totally and unreasonably discomfited. It is as if a great work of art has been sullied by a cheap frame, or a delicate dish dumped upon a chipped plate. To have made all that effort over the basics, only then to give up at the peripherals? Unforgivable.

Maybe that tetchy psychologist was right. Maybe I do need therapy. And yet it is possible that I am already facing up to the demons within, partly, and ironically, aided by the brilliance and innovation of stadium designers and turf technologists.

You see, men's insistence on taming the natural world is bound up in a paradox. Much as we delight in our ability to shape and humanise the natural landscape, sometimes men go too far. No really. When that happens, as in a pristine, manicured Swiss village, perhaps, or a Singaporean shopping mall, the result is to create an unnerving sense of 'placelessness'. In those cases, humans have, in effect, dehumanised their own environment. John Bale might say that they have committed 'topicide'.

In the United States there are even signs of a backlash against the ubiquity of the regulation, blemish-free lawn. Neatness, as I learnt when peering down on my neighbour's garden in Birmingham, is only a wheelbarrow-load away from sterility.

Unquestionably, modern stadiums are heading that same way.

The perfect pitch of today is of course no more 'natural' than a Bonsai tree. Since the arrival of Budding's mower and, a few decades later, the heavy roller, the cricket wicket in particular has become a total artifice; shaved and rolled, bald and smooth as a billiard table, with barely a hint of turf or a patch of green. It is as if the groundsman has had to spend the spring and summer undoing all the work he has put in during the rest of the year.

Pitches for football and rugby, meanwhile, are nowadays laced with all manner of artificial elements, such as pieces of plastic mesh or minute fibres mixed into the sandy subsoil, or even green, fibre strands sewn in at regular intervals amongst the real blades of grass. We used to delight in the differences between stadiums around the country. We could even identify them on the television without seeing the surrounding stands. The sloping pitches. The boggy pitches. The large ones and the small ones. The ones that looked dappled in spring, or like meadows in summer. But those differences are being whittled away by modern expertise.

Does anyone remember mud?

Increasingly the modern pitch has no contact at all with Mother Earth. Thanks to the turf boffins, a perfectly serviceable and flawless pitch can now be grown in sections, on individual pallets, and then delivered to the stadium, to be slotted together on a concrete floor (as at Cardiff's new Millennium Stadium). Or moved in and out on one slab of concrete, like a giant window box, as at Arnhem. Movable cricket wickets are also in an advanced state of development.

Where will it all end?

There was once a novel which tried to predict what football will be like in the future. It was titled *They Used To Play On Grass* (and was co-written by Terry Venables, who used to manage England). I suspect that 'they' always will play football on grass, as will their counterparts in rugby and cricket. Except that the grass of the future, of the very near future, will become so finely sophisticated and appear so absolutely unblemished that eventually no one will think of it as grass any longer. Rather like the pre-packed meat we buy in supermarkets, its true nature and origins will be forgotten.

I cannot bear the thought that this should happen to grass, to God's own carpet.

Instead, I find that lately, gazing out at yet another flawless expanse of turf in yet another modern, state-of-the-art stadium, I am starting to think that here and there some wildflowers and clover would not look amiss.*

*Readers interested to know the state of the author's own modest patch of turf in his London backyard are referred to the old saying, 'I fought the lawn and the lawn won'.

2 TERMS AND CONDITIONS

Hemingway took a slug of vermouth, then looked me squarely in the eye. We were in the Café Iruña, his old haunt on the Plaza del Castillo.

'So, Simey the limey. All that bull about stadiums and amphitheatres, men and grass? What exactly is your point?'

I laughed carelessly, drew on a Gauloise and slouched back in my chair. How should I answer Uncle Ernesto, the great one? What was my point, and why was I even in Pamplona for the fiesta of San Fermin when I had no great love for the *corrida*, the bullfight, and certainly no great capacity for Dionysian excess?

Outside the Iruña, ill-clad *guiris* – 'foreigners' in the local dialect – passed unsteadily along the pavement, killing time between binges. Shuffle, shuffle. Shuffle, shuffle. In the centre of the square, backpackers huddled conspiratorially on the parched, litter-strewn grass. Around them lay assorted bikers, flat out in their leathers and black singlets, their faces pale from excess. Occasionally, an acrid breeze would waft over from dried pools of last night's vomit, flaking in the gutters under the mid-day sun.

A young German couple approached the Iruña. The man walked, arms at his side, chest expanded, so that everyone might see his faded T-shirt, ripped at the belly. A few hours earlier no doubt he had starred in the early-morning *encierro*, had run with the bulls; six snorting behemoths stampeding some 800 metres through the narrow streets of Pamplona from the church of Santo Domingo to the bullring (where they would meet their fate in the evening), accompanied by hundreds of prize lunatics. And here was one who had felt their hornyed ire. His *Fräulein*, clearly, had never loved him more. Oh brave, handsome Hans.

This, partly, was what I had come to witness: this 'paroxysm of celebration', this 'worldwide mecca of diversion', as Pamplona's week-long, annual homage to Bacchus and the bulls has been described by various bleary-eyed veterans. Hemingway himself called it a 'wonderful nightmare'.

'I did?'

'Yes, I think you did. And if you didn't, I will.'

But there was something else.

'I suppose, Ernesto,' I began, 'that I'm searching for the missing link. By the way, do you mind me calling you Ernesto? I know some of the locals call you Papa, but for me that seems a little too familiar.'

'Hey, kid,' Hemingway insisted. 'Call me what the hell you like. I am only a device, after all. This is your party.'

'OK, then Ernesto it is. The point, as I see it, Ernesto, is that the bullring, and the seven or eight days of the Sanfermines in particular, form Europe's last surviving link between the Colosseum of ancient Rome and the football terraces of the twentieth century.'

Hemingway laughed. 'Jeez, Simey. And I thought you were here to enjoy yourself.'

'Oh, but I am. You see, in most sporting arenas in most parts of the developed world, the whole culture and experience of being a spectator, the whole environment of spectator sport, has become sanitised to a degree quite unimaginable only ten or twenty years ago. Go here, go there, do this, don't do that, sit down, be nice, don't swear and oh, do come again and bring the kids and your credit card next time . . .'

'Your what?'

'Oh, it's not so bad really. I mean, it's not as if we're being asked to salute genocidal tyrants or applaud five-hour speeches outlining proposals for agrarian reform. And of course it is still bread and circuses. All spectators sign up to that reality the moment they buy a ticket, whether they like it or not. But it has all changed, Ernesto,' I sighed. 'And I suppose for all sorts of perfectly good reasons.'

'On which, I sense, you are about to expound.'

' 'Fraid so. First comes safety. Boring and obvious but still true. Having spectators die at sports events is not the ideal way to sell the product, let alone preserve one's customer base. And in our country we've had quite a few people dying at football grounds, over the years. So, obviously, something *had to be done*.

'Then there's comfort, because we're all becoming softies these days. And commerce. Always there, of course, but nowadays more highly refined. They used to sell souvenirs and snacks. Now it's "*merchandising*", and "*food and beverage*". Americanisms, naturally. Stadium operators even have a measure of how much we punters are swallowing the bait. It's called "*spend per head*".'

'Ouch, that hurts!' Hemingway interjected. 'Don't forget, I blew my brains out nearly forty years back.'

'Sorry, Ernesto, I meant no offence. What I'm trying to say is that, a bit like the Colossseum or the bullring, going to the traditional twentieth-century sports ground used to be an end in itself. Yet now it's as if you can't possibly be allowed to have a good time unless you're consuming an official brand. "Things go better with Coke" is no longer a mere slogan. It's part of the business plan. As the T-shirt says, *Veni, Vidi, Visa*: I came, I saw, I did a little shopping.'

'Whereas in the bullring in Pamplona . . .'

'Exactly. It's back to basics.'

'Go on, then.'

'The maintenance of law and order is another factor. Closed-circuit television salesmen have never had it so good recently, particularly in stadiums. While we watch the action, there's always someone watching us on a monitor. Watching us picking our noses. Catching us swearing at the referee. And then there's TV itself, because, having spent so many millions on the rights, broadcasters are desperate to present a picture of wholesome entertainment to the folks back home rather than risk showing any hints of anarchy or social unrest. I don't just mean rioting fans either. I mean whole swathes of humanity obeying their own instincts rather than dancing to someone else's tune. Which, incidentally, is usually something awful like Tina Turner wailing "Simply the best".'

'And is she, or it?'

'No, Ernesto, on both counts. No, no, and no again.'

'That's three counts.'

'And then there's the whole relationship between spectators and the stadium. Essentially stadiums used to be public places, albeit often laid on by private enterprise. The masses paid their sixpences or dimes to enter through the gate, but after that they were more or less left to their own devices, as if in a park. Which is maybe why so many stadiums designed to stage the so-called peoples' sports, like football and baseball, are still named "parks", to retain that illusion. If you like, the punter reserved his or her right to remain volatile, to embrace the notion of risk. Yet now that stadiums have become sanitised and, in a spatial sense, privatised, spectators have been seduced, cowed even, into becoming mere consumers. Some experts have called this the "commodification" of sport, though they're probably trying to sell us something too.'

'Whoa, Simey! Sounds like you're ready to bust a few heads. Are you one of those English football hooligan types?'

'Me? Far from it, Ernesto. I'm as passive as the next man; pathetically content with the comforts, the safety, the fact that I can go to a game and get to eat and piss when I want and not have to worry about some arsehole readjusting my features if I happen to be wearing the wrong colour shirt. At the theatre, at rock concerts, at sporting events; the changes have been the same the whole world over. Even if they take a bit longer to occur in some areas than others. Essentially, one day you're a "groundling", standing up in the pit, throwing rotten fruit at the actors and pissing down the leg of your mate's breeches. The next you're slumped in a padded armchair eating overpriced ice cream with a plastic spoon and telling off the people behind you for crackling their toffee wrappers. You know, there are whole stadiums nowadays, open-air ones I mean, in which you can't even have a smoke.'

'No! They can't do that, can they?' Hemingway spluttered on his Havana.

'Oh yes, they can,' I insisted. 'And maybe that's why I've come to Pamplona. I just want one last taste of that so-called "risk society" before I go back to my seat like a good boy. Pamplona during the fiesta is probably one of the last places in Europe where one can experience that "paroxysm of celebration", at least inside a stadium.'

'OK, I get it. You're a wimp, but you like to watch other people get down and dirty. But did I hear you right? Are you saying a bullring is a stadium?'

'Yes, I am. Bullfighting may technically not be a sport, but as a building the bullring does pretty well the same job as the ancient amphitheatres, or for that matter modern stadiums or arenas. Which is why it forms such a vital link between the Colosseum and, say, Wembley or the Albert Hall.'

'Albert who?'

'The Albert Hall in London. It's a bullring with a lid on top.'

'Well, maybe it is but now I'm even more confused. And you keep saying stadiums. Don't you mean "stadia"? Didn't your teachers teach you anything?'

'Yeh, I know, I get picked up on this all the time. To be honest, Ernesto, I use both stadiums and stadia, depending on my mood. But, if pressed, I still go for stadiums, on the basis that most people say *arenas* rather than *arenae* and *circuses* instead of *circii*.'

'There you are, you're doing it again, getting me all confused. What the hell is the difference between a stadium, an arena and a circus? I don't get it.'

'Join the club, Ernesto. Since the days of Anorakos and Vicarius the terminology has got terribly mixed up. In their day it wasn't simple either. You see, the word *stadium* is the Latin version of the Greek word *stadion*. A *stadion* was actually a measurement of length, corresponding to approximately 192.25 metres, and because the track at Olympia was one *stadion* long, that was the name given to the very first race staged at the very first Olympic Games, in 776 BC.'

'So I guess it was just as well for future generations that they didn't start off with a three-legged race for the moms and pops.'

'You guess correctly, Ernesto. But that's the easy bit. The first Greek *stadions* were U-shaped. That is, the slopes on which spectators sat around the single, straight running track were long at the sides and joined up to form a tight curve at one end. When the same U-shaped format, but on a larger scale, was adopted by the Greeks for horse and chariot racing, they called the enclosure a *hippodromos*. The modern-day hippodrome. However, when the Romans built similarly U-shaped racetracks, they used the word *circus* instead, even though there was nothing remotely circular about them.'

'Jeez, I wish I'd never asked.'

'Then, during the first century BC, the Romans also developed a building known as an *amphitheatrum*, because it was in effect two *theatri* put together, face to face, to form a large enclosure in the round. Why they didn't call this a *circus* instead I do not for the life of me know, but what I do know is that you often see ancient Greek and Roman theatres, such as the ones at Epidaurus and Caesarea, referred to in guidebooks as amphitheatres, whereas unless their seating tiers go all the way round to form a complete circle or oval, like the ones at Verona, Arles or Nîmes, strictly speaking they are but theatres. Big theatres, perhaps. Beautiful, evocative and still admirably functional theatres, certainly. But theatres none the less.'

'You know Simey, I was just gonna say that I've seen the amphitheatres at Verona, Arles and Nîmes described also as *arenas*. But on second thoughts I think I might just have another drink.'

'Ah no, I mean yes. *Arena* is simply the Latin for sand. So the *arena* was actually the stage of the amphitheatre. Though not any more. The terms all have new meanings. So a modern-day circus is no longer a racetrack but, well, a circus, as in Big Top, except when it's a large roundabout in the middle of London. And a modern stadium is much more like an amphitheatre, and a modern arena is like a stadium, but with a roof on top.'

'Simey, may I ask a personal question? Do you have many friends?'

'Oh, but it gets worse, Ernesto. You see, there's also confusion between the use of the terms *stadium* and *ground*. The modern sense of a stadium is that of an enclosure which has been designed, if not necessarily built, all in one go, to a predetermined master plan, whereas if the enclosure evolves over the years, to no particular set plan, and has no running track and perhaps only individual grandstands, it is more likely to be considered a ground. But plenty of modern, well-planned football and rugby stadiums are nevertheless referred to as grounds, while, equally, plenty of mix-and-match football and rugby grounds are persistently called stadiums. Mind you, I don't think I've ever come across a cricket stadium that's been called anything other than a ground. Except in India . . .'

'And people say that the bullfight is a bloody and pointless exercise . . .'

'Sorry, Ernesto,' I mumbled. 'But there is just one last thing.'

Hemingway drew on his cigar with menacing deliberation, daring me to continue.

'OK, it's just this. I'll be quick, I promise. In today's terminology, right, stadiums are partially or wholly open to the elements. And modern arenas are fully enclosed, and if they contain any sand at all it's usually confined to the fire buckets. But, during the 1960s, your fellow countrymen started building stadiums with fixed, fully enclosed roofs. Now, instead of calling these "large arenas" – which in effect is what they were – they became known more commonly as *domes*. Which leads me to my final point. What, I ask you, are we going to call the very latest generation of stadiums which, like the one in Arnhem, have roofs which open *and* close? You see, Arnhem's stadium has been named the Gelredome; that is, it's a dome in the province of Gelderland. Yet there's another stadium in the Netherlands which also has a retractable roof, but that has been called the Amsterdam Arena. So, Ernesto, you see the problem. What would you call them?'

Hemingway looked up with one eye open, took a gulp of vermouth and spat, 'I call them both too clever by half, and suggest an end to this debate. Either that or you find someone else to bore rigid.'

We sat for several minutes in silence, until finally Ernesto spoke up.

'All right, all right, Simey, I'll play ball, what the hell. So go on, tell me, what happened to Olympia and the Colosseum in the end? Who was right, Anorakos or Vicarius?'

'Well, Ernesto, since you ask. Actually they both were right, in their own ways. Olympia and the Colosseum ended up enjoying amazingly long runs, absurdly long by modern standards, in fact. Olympia stayed open from 776 BC until AD 369. That's 1,145 years by my calculations, whereas these days a modern stadium does well to last fifty years before the bulldozers tear it down.'

'Anorakos was right, then. Maybe there is merit in keeping things simple after all.'

'Maybe. In fact, Olympia would have survived longer had the ultra-pious emperor Theodosius the Great not formally abolished the games in AD 393. Too much like a subversive pagan ritual, he thought, and of course he was absolutely right. It still is. You can't stage a modern Olympics without Mammon on your team. Put it like this. The ancients managed to clock up no fewer than 287 Olympiads every four years without a single break – despite wars and major political upheaval – whereas we moderns have only got up to number 27 in Sydney, and three of those had to be cancelled owing to the two world wars. In order to match the ancient Greeks' record the current Olympic sequence would have to continue uninterrupted until the year 3041.'

'Will Mammon last that long? Anyway, enough of the stats. I bet you're now gonna feed me some line about the bullfight being the last vestige of the animal shows they had at the Colosseum. In other words, that Vicarius was not entirely wrong.'

'*Bravo*, Ernesto, you're ahead of me. Not only have animal shows survived in the form of bullfights – extraordinary, really, when you think of how everything else remotely dangerous in modern Europe has been banned by the bureaucrats in Brussels – but the notion of the spectacle has been rediscovered by modern man to such an extent that there are now Colosseums in every major town and city in the world. We might call them stadiums rather than amphitheatres, but they're pretty much the same buildings in form and function.'

'With the Colosseum being *El Papa* of them all.'

'Big time. It may be the world's most visited traffic island now, but it managed to survive as a fully functional venue for nearly 450 years, which by any standards surely deserves a bit of applause. If you think about it, why else would the Venerable Bede have referred to it as the Colosseum, two hundred years after it closed, had its reputation been anything other than, well, colossal?'

'Wasn't Bede the Northumberland monk who wrote: "While stands the Colosseum, Rome shall stand; When falls the Colosseum, Rome shall fall; And when Rome falls – the World"?'

'The very same, although the words you quote were Byron's translation of the Latin original, published a thousand years later.'

'Sentimental hokum, if you ask me. Last time I saw Rome it was doing fine with a half-fallen Colosseum. And anyways, why did the Colosseum go belly-up in the end?'

'Well, once Christianity became the official religion of the empire in 330 and Emperor Constantine set up his new capital in Byzantium, business started to drop off. Then the gladiators got the final thumbs-down in 404 from the young western emperor of the time, Honorarius. Shame, really, since a year later they would have been able to celebrate the 500th anniversary of the first ever gladiator fight in Rome.'

'Being a killjoy must have run in the family, then,' said Hemingway. 'Wasn't Honorarius the son of Theodosius, the one who blew the imperial whistle on the Olympics?'

'Hey, Ernesto, for a literary device you're doing really well. You're right, the gladiators were banned eleven years after the last ancient Olympiad. Mind you, animal shows did carry on for another century or so, before the Visigoths and Vandals decided to call in on Rome during their travels. The last recorded show at the Amphitheatre – at the Colosseum, that is – was in 523. After that, decay began to take its toll.'

'Happens to us all, I guess.'

'Which brings us back to the bullring.'

'Hold on, Simey. What about that new stadium Domitian built? And what about the Circus Maximus? What happened to them?'

'Oh, they hung on till the decline and fall of the empire too, although Vicarius was pretty much correct about Domitian's Stadium. Athletics were no great draw in Rome – no change there, then – and the stadium ended up hosting gladiator and animal shows, just as Vicarius predicted. Thereafter the building fell to pieces, although if you visit Rome today you can still trace almost its exact outlines in the form of the Piazza Navona.'

'The Piazza Navona? Well, whadd'ya know! I once had a fight over a girl in the Piazza Navona. By that café where they sold the ice cream . . .'

'And still do, Ernesto. The Circus Maximus, on the other hand, though still on the map, sadly is hardly more than a large expanse of grass in the middle of the city. Huge it is too. Archaeologists now reckon it held as many as 385,000 punters at its peak.'

'Phoo! That's big. And the Greens, and the Reds, and all those Ben Hur types on their chariots?'

'They carried on racing, but in Constantinople, for another couple of centuries. Other than that, any medieval or Renaissance European fancying a bit of spectator sport had either to seek out public hangings or floggings, jousting of course, or, more likely, face a lifetime of blank weekends. Or travel. There were annual events like the *Palio* horse race in Siena or *Calcio Fiorentina* in Florence. The Spanish staged early forms of bullfighting in a few old Roman amphitheatres, or else promoters simply put up temporary stands in town squares. Then permanent bullrings started to appear during the eighteenth century. There's one at Ronda, near Marbella, which opened in 1785, and several dating from the mid nineteenth century, many still in regular use.'

'Ah, Marbella! What a beautiful town. Is it still? I had a fight over a girl there too. Or did I have a fight with a girl? Hell, I just can't . . .'

'There was also a huge, open arena built by Napoleon in Milan, in 1807, where football and athletics were staged between 1910 and 1947. Inter Milan played there before they moved to the San Siro. And there's a fabulous, and I mean fabulous, 7,000-seat stadium-cum-ball court in the Italian town of Macerata, dating back to 1829, where they played a game called *palla al bracciale*. The venue was titled, rather wonderfully, the *Sferisterio*. Do you know, I like that name so much, Ernesto, I think I'll say it again. *Sferisterio*. Otherwise, the bullring was pretty much the only show on offer until the age of the train and the revolution in spectator sport begun by the Victorians in nineteenth-century Britain.'

'Well!' Hemingway declared, 'I sure am better for knowing all that. Now, if you've finished, I guess the real reason that I'm here is that you were saying something about Pamplona and some missing link.'

'Ah yes, the missing link indeed, Ernesto, which in a way is very much your creation. You see, if you hadn't written so damn powerfully about the Sanfermines and the *corrida* in the 1920s and 1930s, Pamplona would probably have tootled along quite nicely as a boring little town with a quaint rural festival attached. Instead of which, largely thanks to you, hundreds of thousands of tourists, and, if you'll forgive me, earnest *aficionados*, flock here every year to run with the bulls and to witness the unpolitically correct slaughter of innocent animals. Whereas you know and I know that real *aficionados* – that is, people who don't just like bullfighting but know it, relish it, cherish it and don't have to keep checking all the terms in the glossary provided at the back of *every* goddam book on the subject – don't come to Pamplona because of the splendour of its bullring or even because it offers the best in bullfighting.'

'Hell, no, that's true. They head to Madrid or Seville.'

'Exactly, Ernesto. Pamplona is where you come to get pissed.'

'And did you?' asked Hemingway, several days later when we bumped into each other in a bar in Montmartre. I was, at the time, trying to persuade Gertrude Stein to accompany me to a football match at the new Stade de France.

'Ernesto,' I said, grinning back, 'I most certainly did get pissed. Which is one reason why the account that follows may be flawed in the extreme.'

'One reason? Is there another?'

'Oh, sure. Three days after I left Pamplona the entire contents of my car boot was liberated by thieves in Nîmes, not far from the Roman amphitheatre, as it happens. My notes on Pamplona, all my taped interviews, cameras, films, underwear, the lot. All the bastards left was a bottle of warm Evian, an old pair of shoes and some novelty fairy lights I'd bought on a whim in Barcelona.'

'And how is old Gertie?'

'Oh, you know, still not much of a sports fan.'

* * *

From 6 to 14 July every year, the whole of Pamplona gives itself up to wantonness and inebriation in the name of the saint San Fermin. During this wild, wild week, the only time one dares not be drunk is if one is crazy enough to run with the bulls. But since the *encierro* begins at eight o'clock sharp every morning and lasts barely three minutes, it at least allows participants a few hours to sober up after the night before.

I arrived halfway through the fiesta, one mid-day, and after a quick trot around the city's football stadium – because I just can't help myself – found an overpriced room in a gloomy *pensión* off the Plaza de la Cruz. The two old sisters who ran the place immediately tried to overcharge me, and when I corrected their sums the dominant one wagged her finger at me, narrowed her eyes and pronounced me to be '*Muy listo!*' Very smart.

'*Muy listo!*' she intoned again, the word 'muy' sounding like a Navarrese nanny-goat. '*Ma-aw-aw-wee leesto!*' it sounded like. What she was really saying, for her sister's benefit, was, 'Just our luck, a Jew who can add up.'

'You'll never get a ticket to the bullfight now,' she continued, watching me unpack. 'Never. The bullfights in Pamplona, it's like the World Cup. Sold out months ago.'

But that didn't put me off, for I was *muy listo*.

Outside the bullring I played the usual watching-and-waiting game, seeing who was buying, who was selling. During six months in Latin America I don't recall ever buying a ticket for a football match or a *corrida* from an official ticket office. Much less fun, and only a touch more expensive. If one is *muy listo*.

But in Pamplona I didn't want just any ticket. Mine had to be for the *andanada de sol*; that is, the cheap seats on the sunny side of the bullring's upper tier, where the *peñas* gather with their booze and brass bands. The *peñas* are social clubs whose members attend bullfights (and football matches) in groups, based round a particular district or café. There are said to be around fifteen or so *peñas* in Pamplona, and if I was to taste the true flavour of what Kenneth Tynan once called 'the loony fair' I resolved that I would have to be among them.

Initially their members seemed easy to spot, or so I thought. During Sanfermines many wear the official uniform; all-white shirts and trousers set off rather rakishly by a scarlet *pañuelo*, or neckerchief, and a red *faja*, or sash, tied round the waist. Said accessories are donned with a whoop (and a song) from the moment a rocket goes off at mid-day on 6 July until the very end of the fiesta on the 14th. Seeing this uniform for the first time I thought I'd bumped into the local Young Communist League on an outing. That was until I saw middle-aged secretaries walking around Pamplona wearing exactly the same garb. And grannies, and teenagers, and self-conscious *guiris* aplenty, similarly attired. Few of them would be members of the *peñas*.

Then I imagined the uniform might perhaps be another link with the past, since custom at the Colosseum required Romans to wear their best white togas. But again, apparently not. I later learnt that in common with so many of Pamplona's 'traditions', the white and red is a relatively recent adoption. More recent still is the 'underpants race' (starting at 3.00 a.m. in the city centre, with breaks for champagne and prizes for the dirtiest knickers). Honourable mention should also be given to a favourite new *guiri* 'tradition' of jumping off the top of the Fountain of Navarreria in the hope that some Australian or Kiwi beefcake below, rather than the shallow water, will break your fall.

But then the entire fiesta of San Fermin seems to consist of one set piece after another – parades, races, songs, recitals, rituals, bull-fights, bull running, heifer baiting – lasting from 12.00 noon to 9.00 a.m. the following morning, every day. Which means that not everyone is in a fit state to attend every bullfight, and, of the rest, quite a sizeable minority have lost all sense of time and place anyway.

Buying a ticket therefore proved not too hard at all.

The *corrida* starts every evening at 6.30, so I had an hour or more to sus out the ticket situation. *Aficionados*, I soon realised, avoid the *andanada de sol* at all costs. They prefer to be in the *sombra*, the shaded sections, and ideally lower down, either in the *grada* (the middle tier) or the *tendido* (the lowest tier), for which black-market tickets are, as one wizened old tout told me all too gleefully, rarer than a fat tortoise at an *encierro*. At least I think that was what he said. Spanish dialect never has been my strong point.

For the wealthy or for those blessed with contacts, the most highly prized ticket in the bullring is for the front row, immediately behind the *barrera*, the wooden fence over which one can lean and smell the fear, the blood and the horseshit. A heady cocktail it must be too; musky, bovine, earthy, like the sole of a cowboy's boot after a night on the range. But tickets for the *barrera* lay beyond the reach of a latecomer with a budget. Besides which, I was determined to stay with my mission.

After quizzing various types who looked as if they knew their tauromachian onions (mostly Australians, plus a few sober chaps from Sussex, wearing BHS casuals and unbranded trainers), and with thirty minutes remaining before the *paseo* – the opening parade – I finally managed to bargain successfully for my ticket. Section 11, right in the heart of the action; 3,000 pesetas to the tout, a 200 per cent profit for him, but not a single grudge on my part. It was still cheaper than watching Premier League football in England.

Back at the *pensión* I kitted up as advised: an old T-shirt and sun hat, with a beach towel for added protection, shorts and old shoes (too old even for French car thieves). In a cheap carrier bag I packed bottled water (not to drink, but to wash my specs), several plastic bags to protect my camera, and a dainty *boccadilla* for the *merienda* – the half-time break which takes place after the third bull. (You see why glossaries are so popular.)

How gauche did I really appear? On a scale of ten? Judging by the way the two sisters tracked my departure with such studied disdain, I'd say nine and a half. No wonder they had insisted on payment up front for the room, in cash. *Muy listas*. Who knows when they would see me again. If at all.

And off I went, an English lamb to the Sanfermines slaughter; an innocent with nineteen years' professional experience of visiting and writing about stadiums; a tentative adventurer who had been to bullfights and bunfights all over the world. Had felt the hot breath of the mob, in Manchester, in Mexico, in Milan.

But the next three hours at the *plaza de toros* in Pamplona? No, this was different. Quite different. This called for a glossary of terms that would make the Devil's own dictionary seem like a manual for boy scouts.

Ever the professional, I can tell you that the bullring is no great beauty. It was opened in 1922, expanded in 1967, and has a capacity of 19,529. Other than that, the word 'pandemonium' does not do full justice to the experience.

Nowadays, being patently drunk and disorderly would bar one's admittance to most stadiums. Not in Pamplona. In most parts of the world, taking any glass bottle into a sports venue is forbidden (except at English cricket grounds, where the gatemen search you only to check on the vintage). In Pamplona the guys on the gate laugh if you turn up short-handed. My single bottle of plonk – my one, oh-so-daring, aren't I being naughty with my little 70 cl. accompaniment, bought on the way to the bullring – was enough to mark me out as a total, teetotal mummy's boy.

The guys in Section 11 could hardly have been more welcoming, nevertheless. '*Inglaterra?*' they asked, making room for me amid the off-licence they had strewn across the concrete benches. I don't mean bottles here, by the way. I'm talking buckets. Big buckets. In fact, very big buckets. Actually, vats. All full to the brim with *sangria* and another popular local lubricant, *calimocho* – a mix of rough Rioja and Coke, designed to keep you happy and peppy and a little bit burpy all at the same time.

It is reckoned that the average human consumes approximately 830 litres, or 1,460 pints, of liquid per annum. If true, how far the rest of us clearly lag behind the lads in the *peñas*.

'*Argentina, Argentina!*' they chanted as I, the Englishman, stumbled self-consciously into their circle. (It's a football thing.) Then, as the parade began down below, all hands in the upper tier turned skywards and a vaguely recognisable tune started up. Some quaint Navarrese folk serenade? An old tradition of the *corrida*, perhaps? And yet its strains filled me with a familiar dread . . . la la la-la la-la la-la, la la . . .

Of course! The Euro-bloody-vision theme music. The first movement of Charpentier's *Te Deum*.

Oh Te Deum, oh Lord, I prayed, spare me from that refrain, and from the memory of the programmes it used to herald.

Introducing *At home with Sacha Distel and guests*.

Or, *On the piste with Charles Aznavour.*

Or, worse, *Jeux sans frontières.*

'And now, live, over to Pamplona in Spain, where it looks like the dashing toreador El Cordobes has a "tail" or two for Kathy Kirby, and, oh yes, an ear too. Bully for you, Kathy!'

No doubt about it, I had suddenly come over all European. So much so that when an American sitting nearby asked what was the tune we were all blabbing like nursery kids, I roared back, 'Oh, you wouldn't understand,' while my new *peña* pals and I exchanged cigarettes and platitudes, then moved on to liquids.

By the time the first bull had met his maker – an act met with silence from the *aficionados*, owing, quite literally, to its clumsy execution by the matador – my paltry bottle was empty, my back drenched and my hat covered in flour. But it could have been worse. In other sections the lads were throwing yellow dye.

As the *corrida* continued, I learnt to take photos in the nanoseconds that elapsed between my standing upright and being subjected to showers of *sangria*. Usually the liquid was laced with soggy fruit. Peaches, I quickly gathered, hurt the most on contact.

Seeing that I was game, my new *peña* pals soon muscled me into some action. Strangers' arms and even stranger armpits locked me in their clawing, intimate embrace. Shoulders entwined, men together, swaying left, swaying right. Rowing forward, rowing back. Standing up, crouching down. Each time to a chant. '*Las Chicas, Las Chicas, yeh, yeh, yeh.*' This matador has *cojones*. That one's mother is a *puta*, a whore. Long live San Fermin. Fuck the Madrileños. *Hijos de putas*, the lot of them. To the left, a brass band. To the right, a brass band. '*Yeh, yeh, yeh.*'

'What're they singing?' shouted up the American at one point.

It sounded something like '*Qué guapa estás, Maria, Qué guapa estás, Maria.*'

'It sounds to me something like, "How cute you are, Maria".'

'Are you sure?' he shouted again. 'Sounds kinda stupid to me.'

But then I thought I heard a song start up about a packet of chocolate, so I gave up trying to translate.

'Of course it's kinda stupid,' I yelled back to the American, but then, all of a sudden, felt an urge to sit down. Down. Down. Had to sit down. Stereophonic discordance. Microwave sun. I was getting pig sick and roasted in the middle, and had hardly seen a bit of the *corrida*.

All that preparation and reading of the glossaries – wasted. This was my fourth or fifth bullfight, so by now I should have been able to decide which side of the *barrera* I was on. Was I for this spectacle or against? Was it true, as I had read somewhere, that more people are killed playing American football than fighting bulls? Could I tell a *veronica* from a *natural*? Could I distinguish between a *derechazo* and a *pase de pecho*? Had that been a good kill or a travesty? As Hemingway wrote, either you get it or you don't.

'And are you getting it, Simey?' A voice came through to me.

'Ernesto, is that you? I'm not even sure I know where I am.'

By the third bull's entry, my *compañeros* had turned their attention to the other tourists around us. Maybe I was too splattered to take any more punishment, or perhaps, as I was later informed, once a *guiri* has proved he can take it, the artillery lay off as a mark of respect. Or maybe it was because a group of shapely young girls had just entered our section.

'*Chicitas!*' went up the cry.

Whoa, and in T-shirts!

In an instant, cups, bottles and beakers were refilled and then emptied with ferocious precision until hardly a dry bosom remained in the aisle. 'Hey, Señor Inglés. You gay boy?'

Reluctantly I joined in, feeling rotten for participating in this crude assault upon the girls, yet noticing their now erect nipples all the same. Well, what the hell. I was drenched too, and they could see my nipples through my T-shirt as well if they wanted.

But then came a diversion. And how. From the vomitory down to our right, up popped the head of a diminutive, elderly Japanese man, wielding an expensive camera, a tripod and an inquisitive expression, as if he'd been sitting down below and had wandered up to see who was making all the noise. I'm not sure what the Spanish is for 'sitting duck'. But it hardly mattered since the lads immediately tried to engage the man in Japanese.

'*Ka-mi-ka-ze, ka-mi-ka-ze!*' they chanted, before unleashing their own Pearl Harbor in bucket loads. I saw the man glance up in our direction, open-mouthed, at the exact moment before a wave of *sangria* cruelly lashed his torso. A naked, knife-wielding assassin leaping out of a potted palm could hardly have provoked in him a more startled expression.

'*Olé!*' cried the *aficionados*, applauding the matador now in the ring. (I really should have been paying more attention, though I knew the score. It read: Humans 3. Bulls 0.)

Back in our bibulous bedlam meanwhile, '*Olé!*' cried the *peñas*, refilling their weapons. Cowering, the Japanese man saw his chance and, with surprising agility, managed to duck and weave, like an infantryman dodging fire, along the aisle into the safety of the next vomitory, down to our left. A lull ensued.

But only momentarily, for a few seconds later, from out of the vomitory on our right, clearly in search of someone, up popped another head. That of . . . a diminutive, ageing Japanese woman. The wife. In a smart Burberry raincoat with a matching Hermes scarf and handbag.

This time I had to look away as the bombardment was renewed. Poor woman. Poor man. Such tales of Europe they would take home with them. Such barbarity they had encountered. Such disrespect for the elderly. Such dry-cleaning bills.

And then it was time for the *merienda* and we all fell back on to our concrete benches, bone-tired and sticky.

Time to eat. Time to catch our breaths. Time, as always, to drink.

Next to me a leary-eyed man of fifty or so, with a cold-box the size of a small car, pulled out an unmarked litre-sized bottle and winked at me in delight. A sideways flick of his wrist and my plastic cup ranneth over.

I stared unsteadily down into its oily depths as my new *amigo* began to toast '*La Reina Ay-lee-za-bet!*' What would I do? Drink and swim, or wimp out and face another hour or so of drenching? Another mouthful of alcohol and my head would have spun away. I vaguely recalled the words of Robert Cohn, one of Hemingway's characters in *Fiesta: The Sun Also Rises*, his novel centred in Pamplona.

'Doesn't this thing ever stop?' Cohn moaned, halfway through the fiesta.

'Not for a week,' came the reply.

I knew how he felt, and this was only my first day. Hemingway hadn't helped much either, making Cohn into a pathetic idiot and a Jewish one at that.

'*La Reina! Da Queen!*' my neighbour insisted. But what was in the drink? I could have sworn it smelled of . . . oh Lord, it did indeed. That sickly aroma conjured up another night of hell, long past.

The drink was *pacharán*, the favourite liqueur of the Navarrese. The smell was anise, mixed with, I was told, bilberries. Sweet ruin. Sweet Jesus.

'*Inglés!*' cried the man once again, raising his tumbler. '*La Reina Ay-lee-za-bet!*'

Somehow my cup rose. My stomach tightened in dread anticipation. I put the cup to my lips . . .

'*La Reina* . . .'

And then, like an angel of mercy, into the aisle reappeared the couple from Japan.

If only I could have thanked them more formally for their timely return. Instead, I did what any gentleman would have done in the circumstances. I offered them my drink. Admittedly not in a container. But they received it all the same. Every last drop.

I was getting the hang of this fiesta lark.

* * *

At this point, in all seriousness and with not a little embarrassment, I should explain something.

Back in England, for the six years before my trip to Pamplona, I had acquired, shall we say, a certain gravitas within stadium circles. After the 1989 disaster at Hillsborough, in which ninety-six football fans died as the result of a complete cock-up by the authorities, I had been invited to sit on various official bodies in order to devote my knowledge of stadiums to weighty matters of public interest; for example, the formulation of new safety standards, the collation of design guidelines, and the implementation of a whole series of stringent new rulings on crowd management. Working hard, working long hours, hand in hand with government inspectors, policemen, architects, engineers and planners, I had come to understand the dangers of an uncontrolled crowd in a poorly managed or badly designed stadium. I was appointed, for heaven's sake, the editor of the British government's official guide to safety at sports grounds.

Trip hazards, design flaws, management lapses: I knew them all, and worked long through the night to help bring about their eradication.

And there I was in Pamplona, vision blurred, brain addled, clothes drenched, watching a pencil-thin Spaniard in an embroidered waistcoat and pink stockings plunge his sword into the neck muscle of an innocent beast, while all around me sat hundreds, no, thousands, of revellers in a state of befuddled anarchy.

Every aisle, I now realised, was blocked by bodies or bottles. Liquid of an unidentifiable nature cascaded down the steps, lapping my shoes and making islands of the sodden newspapers and sandwiches littering the floor. Not a steward was there, not a policeman in sight. With every boozy bombardment, with every unsteady jig I was party to, somewhere from deep within my British reserve, doom-laden possibilities flashed their sober warnings.

Would death come slowly and agonisingly in a stampede for the exit? Or would I choke on my own vomit first? What use would research be when crowd pressure from behind sent me tumbling head first over the balcony rail, a rail which I now saw was patently under the regulation height (1.1 metres measured from the datum) and strength (expressed in kilo Newtons per square metre) required back in Blighty. I could hear my former colleagues with their tape measures and testing gear, loudly tutting with disapproval before closing the whole place down.

Then I remembered dynamic load effects. Caused by the rhythmic activity of spectators. By our pounding, stomping feet. There was a measurement, somewhere in my head: 'a vertical frequency of less than six hertz or a sway frequency of less than three hertz . . .' Was that good or bad? Was the upper tier of the bullring moving, or was it just me?

I was hardly sure of anything now. Just a rather steep rake. Steeper than the recommended maximum of 34 degrees. Dizziness. Dizzier than the recommended limit of ten head wobbles per minute. Narrow aisles. Less than 1.1 metres wide.

'Scuse me, *por favor*, has the bullfight ended? *Finito?* Can't get past. Uneven tread depths. Where's my footing? Fish bones and soggy bread on the steps. Dangerous trip hazards. Can't get a grip. Crowd shoving. Eight-minute evacuation time. No way, José! Wine-stained shirts pressed up against my face. The steaming, intimate odours of an exit queue. That Japanese couple. Still here! Still alive!

Now moving. Moving along. All around me, lads still singing. Steep stairs. Dark concourse. City all lit up outside the bullring. Still moving down. *Peña* pals pushing. Not that way? No? Not going out of the bullring?

'*Inglés! Venga, venga!*'

Vengo, vengo. Hold on, I'm coming. Hold on, I'm coming. Down more stairs. Not enough light. Ooh er, don't like this, Inspector, don't like this at all. No signage. No handrails. *Aficionados* pressing in the opposite direction. Bottle-neck. Neck a bottle. Out on to the lower tier. Suddenly evening light. Moon, violet sky. Families all around. More pushing. *Peña* pals shaking hands. Mums and dads laughing at their boys. More pushing. More singing. Then over a wooden fence. The *barrera*!

'*Venga, venga!*'

Flop. Down on to the sand, in a heap. Ankles OK. Sand? *The* sand! I'm on the arena floor. Smack in the ring. Singing in the ring. Bulls all dead and gone. Just us now, several hundred of us, dancing in the ring. Stands all around. In the round. Round world spinning.

World spinning round.

Eventually, eventually, blissfully, an interlude of stillness. Perspiration drying on the skin. *Peña* pals drifting off across the sand. Standing alone, in the bullring, realising, for the first time, for the very first time, in a cold sweat . . . Jesus oh Lord, not how brave are those matadors to confront wild steaming bulls in this confined space. Brave enough . . . but oh, much, much worse, how must it have felt to be thrown on to the sand of the Colosseum, on sand just like this in a tidy circle, but with 50,000 pairs of vengeful eyes bearing down upon you. No escape. No weapon. Blood-curdling cries echoing down from the crowd. Willing you to die, to die slowly and in agony.

And a slavering beast is coming your way . . .

* * *

'So, Simey, did you run with the bulls?'

'Did I fuck. Ernesto. Didn't get to bed until four o'clock. Got up at five to puke. Then at six, to puke again. *Muy pisto. Ma-aw-aw-wee peesto*. Then I staggered back to the bullring for seven. Was awake just enough to see the *encierro*. Saw the incredible speed of the bulls. Heard the rush of their hoofs down the streets. Saw the steam rise from their snouts. Saw a few guys get close to a goring. Saw a few guys look scared shitless. Saw others look so cool I almost willed them to get a dusting. Saw boys in the ring after the *encierro*, showing off in front of their girlfriends by inviting the heifers to toss them. Then I paid three times the going rate for a lousy croissant and a lukewarm thimbleful of coffee. And finally, one of the sisters in the *pensión* tried to avoid paying back my deposit for the room key.'

'Well, like I said, Simey, either you get it or you don't. I'm just sorry you had such a lousy time.'

'A lousy time?' I shook my head, but then thought better of it. 'Ernesto, don't you understand. I had a brilliant time. Really. Every minute of it. At least, every minute inside the bullring. For those three hours I was alive. My every nerve ending stood up to be counted and was not found wanting. Not for a moment, or at least not for many moments, did I feel in the remotest bit of danger. I may not mix too well with alcohol, but up in the *andanada de sol* I was in the company of seasoned guides. This was nothing like the old football terraces, don't you understand? This was pure, unadulterated, licensed licentiousness.

'Ernesto, Ernest, Mr Hemingway – whatever I should call you – we just can't do that sort of thing in Britain any more. Can't do it. Won't do it. Won't allow it. Too many rules. Too many risks. Not even the Scots get paralytic at Hampden Park these days. Hell, they're not even allowed to take their bagpipes with them. They're considered a "safety hazard". Maybe no one anywhere in the Anglo-Saxon, Nordic, Euro-Disney world does what they do in Pamplona any more. Apart, maybe, from drug-crazed raves in Ibiza, there's only the Rio carnival and Pamplona left. Left of an old world of chaos and risk.

'Believe me, Ernesto, I got what I wanted. I saw what I wanted to see. And I think that in many ways I was right. This whole Pamplona thing is the missing link. A hangover from the past . . . quite literally.'

'Jeez, this modern world of yours sounds awful mousy to me.'

'In many ways it is. Maybe that's why the *corrida* seems to be regaining its popularity in Spain, among locals and tourists. New bullrings are being built all the time, you know. And maybe that's why some Spanish towns are starting to look at Pamplona to see if they can recreate some of the San Fermin mood in their own bullrings. Designer disorder. You never know, it could be the next big thing, when we all finally get tired of good behaviour.'

'Well, ain't that a pretty little speech. So I guess you'll be staying around for a while now?'

'No, Ernesto, I rarely hang around. Always ready to move on, that's me. Things to do, places to see. I have a very short boredom threshold. Next on my list is a rather curious rugby stadium in Beziers, on the other side of the Pyrenees. It's a hard life, but, hey, it keeps me on the streets. So *hasta luego*, Pamplona. *Buenos tardes*, Panadol; and *adios*, Ernesto. It was good talking to you.'

'Hold on there, kid! Did you say you were heading up north, over the border?'

'I did indeed, oh bearded one.'

'Well, maybe you'd like some company. It's a long drive.'

It sure was. Up through the Arga Valley, along the twisting mountain roads to Roncesvalles and the French border. Then east via Toulouse and Carcassonne. I'd be lucky to make it by nightfall.

''Course, if I came along we could just hang out in Biarritz for a few days . . . '

'Biarritz? But, Ernesto –'

'Yeah, I know, Simey. No decent stadiums.'

3
CIUDAD DE LOS ESTADIOS, 1

Tuesday, 19 October. 16.45. On the corner of Avenidas Eva Perón and Carabobo.

El Turco and I had carried on working without stopping for lunch and now both of us had blinding headaches. It was already 4.45 p.m. and still the grey clouds refused to disgorge their maddening electrical charge over the outskirts of Buenos Aires. Steering his battered old brown Toyota along yet another seemingly endless *avenida*, *El Turco* was cursing. 'This city has a million cafés. But out here . . . ' wherever we were, somewhere in the Parque Chacabuco district, ' . . . out here there are none. None! Why have you brought me here?'

I had met *El Turco* only the previous morning and we'd been getting on famously until now. Unbelievably well, in fact, considering how strained it might have been between strangers. But would we be able to last the week? This was not his normal line of work and I have always been somewhat driven when it comes to stadium visits. Yet, slowly and naggingly, I was beginning to wonder whether perhaps this *ciudad de los estadios*, this city of stadiums, this urban sprawl of twelve million souls and ten zillion streets, was too boundless even for my own appetite and stamina.

Poor *El Turco*; stiff from another day's driving, fraught from being directed through parts of Buenos Aires he had scarcely known existed. And it was all my fault. 'Please let there be a café soon,' I begged silently.

I too was in a state. I had still not got over the shock of what I'd seen half an hour earlier, daubed on a wall at the San Lorenzo stadium. My shoulders ached from hauling around cameras, maps and notebooks. My clothes gripped my skin like hot tourniquets. We drove past Korean churches, tyre-fitters, furniture warehouses,

Chinese takeaways. Tall lorries and buses contrived to drive by at just the moment we passed vital street signs, blocking our view. And not for the first time I asked, why? Why must I set myself these absurd Herculean tasks? Maybe my detractors are right. Maybe I'm a train spotter at heart, ticking off the stadiums for no other reason than to say that I've seen them. The words of the American novelist Sinclair Lewis came to mind. 'He who has seen one cathedral fifty times knows something; he who has seen fifty cathedrals once knows nothing.'

Well, Mr Lewis, *El Turco* and I did know something. Barely two days into my crazy quest to see as many football grounds as could be managed in six days we both knew for absolute certain that we were knackered, hungry, thirsty and fed up. And, after San Lorenzo, a little bit spooked too.

Mercifully, an anonymous café with a parking space at the front appeared on the right-hand side of the Toyota, on the corner of the Avenidas Eva Perón and Carabobo. Inside, a tiny but perfectly proportioned waiter served us warmed-up slices of mozarella pizza and *faina*, with bottles of mineral water. Although we were now miles from *El Turco*'s home patch and the city centre, in a dullsville district he had never knowingly visited before, the only other customer in the café appeared to recognise him. But after a few exchanged words it turned out that the man knew *El Turco*'s film director brother, Pablo, instead, so he left us alone to guzzle and brood. In hushed tones, *El Turco* identified him as Cesar Aira, a famously manic genius, novelist and critic who turns out two books a year and is an expert on Orson Welles. He couldn't believe that Aira would frequent such an anonymous outpost of the city as this. Even as we spoke, Aira was feverishly writing at his table. Aware that I hadn't the strength to write so much as a postcard, I stared at him over *El Turco*'s shoulder and remembered how, nearly twenty years before, I had started out with the intention of becoming a serious writer. Before being distracted by stadiums.

But how could I express what was going through my head now? Stuff which had nothing at all to do with stadiums.

Then I also remembered that Jorge Luis Borges, once of this parish, had stated that a great book was one that held up a mirror to the reader, and that its author should remain unaware of the significance of his own work.

This recollection came as a great comfort at that moment. Because at that moment I think I had lost the plot entirely.

Barely two days gone. Nine stadiums down. Twenty-seven still on our master list. We had started, but could we finish? And even if we could, to what end?

Other days. Other times. Las Ramblas and Clerkenwell.

I don't recall the exact moment when I hatched this notion, but I do remember airing it for the first time. It was several years ago, in Andrea and Mario's cave-like studio flat just off Las Ramblas in Barcelona. I said to Mario, 'Mario, next time you're back in Argentina, could you buy for me the very best fold-out map you can find of Buenos Aires. Money no object, I want the best.' Aware of how little Mario cared for football I also asked, 'If you can find anyone to help, can you also get them to mark on the map where all the football grounds are located?'

It is said that in the late nineteenth century the locals in Buenos Aires – *porteños*, as they are called – used to describe the Englishmen they saw kicking around footballs '*los ingleses locos*' (the crazy Englishmen), supposedly because they played in short trousers. In those days *porteños* thought that for adults to show their knees in public was embarrassing. I seemed to meet a similar reaction when I talked about my plans to Argentinians. Out of respect for my boyish enthusiasm they didn't laugh. But you could tell they were asking themselves, 'Why?'

I had concluded from my researches, you see, that there are more football grounds in Buenos Aires than in any other city in the world. Not just dozens of ordinary grounds, however, but a whole string of major stadiums, each reputedly holding thirty, forty, fifty thousand or more spectators, all within a few square miles of each other. A comment in a Buenos Aires newspaper seemed to confirm as much. It read, 'We have more stadiums in the city than public libraries. Never has so much knowledge of football been possessed by so illiterate a people.'

When, two to three years later, Mario delivered the map, in its stiff red folder marked Gran Buenos Aires (Plano de la Ciudad, 1:40.000), with a separate little street index and a truly awful colour photo on the cover, I was transported. It was a large, wonderful map – *gracias*, Mario – sufficiently detailed to gratify my basest hankerings as a cartophile. There probably is no such word, but there should be. How can one love cities yet not love maps? I buy city maps with more care than I do socks, and when their seams tear from use, I feel a good deal sadder. For me a fold-out city map is a portrait of desire, promising delight, frustration and disappointment in equal measure. I can stare at one for hours, absorbing its patterns and names, the paths of rivers and streets, the relationships between one area and another. Bound, A–Z-style street maps are fine for daily use, but show only snapshots, not the bigger picture. Whereas a fold-out map shows it all. Like a centrefold, it is a feast for the eye, a beckoning finger to he who stares. A good map challenges you to step out on to a foreign street and sense your direction without having to look up anxiously every minute, without appearing like a tourist. To nip onto a bus or train without asking for assistance. To be a man, not a mouse.

If you were to ask, do I love stadiums because of what they are, or because of where they take me, my answer would be to unfurl a large city map – if not of Buenos Aires then of Prague perhaps, or Melbourne, or Los Angeles – and simply say, 'Look for yourself. The two cannot be separated.'

Unfurling Mario's gorgeous map, so large it extended from one side of a double bed to the other, I saw that it covered not only the city of Buenos Aires – the Capital Federal, as it is known – but also the outlying suburbs and numerous adjoining municipalities which together form Gran Buenos Aires; from Quilmes on one side of the bed to Tigre on the other, from the Rio de la Plata down by my knees up to the Aeropuerto Internacional curled up towards the pillows. Ringed by the kiosk owner who had sold Mario the map were familiar names such as Boca Juniors, River Plate, Racing, Independiente and Argentinos Juniors. After devouring the map closer, and closer still, further rectangles of green and more club names than I had ever dared to imagine leapt off the shiny, colour-tinted paper like twinkling gems on a Persian rug. Mario and his man had delivered. So had Buenos Aires.

It was then that I accepted my fate. One day, I knew, I would have to conquer this city of stadiums, this *ciudad de los estadios*. I owed it to myself. But more, I owed it to this map.

The years went by. I travelled to hundreds of other stadiums in dozens of other cities. But none came near to the Buenos Aires of my fevered imagination. Not even Rio de Janeiro. Hah! I had managed to visit nearly all the stadiums of Rio in barely two days. But in Buenos Aires I had already counted over twenty, and there were bound to be more.

Eventually, when the time was right, Mario spoke to Andrea, Andrea rang Fernando, Fernando spoke to Carlita, and, as invariably occurs whenever one enters a circle of Latinos, names of friends and friends of friends merged into one, and in time a solution was found. It was arranged: I would stay in Buenos Aires at the Palermo apartment of Enrique, a man – an unusual man, shall we say – with whom my wife and I, plus Andrea and Mario, had shared a French farmhouse holiday several years earlier. Enrique and I had not hit it off. His egotism had crushed mine. His talent, in song, in music, in the kitchen, had reduced me to the role of an embittered onlooker. But maybe this time would be different. His hospitality, at least, was legendary.

Meanwhile, I had to find an interpreter (because my O-level Spanish could now be described as the equivalent of a television company – that is, a *Gran Nada*: a large nothing). I would also need a driver and an expert on Buenos Aires. (I took it as read that anyone who satisfied that last category would also be an expert on football.) Preferably one person able to satisfy all three requirements would emerge. Marcela in London directed me to Pablo in Buenos Aires, who was keen but would be filming in New York. Marcela's 21-year-old sister Jimena was also up for it. But when we met in London she seemed too slight and beautiful for such a demanding assignment. Another contact called Roy had some ideas. Eric at the *Buenos Aires Herald* would do all he could to help, but . . .

I was beginning to think I might have to conquer *la ciudad de los estadios* alone, when, within a few days of leaving, a fax arrived. Pablo was proposing his brother, Mariano (or *El Turco*, as they called him at school, because his surname Salomón sounded vaguely Turkish). I liked what I read about Mariano, and not merely because I was desperate, and so a few faxes later our blind date was settled.

In a Clerkenwell café on the day before my flight I showed Marcela my hit list. By now it had grown to at least sixteen stadiums, with a further ten or so in reserve. I wanted to know, really wanted to know: the distances, the traffic, negotiating streets which stretched across a double bed. Was I crazy? Then there would be trouble with access, surely. Endless phone calls. Accreditation. I had a letter from FIFA establishing my *bona fides*. But getting past the security guards? It would be hell, no?

Marcela insisted otherwise. But she recalled a travel guide which listed ten do's and don't's for visitors to Argentina. The tenth advised, 'Don't expect to work to your own timetables.'

Another book, by journalist Miranda France, said of the capital, 'Everything feels designed to frustrate. It seems that good intentions don't exist.'

Someone else commented that in Buenos Aires even the fast food is slow.

Before I left for the airport, my wife kissed my furrowed brow. 'Just go with the flow,' she counselled. 'It doesn't matter if you don't get to them all.'

What did she mean, not get to them all?

Monday, 19 October. 06.50. Aeropuerto and Palermo.

In those hateful television ads, handsome, smug executives dressed in sharp suits and ties stride off transatlantic flights, ready to conquer the corporate world as if they had just emerged from a week's stay in a health farm staffed exclusively by masseurs. I tend to deplane, as they say, wanting only to shit, shower and collapse. But then, amid the waiting throng at the Aeropuerto Internacional I spotted Mariano, *El Turco* – curly hair, wire-framed specs, well-worn jeans – holding up, rather self-consciously, a piece of cardboard on which he had penned my name in a Charles Rennie Mackintosh-style script, and I thought, 'Hmm, he seems like an interesting dude. This could be fun.'

Even so, as boy strangers do, we toyed with each other during the drive into the city, gauging opinions, trying out witticisms, smelling each other out. The battered brown Toyota, which belonged to Mariano's father, was certainly an excellent omen. Apart from my general dislike of smart cars – to me they reveal a lack of imagination on the part of the owner, given all the other goodies one could buy with the money – in a city as notorious for crime as Buenos Aires it was important for Mariano and me to appear as downbeat as possible, particularly in some of the more unsalubrious *barrios* we were destined to visit.

Mariano did spring one surprise on me, however. In addition

to his passion for football, and for River Plate in particular, his real work was as a psychoanalyst.

On reflection, though, I should not have been at all surprised. The average *porteño*, according to virtually every guidebook to Buenos Aires, is one mixed-up sort of a guy, namely an Italian who speaks Spanish but thinks of himself as British. He despises yet longs for European culture in equal measure, needs at least two jobs in order to maintain a minimum standard of living, and in his every waking moment fears for the survival of his country's fledgeling democracy. 'The Argentinian is unhappy with everything and with himself,' wrote the novelist Ernesto Sábato. Above all, I had read, *porteños* were prone to bouts of *la bronca*, a delitescent rage which reportedly afflicts all inhabitants of the Capital Federal, and which has resulted in there being more pyschoanalysts per head of the population in Buenos Aires than in New York. Three times more, was the estimate.

More stadiums and more shrinks. Maybe there was a link.

By the time we reached the apartment of my host, Enrique, Mariano and I had further discovered that we shared three attributes in common. After a little ritualistic fishing on both sides – his surname Salomón being the bait – Mariano revealed himself to be, like me, Jewish. Or rather, as the theatre director Jonathan Miller once put it, Jew-ish. Moreover, Mariano was aged forty to my forty-three, so that boded well for extra-curricular conversation (life, wife, work, music, films, that sort of thing). Finally, we both smoked the same kind of French-style cigarettes. A computer could hardly have found a better match.

Despite the early hour Enrique was up and as welcoming as if I were a long-lost nephew. Flamboyant in gesture – which is why he had irritated me so much in France – but undeniably warm in spirit, Enrique announced that his apartment, his beautiful *departamento* – 'is *bello*, no?' – was my *departamento*. The contents of his fridge was mine. His Paraguayan maid, Helena, was my maid. I should want for nothing. *Nada!*

Mariano's eyes bulged when he saw the place. I myself, having once visited one of Enrique's chums in Madrid, white-gloved butler and all, was prepared for almost anything. But it was not only Enrique's beautiful *departamento* that so entranced Mariano. It was Enrique.

For Mariano, and indeed for anyone of his generation in

Argentina, the compactly proportioned but big-hearted Enrique who now fussed over our arrival with such theatrical concern was none other than Pipo Pescador, a star of Argentinian television, stage and music. Maybe I should have warned Mariano of this. In France Enrique had spoken quite unashamedly of his personal fame as Pipo Pescador, but I had ignored this as just part of his rather touching, self-centred bluster. If he really had been that famous, surely he wouldn't have brought up the subject so often, I reasoned. But now, in Mariano's sagging jaw, I had absolute proof. Enrique, a.k.a. Pipo Pescador, was indeed Argentina's best-loved children's television presenter, performer and songwriter. He had been as much a part of Mariano's childhood experience as, say, Rolf Harris had been of mine.

So there stood Mariano, intrigued and bewildered at this wholly unexpected start to this uncertain week away from his consulting room, while I, the alien stadium freak, unpacked, showered, feeling a little bit rotten for not believing how famous Enrique really was and wondering, in my deadbeat daze, how I might withstand his extravagant kindness for seven whole days. His ignorance of football, a game he thought far too violent for his taste, came as a blessed relief. I asked if he ever went to games. He did not. He said he never felt comfortable. 'Too *famoso*,' of course. People wouldn't leave him alone.

Once Enrique had left us alone, I thought perhaps that I should make a speech, to mark the formal beginning of our wonderful adventure.

'Mariano,' I would say, 'no one ever said this mission would be easy. Twenty, maybe twenty-five stadiums, maybe more, over the course of six days, is no journey down Easy Street. Sometimes we will laugh. Sometimes we will cry. We will be exhausted, mark my words. But we shall not rest until every one of these highlighted blobs on the map has been visited, photographed and recorded. Well, what do you say kid? This is your last chance to back out.'

But I said nothing of the sort, being far too busy fighting off the moist attentions of Greta, Enrique's tubby little wet-faced bulldog, as Mariano and I sat down to plan our campaign at an immaculately polished dining table, next to a cabinet full of Enrique's delicate, antique Chinese carvings.

I produced my list of stadiums. Mariano produced his list. His was much longer. Mine was tidier. Then he pulled out of his canvas knapsack a copy of the morning's newspaper and a brand-new, thick, ring-bound street map. Another map! Loads bigger and heavier than your average London street map too. Even better, as I drooled over its pages, Mariano said it was mine to keep.

In the newspaper was printed the six divisional tables of the Argentinian football league. Surely, I said, there must be one official publication listing all the clubs, with names, addresses and so on, as *Rothmans* does in Britain, or the *Almanacco del Calcio* in Italy. But Mariano had looked far and wide, and found no such reference. Instead, we would have to go through all the League tables, club by club, and then through the phone book, in order to compile one, definitive master list for the week ahead.

This, I now saw, would be no simple task. There were 104 clubs in the Argentinian football league, divided into six divisions, starting at the top with Primera A Nacional, followed by the Primera B Nacional's two divisions (one entitled Zona Metropolitana, covering Greater Buenos Aires, the other Zona Interior, which we could ignore altogether, encompassing as it did the rest of the country). After that, instead of more defined regional divisions, as one would expect for smaller clubs with fewer resources for travel, there seemed to be three more *nacional* divisions. More bafflingly, one of these lower divisions also was called Primera B, though it was in effect the third division, after which came two more divisions, Primera C and D. (If this is wrong, please indulge me. It was early in the morning, I had not slept for hours, and, besides, Mariano said that the divisional formats often change anyway.)

Of the 104 clubs, Mariano reckoned maybe more than fifty were based in the Greater Buenos Aires area. Of the smaller clubs, he thought, not all had their own *cancha* (or ground), however – and among those that did, many had grounds barely amounting to more than a pitch surrounded by a rail. I assured him that, no, I was not that driven.

Nevertheless, within an hour the highlighted yellow blobs denoting each stadium on my fold-out map had proliferated like sores, and those were just the ones for which Mariano had managed to find addresses.

Each inch on the map was now converted into real driving time, and each section of the map allocated a day, a process of negotiation which easily filled the next two hours. One stadium was not, as I had imagined, just 'up the road' from this other one, but an hour away, traffic willing. That one was not simply across the road from the other one. Hadn't I seen the railway line in the way? And we couldn't possibly cover that distance in the rush hour, so maybe that one would be best left till another day . . . unless, of course, we just missed it out altogether.

Throughout this exchange I thought about asserting my authority. After all, this was my plan. My scheme. It was mine, all mine. But as a *porteño* Mariano surely knew the score better than I, and he was, I would have to remember at all times, a pyscho-analyst. I therefore resolved not to exhibit any manic tendencies – yet – and one by one accepted his cautious recommendations as to our schedule. But in any case, there was an angry voice inside my jet-lagged head which kept niggling away at me. 'Simon,' it pleaded, 'why the fuck are you doing this? No one is forcing you to flog yourself like this. Why not just pop into a few stadiums along the way and spend the rest of the week enjoying the city. No one will ever know.'

Once we had agreed our minimum target, however, I knew there was no turning back. Why not? Because we had made a list. Twenty-six stadiums in six days. Maybe thirty if we were lucky. First, seduced by a map. Now, enslaved by a list.

If Mariano had any doubts himself as we nervously prepared our maps before finally setting out, he said nothing. Besides, he still seemed to be in shock from having just come face to face with the real life Pipo Pescador.

Monday, 19 October. 14.00. Stadium No. 1. Excursionistas.
After *empanadas* in a corner café and a smoke from our new, shared pack of Parisiennes Filters, Mariano and I opted for an easy starter. Closest to Enrique's flat was the Primera C club Excursionistas, in the Bajo Belgrano district, on a street named La Pampa.

In most countries I work on the basis that it is far better to turn up, unannounced, and blag my way into all grounds other than the very largest. Telephoning in advance is a waste of effort. 'You want to visit the ground? A book about stadiums? You need to speak to the FA. About this ground? Speak to Senor Gonzalez. No, he's not here now. Phone tomorrow. Phone next week. Send a fax.' (At one major Buenos Aires stadium I tried to contact in advance from London, the phone in the press office was answered by a child.)

Apart from larger clubs such as River Plate and Boca Juniors, faxing in advance is usually futile too. By the time you turn up on the doorstep everyone denies having received the fax, or the guy you were told to contact, after endless long distance calls, followed by another fax, is either off sick or skulking in a back office pretending to be busy (yes, Senor X, who stood me up after an hour sitting in the waiting room at FC Porto, I saw you). So, other than the big two, River and Boca, no faxes. No phone calls. Just a foot in the door and fingers crossed.

Naturally I was worried as hell, though of course I played it cool in front of Mariano.

Club Atletico Union Excursionistas may have owned a typewriter, but they clearly had no fax. Mariano and I just walked in off the street, through a charming hacienda-style gateway, and there before me lay an instantly familiar sight. Already those thirty-six stadiums on my master list seemed much less daunting.

Basic neighbourhood grounds like that of Excursionistas are a Latin speciality. The essential features are as follows: white-washed, patched-up concrete walls, plastered with ads and graffiti, an apartment block next door; at least one side of the ground so close to neighbouring buildings that there is no room for even a narrow terrace; crumbling terraces without barriers; crumpled chicken-wire fences around the perimeter; a main stand without a roof and with dressing-rooms underneath that appear to have been abandoned several years earlier; floodlights on unsteady, rusting poles and a pitch with the turf equivalent of cellulite.

Neighbourhood grounds like this, without pretension or modernity, and with an old, beer-bellied guy in a vest sitting on a twisted metal chair by the gate, sustain and delight me. The Excursionistas man showed us a sign on the side of the stand. 'Honesty, humility, ethics, loyalty and respect for the member', it declared.

Excursionistas chose their name, the man explained jovially through Mariano, because the players had to make excursions all over Buenos Aires in order to play other teams (rather as several English clubs chose the tag Wanderers or Rovers). It was not much of a reason, perhaps, since every club had to travel in the same way, but the name had a romantic ring to it all the same and, in view of my own excursions, it seemed an apt place to start. The ground could hold, *mas or menos*, 8,000 fans, the man went on, although average gates were nearer 2,000. Automatically I sized up the ground by English standards. I reckoned that with our safety standards they might allow 500. But I wasn't in England, and the sign on the white concrete shed said *Caballeros*, not Gents.

The one fact that any fool can find out about football clubs in Argentina is the date of their foundation. It is there on their crests. On their letterhead. On their stadium walls. Excursionistas were formed on 1 February 1910. The date is significant, since most Argentinian clubs were formed during the period 1890–1914, when the country's population exploded. In 1869 Buenos Aires had 187,000 inhabitants. By 1914 there were over 1.5 million, a figure which would double again over the following fifteen years. Most of the immigrants were European, so forming a neighbourhood football club was as natural as unpacking grandma's pots and pans. Buying a plot of land was also essential. Without a settled home, developers would soon have the club scurrying out to the pampas, on the fringes of the city. Moreover, since those formative years in Argentinian football, no one – not even General Perón or any of the country's subsequent dictators – had dared to suggest mergers or streamlining (as, for example, Mussolini ordered in Italy). So Buenos Aires was now awash with impecunious, community-based clubs like Excursionistas, just about hanging on to dear life while their grounds crumbled around them.

As we bade our farewells some lads hanging around the ground who must have been told about my quest shouted out, 'Please forget to go to Defensores.'

Defensores, a mile or so away, were Excursionistas' great rivals.

Monday, 19 October. 14.45. Stadium No. 2. River Plate.

Big clubs can be so bloody cocky.

'The pride of being the biggest', proclaimed a huge sign outside the Estadio Antonio V. Liberti, home of River Plate.

I felt I already knew the stadium pretty well from television coverage of the 1978 World Cup, and from various photos and postcards in my files. Sometimes, visiting a stadium you already know second-hand can be a revelation. Sometimes, as today, there were few surprises. Casually I said to Mariano, as we strolled around the baking perimeter of the stadium, 'You have to admit, it is rather ugly.'

'Oh, come on, Simon,' he said, with touching familiarity. 'I'll stop work right now.' This was, after all, his spiritual home. Indeed he was visibly nervous about even being there on a non-match day, as if we were trespassing on sacred ground.

But it was rather ugly, as most large stadiums are on the outside. No amount of Coca-Cola or Quilmes beer ads decked around the towering concrete beams of the outer bowl could disguise the fact. Attached to one corner, where an overpass headed off towards the actual River Plate, was a huge, cut-out painting depicting celebrating fans. It could easily have been the work of a Soviet artist, with Coca-Cola taking the place of the hammer and sickle. The sign read: 'River, Champions of the Century'. The club shop was called Rivermania, pronounced River Man 'Ere. But there was no one there, so we made for the stadium entrance and our first major test as a duo; mine as a visiting journalist, Mariano's as an apprehensive, rookie interpreter.

Yet after the swiftest of security checks and only one brief phone call, we were waved through the security gate. Just like that. A further shock was to find River's press relations man, Beto, waiting for us, exactly as arranged via fax and telephone. This is not what I had expected at all.

Rather than enter the stadium bowl straight away, as I had hoped, Beto led Mariano and me on a slow stroll around the ground-floor concourse. Somewhere in the stadium a bell rang. It turned out to be a school bell. On either side of the half-lit concourse were classrooms, gyms, kindergartens, rooms full of computers and of noisy children, sitting at desks next to windows overlooking the pitch. Some school. Apparently several large stadiums in the city were similarly equipped, the result of an aid programme to clubs in the 1930s and 1940s. The government provided generous loans for stadium construction, in return for the clubs providing community facilities. Football, I was to be told repeatedly, is as much an institution in Argentina as the church, the armed forces or the government.

I asked Beto if all the kids at the stadium school were River fans. 'Maybe not when they first arrive,' he said, smiling, with the insouciance of a practised charmer. Apparently a boy did once turn up wearing a Boca T-shirt, but after a quiet word he didn't do it again.

Taped on to almost every classroom window were posters announcing that tickets for the following Sunday's Superderby against Boca were *Agotado!!!* Not just *Agotado* (sold out) but *Agotado!!!* So, er, did that mean . . . ? Beto casually replied that of course he could get me a press ticket for the game. Mariano was immediately taken aback. With half the city going crazy for tickets, I just turned up with a press pass and that was that?

We were now in an area lined by trophy cabinets.

Frankly, trophy cabinets bore me rigid. So full of meaningless cups, baubles, figurines and curling pennants, handed over on the occasion of some meaningless friendly or for victory in a meaningless pre-season tournament. Usually, the larger the trophy the lesser its significance. Still, I had to 'ooh' and 'aah' out of politeness, if not to our hosts than at least to the wide-eyed Mariano, still clearly in awe of his hallowed surroundings. He confided that being in River's stadium, on a Monday afternoon, instead of being with a client, felt like playing hookey. My quest was becoming his adventure.

Further around the concourse we came to a bust of General Belgrano, the nineteenth-century military man who, in his spare time, designed the Argentinian flag, and to whom one section of the stadium was dedicated. A district of Buenos Aires was also named after him (and therefore a football club too, which happened to be next on our list), plus dozens of streets and an ill-fated battleship, sunk by the British during the Falklands war. Two other sections of the stadium (plus sundry districts, streets, parks and so on) were also named after nineteenth-century national heroes: José de San Martin, a general, and William Brown, an Irish admiral who jumped ship to defend the city against his former allies.

Thanks to the British abhorrence of personality cults, I cannot imagine at Wembley or at any of our own stadiums a Churchill or a Wellington Stand, and certainly not a Thatcher Stand (for which we can all cry out 'Rejoice!' as she did when the Belgrano went down), although quite rightly there are plenty of stands named after footballers and cricketers. But in countries like Argentina you can absorb a nation's entire formative history – its most important dates, its great leaders, war heroes, battles, the lot – just by studying a road map. Indeed, each one of the four roads encircling River Plate's stadium was named after a prominent figure.

Antonio V. Liberti, after whom the whole stadium is officially named, was the club president who laid the building's first stone, back in 1933. But no one uses the official name. Rather, as one might expect of a club nicknamed *Los Millonarios* – a tag earned after a spending spree on players during the early 1930s – most people call the stadium *El Monumental*. No translation necessary. Call it the pride of being the biggest.

The name River Plate itself, you will already have noticed, is the English for the Rio de la Plata (the widest river in the world, which flows only a few hundred metres from the stadium). The club's founding members chose the anglicised name in 1901 after seeing it inscribed on large containers down by the docks. Britain was then Argentina's largest trading partner by far, which is how football had been introduced to the locals in the first place (as was the case in most other Latin American countries too). In those early days, River had been near neighbours of their hated rivals, Boca Juniors, until eventually they moved out to a more upmarket part of the city.

El Monumental opened, Beto recounted, as though on autopilot, with a ceremony on Independence Day, 25 March 1938, followed a day later by the first match, against Penarol of Montevideo (the Uruguayan capital on the opposite side of the River Plate). The first goal was scored by River's Peucelle in a 3–1 win. There was a sell-out crowd of 70,000, at that time the largest ever recorded in Argentina. This was a golden era in Argentinian football. Professionalism had been sanctioned in 1931. The local players were full of dash and verve. New stadiums were being built all over the country, generously subsidised by a government who knew just how to win over its football-crazy populace.

Since its opening *El Monumental* had been expanded twice. Originally it consisted of a horseshoe of three curved, two-tiered stands, with one end left completely open. In 1957, explained Beto, River sold a player called Sivori to Italy, and with the proceeds added a single tier at the open end. This took the total capacity up to 100,000. In those days all major stadiums claimed to hold this magical number. No attempt was ever made to substantiate the figure. It was more a matter of national honour.

In 1978 an extra tier was added at that same end, to complete the two-tiered bowl in time for the World Cup. But with seats now installed in most parts of the stadium this reduced the total to 76,000. The current capacity is now nearer 70,000.

Beto said nothing about how the 1978 World Cup had been staged during the so-called Dirty War, or how the country's military dictators had spent vast sums of money – more than any previous host nation – on stadiums and public relations in the hope that viewers back home would be so impressed by what they saw that they would somehow forget the orgy of murder and torture taking place behind the scenes. But, then, why should he? That was all twenty-one years ago. Beto was the young press officer of a football club, with a constantly ringing mobile phone and a Superderby to worry about. So I did not push him. (Besides, the grizzly tale has been told numerous times before and in far more detail than I could possibly manage with at least twenty-four or more stadiums still to visit. I had my priorities too.)

Nor did I ask Beto about the disaster at *El Monumental* when, at the end of a Superderby in June 1968, seventy-one Boca fans died in a crush on the stairs leading down to Gate 12. The real cause was never truly established, or rather never admitted, and no action was ever taken. When I asked Mariano about the disaster later, before he could help himself he remembered, 'The score was 0–0.'

Having completed a circuit of the concourse, we now made our way to meet the stadium manager. Jorge ushered us in, and immediately I felt at home. In common with stadium managers' offices all over Latin America, his was sparsely furnished, with out-of-date photos and a few charts on the wall, a handful of dust-covered trophies on top of metal cabinets, and a large desk which suggested power but remained suspiciously uncluttered. By Jorge's desk, filling one whole corner of the office, was an overwhelmingly ornate and rather depressing bronze of Athena in winged flight, bearing an olive branch. This, apparently, was a gift from the Italian club Torino, sent in gratitude for River's help after the entire Torino team had been cruelly wiped out in the Superga air crash of 1949. So grateful were the Italians, explained Jorge, that there were forty such bronzes dotted around the stadium. I supposed that every office had to have one.

From where we were sitting I could see the pitch through

Jorge's window, and was aching to get outside. But once cards had been exchanged I felt duty bound to ask at least some questions.

Here are some of the answers. *El Monumental* has forty-six private boxes, or *palcos*. River hope to replace their unused grey-shale running track with a proper synthetic one, despite the fact that no one in Buenos Aires gives two hoots for athletics.

The club was able to boast fifteen tennis courts, three training pitches, a pelota court, a fronton court, a table-tennis area, a barbecue, or *asado* area – *de rigueur* in all public spaces and stadiums in Argentina – playgrounds for the *ninos*, various dining rooms, changing rooms and a roller-skating area. The tennis courts, I had already seen, were surfaced in a blinding shade of red shale, contrasting almost unnaturally with the artificial blue of the three neighbouring swimming pools and the neatly planted avenues leading to the stadium entrance. If Buenos Aires's bid for the 2004 Olympics had been successful, said Jorge, the River complex would have been the main site. Meanwhile, the club was spending $1.2 million on a huge glass roof over the Olympic pool.

I asked, 'Don't the football fans resent money being spent on swimming facilities?'

'There's no conflict,' he reassured me, letting slip that River Plate's finances were in such a state of chaos that no one really knew where the money went anyway. ('But everyone knows that,' said Mariano later.) There were, however, plans to construct a roof over the stadium's seating areas, if the club could raise the necessary $25–30 million. No public money would be available, and although River were, naturally, the richest club in Argentina, particularly from sales of star players to Europe, they would still need help from their sponsors, maybe Adidas or Coca-Cola. Still, said Jorge, a roof would help to cut down on maintenance costs, since the structure was so exposed to the elements.

Clearly pleased that someone was interested, Jorge continued to explain that the club was now obliged to install seating in the two sections still left as standing areas. But surely, I interjected, the stadium was already all seated, as all international stadiums must be to stage FIFA World Cup matches.

'Mmm . . .' said Jorge haltingly, officially it was. To satisfy FIFA River had marked out places on the terracing as if they were seats. But of course no one actually sat on them. Of course not. (And of course FIFA turned a blind eye to the practice, as they did all over the world. It was only the dumb, obedient British who did everything by the letter.)

We then rose and I thought, at last, now I can actually enter the stadium. But not quite. First Beto led us to his pride and joy, a private viewing box fitted out specially for representatives from FIFA. This had polished wood, halogen lights and leather seats, accessed from an aisle so narrow I imagined with glee the overweight dignitaries squeezing their way through. I was about to express surprise that the box was completely glazed in at the front when Beto pressed a switch and the screen lowered. A simple but brilliant idea, which I resolved to convey to all those British clubs who installed boxes in the 1970s and 1980s without access to fresh air. As they say in Pamplona, *muy listo*! Mariano beamed with pride, seeing that I was impressed.

A few minutes later the two of us were at last out on the sun-bleached concrete terraces, as Jorge left us alone to wander. Ignoring the heat, we pounded our way up to the highest rows of seats, thighs aching, conversation faltering with every step. From the summit, an almost complete silence filled the bowl, like an invisible soup.

I am quite accustomed to being in large, empty stadiums alone, and have always felt it to be a curiously intimate experience. Mariano, though, had never experienced his beloved *Monumental* in this state of repose. I saw that he too was moved.

A French critic once wrote that 'an empty stadium is a useless thing'. But I prefer to subscribe to the view of the Chinese philosopher Lao-Tzu, who said that the true reality of a room is not its walls but the emptiness they contain. Put another way, 'There is nothing less empty than an empty stadium.' I wish I had written that line. But the Uruguayan novelist Eduardo Galeano got there first.

For Mariano, the emptiness before us conjured up memories of great goals, pulsating crowds, of legendary players and crushing disappointments. For me, the outsider, it conveyed a pregnant dignity, an echoing calm, broken only by the occasional clank of a distant worker somewhere deep within the stadium's bowels, almost like the crack of branches heard in the distant depths of a canyon.

Yet someone else also once said that 'when the snow melts, that is when you see the dog shit'. Stadiums are like that too. Once the crowd has dispersed you see the cracked edges and rust, the leaking pipes and gloomy corners. If anything, this adds to the sense of intimacy, as if one had spied a supermodel without her make-up.

In the section marked Visitantes, I noted graffiti saying '*Gallinas*'. Mariano explained that in the 1966 Copa de Libertadores final, against Penarol, River were 2–0 up and coasting when their goalkeeper indulged in some fancy trickery. This so infuriated his opponents that they soon equalised, before going on to win 4–2 in extra time. Ever since, rival fans had labelled River *Gallinas*, the hens, because they had flapped and lost their bottle. 'I was six at the time,' remembered Mariano, 'and I cried all the way to the dentist.'

El Monumental also became known as the *gallinero*, the hen coop.

In time the River fans turned these insults to their own advantage. Whenever they were winning they would chant, 'In Argentina, in Argentina, all the *boludos* are fucked by the *gallinas*.' *Boludos* are literally 'the big-bollocked ones', but in the context of the chant Mariano agreed that 'wankers' conveyed the sense rather better.

It took us some time, and several strength-sapping journeys up and down dead-end stairways, to retrace our steps to Beto's office. He had found for me a book on the history of the club.

'Can I pay you for this?' I offered.

'Sure,' said Beto, 'by handing us back the Malvinas.'

'Ha ha ha,' we all laughed.

Mariano was livid. 'A River fan all my life and I never had this book.'

I felt so mean. First the promise of a press ticket for the Superderby, now the book.

Back at the car Mariano found that he had left the car unlocked, but that nothing had been stolen. 'Couldn't do that in Boca,' I said with a wink, anxious to keep him sweet.

Monday, 19 October. 18.05. Stadium No. 3. Defensores de Belgrano.

Unbearably sticky, thirsty and now dizzy from lack of sleep, but starting to have a laugh with Mariano, I began to take notice of

Buenos Aires as we drove away from *El Monumental.* Rarely on these trips do I have much time or energy left over for the sights, but one of the few I had often read about now appeared. Past a row of extensive sports clubs, Mariano drove alongside the infamous Escuela Mecanica de la Armada, the naval base which had served as a torture chamber and concentration camp during the Dirty War of the 1970s. Had I not known this I might almost have taken a liking to its prim gardens, not something you could ever say about Auschwitz.

Directly across the road from this former chamber of horrors lay the ground of a club called Defensores de Belgrano, also known as *Los Dragones* (oh, all right, the Dragons). By its entrance, salsa music blared out from a car stereo, around which a dozen or so teenagers were lolling outside the club café.

Though slightly larger than that of Excursionistas, Belgrano's ground also had one side too narrow for spectators on one side, concrete terracing at each end, and a red- and black-striped wall behind one goal, signifying that this was reserved for *locales.* 'Belgrano is a country' declared a slogan painted on a high wall opposite the main stand. More youths lounged on the terraces near where I stood, sending clouds of marijuana scent drifting across the ground. 'What lies behind the high wall?' I asked Mariano. After consulting one of the lads he replied, 'The police club.'

Cool.

A friendly, white-haired man called Nicholas beckoned us to join him in the Secretaría, a room behind the stand where his colleague Mario directed us to sink down upon an old leather settee. Above us, plaster from the high ceiling had fallen away in clumps. The trophy cabinets were coated in dust, their silvery contents tinged bronze with age. An ancient typewriter sat on a desk. The walls were lined by browning team photos.

I noticed a sheet of newspaper leaning stiffly against a trophy on top of a cabinet. It showed a photo of Evita, radiant as always. But then I noticed the date, 1952, the year of her premature death from cancer, at the age of thirty-three. Surely the newspaper was a reproduction, I whispered to Mariano. 'Look, the paper is still white and unmarked by age.'

But it was the real thing.

'Ah!' laughed Mariano, when Nicholas moved out of earshot for a moment. 'Such, it would seem, is the timeless power of Evita.'

'Defensores de Belgrano were formed on 25 May 1906,' began Nicholas, almost without prompting. They moved to this ground in 1918, and the capacity was now 8,500. In the old days a band from the naval base across the road used to play before all the club games. However, once Perón swept into power in 1946, they stopped. The navy did not approve of Perón. But fans of *Los Dragones* chanted the general's name all the same, until finally naval officers came over brandishing guns and ordering them to be silent. It wasn't that the fans were necessarily for Perón, said Nicholas, but, he added, 'You know what kids are like. Anything to be deliberately provocative.'

Surveying the oversized, fading Secretaría and its two wearied old regulars, with gates down to around 1,000 and the ceiling about to fall in, I wondered what was the future for clubs like *Los Dragones*. I imagined Nicholas and Mario must despair at the dilapidation, the loss of hope. 'No, not at all,' said Nicholas earnestly. 'The little clubs like us exist to absorb kids [*los chicos*, he said affectionately] from the street. We offer them a place to play, to keep occupied, so that they may have a better future.' And he meant it. River Plate provided the schools and kindergartens. The *cancha* of Defensores de Belgrano acted as the local youth club.

Apart from the semi-pro players, no one was paid to work at Defensores, Nicholas went on. In 1967 they actually won promotion, but the club president warned *socios* (members) that going into the higher division would stretch the finances too much, so they voted to stay in Primera C instead. Still, at least they had never been relegated, and they did have some resources. They earned rent from three shops adjoining the ground, and had their own pool.

This pool, behind one of the end terraces, was a revelation, complete with palm umbrellas, tropical murals, a cavernous disco and a barbecue area.

'It's just like Honolulu!' exlaimed Mariano.

'This is our future,' said Nicholas, beaming. 'It was the idea of our new club president. He is thirty-two years old.'

As we left, the dope-smoking kids on the terrace shouted out, 'So, what is your conclusion?'

Pointing to the threadbare pitch I replied, 'Your grass is better than the stuff out there.'

I was beginning to like this city. I was beginning to drop. But Mariano and I had one more stop on our schedule.

Monday, 19 October. 19.50. Stadium No. 4. Ferrocarril Oeste. Monday night football, the curse of the modern world. Just when you've resigned yourself to the return of the working week, up it surfaces on television, the fag end of the weekend's fixtures – the game that was not quite good enough for live coverage on Sunday – artificially held back to suit the men in suits. Television executives blather on about how no one complains if games are broadcast live on Tuesday nights, so what possible difference can twenty-four hours make? How little they understand the rhythm of the football week.

So, not much more than forty-eight hours after I had been at Upton Park in east London to watch my own true ones, Aston Villa, draw against West Ham, here I was in the Caballitos district of Buenos Aires to see Ferrocarril Oeste play Estudiantes.

Estudiantes de La Plata! In my youth their name had been synonymous with all that was frightening and fascinating about wicked South American football. Three times they had terrorised European clubs in the World Club Finals. In the third match one of their players had whipped off one of the Feyenoord players' spectacles and trampled them into the ground. (I had never been able to figure out what I found more unsettling about this incident: the act of malice itself, or the incongruity of a professional playing in glasses?)

Ferrocarril Oeste, a medium-sized, inner-city club in Primera A, started out in 1904, on a clear, cool day, as their history has faithfully recorded. As the name suggests, they were the sports club of the Western Railway, a company inaugurated in 1857 and run by the British until well into the twentieth century. Some reports suggest that they first adopted the claret and light-blue colours of Aston Villa (or Aston Ville as one book had it), so I already felt a soft spot for them, even though they subsequently switched to green and white. I was also attracted by the address of their club headquarters: 350 Cucha Cucha Street, where Mariano and I found ourselves looking up at the sort of mock-palatial brick frontage – with castellated parapets, masonry flourishes and gothic archways – much favoured by English grammar schools in the

1920s. In the lobby, next to the tiny Ferro shop, English names on brass plaques abounded; founders, engineers, secretaries, with names like David Simpson, F. J. Day and Wm Beeston. Chattering children and youths brushed past us on their way to the club's tennis courts, gyms and swimming pool.

The stadium, around the corner and behind the clubhouse, turned out to be wonderfully eccentric and misshapen. A real tonic to my flagging senses. It was overlooked at one end by a procession of towering granary silos and, on another side, by two tall blocks of flats. Behind the opposite side, hardly surprisingly, were railway sidings. Stadiums shoehorned like this into their urban surrounds, almost hidden behind graffiti-covered walls and anonymous blocks, have always held a mysterious appeal to me, like Frances Burnett's Secret Garden. I wondered what Mariano would have had to say about that in his professional capacity. (A psychologist in London had once interpreted my love of stadiums as a desire to escape reality and head back for the womb. I was so outraged I nearly had to ring my mother.)

Although it was still far too early for kick-off we bought tickets at a hole in the wall, were frisked half-heartedly by some policemen, and entered, if only to have a chance to sit down for a while.

With a capacity of just under 25,000, the stadium was dominated by a towering main stand to our left, with an extraordinarily slender, curved, concrete cantilevered roof, overhanging the upper seating deck like a sail. Dating from 1971, according to the brass plaque on the side, oddly the roof did not cover the stand's full length. It also bore the inscription Estadio Ricardo Etcheverri, who, far from being a former player or director of the club, was the stand's architect. It was as if he had signed his work to proclaim, 'Yes, I did this, and, yes, it is remarkable that the roof should defy gravity and stay up.'

On the stand's ground floor we could see, through tall windows facing the pitch, a large indoor hall packed with kids playing basketball. Mariano told me that when Ferrocarril's footballers won the Argentinian championship in both 1982 and 1984, their coach claimed to have learnt much about tactics from watching the club's basketball players. The fact that a Primera A game was about to begin appeared to be of no consequence to the kids playing, nor to those swarming around an outdoor five-a-side pitch, tucked in one corner of the site, between the stand and the end terrace where we stood. Schools at River Plate; now a sports centre at Ferrocarril. What the state cannot afford, football clubs provide. Throughout the main football match in the stadium the kids played on, oblivious.

But the true wonder of the stadium lay not on the stand side but on the other three sides, all of which were filled, to my amazement – though I was by now dog-tired and therefore easily impressed – by tall sections of wooden terracing. By this I mean wooden planks bolted on to a slender steel framework, like an old American baseball park from the early 1900s. What the Americans call bleachers and which normally are for sitting on. At Ferrocarril these bleachers rose higher than any bleachers I had ever seen before, high above the paved flooring below, with gaps wide enough between each plank, each springy plank, to be able to gain a clear view down through the steel struts on to the people moving around below.

At the summit of this primitive terracing, angled stays connected the uppermost planks to a wooden back fence, painted in the club colours of green and white. For a few seconds I tried to recall where I had seen this type of structure before. 'Come on, Simon, I know you're tired,' I was castigating myself, 'but think, or else the evening will be ruined by you trying to remember.' Photographs, drawings, where? Where had I seen this before?

And then, as the Estudiantes fans around me started the first of their many rousing songs of the evening, bouncing up and down on the springy planks, I remembered. I had seen this type of structure before in pictures of the wooden terraces at Ibrox Park, Glasgow, in the aftermath of a disaster which occurred in 1902. Twenty-six fans were killed on that occasion, when a section of sub-standard wooden planking gave way, plunging the unfortunates to their deaths below.

I suppose this recollection might have impelled me to grab Mariano and run down the terraces towards *terra firma*. Instead, I could only chortle weakly to myself. It was the irony of it all, I explained to a bemused Mariano. We were experiencing what engineers would call the effects of structural dynamics.

If I may digress. Engineers are a law unto themselves. The fruits of their knowledge and their work surround us twenty-four hours a day, in buildings, bridges, furniture, everywhere. Yet so unfathomable is much of their art – and it is an art – that its practice seems to be about as much as engineers can humanly manage. To have to explain their work in laymen's terms is, if you will, for most of them a bridge too far.

As it happened, only five days before leaving London I had attended a conference at Walsall. There, an amiable, pocket-sized Scottish engineer called Sam Thorburn had been warning delegates of the dangers of poorly assembled, demountable structures, the sort found increasingly at sports grounds (for example at Bastia, in Corsica, where one such structure had collapsed in 1992, causing the deaths of seventeen fans and later also of the local mayor, gunned down by a hit man who held him responsible).

Graph after graph of complex data had been projected onto a screen to back up Sam's solemn warnings, laced with terms like dynamic response, static loading, vertical frequency and, my favourite, synchronised excitation. The non-engineers among us listened politely or checked our watches to see how long there was to go before the buffet lunch.

And yet there I was, five days later, at Ferrocarril Oeste on a breezy, Monday evening in Buenos Aires, bouncing up and down on springy wooden boards as, all around me, the *hinchas* (or fans) of the *pincha ratas* (the, er, pecking rats, as Estudiantes are known) jumped up and down, up and down, up and bloody down, singing song after song after song about following their beloved team while taking cocaine, about their hate of the Ferro green and white, their love for the red and white of Estudiantes, and about how they could think of nothing finer than to be buried in a red and white coffin. Any more bouncing up and down, or, to use the technical term, synchronised excitation, and I felt sure that the *pincha hinchas* would have their wishes granted, taking Mariano and me with them, down into the half-lit void below.

I was imagining the newspaper reports. 'British stadium expert dies in stand collapse in South America.' Was there a certain romance in this, I wondered? Or would some half-baked obituarist comment ironically, 'It would have been what he wanted.'

Still, Sam's graphs now made perfect sense to me. I was participating in a British stadium inspectors' nightmare.

Killing time with these thoughts, I accidentally dropped my Parisienne filter through a gap in the planks, on to the heads of fans milling around below. None of them looked up in anger. Oh well.

And the football was surprisingly good, far more attacking and enterprising than anything I'd seen in the Premier League for a long, long time.

But Mariano and I left at half-time all the same. Thirty-five hours without sleep was taking its toll. All that bouncing was making me feel giddy. And tomorrow would be a big day. Six more stadiums, all in the far southern extremities of the city. I just hoped Enrique would not be wanting to sing to me when I returned to his beautiful *departamento*, and that his salivating hound Greta would be locked in the kitchen.

4 WRIGLEYVILLE

The lengths I go to in order to take a decent photograph. Or, rather, the heights. It's not easy summoning up the courage to press random doorbells at the foot of a block of flats in a foreign land, and then, watched by gawping passers-by, having to explain, via a grubby, crackling entryphone, that I am who I am and that I want what I want.

'J'ai dit, madame, que je suis journaliste de Londres. J'écris des livres au sujet du stades. STADES. Oui. STADES. Oui, bien sûr, ils sont les livres de cette sorte. Madame, s'il vous plaît, est-il possible pour moi d'entrer et photographier le stade de votre fenêtre? Oui. LE STADE.'

If a complete stranger knocked on my door in London and explained in faltering English that he – and it would almost certainly be a he – had a thing about a particular building type, and could he therefore pop up to the bedroom for a few minutes to take a photograph of a building across the road, I would quake with indecision. How to respond? By saying, 'Sorry, mate,' or 'Sure, come in'? To turn away some perfectly decent though mildly eccentric chap? Or to risk attack by a knife-wielding madman?

I like to imagine that the people whose doorbells I have rung in the likes of Paris, Istanbul, San Sebastian and Rio de Janeiro have been wholly untroubled by such moral dilemmas. I say this because nine times out of ten, even after I have tried earnestly, for their own sakes, to offer the occupants an excuse *not* to let me in – by regretting the appalling intrusion, by insisting that the matter is hardly important, that I will fully understand if they say no – nine times out of ten they do not hesitate. They let me in.

They just say, 'Sure, come in.' '*Pas de problème. Entrez, monsieur.*'

In fact so many total strangers have gladly ushered me into their homes – me, the dishevelled, apologetic, pathetically grateful foreigner, sweating under the weight of a camera bag – that it took some time to understand why. But once the penny dropped, pressing on doorbells instantly lost its terror. They were letting me in, not because I reminded them of Hugh Grant or because I have a harmless expression, but because, quite simply, they understood.

Stadiums are special. It really is as uncomplicated as that. You cannot live next to a stadium, or in a block of flats overlooking a stadium, without knowing this to be true. Every day the stadium is there, outside your window: an expansive, concrete-bottomed reality. 'Hey, everyone – get this!' the stadium's stands and floodlights announce to the passing world. 'We're special, and well you know it!'

Having a stadium to look at through your kitchen window or from your balcony is like living next door to a film star. You may not admire their acting, let alone their personal habits; but you can never quite ignore their presence, their routine comings and goings, so near and yet so far, just on the other side of the party wall. You must also concede that if the film star moved, local gossip would never be quite the same. Nor would the neighbourhood feel so . . . so special, so different. In my part of London we have an Oscar winner living just a few streets away, and don't we just love it. Not the actor as such, but the simple fact of her preferring our corner of London to any other. News of anyone remotely famous coming to the area spreads like wildfire.

'Have you heard who's moved into those flats up the road?——!'

'*No!*'

'Yes!'

So when a stranger comes to the door and blathers on witlessly about taking a photograph of the stadium next door, of course the local residents understand. By their very welcome they are saying, 'You want to take a photograph, that's only to be expected. I would feel the same if I were you. There, look at it. You were right. It is amazing, isn't it?'

Then, while I am fiddling around with lenses and filters and trying not to knock over any of the plants or hideous knickknacks blocking my path to the most advantageous window, instead of hurrying me along or looking anxiously at my bag – will I pull out a gun or a baseball bat? – my hosts alway say the same thing. Always. Whether in Paris, Istanbul, San Sebastian or Rio de

Janeiro, they always say, 'Please excuse the mess. We weren't expecting visitors.'

In return, as I click away furiously, praying that the camera won't jam or the skies cloud over, I cannot compliment them enough on their tidiness, on their delightful taste in interior decor, or on the beauty of their quite extraordinary city.

By the time I have finished, the tea things have usually been laid out.

There is an assumption, nevertheless, that to live in close proximity to a stadium must be to live in a state of perpetual misery, to suffer not just occasional sorrow but eternal blight and stunted property values. Imagine enduring the noise, the litter, the invasion of one's neighbourhood. Think of the parking problems, the casual disregard of all those ill-mannered fans.

But don't you believe everything you hear. Certainly in some cities it is hell. But not in all, and certainly not in the north side of Chicago. Not where the Chicago Cubs play, it ain't hell. On the contrary, where the Cubs hang out is heaven; a stadium, or, rather, a ballpark, and a community, perfectly at one with each other. Symbiotic satisfaction.

Friends, it can be done. Up on Clark and Addison, where the wind whips in from Lake Michigan, a few blocks north of the blues bars around Diversey, and not far from the movie house on Lincoln where John Dillinger was gunned down by FBI agents in 1934 – betrayed by his floozie's landlady – Wrigley Field is a jewel of a ballpark, in the midst of a residential district peopled by folk who just love the old place.

'You know what?' as most statements are prefixed in the Windy City. 'We're talking *lurve* here.' So much *lurve* that locals have even taken to naming the district after the ballpark.

Wrigleyville. Now, how could you not fall for a place called Wrigleyville? I know I have. For the last ten years or so an aerial photograph of Wrigley Field and its surrounds has taken pride of place on the wall directly above my computer screen. Even as I type these words I can look up and gaze right over the ballpark to the distant twin peaks of the Sears Tower and the John Hancock building downtown and to the grey-blue waters of Lake Michigan. In the foreground, on a corner of the ballpark, I can see an illuminated sign saying Chicago Cubs. Close by is the glowing golden arch of a McDonald's drive-in, and, opposite that, the corner bar where I nearly got to see John Mayall and his Bluesbreakers.

Wrigleyville, perhaps, is not so much a place as an ideal; a rare enclave of multicultural, switched-on, urban America where you can live and work by day and walk by night. Few of its buildings rise much above three or four storeys. Its main streets are lined, as they should be, by individual shops and bars and restaurants, each funky or pretentious or raucous, with their own neon signs and regular crowds. Side streets are filled by processions of brick and brownstone and clapperboard homes, with none too flashy cars parked outside among the fire hydrants and mailboxes. There are decent bus services too, serving dudes of all colours. In that sense the north side is about as close to a European city as it gets, west of Boston and south of Toronto. And of course there is the El, that venerable, ancient elevated railway which clatters and clunks through Chicago's neighbourhoods and back yards with all the delicacy of a tank, but then makes up for it with cutesie little stations to die for.

You know what? There are other neighbourhoods in the city similar to this. But only Wrigleyville has Wrigley Field at its heart.

Millions of words, most of them sentimental, have already been written about Wrigley Field, so I hesitate to add more. But for those sports fans out there who might enjoy a reminder, here's why Wrigley Field is such an icon in ballpark circles. (Note, a ballpark is, in one sense, a stadium, but only in the sense that a cricket ground is, and also is not, a stadium.)

At the tail end of the twentieth century there were only three genuinely historic ballparks left in the US's Major Leagues, not counting the Yankee Stadium in the Bronx, which was effectively rebuilt during the 1970s. Historic in the American context, incidentally, means pre-1960s.

Of the three, Detroit's Tiger Stadium, opened in 1912, saw its final game in September 1999. Fenway Park, the more charismatic and wonderfully misshapen home of the Boston Red Sox, also opened in 1912, may not survive more than three or four years longer. And boy, that sux. When that old critter comes down, expect to see grown men cry bucket loads.

But the third, Wrigley Field, it would seem, just looks like goin' on and on. Like the Statue of Liberty, Capitol Hill and the Golden Gate Bridge, a US of A without Wrigley Field is almost impossible to imagine. Roger Kahn even went so far as to call the ballpark 'a mystic creation, the Stonehenge of America'. Indeed, such is its status within the pantheon of American sport that over the last decade stadium architects and club owners in places such as Buffalo, Baltimore, Cleveland, Denver and Milwaukee have done their darnedest to build new, urban ballparks that create an atmosphere and setting just like Wrigley Field. Give or take the odd retractable roof and tier of skyboxes, retro-style is now *the* style.

Wrigley Field opened in 1914. It is, frankly, no great beauty. Its double-decker stands are functional rather than grand. Its exterior is mainly utilitarian. But as the one-time Chicago-based architect Mies van der Rohe once famously put it, 'God is in the details.'

Most baseball devotees are familiar with those details. Above the main entrance on the corner of Clark and Addison is a classic illuminated sign, spelling out the name Wrigley Field as prominently as it does that of the Chicago Cubs. Inside the ballpark, luxuriant, dark-green ivy smothers the brick walls that border the outfield. Old-style bleachers (or bench seats) fill one corner, behind the pitcher's mound. Above the bleachers stands a towering manual scoreboard, which, number by number, displays updated scores from games elsewhere in the Majors (thus giving rise to a thriving betting scene amongst the 'bleacher bums' below). Manual scoreboards are even rarer in America than manual gearsticks.

Many of these features date back to the 1930s, to a time when the Cubs' then owner, Philip K. Wrigley – the man who put the PK into gum and whose pop put the Wrigley into Wrigley Field – instructed Cubs announcers to use the term 'Beautiful Wrigley Field' whenever possible. (It was certainly beautiful enough for Al and his brother Ralph Capone to be regular attenders.) One of Wrigley's intentions had been to create, and I quote, 'an outdoorsy feel'.

How well he succeeded. On top of the scoreboard, whose curved rear carries another illuminated graphic saying Chicago Cubs – the one lit up in the photo above my computer screen – tall poles bear the pennants of all the Cubs' National League rivals, hung in the exact order they currently occupy in their respective east and west divisions. When the Cubs win (which is not often) a white flag with a blue W is raised to cheer up passers-by and passengers on the nearby El. When they lose, up goes a blue flag with a white L. At night, blue and white light bulbs relay the same information. Simple, really, for remarkably few stadium operators ever bother to inform outsiders of results within, yet typical of the manner in which Wrigley Field both blends in with, and enhances, its surrounds.

But you know what else? Until recent years, Wrigley Field's hallowed status was also founded not for what it had, but rather for what it did not have: namely, floodlights.

As every American schoolboy knew, Wrigley Field was the last home of the Majors to hold out against the lure of night games. It was one of those things just taken as read. George Washington could not tell a lie. New Yorkers are rude. Elvis was the King. Hollywood is full of shit, and Wrigley Field has no lights. As a song by the Statler Brothers put it: 'Don't wait on me, don't wait on me . . .' And why? Because, as the singer warns, he will only be back 'when a San Diego sailor comes home with no tattoo' or 'when the lights go on at Wrigley Field'. In other words, honey, 'don't wait on me'.

But the lights did eventually go on at Wrigley Field, watched live by viewers all over America on NBC's *Today* programme. They were ceremonially switched on by 91-year-old Cubs fan Harry Grossman at exactly 6.06 p.m. central time on the eighth of the eighth, 'eighty-eight.

The story of how the ballpark finally succumbed to the demands of modern baseball and television during the Eighties in effect runs parallel with the story of how the neighbourhood around the ballpark evolved into the Wrigleyville we know today.

The 'nabe' had grown up at the end of the nineteenth century as a blue-collar area, but by the Seventies was notorious for its vacant lots and dilapidated buildings. Gangs with names like El Rukus and the Latin Kings stalked the mean streets. Prostitution and muggings were rife. The result? 'White flight'. As in every other run-down district of every other American inner city, Wrigleyville was left to its fate as the white middle classes hot-footed it to the suburbs.

But then, slowly, the tide started to turn. In 1981 the *Chicago Tribune* media group purchased both the Cubs and the ballpark from the Wrigley family, a break with tradition which inevitably aroused suspicion among fans and among residents in the surrounding streets. All wanted to know, what would the future hold? The Wrigleys may have made a mint from chewing gum, but over the years their interest in baseball had largely been confined to a paternalistic role. Whereas now, the club was in the hands of a supposedly big, bad media corporation.

Around the same time, the local community began to reassert itself. Neighbourhood associations sprang up. So when the Cubs' new owners started to make noises about installing floodlights – floodlights, at Wrigley Field! – the residents made a few, even louder noises of their own in return. So determined were they to stop the lights that at one of several hostile protest meetings a representative from the *Tribune* stood up and threatened to move the Cubs out of Wrigley Field altogether. Far from shouting him down as a heretic, as might once have been expected, the locals applauded. They were that angry.

That could have been it for Wrigley Field. According to the *Tribune* (and sundry other doom-mongering analysts), as long as the ballpark remained as it was, not only without floodlights but also with its limited capacity, its lack of skyboxes, its poor facilities and minimal parking, the Cubs could not possibly hope to compete with their wealthier, flashier, superbowl-owning rivals. No wonder the team never won anything, sneered the critics.

In response, anxious residents claimed that floodlit games would bring hundreds of drunks on to their streets at night. The gutters would overflow with urine. No one would be able to park. There was even a fear that property owners would be tempted to demolish their decaying, five- and six-flat blocks in order to make easier money from parking lots.

For a while things became rather heated. But, while they did, bit by bit life at the ballpark started to revive under its new owners. In 1984 the Cubs won the National League, Eastern Division, championship, their best effort since making it to the World Series in 1945. Attendances at Wrigley Field topped two million for the first time ever, nearly double the norm during the previous decade. Suddenly the Cubs, or at least the Cubs at Wrigley Field, or even just Wrigley Field itself – as the embodiment of the authentic baseball experience – became a hot ticket.

Moreover, after the lights were finally installed in 1988 – as part of an overall $30 million refurbishment – contrary to all expectations, the essence of Wrigley Field not only survived but improved, as do so many stadiums when bathed in the warm glow of several thousands watts. Inevitably the local authorities imposed conditions. Only eighteen night games a season were to be allowed. No beer could be sold after 9.20 p.m., and no organ played after 9.50 p.m. (Live baseball without chintzy organ music is as unimaginable as an American movie in which no one gets to say 'I love you'.)

The result was that fans leaving the ballpark at night were not all legless, as had been feared. Neither they, nor local residents, were subjected to serial muggings. No cars were trashed. Nuns from the local convent did not have to flee in terror.

Thus Wrigleyville slept rather more easily than had been anticipated, as, to an extent, did the rest of the baseball nation, knowing that Wrigley Field, though floodlit, was at least safe for the foreseeable future. For this was no parochial matter. While the majority of American fans, including those of the White Sox down on Chicago's south side, were finding themselves increasingly shunted into modern, identikit ballparks dedicated to blandness and Mammon, Wrigley Field had managed, through Depression, Prohibition, Cold War, the Summer of Love, and now the advent of night games, to retain its links with baseball's more heroic, if mythical, past.

But the revival was not confined to within the walls of Wrigley Field. As the Cubs picked up, so too did life on the streets. Smart developers started to buy up and gentrify old buildings. Rents in the district rocketed. Regardless of the ballpark, Wrigleyville still had plenty in its favour, being close to downtown, with good public transport links, and a burgeoning street life that few other Chicago districts could match.

The allure of Wrigley Field could never quite be omitted from the equation, however. Ernie Banks, a player from 1953–71 – now reverentially known as 'Mr Cubs himself' – had once described Wrigley Field as the 'Friendly Confines', an expression which now adorns the roof of the visiting team's dug-outs. 'Welcome to the Friendly Confines', it reads.

And now those friendly confines were spreading. As one local real-estate broker, Geoff, confirmed, 'More and more people like to live close to the energy generated by Wrigley Field.' New York's *Daily News* (concerned about the lack of a community feel around the Yankee Stadium) quoted one resident, recently moved into Wrigleyville, as saying, 'I was looking at this apartment, and while they were showing it to me I heard the crack of the bat, the roar of the crowd, and it was like a movie. I said, "This is it."'

She was not alone. According to Geoff, who, you know what, had a queue of willing buyers, a top-floor apartment with a view of the ballpark could easily command $2–3,000 a month. Lower ones with no view had been fetching around $1,700 a month. Generally speaking, said Geoff, the nearer to Wrigley Field the better, so that the price of a house on the same street as the ballpark would be double that of an identical building one or two streets away; the difference between, say, $1 million and $500,000. These were, naturally, only ballpark figures.

Which came first is hard to say: the property boom or the rebirth of the Cubs. But it hardly matters. Whether gentrification occurred by symbiosis or not, the 'feel-good factor' fed itself. What is good for Wrigley Field has turned out to be good for Wrigleyville, and vice versa. Bars and restaurants are now always packed on match days (of which there are over eighty per season). Some North Siders even compare the street life to that of New York's Greenwich Village. Maybe that's pushing it a little. But Wrigleyville does have its fair share of tourists, travelling up on the El from downtown Chicago in pursuit of the famed Wrigley effect and, since 1998 especially, a pennant or a mug or a shirt or anything bearing the name of Sammy Sosa.

To have had Sammy Sosa fraternise one's establishment has become the *sine qua non* of business respectability around Wrigleyville. 'You know what?' I would hear on several occasions. 'Guess who was in here last fall, on that very bar stool you're looking at now?'

When Sosa, an outfielder from the Dominican Republic, was vying with Mark McGuire of the St Louis Cardinals for the record number of home-runs in one season, during 1998, one baseball souvenir shop on Addison kept count on a prominent, electronic Sam-ometer.

But there is one other characteristic of Wrigleyville that is also unique. Or even 'very unique', as they say in America, if not 'totally unique'. Should anyone fail to obtain a ticket for one of the ballpark's 38,957 seats – which happens more often than might be imagined considering the Cubs' notoriously uneven form – they can always try to catch the game from one of the rooftops lining the streets on two sides of the ballpark.

Nowhere else in the world is there a major stadium blessed with so many prime seats located on the outside looking in. The Oval cricket ground in London has its share. And there are plenty of small football grounds all over the world with houses or blocks of flats whose windows overlook at least part of the action. Believe me, I have rung on more doorbells than I care to remember with my cameras and excuses at the ready.

To my knowledge, though, there really is nowhere like Wrigleyville for Peeping Toms. This is because two sides of Wrigley Field, backing on to Waveland and Sheffield Avenues, consist of open seating decks so low that, from the windows and rooftops of maybe a dozen or so neighbouring buildings on the opposite sides of the roads, one can gain a near perfect view of the diamond and, in several cases, most of the outfield.

From the first day the ballpark opened in 1914, the very same windows and rooftops were packed with 'rubberneckers'. Most other sports clubs would have taken action to prevent this, sooner or later. My own favourites, Aston Villa, erected in the late 1890s a huge advertisement hoarding to stop freeloaders watching matches from the slopes of the adjacent Aston Park. The Philadelphia Athletics built a similar barrier at Shibe Park in the mid 1930s. Fifty feet high, it was known, unsurprisingly, as the Spite Fence. (Shibe Park, incidentally, was the venue for the famous 1929 World Series, staged during Prohibition, when baseball fans were heard to chant loud and clear – sixty or more years before the creation of Homer Simpson – 'We want beer! We want beer!')

No owner of the Chicago Cubs has ever dared to try such a low-down, high-wall trick as that. Instead, a sense of fair play has always permeated the air around Clark and Addison. Wrigley Field's creator, 'Lucky' Charlie Weeghman (who rose from a waiter to a millionaire in a matter of years), was, for example, the first baseball-club owner in America to allow spectators in the crowd to keep any ball hit into the stands, a policy now accepted as one of the sport's best-loved traditions. Weeghman would not have put up a Spite Fence. Nor would his successor, William Wrigley Junior, who took over in 1919, nor Wrigley Junior's son P. K. (who always insisted on plenty of game-day tickets being available for the ordinary fan on the street); nor would P.K.'s son, also William Wrigley, and nor would the current owners, the *Chicago Tribune*. After all, why risk a slump in circulation over such a relatively minor matter?

Actually in 1989 the *Tribune* did consider erecting a barrier, albeit a small one, but that was specifically to block off the view from one of the roofs on Sheffield Avenue, whose owner had erected a formal viewing platform for fee-paying members. 'It's not the money, it's the principle,' roared Cubs president Donald Grenesko. 'They are clearly stealing our product and that just grates on us.'

But the founders of the Lakeview Baseball Club at 3633 Sheffield held on to the high ground. It was not, they argued, as if they were taking business away from the Cubs' new skyboxes, which had all sold out, and it wasn't as if there were thousands of empty seats in the ballpark. Besides, the Cubs had been quite happy to feature happy fans watching from the other rooftops in their television advertisements.

You know what, though? Those other fans, said Grenesko, were different. They were just friends of the people living in the buildings. No money changed hands. They were, he repeated, 'part of the unique charm and character of Wrigley Field'.

Grenesko soon dropped his stance once it became obvious how petty it appeared to the public, and how ugly and obvious the barrier would have looked. But from then on, life up on the roofs started to change. There was a report that after one fan had been seriously injured falling over a parapet, building owners were making guests sign insurance waivers. Meanwhile, ordinary guys who lived in the buildings started to be turned away from their own rooftops. Their landlords, it was revealed, were now renting out the space to corporate clients. A single roof could earn $5,000 a game, it was reckoned.

Baseball was now becoming hip and, even more so, the Wrigley Field rooftop experience was catching on in fashionable circles. What had once been a casual undertaking for real fans, mostly dependent on whether they could befriend any of the tenants, now became a serious business. Soon the rooftops began to fill up, even the ones that could only be reached via ladders and through dusty lofts.

Alderman Bernie Hansen, the stocky, pugnacious and always-open-for-business councillor for the city's 44th Ward – a Cubs man through and through – watched the situation change. Amid a succession of phone calls in his bustling, high-street office, this is what he told me.

'For twenty to twenty-five years the people going up on those roofs were, you know, Joe Sixpack and his buddies who lived on the second floor and went up to watch some games. Will you excuse me, Simon. Hello. Yeh, no, yeh. A speed bump? I'll see what I can do. Sorry, Simon. So, anyway, it had been going on a long time on a very small scale until the Lakeview private club turned up and gradually one rooftop after another started inviting more friends, and then it turned into a profitable business. Wait a sec. No, yeh, no. They can't do that. Fax my secretary. No, I promise. His attorney should know that. I'll talk to the DA tomorrow. Sorry, Simon. A few years ago, around '96, I'm looking at the rooftops and I see a whole lot of people up there and I'm thinking, "Now, hey, wait a minute, what is the structural strength of that building?" I mean, this wasn't just fifteen to twenty people. This was a lot of people.'

Bernie is clearly not the type of local politician you would try to hoodwink. Hell, he had a photo of himself and Bill Clinton on his office wall.

'So a building commissioner and myself did some preliminary investigations, making sure the buildings were safe. Then the City's Department of Revenue came in and decided to regulate. Then it got to licences and all kinds of stuff. But who's complaining? These guys are making plenty of bucks.'

The man generally accepted, or blamed, for being the first to exploit the rooftops' potential is Bob Racky, top man at the Lakeview Baseball Club. Despite being born a White Sox fan on the south-west side of Chicago, Bob has lived in Wrigleyville since buying his first property in the area in 1972. In that time he has done up about thirty others, all within a few blocks of the ballpark. The one where the Lakeview is based had been a total wreck when he bought it in 1988 for $250,000 – with the express intention of starting the club – and he'd spent 'a fat million' on it since.

'We have a good relationship with the Cubs now,' he insisted when I called into the club. And then he laughed. 'In fact, the guys over there even call to make reservations for our roof when they've sold out the ballpark! But you know what? Their primary income is not from selling seats and hot dogs anyway. It's from TV and radio rights. The cable network gets them to 150 cities. They don't need to worry about us.'

Bob said a whole lot more, but, to be honest, I couldn't help but be distracted by all the baseball memorabilia displayed around his club walls. Seeing my eyes wander across the black-and-white photos, scoresheets, newspaper cuttings, and signed baseballs, Bob guided me through them all, pronouncing each name in his musical, Chicago drawl.

There was Stan Hack, Peanut Lowry, Phil Cavarretta, Swish Nicholson ('he struck out a lot'), Ernie Banks ('Mr Cubs himself'), Hank Wyse, Harold Vandenberg, Ryne Sandberg, Fergie Jenkins, Joe 'Dago Joe' Pepitone from New York ('he didn't like that nickname at all'), Leon Durham, Pete Rose (sigh), Lenny Merullo.

Only a few of the names meant anything to me. But the rhythm, oh the rhythm! The devil may have all the best tunes, but sure as hell the Americans have grabbed all the best names.

Bob then showed me a chewing-gum wrapper depicting the Sultan of Swat himself, Babe Ruth. A tiny, coloured scrap of waxed paper dating from 1929, it was now said to be worth $6,000.

Babe Ruth has a special place in the hearts of Wrigley Fielders. When playing there for the Yankees in the 1932 World Series he was said to have 'called a shot', meaning that he pointed to a spot in the stands where he intended to hit the ball – just about the most arrogant stunt any batter can pull – and then proceeded to hit that spot, on the button. Or, at least, so the legend goes. 'Actually,' said Bob, 'I saw some grainy black-and-white footage of the incident and it looks like all Babe Ruth was doing was pointing out some activity in the stands that was putting him off. No one heard him actually call the shot.' But in baseball, as in so much of American folklore, truth has seldom been allowed to get in the way of a good story.

I should add, at this point, that on a previous visit to Wrigley Field I had made certain vows about baseball. These were:

1. That, as with bullfighting, much as I enjoyed the experience of attending baseball, I would never fully grasp its subtleties. I should therefore just relax and enjoy the apparent absurdity of it all. Much of what Bob Racky was telling me went right over my head, but what the hell. The words sounded good. They had a

poetry all of their own, and for me that counts a lot.

2. That there are few more embarrassing sounds than those of an earnest Brit, like the one I once heard in Chicago, trying to steer his stuffy vowels around the all-American, shorthand patter of baseball. 'Way to go!' Not my way, pal. I wouldn't know a knuckleball pitch from a southpaw pinch-hitter, and I ain't ashamed of admitting it. Ballpark mania is quite enough to be going on with.

3. That, damned tempting though it may be, commercially produced Americana is best left in its natural habitat – that is, on the shelves of souvenir shops. I refuse, especially, to be lured into reckless spending on baseball memorabilia. Take it away from me, I declare. But when Bob Racky showed me a white plastic radio, given away as a promo by the Chicago White Sox in the 1950s, complete with a dial, dinkily shaped like a baseball, I broke my own vows and the tenth commandment to boot. Covetousness beckoned me into its sapping embrace. I wanted that white tacky radio. Wanted, wanted, wanted.

After I had calmed down, taking deep breaths and being careful not to look back at the radio, Bob showed me on another wall some stuff relating to Sammy Sosa. Or 'Seami Sowzar', as he pronounced it. Surprisingly, he did not claim to have had Sammy Sosa in the club, but he did often host executives from the cable network ESPN. 'They like it here. The food is better than over the road. It's a better deal, and it's private.'

Up on Bob Racky's roof I could see why. So good was the view that, if you did not look down on to Sheffield Avenue, you would swear you were on the upper tier of a stand inside the ballpark.

Looking left and right, Bob pointed out only one other building with a view that did not have bleachers on its roof. That was Bob's neighbour's, and for a good reason. One of Wrigley Field's many quirks is that the Cubs have rarely allowed any advertising hoardings inside the ballpark. In any other joint, in any other town, in any other country, such a self-denying policy on the part of a stadium operator would be dismissed as ludicrous. In the United States the idea borders upon blasphemy. Given Will Rogers' dictum that 'One ad is worth more to a paper than forty editorials', it is also remarkable that the *Tribune* has maintained the policy since it took over Wrigley Field.

Almost as remarkable is that in 1954 a city ordinance was

passed banning any new hoardings being erected on the rooftops *around* Wrigley Field. Only two survive until the present day, both tolerated only because the buildings had carried ads before 1954. One can be seen on Waveland Avenue, a garish red eyesore extolling the virtues of Budweiser. The other is on the roof of Bob Racky's neighbour, advertising an auto and oil distributor called Torco. This exclusivity, plus the fact that the sign can be seen clearly by over two million Cubs fans per year, plus zillions more viewers on TV, has been worth more trouble-free dollars to the building's canny owner than any rooftop club could possibly manage. Mind, he must have hit the roof, as it were, when a few years ago, according to Bob, Torco sublet the hoarding to Southwest Airlines for just one season, for an estimated $1.25 million.

Actually, two other signs are clearly visible from inside Wrigley Field. Both are fixed to the front of the Lakeview building.

One reads 'Eamus Catuli'.

'Let's go, Cubs!' explained Bob.

'And the other: "AC – 9 – 53 – 90"?'

'Yeah,' he smiled, clearly anticipating that one. 'OK, well, AC means Annus Catuli, the year of the Cubs. The 9 refers to the number of years since we last won our division. The 53 stands for fifty-three years since being National Champions in 1945, and the 90, well, the 90 is for the ninety years since winning the World Series in 1908. My dad was born in 1908 and never lived to see Cubs win a World Series. I'm fifty-seven and I've never seen it. I have three sons and I sure as hell hope one of 'em will.'

And if it does happen, at least Bob can be sure of getting a prime view of their progress.

'When this building came on the market, I was taking a big chance. I didn't know if people would be willing to join a social club focused on baseball, and the fact is it took a long, long time to take off after we opened. Since then it has grown slowly. At first we just built out the rooftop. Then we added an upper deck of seats in 1995. Now we have two levels with 140 seats total. But, yeh, it's going to take a long time to recoup the investment. I mean, this is no get-rich-quick scheme. I don't make my primary living from this. We don't even sell out for every game.'

Racky preferred smaller crowds anyway, he assured me. Every applicant had to be evaluated. 'Most members are personal recommendations and I'm proud of their deportment. We've never had any complaints from neighbours, and never any violence.' Pause. 'Unlike some of the other rooftops,' he added, waving in one direction.

That direction – though not necessarily Bob's imputation – led me to call upon Jim Murphy, proprietor of the eponymous Murphy's bar on the corner of Waveland and Sheridan, a short hop's distance from the rear of the old scoreboard. If sports bars are your thing, his is one of the best. Hot fries, cold beer, neon lights and, once again, enough memorabilia on the walls to keep you browsing long after you have lost the ability to stand upright.

'The rooftops started out just being a friendly thing,' Jim explained over a beer. 'Never charged anyone for anything, not even for the '84 play-offs. It was just "Come on up". In those days we had our own cheering team up on the roof. The Bleacher Buns, we called 'em, dressed in these outrageous cheerleader oufits. Man, they were cool. I mean, these were good-looking girls.' His eyes rolled at the memory.

'Then in '89 we decided to train lights on the girls and, whadd'you know, the umpires down in the ballpark would not start the game till we turned off the lights. A whole load of coppers [yes, 'coppers'] came over and asked us to switch them off 'cos there was so much attention on these *zaftig* girls.'

'Zaftig?'

'Yeh, zaftig. You don't know what zaftig means? It means large-breasted.'

Murphy's sundry regulars sitting at the bar then proceeded to hold a heated debate as to whether 'zaftig' was a real word or just Chicago slang. Jim sent for a dictionary and thereafter matters all became rather confused. One guy offered to get me into a nearby club where I could meet with all the zaftig girls I could handle. It had clearly been a good lunchtime session.

But, anyway, because of Alderman Hansen's new regulations Jim had had to spend $500,000 on renovating the roof, building a new parapet wall and new steel stairways. Then came the fire inspectors and the building inspectors, and new rules about not cooking on the roofs or selling tickets on the day, and a limit on the numbers. Jim then launched into a monologue about the city, the county, and this tax being imposed for a car lot, or that tax withdrawn. But he lost me completely, so I asked if I could see his roof.

On our way up he showed me the first-floor clubroom, where there stood, amid a ragtime piano and more memorabilia, his pride and joy, a table-top model of Wrigley Field. When finally he found the switch, its tiny lamps lit up his ruddy cheeks like the flickering candles of a birthday cake.

'I did this for love,' declared Jim emotionally, as we continued up the stairs to the roof and looked out, at last, over Wrigley Field.

Fifty or so seats were set up facing the ballpark, like a mini-grandstand. Tickets were $60 each, nearly twice that of a good seat inside Wrigley Field, but at Murphy's the cost included all one could eat and drink. There was a small bar and food counter, and the roof was covered in Astroturf. I wouldn't have described the view as the best view in the house. But for a building across the road, it was still remarkably good.

'We're the only ballpark in the country that has these rooftops, so why wouldn't I do this?' he went on. 'It was a labour of love. That Grenesko, he didn't have a clue. He was a hard guy, but he had no idea about baseball.'

'Everyone's been up here,' he added, though he could not quite recall who. But as we made our way down the back stairs, two names came to him. One was Ernie Banks. 'Mr Cubs himself.' The other, of course, was Sammy Sosa.

Sosa, I was later told, had also left his calling card on one of the other rooftops. It was during a game against the Philadelphia Phillies, in June 1998, when one of his sixty-six homers that season sailed effortlessly over left field, over the road, and on to one of the rooftops on Waveland Avenue.

But even Sosa couldn't match the range of the Cubs' epic slugger of the late 1970s, Dave 'Kong' Kingman, who once managed to hit a ball through the roof of the Metrodome in Minneapolis, and was only half-jokingly described in *Sports Illustrated* as using the buildings on Waveland, 500 feet from homeplate, as target practice. The Cubs did pay for windows to be repaired, but, as one resident commented, the club might at least have allowed her to keep the balls as souvenirs.

One of the most memorable rooftop encounters occurred in July 1993. A visiting player called Kevin Mitchell had just hit a home-run for the Cincinatti Reds when he noticed some guy waving frantically at him from a rooftop in Sheffield Avenue, beyond the right-field bleachers. Spying a TV camera stationed by the dug-out, Mitchell had the cameraman zoom in on the figure and saw that it was Tom Browning, one of his team-mates.

'Wait a minute,' thought Mitchell, 'I just saw him a few minutes ago.'

Which was true, except that after the Reds had gone into bat again, Browning had sneaked from the dug-out, slipped on a sweatshirt to hide his uniform, and left the ballpark, from where he made his way up to one of the roofs. At first none of the fans there would believe he was the genuine item. Once they realised, they plied him with beer and dogs (all of which, he said later, he refused). Before long the TV cameras had picked him out and the annals of baseball had yet another all-time prank to add to its list.

Accepting his manager's $500 fine after the incident, Browning described his unauthorised outing as 'kind of neat'. In his defence, one of his fellow Reds said, 'A little levity never hurt anybody . . . we're not a bunch of stuffed shirts or accountants.'

And the point of all this?

Well, you know what? The point is that while there are legions of stuffed shirts and accountants running stadiums all over the world today, there is only one Wrigleyville. And what Wrigleyville demonstrates is the one very simple fact which all sports fans already know without me telling them: that the best place for a stadium, be it a ballpark, football ground or whatever, is in the heart of a community. Not stuck out in some remote no-man's-land where the only bright lights are traffic lights and where the only signs of life are on match days, in the barren spaces between the car parks and the turnstiles. Ask the supporters of the Cubs in Chicago, of Arsenal in London, of Hearts in Edinburgh, of Sampdoria in Genoa, of Vasco de Gama in Rio, of Northern Spirit in Sydney. Would they swap their traditional grounds for a superbowl by a motorway? I think not.

And the best way for a community to feel at home with its stadium is for the stadium operators to embrace, and to respect, the local people and make them feel proud of the extraordinary building in their midst. It's a two-way thing, and of course it doesn't always work out.

Yet nine times out of ten when you ring a doorbell in the vicinity of a stadium and tell the occupants you want to take some photos; nine times out of ten they let you in. Because they understand.

Stadiums are special.

5 SOUND, LIGHTS, ACTION

There is an old Maori saying: '*He aha te mea nui o te ao? He tangata, he tangata, he tangata.*' 'What is the greatest thing on earth? The people, the people, the people.'

It reminds me of an expression much favoured by estate agents: 'What are a property's three most important assets? Location, location, location.'

But what happens when the people, the people, the people, and the location, location, location, are not in harmony, as is the case in Mount Eden, a suburb of Auckland which has in its midst Eden Park, the *de facto* national stadium of New Zealand? At what point should the interests of people actually living in the location prevail over the interests of the 'people' to whom the property is supposed, in effect, to belong?

Now that is a tough one.

Bloody stadiums. As powerful as the passion they engender within their confines is the hostility they often provoke without. Not all host communities are as hunky-dory as Wrigleyville.

Bloody stadium operators too. Talk about insensitive. Some of them think that life begins and ends at their stadium gates; that if it's good for sport (that is, their own branch of the business), then it must be good for everyone else in town too. So if the neighbours don't like the plans to enlarge the stadium, or to play games on Sundays, or to turn up the volume on their public-address systems until Johnny's pet rabbits have died of fright in their hutch, then it's tough. But it's sport. And in sport, where there's a winner . . .

Frequently caught in the middle of this war of nerves is the professional adviser. Either in defence of the local community (that is, the voters) or in the service of stadium developers, he may be called upon to draw up forecasts of economic impact and environmental impact, along with traffic management and feasibility studies, each of which might take months to complete. My own files are literally bulging with such weighty reports. Occasionally my bank account has bulged too, from the proceeds of being consulted by the consultants. Reader: I am an interested party.

Stadiums have often been called 'theatres of dreams'. But the world's sporting map is also littered by stadiums more accurately dubbed 'theatres of conflict'. And although it is tempting to caricature the main protagonists in these conflicts as either goodies or baddies, for the most part they are just ordinary men and women, fighting to protect their own corner. In north London, to take but one example, the residents around Highbury Stadium have protested so successfully against Arsenal Football Club's plans to expand – plans which would have necessitated the demolition of several, perfectly fine Victorian houses behind one stand – that the club is now considering relocating altogether. This is no small matter. Millions of pounds and nearly ninety years of tradition are at stake. Some of the home owners clinging steadfastly to their properties are even Arsenal fans. They know exactly the consequences of their stance, and feel rotten about it. Rotten, but determined all the same.

Then there are the many suburban and rural communities that have banded together to oppose the construction of a new stadium in their midst. And so the battleground moves on. In Britain, so many individuals and businesses have been affected by stadium proposals in recent years that a Federation of Stadium Communities has formed. Its newsletter is called *The Shadow*.

When people ask what on earth I find so interesting about stadiums, I wish I could take them to one of the church halls or community centres where residents (the 'us') are to be found hammering out their grievances against the stadium operators (the 'them'). Mistrust pervades the loaded air. Tempers get frayed. Slide presentations go comically haywire. Suave operators accustomed to dealing with prime ministers and megabuck transactions are reduced to perspiring, mumbling wrecks by stooped pensioners. Architects' plans are wilfully misunderstood, as if they were secret codes. And there's always someone shouting, 'Can't hear you at the back!' or leading the choruses of 'Shame! Shame!'

For any neutral observer, these locked-horn meetings make for palpably tense drama. But for those of us who strongly advocate the maintenance of stadiums in cities rather than their consignment to barren, out-of-town wastelands, what we hear and what we learn at such gatherings places us in a most uncomfortable quandary.

By the time I reached Auckland the Eden Park Neighbours' Association was just entering its third year of campaigning.

A few streets from the stadium and in the midst of a residential area that seemed one part California, one part Scotland and one part Aussie Soapland, eight of the EPNA members gathered to tell me their side of the story. I was ushered into a stunningly renovated, single-storey wooden house dating from the early 1900s. The décor was tasteful. The wine flowed sedately and the barbecue was already lit. (It is deemed unpatriotic in New Zealand to have a gathering of more than three adults without serving alcohol or cooked meat.) From the lush back garden I could see the silhouetted hump of nearby Mount Eden – one of several verdant hills that punctuate the sprawling city – and, above rootops in the distance, the neon-bathed Sky Tower in Auckland's central business district. Yet the only sounds were of crackling charcoal, rustling trees and the reassuring patter and chatter of suburban, family life at sundown on a summer's evening.

From an outsider's perspective it is hard enough to imagine Kiwis getting worked up about anything, such is the easygoing nature of the country. Certainly this group of comfortably dressed, articulate, middle-class suburbanites appeared to be about as militant as librarians. Not at all the steamy rebel rousers I had been led to anticipate. Round-shouldered and soft-skinned in a land of beefcake and sheep shearers, softly spoken in the home of the Haka, I could not help but wonder if these EPNA members were typical of the urbane yuppies I had heard frequently disparaged by other New Zealanders as JAFAs; Just Another Fucking Aucklander. Yet I had earlier been told that some JAFAs considered the EPNA activists to be righteous zealots.

I had also been forewarned, 'There's a lot of "he said, she said" in all of this.' But then that was only to be expected. There always is.

'The biggest impact [of the campaign against the redevelopment of Eden Park] has been on my family life,' lamented Chris Chittenden, a publisher with a background in teaching geography and a woolly jumper to match. In the local press Chris had occasionally been painted as an obsessive. Yet in the flesh he seemed charming and not at all screwy (though the evening was young). 'I have a wife and two young boys, and the campaign has intruded hugely, partly out of my own personality but also because I was just so bugged by what I saw as the whole irrationality of the Eden Park proposals. I felt quite affronted by their approach and by that of Auckland City Council.'

For Mike Oberdries, who worked in computer mapping and database technology, the campaign had been a real eye-opener. 'I guess I'm now much less naïve about local government and politics. While the philosophy [of the planning regime] appears to be trying to encourage public participation, the reality is that a lot of it depends on lip service. When a community group like ours is up against what amounts to a corporate entity, which has people fully employed to fight its case, forty hours a week, you quickly realise that the notion of democracy actually costs, and not just in a monetary sense.'

One of the brickbats most frequently hurled at those who live near stadiums is that they have no right to complain. After all, wasn't the stadium there long before they moved in? Didn't they realise what they were letting themselves in for?

Chris rejected this out of hand. 'The whole argument is quite specious. When the ground was originally built here the area was already residential. When they made plans to expand it was already residential. When they made the decision to modernise it was residential. So you could equally say to the Eden Park Trust Board, "Well, surely when you made these plans you must have known that this was a residential area." You can turn the argument round. One of our members was born within spitting distance of Eden Park and has lived in the area all her life. She's now eighty and is really affronted by what's happening.'

And what was happening?

The Eden Park Trust Board wanted to build a new stand and erect floodlights. In my world, at least, that seemed like a fairly routine occurrence. Hardly radical or earth-shattering. Inconvenience would arise, for sure, especially during the building work. But new stands are being built all over the world, often in much tighter locations than Eden Park. And as for floodlights, north Americans have been living with them since the 1930s (Wrigleyville excepted), Europeans since the 1950s. It is possible that my research was lacking, but I had no clear evidence of wholesale misery having been caused as a result. Furore over a motorway or a supermarket next door I could understand. But one new stand and floodlights?

But as I was patiently informed by the EPNA members, the new proposals for Eden Park were symptomatic of a much greater threat. It was not, they insisted, that local residents had become suddenly less tolerant. It was that the stadium in their midst had changed. Changed quite radically. More spectators were arriving by car. The physical structures of the stadium had grown. In the boardroom, bumbling amateurism had given way to thrusting commercialism. More games were being staged and, in some cases, in an atmosphere of such hype that it was getting harder to close one's doors and windows against the blare of music systems, of helicopters flying overhead and of pumped-up fans parading outside in the streets, many of whom arrived already tanked up because the area around Eden Park happens to be 'dry'. (Apparently some local residents used to do quite well selling homebrew from their front gardens, but that trade had dried up since the stadium obtained its own liquor licence.)

Lynn Webber, who described herself as one of the EPNA's foot soldiers, said, 'I came here about 1989. I went to the Zimbabwe cricket match recently, hoping the New Zealand team could finally beat someone, and the Eden Park Trust Board wouldn't even cut the noise down so that the people inside the park could concentrate on what was going on. They were much more interested in playing music between overs and running the whole thing as an entertainment package. Now we have this crazy game called Cricket Max which teaches players only how to survive ten overs, and it's been driving people crazy. An old couple close to me were driven nuts by the music. It has changed, no doubt about it.'

All right, I conceded, but changed from what?

Cricket first appeared on the former farmland at the turn of the twentieth century. This was at a time when Auckland's population was set to double in less than two decades and when virgin fields such as those undulating around Mount Eden and Kingsland were being carved up into streets and plots. Despite creeping suburbanisation since, the area still retained some vestiges of impermanence: telegraph poles, wooden houses on blocks, single-storey shops. But that was part of its charm. That, plus its proximity to the city centre, had drawn hundreds of young families to Mount Eden during the Seventies and Eighties to what had previously been a comparatively working-class, run-down district. Now it had all the trappings of a cosmopolitan social mix: smart homes next to rooming houses, young families next to pensioners, trendy restaurants and cheap take-aways. Slowly but surely, Vegemite and corned beef were being nudged from the shelves of local shops by pasta and balsamic vinegar. Shades of Wrigleyville indeed.

Rugby, the true religion of the Kiwi nation, arrived at Eden Park in 1921. Five years later a formal Deed of Trust was signed to ensure that the ground would be run entirely for the benefit of all cricket and rugby in Auckland under a newly established, non-profit-making Board of Control. The Board's functions were then formalised by the passing of the Eden Park Act in 1955. In the meantime, Eden Park played host to the 1950 Empire Games. There were just two stands in those days; the Number 1 and Number 2 stands. The rest of the ground was surrounded by a bowl of open banking, capable of squeezing in just over 61,000 at its peak.

As, one by one, new stands and terraces were built, Eden Park's international profile was raised by the staging of the inaugural Rugby Union World Cup in 1987, the Rugby League World Cup a year later, and in cricket, one-day extravaganzas such as one against Australia in 1982 that drew a record gate of 43,000. Meanwhile, on Eden Park's Outer Oval, immediately adjacent to the main stadium, corporate hospitality tents started appearing during the Eighties. Houses on the south side of the block were demolished to make room for car parking. Then in 1989 the first executive boxes were added above the roof of the South Stand in a $7.5 million revamp. This was followed three years later by new West and South-West Stands costing $11.2 million, built in time for the cricket World Cup of 1992.

By the mid Nineties Eden Park had thus become a quirky mish-mash of old and new. Hardly a stadium at all, in fact. More like a moderately comfortable English-style cricket ground with no cohesion but several popular sections, each with its own set of regular patrons. I mean this not as a criticism. For while the North Americans and Europeans have always tended to design and build 'stadiums' in a controlled manner, according to a master plan, until recent years the British and their colonial cousins down under usually preferred to assemble 'grounds' on an *ad hoc* basis. A number of factors help explain this; not least being that in Britain, Australia and New Zealand most stadiums and grounds are privately owned. Class divisions have also played a part in shaping the design. But so too has the quintessential notion that advanced planning and strict uniformity are somehow unBritish. When the German exile Nikolaus Pevsner, author of the mammoth *Buildings of England* series, described Lord's in London as 'a jumble without aesthetic aspirations, quite unthinkable in a country like Sweden or Holland', he revealed as much about his own Continental sensibilities as he did about those of the British.

But however idiosyncratically Eden Park evolved, it is also the case that cricket lovers have never rated the ground particularly highly. Their main complaints are that the wicket is too slow and the boundaries too short. Rugby fans, for their part, have described the viewing distances as too long and the terracing too shallow. Eden Park has thus been dubbed the 'rucket and crigby ground', and not always with affection. But New Zealand has several such rucket and crigby grounds, if only because the population of 3.8 million is too small and gates are too low to sustain individual venues for different sports. Even a new and much vaunted stadium that was then being built in Wellington was a compromise (albeit a good-looking one), shared between rugby and cricket.

Until the Seventies, the main bugbear of residents around Eden Park had been the sheer volume of crowds congregating in the surrounding streets. Life was particularly unpleasant, some locals recalled, in the build-up to major games, when crowds would queue for up to two or three days in advance, camping out on the pavements, littering the streets and relieving themselves in front gardens.

The first inkling of concerted action by residents came in 1982 when, a few months after anti-apartheid protests had disrupted a controversial Springboks tour, the Eden Park Trust Board applied to the local council for permission to erect floodlights and stage twelve night games per year. Floodlights were going up all over Australia. New Zealand's national stadium, it was argued, should not lag behind. The Board agreed that no alcohol would be served at night-time, but, as in Wrigleyville around the same time, the Eden Park residents were incensed. After 448 objections were filed, the Board withdrew to lick its wounds.

To head off any future applications, the residents then successfully lobbied the council to make it a written condition of the District Scheme (a document which lays down official parameters for all planning in the area) that no night games would ever be permitted, because of their likely impact on the surrounding residential neighbourhood.

'And that was it,' said Chris Chittenden, topping up my wine glass. 'We foolishly got on with our lives, thinking the issue was done and dusted.'

But it was nothing of the sort. In 1993, Auckland City Council issued the draft of a new District Scheme. Buried somewhere in this thick tome was a brief clause proposing that night games at Eden Park be no longer banned absolutely but open to consideration as a 'discretionary activity'. Notice of this change was confined to a small ad in a newspaper. Nine residents managed to spot it. But their objections were in any case overruled. Cricket, and especially rugby, has too many friends in high places. As one Aucklander told me, in order to separate the top brass in sport from the politicians in New Zealand you would first need a microscope to detect the join, and then a very large bucket of freezing-cold water. 'But even if you could split 'em, you'd still be hard pressed to tell 'em apart.'

Another Aucklander reckoned that such was the importance of sport in the country that, 'When the All Blacks lose, half of New Zealand goes into denial.' He may well have been right. After the Kiwis' defeat by France in the 1999 Rugby World Cup, one New Zealand university set up a grief-counselling service. Some commentators felt that the result would even have an effect on the forthcoming elections. In other words, sport is not just newsworthy in New Zealand. Often it *is* the news.

I had already gained some inkling of this within half an hour of arriving in the country. I was just about to leave the airport terminal when, purely by chance, I was introduced to a high-profile, no-nonsense sports presenter called Murray Deaker and invited to appear on his radio phone-in. Naturally I agreed, immensely flattered, somewhat amused, but aware that stadium chat is hardly of universal appeal. 'How long will you need me? Five, ten minutes?' I enquired, thinking of the time slots usually allocated to the subject on British radio.

'Ah no,' came Murray's reply. 'The full hour.'

And when the programme went out they had so many callers –

heaps and heaps, as they say in New Zealand – they invited me back the following week. For another hour.

So no doubt about it. The Kiwis wanted to talk about stadiums.

But to return to Eden Park. In November 1995 – significantly, noted the EPNA, a month *after* local elections had been held – the Eden Park Trust Board at last unveiled its plans to transform the stadium. Under the grandiose title of 'Genesis' (this being a park in Eden), the twenty-five-year phased redevelopment proposed to raise the capacity only marginally to 50,000 – albeit still the largest in New Zealand – but with a whole range of new facilities, starting with a 12,300-seat, two-tiered North Stand, plus executive boxes, lounges, video screens and so on, promising a 'total entertainment experience'.

Apart from their distaste for the concept itself, not to mention the prospect of having to live opposite a building site for years to come, most disturbing of all for the neighbours was this passage from the glossy brochure: *The name Genesis captures the essence of the vision for Eden Park. It is a vision of creation and renewal. Like the creation story, it will also be developed in seven stages, and the first stage begins with the command 'Let there be light.'*

Within days, some 250 angry residents gathered at the local Kowhai Intermediate School, almost opposite Eden Park, and with a dashing young lawyer called Vincent Carmine at the helm the Eden Park Neighbours' Association was set up. No one denied that Auckland needed a modern stadium. Indeed – and this was to become a familiar cry – many of the protesters claimed to be ardent sports fans themselves. But a residential area like Mount Eden, they reasoned, was simply the wrong place to build such a large new facility, particularly one destined for night use, and with drinking and betting facilities to boot. Eden Park was now dubbed by the EPNA as 'the 21-acre pub that wants to be a casino'.

'Bunch of lefties!' came the response from equally ardent sports fans. Carmine refuted this, saying he was about as right-wing as one could be. Besides, the EPNA was above party politics.

It was, however, extremely organised, with official spokespersons, a media group, street co-ordinators and, pretty soon, a slogan. Writ large on a hoarding near the stadium, this proclaimed 'No Lights, Silent Nights'.

The Board responded by putting up a sign inside the stadium

saying 'Let's Light Up Eden Park'. It also fostered the formation of the Friends of Eden Park, a group instantly dismissed by the EPNA as the 'blazer-and-brass-button brigade'.

Without lights, argued the Board, Eden Park, home of the All Blacks, mecca of the rugby universe, was in danger of becoming a sporting backwater. It was bad enough business having to stage Auckland Blues matches in the prestigious Super 12 competition on midweek afternoons, when gates would sometimes dip embarrassingly below 5,000. The same games staged at night might have drawn nearer 35,000. But the Board's all-important television income also suffered. Even in New Zealand not many workers could slope off during an afternoon to watch rugby on TV.

'If the lighting proposal is stopped the world-class sport we enjoy will stop too. It's that simple,' said the Friends' spokesman, former All Black David Kirk.

But not everyone was swayed. One protester wrote to the *New Zealand Herald*, 'When will the one-eyed sports players and fans in this country realise that not everyone is sports mad? New Zealand should be known around the world for what it contributes to peace and conservation, not sports hysteria.' It was signed by a woman called Fenella, which no doubt raised a few ribald laughs around the bars of Auckland's rugby clubs. But Fenella's was by no means a lone voice.

By March 1996 the number of responses to Genesis sent to Auckland City Council had topped 2,250, three times the number recorded for a far more controversial scheme involving a transport terminal in the city centre. Of the responses, 52 per cent were in opposition. The bulk of the remainder, claimed the EPNA, were on preprinted forms issued by the Friends of Eden Park and filled in by people who lived outside the affected area. Ah yes, the 'people' again. The 'people' vs. the 'people'. 'He said, she said.'

But it was not long before some of the 'people' on the other side of the fence started growing rather peeved by the EPNA's stance.

'Forty years ago,' wrote the *Herald*'s Bob Pearce, 'it was acceptable to have two-day queues along Sandringham Road for the privilege of sitting on exposed terracing, where Broadway pies doubled as food and ammunition, and beer bottles quenched the thirst and absorbed the excess.' But no longer. Eden Park was falling behind. A *Herald* editorial agreed. Floodlights were a reality of modern, professional sport, it argued. Furthermore, if Eden Park were to be jettisoned, a part of Auckland's heart would go with it. 'A solution is essential,' came the plea. 'Turn on the lights!'

For three years this war of words continued, in hearings, appeals, on the streets, in the newspapers, on Murray Deaker's radio phone-in and on television. Soon the whole of New Zealand would know that the residents around Eden Park were fed up with drunken or violent 'hoons' reeling about in the streets. The police, complained the residents, did nothing, and Eden Park's management did even less.

Eventually the issue was formally aired at an independent planning hearing, staged at the 'Delightful Lady Lounge' at Auckland's not-quite-so delightful Alexandra Park Raceway, in September 1996. After ten days of deliberation in front of a sparsely populated public gallery, the lights were approved, albeit with forty-four conditions attached to their use.

Martin Weekes, Eden Park's recently appointed chief executive, was delighted, claiming that thirty-five of the forty-four conditions had been drawn up by his team of consultants anyway. The crestfallen EPNA described the result as 'Big Business 1, Residents 0'. Yet despite the association now being heavily in debt and needing to raise a further $40,000 if it wished to appeal, its members made the bold decision to fight on. They had gone too far to back down now.

So once more the parties prepared for battle, only this time the EPNA found itself challenging both Eden Park and Auckland City Council (which was now a party to the earlier verdict).

At this second hearing, conducted under the aegis of the Environment Court, a further mass of detail was considered: alternative stadium sites, light levels, sound levels, conservation issues and even property values (which apparently had not suffered, as Vincent Carmine found when he sold up for a nice profit and moved on soon after). For the EPNA a university professor explained how the 'physiological arousal' experienced by fans when watching competitive sports often continued to be dissipated after they had left the stadium. Hence the possibility of such post-match actions as 'sudden shouts or calls, vigorous actions, jumping, swinging on objects, mock scuffles and horseplay'.

Who would have thought it?

One protester feared that once night games began children might easily be run over in the dark. A seven-year-old boy who liked to play in the garden expressed his fear of abduction. A parent voiced fears of HIV-infected syringes being discarded by night-time concert-goers.

EPNA members showed photographs of illegally parked cars and of urinators in mid-stream (examples of which I was shown during my visit, featuring all kinds of poses next to buses, fences, garden walls and gutters). One resident said that she had taken to dousing with a hose anyone who piddled in her garden, and that she wielded a fencing sword in case of retaliation. Then the anti-smoking lobby joined in, prompting the Eden Park board to promise that it would canvas its 10,000 members on a smoking ban (they approved it).

One EPNA proposal was to ban non-residents from parking within a two-kilometre radius of the stadium. 'But what if,' asked the Council's counsel, 'you were dropping off a knitting pattern, say, in [the neighbouring district of] Ponsonby, at the same time as a match?'

'Or attending a Tupperware party, perhaps?' chortled the presiding judge.

By now, according to newspaper reports, there were only a couple of onlookers in the public gallery.

And so it continued, going on into overtime and then adjourning for another few months before the judge and his three environment commissioners finally reached their verdict in October 1997. Once again the EPNA was overruled, apart from the fact that the number of conditions had now increased by one, from forty-four to forty-five. So that must have seemed to all concerned like time and money very well spent.

From then on the residents' association assumed the role of eagle-eyed watchdogs. Illegally parked cars were diligently logged and reported. Urinators continued to be snapped on camera. The construction of the new North Stand was monitored for any breach of noise regulations. The EPNA also wrote protest letters to companies considering investing in facilities in the new stand.

Meanwhile, the EPNA had to continue the exhausting process of raising campaign funds. There were street parties and wine-and-cheese evenings, film shows, lectures and garage sales. Local artists donated work for auctions. Residents also raised cash by selling grilled sausages to fans on their way to the stadium, the irony of which was no doubt savoured by both parties.

According to Mark Donnelly, a fresh-faced, thirty-something accountant who was now the EPNA president, all these events and hundreds of hours of hard slog went only part way towards paying off their legal costs of $100,000, whereas he reckoned that, between them, Eden Park and Auckland City Council had spent between $500,000 and $1 million. 'Basically,' he concluded, 'you get the justice you buy. Although it may seem that we spent a lot of money, it was probably only a third of what we needed to be effective.'

To what end, though, I asked again. Did they really, honestly believe they could have prevented floodlights being installed? To my knowledge no neighbourhoods have descended into a sulphurous abyss with the advent of night games – at least, no more so than they did during daytime matches. Consider the people of Wrigleyville, I suggested. They had fought the same battle and lost, yet now few of them can even remember what all the fuss was about. I wanted to say, 'Weren't you just pissing into the wind on this issue?' until I realised that I'd never heard the words urine, urinating and urinator mentioned so frequently, all in one evening. Come to think of it, I don't think I'd ever heard the word 'urinator' at all before that evening. But all the same, I couldn't help feeling that their undeniable energies had been ultimately misdirected.

On the contrary, they assured me. The fact remained that, lights or no lights, in the overall context of Auckland, and in particular regard to its congested roads and its painfully inadequate public transport system, Eden Park was still, irrefutably, in the wrong place. And that, they felt, had been the one issue no one in Auckland had ever been able to debate frankly and openly.

After I left the EPNA members that night, I had to admit that among the people I had met that night, gathered around the tasteful kelims, designer furniture and heaving bookshelves, I had felt pretty much within my own social milieu. In fact, after a few glasses of Kiwi red and a tender lamb chop or two (with green salad on the side), I felt more sympathetic towards their cause than I would ever have imagined.

'Bloody stadiums!' I cursed as I drove off through the night. 'Bloody blazer-and-brass-button brigade!' In Auckland, as everywhere else, old thinking and new money had always made for an unpalatable cocktail.

Still with these bitter thoughts swirling around in my head, the following day I returned to the neighbourhood and chanced upon an elderly resident leaning against his gate on Cricket Avenue, behind the East Terrace at Eden Park. Every week, he told me, he crossed the road to take photos of the new North Stand going up. 'Should have seen the place thirty-five years ago,' he said. 'Bloody terrible. People all over the street, queueing for days. Now it's all pre-booked tickets there's hardly any trouble at all.'

Hardly any trouble? *Hardly any trouble*?

I asked him about the EPNA's campaign.

'Dah, they're all newcomers, aren't they? Only been here five minutes.'

Matthew, in his late twenties and living on Walters Road, directly opposite the new North Stand, was similarly scathing. 'Sure, it's noisy, but, I mean, this is Eden Park, isn't it? History, emotion. This is where the All Blacks play. You can get quite emotional about it.' He could say that again.

I met another local who was just about to move from a nearby street on to Walters Road. So the redevelopment hadn't put him off? Absolutely not, he insisted. He'd lived in the shadows of Eden Park for years. No, his only problem was that he would now have to switch his season ticket from the South Stand to the North Stand, to save him from having to walk around the block.

Wearing the expression of a man who spent his life trying to appear reasonable but deep down wanted to scream out loud with indignation, Eden Park's chief executive, Martin Weekes – a pom as it happens – hedged with me at first. After a spell buying women's lingerie for Marks and Spencer in England, Martin had come to New Zealand for a holiday. As soon as he got off the plane he decided the country was for him. Since taking up his post at Eden Park three years earlier, he'd had some pretty bad experiences with reporters. I could see him sizing me up, working out whose side I was on.

I told him about my previous evening's meeting with the EPNA and he sighed.

So now it was his turn.

'You're talking about some very extreme perspectives,' Martin assured me, handing over a sheaf of newspaper cuttings. 'You might think that there's a battle zone here. But there really isn't. There are around 17,500 residents in total in the area. At the peak of their opposition the EPNA had about 500 members. Within the same area there were about 500 people who supported us. Which leaves approximately 16,500 people who, given all the sustained publicity, the letters, the newsletters put through the door, were still not motivated either way.

'There were concerns about litter. We put bins out the night before every game, and collect them the following day. And you know the complaints then? "I don't want a bin outside my house."

'We employ security guards out in the street. Do you know what complaints we received about that? "We don't want to live in a police state."

'The next thing was urination.'

First urinators, now urination. My urological vocabulary was now fit to burst.

'We provided portaloos in the streets,' said Martin. 'Then we had complaints from people saying, "I don't want a portaloo in the street." '

I wondered if he or any other senior officials at Eden Park had fully considered the idea of building a new stadium elsewhere in the city.

'There was no real debate,' he conceded. 'This is the national stadium, but it is also a private stadium, owned by a private trust. It has never received government funding. Now if someone had come to us and said, here is $150 million to build a new national stadium for New Zealand, go and find the ideal site, maybe or maybe not this site would have been redeveloped. However, nobody has ever put up the money to do that, and not one of the sites raised by the neighbours was suitable from a planning perspective, let alone a cost perspective. So the argument to relocate was never really pursued.'

Besides, he added, according to an economic-impact study conducted in 1995, the very existence of the stadium was worth $24 million to the locality.

'Now to opponents of Eden Park the economic-impact argument just serves to reinforce the image of us being a big business. So you see, everything can be turned into a negative if you're that way inclined.'

Martin was now getting into his stride.

He reckoned that the EPNA's protest had delayed the start of Genesis by two to three years and had thereby added $6–7 million to the bill. Construction costs had risen around 3 per cent per annum, while instead of receiving an expected lottery grant of $4 million – the same as was allocated to the new stadium in Wellington – by the time Eden Park's redevelopment was cleared to start, lottery income had dipped so severely that a grant of only $1 million was all that could be managed. And the EPNA had even lobbied against that being handed over, on the grounds that the main beneficiaries would be 'Rupert Murdoch and the globalised television entertainment industry'.

'What has gone on here I don't think would have been tolerated in any other country. Maybe it was our fault for letting the matter get out of hand too early. I mean, all we are talking about is transferring some of our games from 2.30 kick-off to 7.30.

'We know there'll be problems, we all know that, but not on the scale they've been talking about. So all I'm saying is let's address these fears together.'

During the following days, as I travelled round visiting Auckland's two other major stadiums, then the new venue in Wellington and several other sporting gems on the North Island, I knew that sooner or later, and at the very least on my return to Murray Deaker's radio phone-in, I would be asked where I – 'Simon Inglis, visiting UK expert on stadiums' – stood on the Eden Park issue. Watching the seemingly unending and awesome beauty of the New Zealand landscape passing by my car window, day after day, these were the thoughts that coursed through my mind.

OK. Since I contend that stadiums are crucial to the life, soul and identity of urban communities, I would surely be expected to support the Eden Park Trust Board's position, whether or not I identify with the blazer-and-brass-button brigade. I would further add that, ever since the days of the Circus Maximus, stadiums have deserved their place on the civic map no less than libraries or theatres, opera houses or parks, all of which have been traditionally subsidised by the public purse. I might therefore castigate those complainants who are only too happy to benefit from the good life that cities can offer yet refuse to accept the inevitability of change within the cycle of urban renewal. Hey, buster, I could retort, how the hell do you think that nice street of yours or that shopping centre or that new cinema got built in the first place? Not by artists and craftsmen working at the behest of concerned philanthropists, I'll warrant, but by speculators and profiteering contractors. What do you think was there before your nice street was built? For everything that goes up, something else must come down, be it a tree or a hedgerow or a rotten old slum.

Losing my temper only slightly I might continue by saying, honestly, you go all gooey-eyed and conservationist about some crappy old worthless building or grandstand put up fifty years ago or whenever, yet spit blood should anyone dare to propose a properly designed modern edifice to take its place; as if the long-forgotten jobbing builder responsible for the old building somehow had more soul and sensitivity towards his environment than might any contemporary developer.

But that's not all. I might also want to say that the emotional ties to Eden Park – to the turf, to the name, and, yes, to the very soul of the place, with all its memories and echoes of past triumphs and torments – be they felt by the New Zealand public at large, by regular supporters or by members of the Eden Park Trust Board, cannot and should not be lightly dismissed either. History and tradition within sport are no less worthy than any of the other cultural values which do so much to underpin our sense of identification with a nation, a city or a neighbourhood. Did you know they had signs up at Eden Park in Japanese. Why? Because coachloads of Japanese tourists regularly flock to Eden Park as reverentially as they would to a cathedral. Doesn't that mean something?

I could go on further. And on. And on some more. (I often do.)

But if anyone were to ask how I would respond to a proposal to build a stadium in my own neighbourhood . . .

So, taking a deep breath, I will concede that the stadium business is indeed a minefield for hypocrites, of which, I guess, I am one. I may not be a 'Banana' (who insists 'Build Absolutely Nothing Anywhere Near Anything'), or a 'Note' (who adds, 'Not Over There, Either'). But I am, at heart (and so are you), a 'Nimby' in waiting: that is, someone who would chorus 'Not In My Back Yard' the minute my domestic environment was ever threatened.

I therefore prefer my stadiums (like my theatres, cinemas and libraries) to be alongside cafés and pubs and shops, in the heart of bustling communities, but don't fancy a stadium in the middle of my own.

What, then, did I say when, predictably, a caller on Murray Deaker's radio phone-in asked for my views on the redevelopment of Eden Park? What pearls of wisdom was I able to impart after my days of deep thought and soul-searching on the issue?

As is the wont of a true 'expert', when it came to the crunch I decided not to give a clear answer at all. Instead, I opted for the last refuge of all scoundrels and politicians by recounting an anecdote.

A rabbi is visited by a feuding couple. The husband tells his side of the story, to which the rabbi responds by saying, 'Mr Cohen, you are absolutely right.' The wife then counters with her completely opposite version of events. 'Mrs Cohen,' responds the rabbi, 'from what you say, I cannot find fault with your actions. You are entirely right.'

At which point one of the rabbi's students raises his hand and says, 'But rabbi, first you tell Mr Cohen he is right. Then you tell Mrs Cohen she is right. How in God's name can they both be right?'

To which the rabbi replies, after some thought, 'Mmmm, yes. You also are right.'

Except that when I narrated this tale on New Zealand radio – not, I imagine, a medium normally attuned to cadences of Yiddish folklore – it went down like the proverbial lead balloon. With it, no doubt, went my reputation as an expert.

Murray Deaker was polite all the same, and after the broadcast I tried to cast the whole business from my mind over a curry with an old Auckland friend.

Since then? A few months after my visit, the North Stand was finally completed and the first floodlit match staged at Eden Park, in March 1999. At the time of writing, several months later, a further nine night games had followed. So, I hardly dared inquire . . . how was it going? In certain respects, it transpired, fine. In others, don't ask.

As far as I could ascertain, happily there had been no cases of match-related rape, murder or child abduction in the vicinity, and no HIV-infected syringes found in front gardens. Nor, rather more surprisingly, had there been any arrests at any of the floodlit rugby games. Arrests for the one day–night cricket match held so far had been lower than was usual for a routine day game, despite the crowds being 30 per cent larger. All the controls put into place were working well, and, according to Martin Weekes, the only complaints on the hotline had concerned illegally parked cars.

Between Eden Park and the EPNA relationships appeared not to have improved one iota. There had been more 'he said, she said' letters in the press, more street patrols by concerned residents and more arguments over the use of floodlights for training. Most notably there had been another almighty row over an application to stage a concert. 'And the nature of the concert?' I asked, expecting to be told maybe Def Leppard or Metallica. But, no, the artist in question was Pavarotti.

Luciano Pavarotti. The great Italian tenor whose *Nessun Dorma* had turned a billion deaf ears towards the delights of Puccini. Who better, I thought, to bring together warring factions and to appease the more sensitive souls around Mount Eden? What better aria for the troubled area? *Nessun Dorma*. 'No one sleeps.' If nothing else, what a brilliant opportunity for the EPNA to leaflet the great and the good, few of whom would have dared to miss the event.

Alas not. Apparently not even the man mountain from Modena was to be tolerated on the gentle slopes of Mount Eden. Think of all those wine-boxes strewn across the pavements. Think of all those fans – some, heaven forfend, of rival tenors Carreras or Domingo – slugging it out on the streets, still physiologically aroused after the concert, still humming loudly. The lawns littered with broken opera glasses, the fretful parents vowing never to touch fettucine ever again. No, if it was Pavarotti today, it would be Marilyn Manson tomorrow.

Thus the EPNA returned to the Environment Court once again, but this time with a difference. The Council backed down. The concert was blocked. Victory at last for the association. Pavarotti sang instead at another, smaller stadium on the other side of Auckland.

As I write, the EPNA is apparently going to court again, this time to try to stop Eden Park from having a liquor licence in the new North Stand. The neighbours were also attempting to curb the proposed opening of a Rugby Hall of Fame and a conference centre in the stand.

Chris Chittenden, the publisher, described the situation to me as an ongoing 'war of attrition' which it seemed neither side could win.

Another Mount Eden resident said of the EPNA, 'You know, those guys really should get a life.' He had been really looking forward to the Pavarotti concert.

Meanwhile, house prices in the area were continuing to rise. Public transport links to the stadium remained poor.

Martin Weekes decided to move to Canada.

As for me, I await an inevitable stream of letters from Auckland, listing all the mistakes and omissions I have perpetrated in this chapter, point by point. He said, she said. You said.

Naturally I will admit to every single error. Like the rabbi in my unfunny ancedote I'll say to all and sundry, 'You're right!'

But I will also say this. I may not be so wild about rugby or cricket, and on the whole much prefer Tom Petty to Pavarotti. But by heavens I do like living in a city where things are happening, where things are moving, where people say 'yes' more than they say 'no'. Where the lights go on seven evenings a week. Where the pavements hum and the air sizzles. Whether it's a stadium or an opera house, a pub, a street market or an all-night bagel bar, or an evening barbecue with interesting, opinionated neighbours, it is what makes city life so exquisitely tolerable.

Nessun dorma, nessun dorma . . .

No one sleeps. No one sleeps . . .

Dilegua, o notte! Tramontate, stelle! All'alba vincerò, vincerò, vincerò!

Vanish, o night! Set, the stars! At daybreak, I shall conquer, I shall conquer, I shall conquer!

These are the cries of the people, the people, the people. These are the sounds of the location, the location, the location. Day or night, they are part of the territory. Day or night, the rough with the smooth.

Sometimes, just sometimes, you have to let go.

6
CIUDAD DE LOS ESTADIOS, 2

Tuesday, 20 October. 09.55. Stadium No. 5. Vélez Sarsfield.
It isn't only stadiums that make for noisy neighbours. At around six o'clock in the morning, the building workers next to Enrique's flat in Buenos Aires decided to hold a competition. Not who could hammer in their nails the loudest, but who could sustain the same rhythm the longest. I thought they all did exceptionally well.

Enrique, bless him, had laid out for me a delightful breakfast of yoghurt, nuts, fruit and crackers, most of which I just had time to scoff before Greta, his slobbering bulldog, emerged from the kitchen to reacquaint herself with my trouser leg. I was saved from another soaking by a ring at the front door, where stood my new friend and guide for the week, Mariano, ready for day two of our attempt to visit as many stadiums as we could manage in six days. I still wasn't entirely sure why I was undertaking this quest. Was I a serious writer or merely a collector of stadiums? Was I a professional specialist, or a list-driven obsessional?

Certainly our day's schedule – six stadiums, all located in the southern extremities of Buenos Aires – would have seemed challenging enough in any city in any country of the world. In the Capital Federal of Argentina it may well have been madness, particularly with a navigator who was rather less than fresh from London and who was also a touch twitchy following his earlier than expected wake-up call from the builders next door.

First on our day's list was one of Argentina's leading clubs, Vélez Sarsfield, located twelve kilometres away along the snaking route of an *avenida* named splendidly after one Juan B. Justo, in the municipality of Liniers. Although Vélez were one of the top clubs in the capital, unlike for River Plate and Boca Juniors I had not rung in advance. Mariano and I were both thus a tad apprehensive as he wove in and out of the steady stream of rush-hour buses and trucks, crossing intersection after intersection; Cordoba, Corrientes, Warnes, San Martin (him again), Segurola, Carrasco, Lope de Vega, Victor Hugo. That Juan B. Justo just kept on rolling on and on, until finally, just before it hit the Avenida General Paz, which marks the south-eastern boundary of the city, the startling mass of the Vélez Sarsfield stadium loomed into view above the anonymous sprawl of the outer city.

If there's one thing I love more than a good map it is a great stadium at the end of a long bout of map reading.

Although I already had some sense of its form from press and TV coverage of the 1978 World Cup, up close the stadium bore a remarkable resemblance to an American college football stadium, particularly its vertiginous, slab-like open tiers on two sides and its no-nonsense, concrete and glass institutional façade, painted in sickly pale-yellow and green. Officially called the Estadio José Amalfitani, it was quite the largest mass for miles around. I could see why Velezanos called it *El Fortin* (the fort).

Inside the enormous foyer, next to the members' café, Mariano and I came face to face with an oversized bust of Amalfitani – Don Pepe to his admirers – sporting a pair of welded spectacles large enough to have served as a shop sign for an optician. Amalfitani was a former president of the club who had moved heaven and, quite literally, a great deal of earth in order to secure the site for Vélez in the early 1940s. Apparently the land, a lagoon more or less, had belonged to the then British-owned Ferrocarril Oeste (the Western Railway, whose own club stadium we had visited the night before). When Vélez first tried to reclaim the land, its boggy depths swallowed everything they could dump on it. Amalfitani persuaded the railway company to throw in all the surplus junk they could spare, then managed to redirect much of the rubble left over from road and bridge-building works in the area, until, 77,000 cubic metres of spoil later, the lagoon's appetite was sated and the ground could be levelled for use. Without Amalfitani, Vélez might well have sunk without trace.

Now, Mariano told me, they were one of the best-run clubs in Argentina, always living within their means, never getting into debt. Because of this, certain Vélez players had apparently refused to be transferred, even to mighty Boca, because they at least knew that at Vélez their wages would be paid. One of their current stars was the eccentric Paraguayan goalkeeper José Luis Chilavert, famous for scoring goals as well as saving them.

As to the name of the club itself, Dalmacio Vélez Sarsfield was a nineteenth-century constitutionalist – apparently of Irish descent – who drew up Argentina's first Civil Code and was a passenger on Argentina's first ever train. Later, a railway station in the district of Liniers was named after him. Then in 1910 a group of local footballers decided that the name of this railway station would also make a good title for their newly formed club. Given a vote, I don't think I would have agreed, but the name is at least unusual.

I knew of only one other fact about Vélez: that their former ground, a mile or so down the railway line, near Villa Luro, staged the first floodlit match in Argentina, in 1928.

After several uncertain minutes waiting in the lobby – another trophy cabinet there for us to admire – followed by further entreaties to the Secretaría, Mariano and I were eventually allowed into the stadium in the company of a burly security guard called Julio, whom I left in Mariano's safe hands while I scurried hither and thither taking notes and photographs.

Julio, it transpired, was actually a policeman, working a second, plainclothes shift for Vélez, just as Mariano, a psychoanalyst, was for a week working as my guide and interpreter. This was not uncommon, said Mariano later. Policemen in Argentina were notoriously underpaid, hence their susceptibility to corruption. As soon as I had left the two of them alone, Julio had apparently asked Mariano how much I was paying him, on the basis, he said, that all foreigners are, by definition, rich. Mariano was appalled. Not so much by Julio's presumption, but by the very fact that he, Mariano, found himself in conversation with a policeman. This was not the sort of thing that routinely happened to nice middle-class Jewish boys in Argentina. Too much bad blood.

'First I meet Pipo Pescador, now I am talking to a cop. This is all very different from my quiet consulting room,' he confessed.

'That's what happens when you consort with rich foreigners,' I replied.

As for the stadium, it held just under 50,000 spectators and was tailor-made for frightening the pants off the opposition. Apart from the slab-like stands on both sides, at each end were deep, open terraces, liberally decked in broody, terracotta paint, with randomly scattered crush barriers topped in gun-metal grey.

None of the barriers would have remotely passed muster under English standards, but for heaven's sake I had to forget all that. I was not there to do an inspection. I had to keep reminding myself of that.

Not. There. To. Do. An. Inspection. All right. But for what, then? Up and down those terraces, my thighs were aching already, and the day had hardly begun. So I had to concentrate.

Each terrace, I then noted, was lined along the front by absurdly tall perimeter fences, some 20 metres high, with a generous roll of barbed wire attached at the midway point. Julio was pleased they were so tall. Before last season they were only half the height, he said, and fans still managed to climb over.

All over the world fences were coming down at stadiums, condemned as no longer socially acceptable, no longer efficacious. Treat fans like animals and they will behave like animals, as I wrote nearly twenty years ago. Yet in Argentina the fences were not just staying put, they were growing taller. And still the country's serious crowd violence continued to escalate, and still no one made the connection. Certainly not Julio. He was amazed to learn that the British grounds had no fences at all. Nor much violence any more, at least not inside the grounds.

As an added line of defence, in front of the fences many Argentinian stadiums also had moats. At first I assumed the ones at Vélez were grassed over, until a closer look (and smell) revealed their contents to be stagnant water, covered in algae.

Another problem at Vélez, said Julio, were the *punguistas* – the little thieves – who picked pockets during *avalanchas,* or crowd surges. But at least the authorities had now banned fans from bringing in the huge banners which had once been so popular (and which English fans so envied). When unfurled across the terrace, according to Julio, the banners would allow fans underneath to smoke dope and snort coke without detection. Then the *avalanchas* would get really crazy.

As Julio was telling us this, I noticed a wall cut into the lower reaches of one of the end terraces. Odd enough that this should turn out to be the wall of a toilet block – slap bang in the middle of a viewing area – but odder still was a delicately inscribed piece of graffiti, painted in tiny white letters on the terracotta background. I expected some routinely vicious rhyme about *putos* (gays), *putas* (whores) or at the very least *cuervos* (vultures, meaning fans of rival club San Lorenzo), the standard fare of Argentinian daubings. Instead, this is what it said:

Una sola alma nacida en el cielo se divide en zespiritus gemelos y luego caen como dos estrellas fugaces en la tierra donde por encima de oceanos y continentes, grandes ciudades y de solados campos, sus fuerzas magneticas velvén a unirlas fundado de nuevo las dos mitades, solitarias y perdidas.

Mariano translated as follows: 'A single soul, born in heaven, divides into twin spirits, which then fall as two shooting stars towards the earth, where over and above oceans and continents, great cities and sun-bathed fields, their magnetic forces reunite once again the solitary and lost halves.'

It was signed, Ana Maria.

Tuesday, 20 October. 12.15. Stadium No. 6. Nuevo Chicago. From the late nineteenth century until the Depression, in addition to its thriving export trade in sheep and cereal, Argentina exported enough beef to Europe to have filled in the English channel. And without copious shipments of leather from Argentina, the troops in both World Wars, on both sides, would have been reduced to wearing braces and fighting barefoot. The Argentinian *estanciero*, or rancher, of the period enjoyed a level of riches and a reputation for extravagance we associate more today with oil sheiks and software barons.

For millions, if not billions, of cattle, the long journey from the *pampas* ended on the southern outskirts of Buenos Aires, at stock-yards located around four kilometres from Vélez; a place where giant *mataderos*, or slaughterhouses, worked day and night to keep up with the world's insatiable appetite for beef in all its forms. So plentiful was the supply, according to travellers of the nineteenth century, that instead of extracting profit from every last hoof and hind of every animal, piles of unwanted carcasses were left rotting on the ground, creating an indescribable stench. As processing methods improved, many of them imported from the world's foremost meat-packing city, Chicago, thousands of immigrant workers flocked to the area. As in every other part of Buenos Aires, these new arrivals formed a football club, in 1911. They called it, after their new *barrio*, Nuevo Chicago.

As soon as we parked and opened the doors of Mariano's

battered brown Toyota, we knew we'd found the right place. Although the stockyards stood mostly idle that day, decades of slaughter had infused the air with an all-pervading stink of raw meat and dung. Worse, the air was now so stiflingly hot that I felt as if I were being slowly cooked inside my clothes.

Around the ground lay street after street of low-rise, 1960s working-class estates; their fading white walls offering local graffiti artists plenty of scope for self-expression. Some had been busy at the ground too. The street-facing wall of the main stand bore a slogan 100 metres long in green and black, saying, 'Chicago needs you, enrol as a member.' What the club really needed, though, was for the builders to come back and finish off the main stand.

The usual daytime idlers hung around inside the ground, watching the players train, but none was in the mood to talk to strangers. So we wandered off towards the small house of the *intendente* in one corner, until the first few drops of rain exploded on our heads. (South American rain can be like that. Rather than starting as a drizzle, it announces itself with a series of intermittent water bombs.) Within less than a minute the air filled with the sound of rejoicing birds.

I shall not bore you with a description of the ground, other than to say it had an unsatisfactory mix of newly built terraces and open stands, around a scrubby shale track, lined by chicken wire and barbed wire. If we wanted any information, muttered the *intendente*, we'd have to go to the club headquarters, or *sede*, across town. Having seen the ground, I didn't really want to know much more. But nor did I want Mariano to think I wasn't serious in my quest. So we climbed back into the car, trying to decide which was worse; windows open to let the rain cool us down, or windows shut to keep out the pungent odours of the stockyards.

As I have indicated earlier, most Argentinian football clubs are general sports clubs, with a stadium, a social centre and a sports centre. In some cases these are all located on one site, as at River Plate or Ferrocarril. In others, all three are separate. To get to Nuevo Chicago's *sede* we drove past the vast cattle markets, got lost among the housing estates, and ended up cruising down a main street lined by mature trees, small garages, very few shops and several old colonial buildings, all well past their best. We passed a statue of a *gaucho* on his horse in a small square, where

Mariano told me that every Sunday tourists come for a taste of *gaucho* folklore and grilled beef. I could just imagine the disappointment of Americans as they took in the decay. Once, no doubt, the street was a bustling hive of activity; of bars, brothels and cheap *pensiónes* where the *gauchos* would live it up after days out on the *pampas*.

Naturally the club's *sede* turned out to be closed, but since we were told that Nuevo Chicago's sports centre lay at the end of the same street we drove on, to find, set amid open fields, a large, modern-styled complex also well past its best, with chipped tiles and leaking roofs. We found no staff around to ask for information, but on a blackboard inside the centre someone had written:

> 'Chicago is an inexplicable feeling.
> So much love.
> Chicago doesn't buy, doesn't sell.
> We're going back to the first division, and then there will be a feast.'

'What a great idea! Let's have some lunch,' we both agreed, and sprinted back to the car under a bombardment of rain now so heavy that we literally had to bellow at each other above the din. We fell into the Toyota, soaked to the skin, laughing.

Tuesday, 20 October. 13.20. Stadium No. 7. Sacachispas.
Still no lunch, but that was not my reason for feeling nervy at this point. Already we'd had to strike off two stadiums from our schedule – two! – both in the general vicinity of Vélez; one (Lugano) because we couldn't find its address, another (Lamadrid) because it would have pulled us too far west. This was not like forgetting to buy the tomato sauce at the supermarket. This, I knew, was final. I would not be coming back for these two later. I had to learn to let go, not to be enslaved by the list.

Mariano, meanwhile, was driving us through territory previously unknown to him and, judging by the lack of other vehicles on the road, to most other forms of life too. He exclaimed, 'I am forty and have lived in Buenos Aires all my life, but I was never here before! Never!'

This was no loss. We were motoring through the Parque Almirante Brown (the Irish admiral again), an unlovely park of such monotonous flatness and so devoid of any human life that it reminded me of some abandoned People's Park laid out amidst the forests of outer Warsaw. Further on, to our immediate left we passed a police cadet school, where young poseurs in braid and shades were strolling along the pavement self-importantly. On the opposite side of the road lay one of the city's numerous *villas miserias*, or shanty towns. In Buenos Aires they pronounce 'villa' as 'viz-ja'. If asked what team I supported I would therefore have to remember to say Aston Viz-ja, and not Villa. Many of the *villas'* inabitants, said Mariano, were immigrants from Paraguay and Bolivia. Had we veered eastwards an extra few miles we would have reached Villa Fiorito – the birthplace of Diego Maradona – on the other side of the Riachuelo (a famously polluted tributary of the Rio de la Plata).

So busy were we gawping at the *miseria* of the *villa* that we drove straight past the low white wall of our next destination, the ground of the Primera D club, Sacachispas. Eventually realising our mistake, we found ourself bumping along an unmade, pot-holed lane running underneath the skeleton of an unfinished overpass, which came to an abrupt halt, coincidentally, parallel with the corner gateway of the ground. Loose horses grazed along the verges. Above their heads, rusting reinforcement rods poked out of the abandoned structure. Although not that far from the metropolis, this felt truly like the end of the road. If there ever had been a reason for the road, either it had been forgotten or the money had run out. Probably both, reckoned Mariano. There had been a lot of that sort of ill-conceived construction during the dictatorship.

Sacachispas were the lowliest club on our list. The fact that their ground, or *cancha*, turned out to be so basic was, therefore, rather like its location, neither here nor there. Surrounded by a white wall resembling that of an *estancia*, it consisted of hardly more than a pitch – covered in clover and dandelions – with a few uneven concrete steps around the perimeter, plus a shed marked Secretaría and a tropical mural by the entrance. And that was it. Normally I'd not have stayed a moment longer. Tick. Done that. Now move on. But I was intrigued by the name Sacachispas. It means the Spark Makers, or Sparklers.

Surprisingly, for the surrounding roads and dirt tracks were virtually deserted, there were several characters milling around inside the ground. One introduced himself as Juan Carlos. A typical former footballer with a strong torso, huge thighs and a firm, protruding belly, Juan told us that a match was due to start at four o'clock, versus Claypole ('Aha!' I remembered, one of the clubs *not* on my list), and that we were welcome to stay. We exchanged looks, but decided that, no, the schedule would not allow it. No, no, no. We were not there to enjoy ourselves.

Anyway, we were enjoying ourselves, so why let a fifth-division game of football break the spell? I was keen nevertheless to learn more about the name Sacachispas.

This was Juan Carlos's version of the story, to which I have added a few details of my own, gleaned from people we met later.

Back in the late 1940s, at the height of General Perón's popularity as the recently elected president of Argentina, the mass-circulation sports weekly *El Gráfico* ran a much loved column. Written by one Borocotó – the pen-name of a journalist called Ricardo Lorenzo – the column described the wacky exploits of an imaginary scratch team of *descamisados* (shirtless ones) from one of the poorest *barrios* of Buenos Aires. Their name? Sacachispas. And the reason I might have heard the name before was that in August 1948 a full-length feature film called *Pelota de Trapo* (Rag Ball) had been made about the fictional Sacachispas, depicting the rise of one of their humble players to the national team. My friend Marcela in London had lent me a tape of it shortly before my departure. (If you can stand listening to pre-pubescent kids shouting at each other for the first twenty minutes, and can forgive the blatantly Peronist message – which in its own way seems hardly more overt than the sort of propaganda found in any British, Ealing film of the era – *Pelota de Trapo* develops into a touching period piece, with some of the most clumsily edited football sequences ever to have left a cutting room.)

Anyway, on 17 October 1948, barely nine weeks after the film's release, a group of lads decided to form a team of their own, and to name it Sacachispas. That might have been the end of the story, except that pretty soon life began to imitate art. Firstly, Borocotó became one of the first members of the Sacachispas club. Then, as part of the new government's drive to promote better health and social cohesion, General Perón's enormously influential wife and *de facto* joint president, Evita, gave her support to a new football competition, El Campeonato Infantil del Gran Buenos Aires, open to boys aged thirteen to fifteen. All entrants had to do, like the founders of the Sacachispas, was to form a team. It mattered not if they played on the street or on waste grounds. The Peronists' Social Aid Foundation would supply boots and shirts. The only condition of entry was that all players had to undergo medicals and show evidence that their parents were married, for this was the Peronist way of encouraging a new social order based upon family values. Hundreds of teams entered the competition, which immediately became known as the Evita Championships.

It was not long before the Sacachispas started living up to their name. They sparkled in the competition. So much so, in fact, that they won game after game, sometimes by huge scores, until eventually, in the finals at the River Plate stadium in 1950, they beat opponents from Rosario and received the trophy from Evita herself.

As their reward for this triumph, concluded Juan Carlos, the Sacachispas were granted a portion of land, the land on which we now stood in the shadow of the forgotten overpass.

Mariano was even more enchanted by this story than I, remembering that his first pair of football boots had also been called Sacachispas. In Argentina, he remembered fondly, they had been as popular as Adidas or Nike are now. He could still picture the advertisements in the magazines, and although I had never seen these I felt I could picture them too. A man never forgets his first pair of football boots.

We drove away through the *villa*, sighing with memories of our youth like two old farts, hardly noticing the rotting garbage piled up alongside the road, and only vaguely aware of our empty stomachs.

Beyond the *villa*, past a Christian radio station, we entered an area comprising acres and acres of flat, green land, almost all of which was occupied by various sports clubs. And then, at the end of a long, straight and empty road, there appeared a huge stadium in the distance. No wonder we were so hungry. Judging by the look of the stadium it was as if we'd driven all the way to a university campus in Texas. Except that we hadn't passed a single McDonald's.

Tuesday, 20 October. 14.15. Stadium No. 8. San Lorenzo de Almagro.

At the security gate, still some way from the stadium across an empty car park, the guard roused himself from his cabin and studied my press card, more baffled than suspicious. Foreigners just turning up, unexpected. On a Tuesday afternoon? He picked up his radio.

'Alicia . . .' he intoned, slowly and deliberately pressing down the all-important button, huffing in our direction as he prepared to explain the situation.

'Alicia . . .'

At the other end we heard a crackly Alicia give us the brush-off. There was no one here to help, she seemed to be saying. Maybe we could go to the club headquarters. Maybe we could send a fax. The guard shrugged at us. What could he do? He'd done his best. He'd done his bit. He started back to his cabin.

I nudged Mariano forward. In such situations one has to be insistent.

So Mariano insisted, in the nicest possible way, and with an even more pronounced huff the guard returned to the radio. A horse and cart passed lazily by on the otherwise deserted dual carriageway behind us, while I studied a bust of Lorenzo Massa, *El Padre*, the priest who had given the San Lorenzo club both its name and its colours of red and blue in 1908. We had been warned that this area was not safe, because of the *villas* in the vicinity and because a visiting fan had been murdered on the surrounding streets less than a year earlier. But with hardly a soul in sight it seemed more likely that I would end up being the one to resort to violence. The atmosphere was now so suffocatingly airless that the distant stadium had assumed the shimmering semblance of a mirage. I had to get to it. The schedule demanded it. No one could stop me. No one!

'Alicia . . .' repeated the guard, reluctantly. Really, this was all too much.

'Alicia . . .'

Finally, after more button pressing and disconnected dialogue, he directed us across the car park, clearly grateful to be shot of the responsibility. We could just imagine him going home to his wife and telling her she wouldn't believe the nonsense he'd had to put up with at work that day. We left him to his solitary brooding.

Five minutes later, approaching the outer road around the base of the stadium – its hulking great structure of concrete struts and exposed raker beams now looking down on us like an ancient ruin – we saw another guard standing quite still ahead of us, watching our every step. By the time we reached him he had clearly decided to be an obstacle. We explained that his colleague had sent us to the stadium office, but of course he was having none of it. Oh no. So now he took up his radio.

'Alicia . . . ?'

As it happens, when finally we found her in an office under one of the towering stands, Alicia turned out not to be the harridan we had expected but a mild, middle-aged woman who clearly treated all her security staff like stupid children. There was genuinely no one around, she explained, but we could go into the stadium if we really wanted . . .

From the shadows of the concourse a man then appeared, as if he had been waiting hours for strangers to pass by. He was, he explained affably, a 'collaborator' of the club's architect, which was no doubt much less sinister than it sounded. I think he was actually delighted to have someone to talk to in this barren landscape. The stadium might even have been his shelter, his refuge from the dispiriting nothingness all around. He said his name was Julio and that we'd be welcome to look around, when at that moment the heavens renewed their watery blitz, sending the three of us scuttling for cover into one of the stadium's vomitories, halfway up the nearest end stand, a stand which had no roof.

From the shelter of the vomitory, a narrow view of the cavernous, rain-lashed concrete arena appeared before us. Thousands of dull, orange plastic seats were filling with small puddles. Above the rim of the stands, the steamy horizon of the distant city centre merged with the great, grey void encircling us. For a better view I stepped forward from the vomitory, only for the blowy, wet air to send me scuttling back with an exhilarating force. And then I stepped out again to feel more of its joyous slap, for this was a sensation I had come to know well on my travels around the stadiums of the world. Better than heat, better than cold, it was the nerve-awakening sting of exposure.

Mine is an odd vocation, I reflected momentarily.

Julio, meanwhile, was talking. I realised I had asked him questions and now he was answering them. San Lorenzo had endured a tough time in recent years, he was saying. They'd been one of the leading clubs in Buenos Aires, based at an old but popular ground nicknamed *El Gasometer*, because it stood next door to one. In 1979 San Lorenzo fell so heavily into debt that they could no longer afford to rent *El Gasometer*, so the landlord sold the whole site for a Carrefour supermarket, causing much gnashing of teeth and despair among the fans. The loss of an old ground is always a heart-breaking affair, but when there is no ready-made replacement to assuage the sorrow, bleak uncertainty sets in. No club can retain its identity for long without a ground of its own. It is one of the universal truths of the game.

So off went *pobre* San Lorenzo to share with nearby Huracán (who had been skint for even longer), where they soon found themselves suffering the indignity of relegation. Rival fans taunted them by singing: 'San Lorenzo, San Lorenzo, San Loré, You have no ground, and you went down to the B.' (It helps to know that in Spanish this rhymes.)

Eventually San Lorenzo were offered this new site, seemingly remote but in fact not too far from *El Gasometer*. The land was, however, rather prone to flooding, which is presumably why no one wanted it before them. When one match was postponed at the new stadium because of this, Huracán fans turned up at the next game there wearing lifebelts. Ha ha!

Wet and laughing again. God, but we needed to eat.

Julio explained that work on the stadium had started in 1989, a crazy time to build because of the country's hyper inflation, and had taken four years to make ready. When finally it opened in December 1993 the capacity was 38,000. Since then, two corners had been filled in so that the current total was now around 44,500. If they could fill the last two corners the capacity would rise to 55,000. Until they did, said Julio, rival fans would carry on calling the stadium 'the ashtray'.

The ashtray?

Because the two corners were still open. Like an ashtray.

Right.

San Lorenzo fans called the stadium *El Nuevo Gasometer*.

There wouldn't be any more building work at the stadium for a while yet, though, said Julio. The club had already spent $20 million on the place. Besides, crowds were much lower these days. Too much football on television, he bemoaned. I wondered if the stadium's bleak, isolated location might not help. So many fans I met said 'Phoo! San Lorenzo, *muy peligroso*. Very dangerous place.' But Julio thought not. Although there had been one problem. Since the stadium opened, a *villa miseria* called Nuevo Pompeya had sprung up directly opposite the main entrance, forcing the club to redirect VIPs into the stand from the other, distant entrance, the one we had come in from. The *villa*, Julio said, had arisen as a result of democracy, and was inhabited mainly by immigrants fleeing from the poverty of Bolivia, Paraguay and Peru. None of them could afford match tickets, but at least some of their kids were able to attend the club's kindergarten.

As he was explaining this I happened to glance at the concrete wall of the vomitory, just behind where Julio and Mariano were standing. On the wall was scrawled the words 'Jonathan 1997.' There was no other graffiti in view. Just the name and the date.

Once the rain stopped, Mariano and I thanked Julio for his time and set off back across the car park to find the Toyota. As we walked there were many things I wanted to say to Mariano, about how great a sense of loss San Lorenzo fans must have felt to have left behind their old familiar *Gasometer*, to have been homeless and shat upon for four years, and then to have found refuge, rather like Julio, in this unlovely, concrete windbreak in the middle of nowhere. I also wanted to express how good a team I thought we were becoming, Mariano and I, and how the stadiums were really becoming just an excuse for us to mess around and get to know each other. How my quest was becoming also his quest.

But instead I told him the one fact that, above all, he needed to know about me, not in his capacity as a guide, but as a new friend. And that was that I once had a brother whom I loved dearly. And that my brother's name was Jonathan. And that he was killed in a road accident. And that the year in which he was killed was 1997.

There was not much either of us could say for a while. Mariano too had seen the graffiti in the stadium, and had no explanation either.

I started to think about what Ana Maria had written at Vélez: 'A single soul, born in heaven, divides into twin spirits, which then fall as two shooting stars towards the earth, where over and above oceans and continents, great cities and sun-bathed fields, their magnetic forces reunite once again the solitary and lost halves.'

A solitary half and a lost half, divided, reunited, and now divided once more. I had come a long way to be reminded of that.

Tuesday, 20 October. 15.15. Stadium No. 9. Club Deportivo Español

A short drive across the flat parkland took us to the ground of a small club called Riestra. As soon as I saw its railings from the road I asked Mariano to drive on. If Sacachispas was basic, this barely registered as a *cancha* at all. Actually it was a relief. Neither of us was in the mood. So we continued, hardly talking, for another few kilometres across the green plain, heading for a set of floodlights we had seen earlier on the horizon, from the other side of the Parque Almirante Brown. The lights belonged to Club Deportivo Español of Primera B Nacional (that is, the Second Division), whose stadium, when we arrived, happened to be hosting a Primera B match (that is, Third Division) between Deportivo Italiano and Argentinos de Quilmes. Spanish. Italian. Argentinian. But, would you believe it, not a snack bar in sight.

We didn't stay long, even though the match was just starting in front of a crowd of maybe two or three hundred. The stadium itself was worthy enough, but uninspiring: a low, concrete bowl in the middle of fields, with three sides of terracing and one of seating. Deportivo Español were a young club, Mariano explained. Formed in 1956, they had been bought up by an autocratic Spanish wheeler-dealer, whose largess impelled them up through the divisions in a fairy-tale, Wimbledon-like fashion, from obscurity to fame all within a decade or two. In 1980, a man informed us, the club had spent $800,000 on this new stadium. Originally it held 15,000, most of them standing. But onwards and upwards the team had continued to rise, right up to Primera A by 1984. A further 3,500 places were added to cope with the expected rush, but the stadium had only once got near to capacity, for a match against River Plate ('Naturally,' said Mariano) in 1996. And now, two years later, the dream looked as if it were over. Deportivo Español were back in the second division. Gates had slumped to under 2,000. And weeds and tall grasses were now growing up around the stadium's stained, concrete exterior, where they were being hungrily chewed by a number of emaciated police horses.

Tuesday. 16.45. On Eva Perón and Carabobo

Half an hour later Mariano and I were sitting in that café I told you about many pages ago – the one on the corner of the Avenidas Eva Perón and Carabobo – where we were to be found hungrily stuffing pieces of mozzarella pizza into our mouths as if we could eat our headaches into submission; the café where the famous and prolific Argentinian writer Cesar Aira was sitting a few tables away, writing, writing, writing.

It had taken us some time to get there, and I don't just mean to the café. I'm certain that I would have told Mariano about Jonathan sooner or later. *Inter alia*, we had already talked a little about our families. But I hardly expected a random piece of graffiti to act as my prompt. I also recognised that however accustomed he may have been, as a psychoanalyst, to hearing about personal tragedy, Mariano had a brother of his own. Pablo, the film director. I was pretty sure they were close, too. Maybe Mariano was now thinking what it would be like for him to lose his brother, like I lost mine. It feels bloody awful, I told him anyway. More awful than I could ever describe.

And now after San Lorenzo I was beginning to find meaning in every little thing that I'd seen that day.

In the fact that we had come across Ana Maria's offering as we did and when we did. In the fact that of all the twenty or more different entry points we might have chosen within the San Lorenzo Stadium, we happened upon the one that had 'Jonathan 1997' daubed upon its wall. In the fact that after searching interminably for a café in a dreadfully ugly part of the city we happened to have found the one occupied by a famous writer who happened to be acquainted with Mariano's brother. In the fact that I had just been talking to Mariano about my brother when we had met this writer.

And why had this writer, this serious writer, appeared from nowhere at that very moment, if not to remind me of my own lassitude, born perhaps from the futility of my own, self-imposed, vacuous quest to visit as many football grounds as I could in six days? Or was the quest just another excuse to blank out the grief?

Then, when we rose to leave, a gaunt beggar blocked our path. He said he was a veteran of the Malvinas war and was suffering from Aids. Mariano gave him a peso. I think I gave him a dollar. I wasn't sure what the note was. I wasn't sure of anything at that point, not even where we were.

I had lost the plot. And, worse, by my own reckoning, I had lost my place on the map.

On the pavement outside, Mariano pointed up to a street sign that reminded us we were standing on the corner of the Avenidas Carabobo and Eva Perón. Even this, Mariano had to admit, conveyed a certain resonance.

Carabobo, he explained, meant 'simple, or stupid, face'. As for *Evita*, well, her pale, pretty face had evoked whatever meaning her admirers had wanted it to. Unlike the writer Jorge Luis Borges, she certainly had not remained unaware of the significance of her own work.

But as for Mariano and me, which path would we take from there? Would we remain fair-faced with each other and just buck up and get on with our schedule, however arbitrary its true nature? Or would we go to the opposite extreme and put on simple faces, going all limp in the process, and feel sorry for ourselves in the heat and with our aching limbs, and forget how much fun we had actually shared in less than forty-eight hours in each other's company?

Barely two days gone. Nine stadiums down. At least seventeen, maybe as many as twenty-seven, still to go.

As we drove away, I saw Cesar Aira still sitting by the window of the café, still writing. Still being clever. And so I resolved there and then to be strong. We had started, so now we had to finish, come what may.

Just before he dropped me off back at Enrique's I remarked to Mariano, 'You have a nickname, *El Turco*. So many people I have come across in Argentina have nicknames.'

'*Apodos*,' said Mariano, translating. And yes it was true. The country's president, Carlos Menem, was a *turco* too, simply because he was of Syrian descent, and that was near enough. Red-haired men were *polaco*, even though they had probably never gone near Poland. The footballer Mario Kempes was dubbed *El Matador*. Maradona was *pelusa*, or fluff. Fat men were *gordo*, thin men were *flaco*. Then there was Don Pepe. And Borocotó. And of course Pipo Pescador.

'I'd like one too,' I said to Mariano. 'Can you think of an *apodo* for me?'

7 A TALE OF TWO STADIUMS

I was polite, I was respectably attired. Outside, the temperature was 90 degrees. But still the barman at the Brabourne Stadium's Wet Wicket Bar would not serve me. Not even a glass of water to wet my wicket. They don't take cash in the Cricket Club of India, the barman explained, and, besides, I was neither a member nor a member's guest. So instead, waiting for the CCI's secretary to see me, I bided my time in the lobby, content if only to find myself in relatively cool and pukkah surroundings after the stifling dust, disorder and din of the streets outside.

Bombay – or Mumbai, as the city's fundamentalist Hindu leaders insist we now call it – appears to the casual western visitor to be a city out of control. A victim of corporate greed and unchecked poverty, and blighted by swathes of ugly, speculative architecture, the commercial hub of India is throat-throbbingly polluted and hopelessly overcrowded, with an estimated 2,000 rural migrants pouring in every day to swap their place in the sun with a few square feet of pavement, rough earth or concrete. Anywhere will do, even alongside the outer lane of a busy motorway. Individually, these people's lives might be small and wretched, their hopes limited, their expectations zero. But on the streets, as in a stadium crowd, the sum of their parts is awesome. Overwhelming, even. In most cities the majority of people on the streets are on the move, in between their homes, offices, shops and restaurants. In Mumbai the streets fulfil all those functions. Soon, it is said, Mumbai will be the world's second largest city. Soon after that, there will be more people in India than in China.

After only a few days in town I was going through all the classic responses of a first-time visitor to urban India, alternating between fascination and despair, amusement and anger. How to absorb the reality of all this factionalism, communalism and what one observer has described as 'Indian dissolution'? In a taxi, caught in a jam *en route* to the Brabourne Stadium, a disfigured hand reached up to touch my elbow through the open window. I looked down on to the road to see a tiny, leprous creature with no legs, zigzagging perilously in and around the cars on a makeshift trolley. And instead of parting with a measly ten rupees, I froze. V. S. Naipaul once wrote of how hard it is to confront 'the knowledge of the abyss'. Enough will never be done, he said. Despair soon turns to weariness.

If I did not then comprehend a fraction of the issues out there on the streets or in the gutters, however, I hung on to a sense that I often experience abroad: that if only I can find my way to the stadium, I might yet come to a closer understanding of the city itself.

'By their stadiums you shall know them' might seem a fairly shallow maxim for any traveller. But it sort of works for me. If only you know how to read the signs, a stadium – whether empty or full – cannot help but reveal a good deal about a place and its people. I dare say specialists in public transport, or medical provision, or education, or even refuse collection, feel the same about their disciplines too. Doors marked 'private' open up. Staff talk, and, gradually, different interiors and realities are revealed, beyond the eyes or reach of the ordinary tourist.

So I lingered on in the lobby of the Brabourne Stadium, waiting to see the club secretary. A cool breeze skipped across the polished floors, rustling the potted plants and causing distant doors to flap on their hinges. Guests at the clubhouse hotel idled down the marble staircase and drifted through the front doors to waiting taxis beyond. Through the windows of the bar I could see the cricket pitch, but not approach it. Not a member, you see, nor a member's guest.

Membership of the Cricket Club of India is open only to the few. But it is well worth it. Members may swim in the stadium's outdoor pool or sunbathe in its efflorescent gardens, play tennis, badminton, squash or billiards, eat at the Chinaman Restaurant, browse in the library or use the fitness club under one of the stands. According to the members' noticeboard in the lobby, bridge and rummy were particularly popular pursuits, although under by-law seven of the club fifty or so individuals were banned from the Card

Room until their dues were paid. I also noted that over eighty members had passed away during the previous year. That would have cut down the waiting list.

On other walls I surveyed the usual parade of pavilion portraits of past and present worthies. Among them was the massively wealthy nineteenth-century industrialist J. N. Tata (the man who built Mumbai's sumptuous Taj Hotel in a fit of rage after being excluded from Watson's, an English club which decreed 'Indians and dogs not allowed'). Tata was a Parsi. Cricket, it has often been remarked, is an Indian game accidentally discovered by the English. But in old Bombay, of all the locals it was the Parsis – the descendants of Persian escapees from Islam – who first took up the bat and ball, and before long were showing the rest of India how to beat the English at their own game.

Another name I recognised among the portraits was that of the Maharaja Bhupinder Singh of Patiala. The turbaned Maharaja, portrayed in all the regalia of the Raj – medals, sashes, jewels and waxed moustache – is revered as the 'father' of the CCI and as a link with India's first great cricketer, Ranji. On the honours' boards were other names, evocative not only of cricketing history but also of the pressures on Parsis to shape their identities in order to please their new colonial masters; H. N Contractor, K. S. Engineer, Vijay Merchant and J. S. Lawyer. But nowhere did I find a single reference to forthcoming cricket matches at the stadium.

In recent years the CCI has been labelled by its detractors as the Card Club of India. The watching or playing of cricket, it seems, has long ceased to be the club's *raison d'être*. Facing the clubhouse on three sides of the stadium and sheltered by cavernous, overhanging roofs, the Brabourne's three public stands are rarely used for their intended purpose. Instead, they serve as barriers against the outside world, turning the stadium into a cloistered bastion of polite manners and order in the midst of an unruly, brash metropolis. Indeed, the CCI's small hotel, sports complex and clubhouse could exist quite happily without the rest of the stadium. And as for the cricket field, apart from school sports, junior matches, very occasional first-class games and an international fixture once in a blue moon, its main use appeared to be as a setting for a quaint, daily ritual.

As I would later witness, this takes place on the pitch in front of the clubhouse every evening around five o'clock. Wicker armchairs are humped out from under the shadows of the stands by groundstaff, to be placed around tables on the outfield. In time – they never hurry – young businessmen and their chums, plump old men in blazers and fine ladies in saris emerge from the bars and terraces to take their seats, where they are served with masala tea, G & T and Scotch by waiters wearing black bow-ties and red waistcoats. Every evening. And while this incongruous display of studied ease continues on the pitch, the only activity to be seen in and around the 35,000 seats of the surrounding stands is that of a few kids running up and down the steps, or of barefooted groundstaff snoozing in the shade under the roofs. A notice on the edge of the pitch reads: 'Ayahs, Servants, Maids of Members, are not permitted on the main Lawn.'

As I said, it is all a question of reading the signs.

So how did it happen that such a well-appointed cricket ground should be reduced to such a futile, if genteel, existence? Part of the answer I already knew. It was to be found a few hundred metres north of the Brabourne Stadium, further up the Marine Drive promenade which fronts the Arabian Sea. Tucked between Marine Drive, D Road, F Road and the main commuter railway lines leading from Churchgate Station lies the root of the Brabourne Stadium's dilemma. It is called the Wankhede Stadium.

This, then, is a tale of two stadiums.

Opened in 1975, the Wankhede Stadium is the property of the Mumbai Cricket Association. Relations between the MCA and the CCI are said to be much improved these days. But three decades ago, when the MCA was still known as the Bombay Cricket Association, they were sufficiently venomous to persuade a few of its leading lights to turn their back on the Brabourne Stadium and build their own house of cricket, with unfortunately depressing consequences for both parties.

It would be tempting to conclude, 'Only in India.' Yet find two stadiums suspiciously close to each other in any city of the world and the chances are you will find, buried somewhere in the past, a bitter feud. Perhaps the most famous example is in Liverpool, where in 1892 members of the Everton football club fell out with each other at their ground on Anfield Road, forcing one faction to set up a new stadium, Goodison Park, a short distance away on the other side of Stanley Park, while the rump remained at Anfield and established a completely new club, called Liverpool FC. There have been other significant footballing splits, in Milan and Seville. But none of the stories behind these divisions comes close to matching the sheer pettiness and ruinous spite which led to the construction of the Wankhede Stadium.

And so there I was, having followed the trail of my own curiosity, in Mumbai, waiting to see the Secretary of the CCI, and gasping for a drink.

* * *

If the Cricket Club of India was an attempt to emulate the hauteur and spirit of the Marylebone Cricket Club, the Brabourne Stadium was, in its heyday, indisputably the Lord's of India. Actually, many thought it superior in certain respects. Until the late 1960s it was not only the cricketing centre of Bombay but of all India. The stadium was also a magnet for the city's establishment. The Indian National Congress celebrated its centenary at the stadium. Bombay's influential Parsi community hired it to honour the Shah of Iran. One report suggests that the Aga Khan was once weighed there in diamonds (which, if true, must have presented the stadium staff with a security nightmare). For several years until recently, thousands would also gather in the stands to hear the prominent economist and jurist Nani Palkhivala deliver his verdict on the government's latest budget.

Despite an overworked wicket which made it a batsman's paradise, the Brabourne Stadium was a pretty good cricket ground too, unique in particular for having its own hotel, with rooms overlooking the pitch. Apparently during one match the West Indian captain Frank Worrell appeared on the balcony of his bedroom in a dressing-gown and watched play until it was time to pad up and head out for the wicket.

The English cricketer Keith Miller called the Brabourne 'the most complete ground in the world'. After a day's play, he recalled, a dance floor would be laid out on the pitch. 'There, under the soft Indian night with millions of stars twinkling overhead, you can waltz to the strains of a carefully concealed orchestra. When you feel the need for refreshments you walk a few yards to a perfectly equipped bar.'

Before the Brabourne Stadium opened in 1937, major games in Bombay – such as the city's popular Quadrangular tournaments – were played a short distance away at the ground of the Bombay

Gymkhana, where the Gymkhana's predominantly British team played off against teams representing the Parsi, Hindu and Muslim communities. However, apart from a delightful mock-Tudor pavilion, the ground was (and still is) barely enclosed. Tents were set up around the boundaries, but the majority of spectators watched for free from surrounding tree tops and rooftops or from the edges of the adjacent 'maidan' (an expanse of dusty, stony and barely turfed open ground which forms a spine through the centre of Mumbai and which, despite being criss-crossed by heavily used paths, has long been the stage for the city's thriving amateur cricket scene). But with its total lack of spectator accommodation and its hateful rules banning Indians from membership, the Bombay Gymkhana was so clearly unsuited for senior games that even as it staged, somewhat chaotically, India's first test match in December 1933 (against the mother country, of course) plans were being made to create an alternative.

Thus the CCI was launched, to promote the game as a whole and to raise funds for a new ground which Indians might enjoy, and which Bombay could offer as a decent test venue in competition with Delhi, Madras and Calcutta. But where could this ground be built? So little space was there in the city even then that the only possible site was on land being reclaimed from the sea as part of the Backbay Reclamation scheme. Much of modern Mumbai is built on such land. But such land did not come cheap.

Not that the CCI's Secretary, Tony de Mello, was deterred. A charismatic go-getter from Karachi, de Mello approached the cricket-loving British Governor of Bombay, Lord Brabourne, with this none-too-subtle appeal. 'Your Excellency,' he said, 'which would you prefer to accept from sportsmen: money for your government or immortality for yourself?'

Brabourne departed Bombay for the governorship of Bengal before the stadium was officially opened in December 1937, but he could not have wished for a more magnificent memorial. At the inaugural match the visiting English captain, Lord Tennyson, declared that there was not a ground like it anywhere in the world.

And nor was there. So many cricket venues, whether in England, Australia or elsewhere, had, up to then, been developed in a piecemeal fashion; stand by stand, with little sense of architectural or aesthetic unity. They were 'grounds' rather than 'stadiums', and, to an extent, remain so. Even Melbourne's giant cricket palace – the largest and most modern cricket stadium in the world – retains the name 'ground' to maintain its foothold in tradition.

The Brabourne Stadium was, on the other hand, a genuine stadium from the very beginning; conceived, planned and erected as a balanced ensemble. Along with Arsenal's Highbury Stadium in London, the Stadio Comunale in Florence, Bordeaux's Parc de Lescure and Montevideo's Estadio Centenario, it represented a high point in 1930s sports architecture. (I would also put in a claim for another art deco gem, the lesser known but quite stunning Glenferrie Park in Melbourne.)

Two streamlined pavilions flanked the CCI's stately, four-storey clubhouse; all three buildings being faced in pale-blue and white stucco and linked by a gracefully curving, elevated terrace. There were seats for 35,000 spectators on the other three, more modest sides of the pitch, plus a grand carriage drive, a swimming pool and tennis courts. The pitch, having been prepared on marshy, reclaimed land in remarkably short time and in the midst of two monsoons, also came in for glowing praise, even if it would soon start sinking, once the ground settled. Thereafter a succession of groundsmen would roll its wickets, relentlessly and repeatedly, into lifelessness. (The pitch had originally been laid under the direction of an itinerant Australian cricketer, Frank Tarrant, who was said to have made more from gambling on horses than from his entire career as a professional cricketer.)

Unsurprisingly, given the quality of the works, the stadium's construction veered hopelessly over budget. Indeed, the costs might well have bankrupted the fledgling CCI had it not been for the generosity of various patrons and the firm of contractors, whose directors were persuaded to accept debentures in lieu of payment (a familiar enough tale in the annals of stadium construction).

As fate would have it, few of the stadium's more active proponents were able to enjoy the fruits of their endeavours. The eponymous Brabourne died suddenly after moving to Bengal, having never once seen the stadium. Sir Nowroji Saklatvala, a nephew of J. N. Tata and the man responsible both for the all-important debenture scheme and for the subsidy that enabled the clubhouse to be completed, died in 1938, less than a year after the inauguration. The Maharaja of Patialia also died in 1938, at the age of forty-six.

Tony de Mello, meanwhile, was obliged to resign as CCI Secretary that same year when the size of the debt was revealed. Described by the stadium's chroniclers Vasant Raiji and Anandji Dossa variously as an incorrigible dreamer, dictator and dedicated self-publicist, who went from one grandiose scheme to another, leaving others to worry about the more mundane details of finance, de Mello had hoped to build other new stadiums in Delhi, Calcutta and Madras. To pick up all the latest ideas he often toured Europe. But in 1951 he finally bowed out, resigning as president of the Board of Control of Cricket in India after a tense and boozy nine-hour crisis meeting. 'I leave cricket never to return,' he declared somewhat theatrically. Ten years later he died, and was buried in his MCC colours.

De Mello's original vision in Bombay was not misplaced, however. From 1937 onwards, and particularly after independence in 1947 until the early 1970s, the Brabourne Stadium was the most successful, most glamorous and most prestigious cricket venue in the whole subcontinent. As journalist Mihir Bose has written, membership of the CCI in those golden years was as exorbitantly priced and as difficult to secure as was alcoholic refreshment in what was then a 'dry' city. And because, unlike at Lord's, women were allowed and even encouraged to attend, test matches at the Brabourne soon assumed a prime billing on the social calendars of the rich and influential in Mumbai society.

Beyond those privileged few in the clubhouse and its adjoining pavilions, other more affluent members and guests congregated in the North Stand, where there were proper seats and cushions, while the East Stand, often notoriously rowdy and overcrowded like an old-style English football terrace, was reserved for the more vociferous elements. After a riot in 1969 it was caged in by fencing, exactly like an old-style English football terrace. Although Bombay crowds were generally commended for their knowledge and appreciation of the finer points of the game, the East Standers were said to have been so intimidating that during one match against New Zealand the Indian captain had to plead with them to show some decorum towards the visitors.

Finally there was the Gymkhana Stand, reserved for members of the city's numerous cricket clubs and gymkhanas that each belonged to the umbrella organisation, the Bombay Cricket Association. It was the BCA's frustration with the ruling élite of the CCI that would finally lead to the downfall of the Brabourne Stadium.

* * *

After the cool calm of the lobby, the hustle and bustle of the CCI's offices on the first floor of the clubhouse came as quite a shock. Secretaries and clerks fussed busily about their business, ferrying files, papers and dockets to and fro in the narrow spaces between desks, cubicles and heaving cabinets. Rubber stamps went thud. Antiquated telephones rang likes props in a Whitehall farce. Typewriters and adding machines clicked and clacked. Yet what, I wondered, could possibly be keeping all these desk-wallahs so busy? And the rest of the stadium's purported roster of 400 staff?

Not cricket, that was for sure. Chasing subs and sending out renewals occupied considerable time, explained the urbane secretary and chief executive of the CCI, Mr R. N. Renjen, in the relative calm of his side office. The CCI, he said proudly, had 8,000 members, more than any other club or gymkhana in Mumbai, and a waiting list of 2,000, some of whom had been waiting since 1988. (I knew how they felt.) Only men could apply, but once they were accepted their wives automatically became members too. If they had no wife they could invite one daughter instead, provided that she was unmarried. The only part of the club a woman could not enter was the siesta room. No one, male or female, could use a mobile phone while on the premises.

Although the cricketing traditions of the city lay in its communal divisions – Parsi, Hindu, Muslim and Catholic – the CCI had always been cross-cultural, said Mr Renjen. ' "The presiding deity of Bombay cricket",' he quoted. 'That is how the Brabourne Stadium was described in its heyday.'

And now? Now that few of the matches staged attracted more than a smattering of spectators?

'Now we survive on our investments,' lamented the secretary. The sports sections of the club ran at a loss, he admitted. The hotel ran at a loss. The catering ran at a loss, although weddings were good business. They did try to raise money by staging a concert on the pitch in 1991, but residents living in the flats backing on to three sides of the stadium complained. There was also a half-baked plan to try greyhound racing, but the members were 'too straight-laced for such things', as someone later remarked. But now the clock was ticking away. Although there was no shortage of people wanting to join, the investments would surely not last for ever.

In fact the annual report Mr Renjen handed me for 1997–98 showed that the club had made a small profit. But it was clear that cricket now formed only a modest part of the club's business. The CCI earned more from its health and fitness centre.

And all because of the row with the Bombay Cricket Association.

'It should never have happened,' said Mr Renjen, shaking his head with genuine regret. 'Never. It was a sad, sad affair, and it could so easily have been settled.' And then, as he rose to pass me on to one of his minions, he added, 'You know, the man you should really talk to is K. N. Prabhu. He was around then. Used to be the sports editor of the *Times of India*. He wrote all about it. "Prabs", they call him in England. Everyone knows Prabs.'

I was then introduced to the stadium curator, Madan Pande, a kind, gentle man who gave me a splendid tour of the facilities, and at last, a long, cool drink. A few hours later found me in the small club library, leafing contentedly through dusty old cricket books whose pages smelt of wood pulp and wisdom, while in the adjacent siesta room a few old gents snoozed peaceably under ceiling fans, oblivious of my presence or of the still heat of the late afternoon.

Down on the pitch, wicker chairs were being laid out for tea.

* * *

The venerable doyen of Indian cricket writers, 'Prabs' was a thin, bespectacled man, living in retirement with his wife and daughter in a modest flat down in Colaba, a residential area on the peninsular which forms the southern tip of the city, beyond the docks and the cheap hotels much favoured by backpackers and seamen.

'My family call me Niran,' he said, pouring me a large tumbler of Johnny Walker the following evening. 'So do my Australian friends. But British journalists all know me as Prabs.' So Prabs it was.

'In a place like this you can hardly breathe,' he complained, gesturing through his open window towards the flats opposite. Somewhere in the lamp-lit street below a Hindu wedding party was in full flow. 'Hear that noise! Bombay! What a city it was when I first came here. Neat and clean. I could stand in front of my window and see all the way to the Taj Hotel. But look at all the high-rise buildings that have come.'

Overdevelopment was one of several reasons Prabs had decided to oppose the construction of the Wankhede Stadium, over twenty-five years previously. 'In a city gasping for breath they built a stadium on a playground where children used to go and play.' And then he laughed. 'I took a stand against all those conservatives and fascists, and now that's what my daughter calls me!'

Amiably, Prabs chatted on, about cricket in old Bombay, his Jesuit schooling in Madras, his years on the *Melbourne Herald*, about old pals in the press box, former enemies, great players and scoundrels in government. And somewhere, in between his genial meanderings and occasional asides to his wife – 'No, Mummy, there were not 30,000; maybe 10,000 at the most!' – he brought out his flaking scrapbooks and told me the story of the row between the CCI and the BCA, the row that had led to the construction of the Wankhede Stadium.

Ostensibly there were three issues, he explained. The allocation of tickets for test matches, the distribution of profits, and a clash of personalities. But, really, the dispute was part of a much larger crisis in India and Bombay. The 1970s, I had to understand, were a time of great turmoil and change. The Indian prime minister Indira Ghandi had suspended the constitution and declared a state of emergency. There were strikes, violent protests and regular clashes between the police and students. Democracy, in the world's largest democratic state, was under the severest of pressures. It could have gone either way.

So what began as a relatively petty dispute between two sporting bodies in fact evolved into a more fundamental battle between the representatives of old money and new money, between the established, wealthy Gujerati and Parsi merchant classes of Bombay and the up-and-coming ranks of Maharashtran middle-class businessmen, entrepreneurs and social climbers.

Maharashtra, explained Prabs, is the state of which Bombay – he could not agree with all this Mumbai nonsense – is the capital, although the state's former seat of power had been Pune ('Poonah' to the British). Some would argue that, culturally at least, Bombay had never been a truly Maharashtran city at all, more a trading centre peopled by immigrants, like New York. That was partly why, even now, a team representing Mumbai competed in India's national cricket championships, the Ranji Trophy, in tandem with another team representing Maharashtra, based in Pune. No other Indian city enjoys such a separate status in sporting circles.

A crucial influence at the time of the big split between the CCI and the BCA was the recently formed Shiv Sena party, founded by an extremist Hindu, Bal Thackeray, a man who had once professed an admiration for Hitler and who, during the 1970s, espoused a virulent policy of 'Maharashtra for Maharashtrans'.

Although comparisons with western politics are always fraught, in cricketing terms, said Prabs, 'You can think of Maharashtra as a bit like Yorkshire.' Its people share the same, inbuilt wariness of the establishment and, in Mumbai, a concern to look after one's own. Also like Yorkshire, Maharashtrans consider their state to be the cradle of Indian cricket and a place where club cricket flourishes like nowhere else. The Parsis and the Gujeratis may have held the whip hand at the CCI and the Brabourne Stadium, but back in the 1970s, as far as the increasingly vociferous Maharashtrans were concerned, it was pay-back time.

Put in its simplest terms, the Bombay Cricket Association, with its membership consisting of individual clubs and club secretaries, should really have been in overall control of cricket in the city. It was, for example, through the auspices of the BCA that test matches were staged at all at the Brabourne Stadium. Yet the CCI, with its old committee-men and their time-worn self-assurance, continually refused to hand over to the BCA more than a certain number of tickets for test matches. At the height of the dispute the total had been nudged up to 10,000 – less than a third of the Brabourne's capacity – but even that was patently insufficient to meet demand. The CCI repeatedly argued that the burden of maintaining the ground to a test standard was escalating, that the club was already running at a loss, and that, in any case, there was no room for more ticket holders. (There could have been had the CCI not reserved so many seats for its members, each of whom was allowed free entry for all matches. But the club insisted that it could not possibly amend its own constitution.)

For more than a decade the two organisations fought over the issues, the CCI always in the driving seat, never imagining that one day the BCA might gain sufficient self-belief, let alone the resources, to go its own way. Until finally, in 1973, the BCA's patience ran out.

Two characters stood out in the feud. Batting on behalf of the CCI was its president, the legendary Indian cricketer Vijay Merchant. Beyond criticism as a player, Merchant turned out to be stubborn beyond reason when it came to the BCA.

'Vijay was a strange man,' recalled Prabs. 'A truly great batsman and personally a very rich man. I think his family owned cotton mills. John Arlott once said that it was almost impossible not to like him. But as an administrator, although he was very upright, Vijay was also gullible and naïve, and I am sure that he was misled by other leading figures at the CCI. If you, Simon, were to tell Vijay that "Niran Prabhu is a rogue," he would believe you. But if I were then to go in next and say, "No, no, that Simon is up to no good," he would believe me too. He sat in that very same chair as you are sitting now and my daughter could not believe it. Two years before, in 1969, I think, he had threatened to take me to court because I criticised his team selection in the newspaper. Yet now he was in my home calling me Niranjan bhai. Niran brother. My daughter saw him and called us all such hypocrites, so I told her, journalists don't have any permanent interest. We just go by the book.'

When Vijay Merchant was sitting in the seat I now occupied, in around 1973, Prabs told him it was ridiculous that, just because of a stupid disagreement over tickets and money, another stadium should be built anywhere in Bombay, let alone one within a stone's throw of the Brabourne.

'It would have been like building a test ground at the Clarendon Court Hotel in Swiss Cottage,' Prabs declared with a wink, seeing from my business card that I lived in London, not far from Swiss Cottage or Lord's.

The BCA's resolve nevertheless became considerably firmer once its longstanding president, a Congress Party politician called S. K. Wankhede, entered the fray. Had he wished, said Prabs, Wankhede could have used his political muscle to force a settlement. Instead, he chose to take on the old guard, and thereby show who was boss in the new Bombay.

'Wankhede,' said Prabs, 'was actually very gentlemanly and courteous. A nice man to know.' But he was a politician through and through, and as finance minister in the local government he had one major trump card to play in the dispute with the CCI.

And what was that trump card? The ear of Indira Ghandi, perhaps? Some incriminating photographs of Vijay Merchant? No, no. The trump card was cement. Without it, you cannot hope to build a stadium. Yet in India in the mid 1970s, cement was as scarce a resource as fresh water in a Bombay slum.

As Prabs himself demanded to know in one of his *Times of India* tirades, once piling had begun on the new stadium, 'Where is the cement coming from?' Naturally he had his suspicions. So did others in Mumbai, who told me, in confidence and still in whispered tones, despite the passing of over twenty-five years, that the cement for the Wankhede Stadium had almost certainly been diverted from approved social projects financed by the World Bank. That no one could justify building this new stadium either on sporting or economic grounds was therefore bad enough; but in a nation crying out for more houses, schools and hospitals, it was also morally indefensible.

In his book *A Maidan View* Mihir Bose expressed little doubt that funds for the Wankhede Stadium came largely from the 'number two' accounts of its leading patrons, the ones they kept hidden from the taxman.

In yet another dusty, cramped but immensely comforting library in the city, I also learnt that, according to a former Indian civil servant S. S. Gill, corruption distorted India's entire planning and development process during the 1970s, and that Bombay had suffered from some of the worst excesses. Entire schemes aimed at the alleviation of poverty and disease had foundered. Modern shopping malls had risen up next to crumbling hospitals. Floors were added to low-rise buildings, in clear violation of planning controls, while other more worthy projects, such as Mumbai's long-discussed but never realised underground railway, remained on the drawing board. The result, concluded Gill, was property prices higher even than London, and some 'fabulous kills' for those in the business.

Strange then, one would have thought, to plan what would certainly be a loss-making stadium rather than, say, a hotel or an office block. But perhaps S. K. Wankhede had more honourable intentions. Certainly he was a devotee of the game, occupying various positions on cricketing committees as well as his presidency of the BCA. Moreover, the land on which the stadium

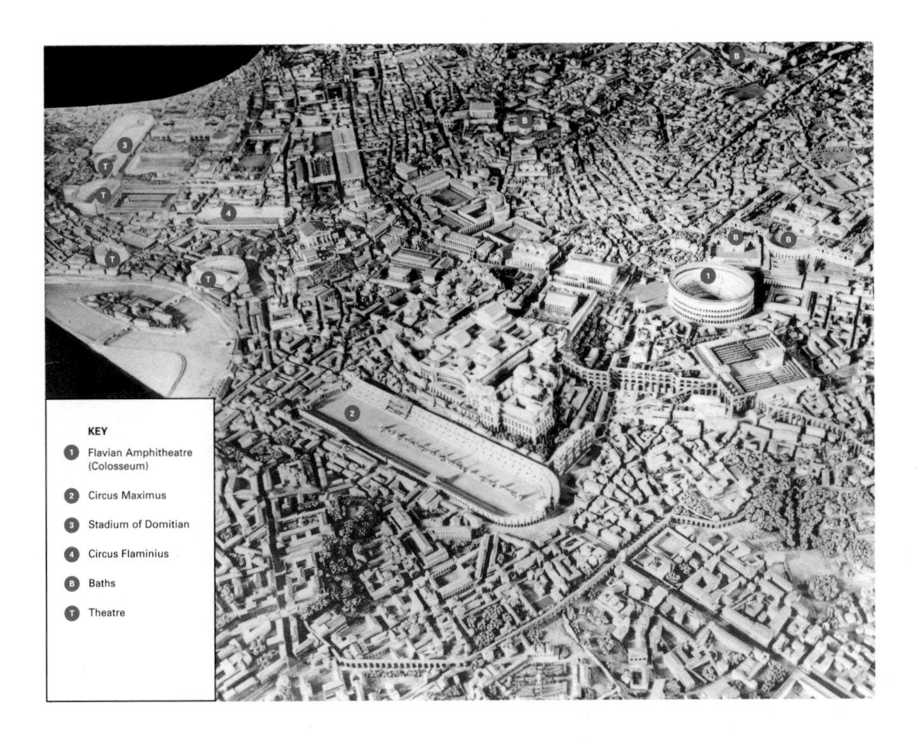

Rome
A model city for spectators and pleasure-seekers, as it would have appeared in the 4th century AD.

Olympia
The original players' tunnel at the entrance to the stadium.

Wrigley Field
Up in the stands, out on the streets, up on the roof – all hail Chicago's Wrigley Field! May its turf be ever edged so neatly.

Eden Park
Auckland's cricket and rugby ground starts to dominate the plot while the residents highlight their side of the story.

Brabourne Stadium
Time for tea – setting the boundaries at the C.C.I. in Bombay.

Croke Park
All-Ireland Day in Dublin – Galway's minor captain John Culkin psyches himself up for a spot of public speaking.

Cité Sportive
Beirut, where the grass is not always greener on the other side of the fence.

El Monumental
River Plate, mountain high.

La Bombonera
Boca mural, do or die.

Sacachispas
The spark makers on parade.

Tigre
Under the bleachers, a secret garden.

Banfield
Ticket windows '98.

Independiente
Sitting pretty in the stadium's backyard.

Houston
Echt-Texas at the Astrodome, the Colosseum of the 20th century.
Judge Roy Hofheinz, the Great Huckster (bottom right).

was built had been granted to the BCA a few years earlier, in 1968, for junior games and training. And the BCA was already planning a clubhouse in one corner, with money donated by a wealthy textile enterprise called Gaware.

Maybe, therefore, like Lord Brabourne before him, Wankhede was seduced by the promise of immortality. After all, few people beyond local political circles had heard of him before the stadium was built.

'In fact,' said Prabs, laughing, 'a friend of mine once joked that Wankhede was the first man ever to be named after a stadium!'

As it happened, this did him more harm than good, for whether he had diverted cement from social projects or, just as likely, used his muscle simply to procure the materials from supportive businessmen, Wankhede lost his seat soon after the stadium opened. Less tainted was the engineer Wankhede had chosen to design the new stadium. He went on to work on several major projects elsewhere in the city. His name, coincidentally, was also Prabhu. Sashi Prabhu.

'But he was no relation of mine,' Prabs interjected. 'Fortunately. Have you seen the stadium? You can judge him by that, I think.'

I promised I would look closely when I went to the Wankhede Stadium the following day. But I was more interested to know how Prabs had felt during the dispute, speaking out against so many vested interests.

'The problem was that no one believed the BCA would go as far as they did. We all thought an intermediary would come forward – there were several likely candidates – and knock heads together. We ran several stories on the matter.'

He showed me one, dating from December 1973. The headline read: 'Goodwill and reason should prevail.' Underneath, Prabs argued that if the BCA did have the money for a new stadium, they should spend it instead on grass-roots cricket. By that stage the new stadium's clubhouse had gone up, though it was still not too late to halt the other works and turn the clubhouse into a cricket museum with indoor-coaching facilities. In another article it was argued that the best compromise would still be to enlarge the Brabourne Stadium by building an extra tier to the East Stand and by adding more seats to the two pavilions.

At one point Prabs was banned from the press box for speaking out.

'I was a lone voice, that is for sure. But I was lucky in that the *Times of India* editors were not interested. They left me alone to write the way I wanted to. Some of the top guns used to come and see our managers. They thought they could bring pressure on me to stop me writing about the cement and how this stadium would spoil the environment and how there was no need for it. Even after the stadium was built I made a plea. I said they should take football there, because soccer was becoming more popular at that time and it would at least make the stadium pay. Then we could leave the cricket at the CCI. But in this country no one listens to writers.

'And I was appalled also when my other Indian journalist friends – I'm sorry to say, because they're long dead – were all very happy about the news of this new stadium because they would be able to enrol at concessional rates and see cricket free with their families, which they couldn't do at the CCI.'

Once the BCA had grasped the nettle, it did not hang around. When the visiting West Indian team arrived in Bombay at the beginning of their five test series in late 1974, apparently all they could see on the site was a huge hole in the ground. By their return, for the final test in January 1975, the new stadium was all but completed. Yet although it had cost an estimated 30 million rupees ('Though it's impossible to know what anything really costs in India,' Prabs added), there was surprisingly little fanfare to mark the occasion. Even the programme for the inaugural test match barely mentioned the existence of the new stadium, other than to give its capacity as 44,000.

Grudgingly, Prabs would admit that the Wankhede's press box was far superior to that of the Brabourne. But otherwise he disliked the stadium intensely. Cramped, ugly and shoddy, he reckoned. 'The members had to watch from behind barbed wire. It was like a stalag.'

But if the BCA's coup symbolised the ascendancy of the new monied classes in Bombay – I would also hear them described as '*nouveaux riches*' and 'smugglers' – so too did the behaviour of the crowd at the Wankhede Stadium's opening match reflect the uneasy mood of the period. As Prabs recalled, 'A boy trespassed on to the pitch to congratulate Clive Lloyd, who had made 242 not out. But the police were very nervous and instead of leaving the boy alone they arrested him.' This incited the rest of the crowd, forcing the game to be suspended for over an hour as running battles ensued between the crowds and the police. Although hardly a new occurrence in Indian cricket, the fact that the unrest spread to the other stands, and even into the pavilion, suggested a darker mood.

Following a further outbreak of crowd misbehaviour during a later match at the Wankhede Stadium, against England, Mihir Bose quoted one Indian as remarking in disgust, 'This sort of thing would never happen at the Brabourne Stadium.'

In one sense he was correct. Less than forty years after it had opened, one of the best cricket grounds in the world had faded into oblivion; upstaged, outmanoeuvred, and left to feed on the scraps of the local cricketing calendar.

* * *

Apart from the impromptu action I kept encountering on the maidans – the Hackney Marshes of the East, but filled seven days a week – I had hoped to see at least one day of first-class cricket whilst in Mumbai. But even with two large stadiums in the city, not a single game was scheduled during the entire week. Nor would the city be staging any of the test series then taking place against Pakistan. A few days before my arrival, Hindu fundamentalists had smashed up the offices of the BCCI (the Board of Control for Cricket in India) – located just behind the Brabourne Stadium, as it happens – in protest against the series taking place at all. As the attackers went on the rampage, smashing trophies and attacking officials, the BCCI's executive secretary was reported to have cried out, 'I have nothing to do with this, I am just a paid servant.' He also told the press, 'Luckily, they spared the TV set.'

So in my free time I went to the cinema instead and caught up with the latest offerings from Bollywood. I also managed to blag my way on to the roof of an astonishingly decrepit office block, owned by the government, in order to take photographs of the Wankhede Stadium. I had to wait an hour for the man with the key, but it was well worth it, if only to see the look of delight on the face of the press officer who accompanied me. Twenty years he had worked in that building, and never once had he been on the roof. I later had lunch in the canteen on the seventh floor, watched by dozens of amused office workers, several pigeons and the odd mangy cat. And, no, I was not in the slightest bit sick. The meal was a treat, even if the washer-up boy did insist on giving me a spoon he had just wiped on the inside of his pocket.

The day after I went back to the Wankhede Stadium to meet Professor Ratnakar Shetty, joint honorary secretary of what was now called the Mumbai Cricket Association. He offered me masala tea straight away.

Apart from its orderly, if suspiciously uncluttered, offices and its towering floodlight pylons, the rest of the Wankhede Stadium was immensely depressing. Prabs had been right. It was shoddy. No more so than hundreds of other buildings in the city, but in my eyes more poignantly so because of its needless creation. Had it been more impressive one might have accepted the Brabourne Stadium's demise more readily. But those areas that the Wankhede's unsmiling security guard did let me see, appeared, in their crudity and rough edges, quite at odds with the ethos of cricket.

The dressing-rooms were dark and dingy. Several filthy, malnourished men – builders, I was assured – sat idling in the morning sun. Their tattered laundry fluttered from washing lines tied to the underbelly of one of the stands. Inside, the spectator areas were gloomy and fenced in. The police box was packed full of old mattresses. The bench seats cried out for several licks of paint, as did the rusting steelwork and the stained concrete of the concourses. On one outside wall, alongside a busy railway line, I noted a large advertisement for steel construction rods. It read: 'The everlasting way to fight corrosion.'

One of the stands, I also noted, was named after Vijay Merchant.

Professor Shetty did not find this at all ironic. 'You must realise one thing,' he told me. 'Although it was Mr Vijay Merchant who was responsible for the CCI's decision about the tickets, Vijay was one of the greatest cricketers Bombay has ever produced, and that is why he has a stand named after him here. As far as we are concerned the past is all forgotten.'

He acknowledged that neither party had really won, however, for as the present situation made clear, there were now barely enough profitable games on the calendar to support even one stadium, let alone two. Although the Wankhede staged maybe 150 games a year, only five or six of those were first-class, and in 1999, as in 1992, Hindu protests had ruled out Mumbai altogether from hosting a single test. Of the other fixtures, the day/night ones attracted gates of 10–20,000, but many more drew fewer than 500. In those instances it was not even worth hiring gatemen, so spectators were allowed to enter free of charge. Only test matches, said the Professor, yielded any profit. Otherwise, the MCA was living off the proceeds of earlier games, going right back to the World Cup in 1987. The last full house of 35,000 had been in 1996.

That would explain the state of the stadium, the swimming pool and the adjacent hockey pitch – its synthetic surface dangerously ripped and uneven. But what of the building I had seen near the main entrance? Was that half built or half demolished, I asked the Professor tentatively, since it wasn't easy to determine amidst all the rubble.

His reponse was not what I had anticipated. The building, he explained wearily, was supposed to be an indoor cricket school. But there had been problems.

'Problems?'

The Professor sat back in his seat and sighed. Apparently, some time ago the administration of the Gaware Clubhouse, the social hub of the stadium, had been deliberately separated from that of the BCA, purely for tax purposes. The idea had been to free up more of the club's profits for handing over to the parent organisation. Unfortunately, some of the Gaware committee members had taken this new-found independence rather too literally, and to widespread consternation had resolved to keep all the profits for the club.

'As if,' I said, 'the son had turned against the father.'

'Acha.' The Professor nodded. 'Yes. But we're hoping the mess will be settled by arbitration next year, because it has already cost us about a crore [10 million] of rupees on litigation. A real waste of money, just to get our own property back. The Gaware people must have spent an equal amount. Between us we have made quite a few lawyers happy.'

I was dumbfounded. 'Don't you think it somewhat ironic that you broke away from the CCI because of arguments over money, and now you are in dispute with your own members.'

'It is very ironic,' agreed the Professor.

'And how long has this been going on?'

'Since 1979. Twenty years.'

In other words, the quarrel had begun only four years after the stadium opened.

As I was leaving I asked the Professor if he ever went to the Brabourne Stadium.

'I watched many matches there when I was small,' he told me, and as an ordinary fan had not thought much of it. Then in 1998 the CCI staged one of its very few, first-class games of recent years, a three-day international against Australia. On that occasion the Professor had been invited to watch from the pavilion.

'Definitely, sitting in the pavilion . . .' he said in a faltering voice, 'I'd never watched a match from there . . . it was . . . well, something different. Watching from there, I thought it was great. Personally, I think it is a great loss.

'Such a beautiful stadium,' he said, shrugging. 'Just lying idle.'

8 A GREAT MINGLING

05.30 on the second Sunday of September. In Leeson Street the several floors of the Hotel Burlington hum gently to the snoring rhythm of a hundred hangovers, waiting to spill out of their hundred, fragile skulls. Down in the hotel's cavernous bars the air hangs heavy from last night's jamboree.

Christ, but it's cold. Eighty degrees it was in London, yesterday afternoon.

'Take a coat,' she said. 'It'll be cold in Dublin.' She'd looked it up in the paper.

'Bollocks,' said I, sweating on my way out of the house. And guess who's sorry now.

Cork are in town. The Red Rebels. The team arrived at the Burlington yesterday evening, around five. There was no commotion or anything when the coach pulled up. Not like your pro soccer players or pumped-up athletes. Just Timmy McCarthy the farmer, Donal Óg Cusack the electrician, young Neil Ronan the student and all the lads with their hurleys and haircuts. Not, 'Hey, look at me, I'm wunnerful,' autograph, autograph, but, 'Hi, Ma; hi Da; hi, Cousin Mona from Limerick. Glad you could make it.'

Soon after they arrived the players all trooped off to the Gaiety Theatre on South King Street for a production of Sean O'Casey's 1924 classic, *Juno and the Paycock*. Not your usual outing for an eve-of-final get-together. But then the All-Ireland Final at Croke Park, Dublin, is not your usual final. No way.

Best day of the year if you're part of it. Best day of your life if you're on the winning team. Worst for the losers. In a fortnight it'll be the All-Ireland football finals. Gaelic football, that is. Today it's the hurling: 1.30 p.m., the Minor Final, Galway vs. Tipperary; 3.30 p.m., the Senior Final, Cork vs. Kilkenny. The Red Rebels vs. the Black and Amber Cats. Old adversaries. Paired in eighteen All-Ireland hurling finals since 1893.

On the early-morning radio they're saying there'll be heavy rain in Dublin today, and everyone knows the Cork team can't do it in the rain. Anyway, Kilkenny were last year's losers, so they'll be more fired-up. And if they're not, well, what the hell, there'll be a mighty session anyway. Ah yes. Life is grand when you're into the hurling. That's what they tell me.

Upstairs in the curtained dawn, the menfolk loll and fart in their hotel beds, realising, blink by blink, stretch by yawn, what day it is. But one of them has no time to idle or dream. Pat Guthrie, presentation and protocol steward at Croke Park, winces at the alarm's insistent buzz. Two months planning, all for today. Pat's fifty-five and has faced many a day like this before. That's why he didn't touch a drop last night. Too much to do. Got to keep a clear head. All the world and his wife will be watching, watching on All-Ireland final day.

06.30. Down in the Burlington's deserted lobby, the Guinness and Murphy's taps lay silent and drained. 'Mr Guthrie for Croke Park,' calls out a driver from the forecourt. Through Dublin's deserted, lamp-lit streets they drive. Sleepy-eyed cleaners and chambermaids stare out of the fluorescent-lit buses on their way into town. Grafton Street, pavements sticky from the excesses of the night before. The Liffey, catching the twinkling of traffic lights on its flecked surface. Last night's take-away cartons bobbing beneath O'Connell Bridge. But none of the usual stop-start, stop-start. A time to remember that Dublin is really not such a big place at all. Only the grinding daytime traffic makes it seem so. So much for the 'Celtic Tiger' they're all on about. Prosperity without planning. Then almost before Pat knows it, the taxi pulls into Jones's Road, under the shadows of the Hogan Stand.

07.30. Cars now pulling into the driveway. Doors swinging open. The Gaelic Athletic Association's director general, Liam Mulvihill, has just arrived, smiling as ever. There's the overnight security crew, the heads of various sections of the stadium, officers of the Gardai. Passes are checked. Greetings exchanged. Throats cleared. In the lightening sky, Croke Park's silhouette emerges above the terraced houses and warehouses huddled around its walls. Tallest of all, higher than any building on Dublin's northside, is the new £40 million stand, named after the GAA's founder, Michael

Cusack; four tiers of 25,000 seats it has, executive boxes, premium seats, lounges, museum, the lot. Ten years ago the idea of the Dublin business community coughing up serious money for a corporate bash at Croke Park would have been laughable. Ho ho! The GAA, that hidebound load of old conservatives? Hurling? All those rustics fighting with sticks! Croke Park, that old dump? Pull the other one.

And yet, the Nineties are being touted as hurling's greatest decade. Another new stand at the Canal End, now half completed, is flanked by two cranes. From one flutters the green, white and orange of the Irish tricolour. From the other, a red and white Cork flag. How the fuck did that get up there, mutters someone.

Opposite, at the Railway End, the ground's last section of open terracing is still in shadow. Though hardly more than a hump, they call the terrace 'Hill 16', since it was built up from rubble left over from the 1916 Easter Rising against the British. In modern Ireland the past is much less a foreign country than it used to be, while Croke Park – *Páirc an Chrócaigh* in Irish – is more than concrete and steel, gravel and turf. Far more, even, than a stadium. It is, in effect, the national playground, where thousands of schoolkids and juniors, girls and boys, get to play the traditional Gaelic sports of hurling (or camogie for the women) and football in front of a crowd. Take Kilkenny's current stalwart, D. J. Carey. His first Croke Park outing was as an eleven-year-old, and now he's here as a Senior for the All-Ireland.

But more than a playground too. For today Croke Park will be the epicentre of the entire Irish world. Dublin, Cork, Kilkenny, Boston, Chicago, London, Melbourne: they'll all be watching, listening, following the match. No other sporting organisation on earth runs so thickly through the blood of a people as does the GAA. They say that only the Catholic Church is more important. Over 2,800 clubs are registered. Over 800,000 members belong, in a population of only five million, north and south of the border. From the cradle to the grave, the GAA defines the nation, with Croke Park the beating heart at the very core of its existence.

08.15. A room in the Hogan Stand. The main men, twenty-five or so of them, gather for Mass. 'We like to gather in the quietness of the stadium to ponder the events of the day,' says Pat Guthrie. 'Ireland is a fairly spiritual country, not maybe in that strict sense of spirituality, but for us the GAA is a religion too. It's an extraordinary feeling, there in the bowels of the stadium with Father Seamus Gardiner. He's like a chaplain to us. There's a calm and a stillness, a great peace before 63,000 people start descending on the ground.'

Later on in the morning the Cork and Kilkenny players will attend their own Mass too.

08.40. Time for *bricfeásta*, as it says on Pat's timetable. Orange juice, cornflakes or porridge, bacon and egg, black and white pudding, fried mushrooms, you name it, and plenty of soda bread and marmalade. 'For most of us,' says Pat, 'this'll be our last sighting of food for maybe another twelve hours. Running from this job to that, we'll have no time to stop.'

Most of the men chomping and slurping hungrily away around the table speak Irish fluently, if not exactly as their first language then at least as equal first with English. They think nothing of switching between the two. It's the same in the newspapers. Liam Mulvihill suddenly appears in one paragraph as Liam Ó Maolmhichil, as the text slips from English to Irish then back again without warning. Keeps you on your toes though.

Barely 1 per cent of Ireland's population speaks Irish only. Of the other 99 per cent, not many manage more than a smattering. But this is the GAA – the *Cumann Lúthchleas Gael* – and if *they* don't promote Irish, who will? The match programme is full of it. Not Cork vs. Kilkenny but *Corcaigh vs. Cill Chainnigh*. Today's referee, or *an réiteoir*, is listed as Pat O'Connor, not from Limerick, as we know it, but *Luimneach*.

As plates are cleared and second cuppas consumed, the *craic* starts. The one word of Irish everyone knows. The crack. The bilingual banter. How the day will go. Who will have to be on their guard. Someone reminds them, there are eleven closed-circuit cameras at Croke Park, so if they're not doing their job, it'll show. No place to hide. There's quiet laughter. This is a good team. You can tell.

09.30. Pat and the others meet in Liam Mulvihill's office to check over the day's arrangements, check what's happened overnight, see if there are any new arrangements for VIPs. Security is paramount. They've got the British Northern Ireland Secretary, Mo Mowlam, coming to the game. 'Highly sensitive,' says Pat. And the British ambassador. And Bertie Ahern, the Irish prime minister, or *Taoiseach* (which is pronounced very much like 'T-shirt'), and most of his cabinet, and the head of the army, and the leading people in the judiciary and the civil service, and the president of course, Mary McAleese. 'A lovely woman,' everyone agrees. 'You name it, the whole of Ireland will be here,' says Pat with pride. 'There's no other event like it. It's like a great mingling.'

10.45. Filling up with staff now. There'll be over a hundred Gardai on duty inside Croke Park, a few hundred more in the vicinity. Never any real crowd violence, though, says Pat (though there was one year when some 'eejits' on Hill 16 tried to break into a covered stand when it started pissing down). Otherwise the fans'll mix like they always do in Gaelic sport, but especially at the hurling. Hurling's just that little bit different. Everyone says so. Then you have maybe 800 stewards and volunteers manning key areas. On top of that there'll be the toilet attendants, the gate keepers, the door keepers, programme sellers, catering staff, plumbers, carpenters, welders. Every eventuality has to be covered. 'There'll probably be close to 2,500 people who won't be able to see the game,' Pat reckons. 'I've been to every All-Ireland since 1980, but I haven't seen one game, because I've a job to do and you cannot be watching the match. I'll only find out later when I see the game on the TV.'

Like the others, Pat is a GAA man through and through. Stocky, medium height, round-shouldered, with grey hair straggling across the back of his bald pate, he has the concentrated frown and tight-lipped expression of an ex-copper. In fact he's a primary-school teacher at St Michael's, a Christian Brothers School on an estate at Inchicore, just a few miles from Croke Park. Michael Cusack was a teacher too, and, like Pat, also from County Clare. Cusack set up the GAA in 1884 to organise and revitalise traditional Irish sports after centuries of disparate, local effort and the devastation of the famine in the 1840s. Also, because cricket was catching on fast by the middle of the century. But why the name Gaelic Athletic Association? Well, Cusack loved athletics so much that for a while he was prepared to overlook the increasing exclusion of his fellow Irishmen from Dublin events in favour of gentlemen amateurs with leanings towards London. But he soon grew tired of the burgeoning control by the British, and of all the cheating and gambling at the races. Muscular Christianity came into it too, same as it did with his contemporaries across the water in soccer and rugger circles.

Within months the GAA message had spread across the island, 'like a prairie fire', Cusack later wrote. But athletics were soon cast aside. What the people wanted was Gaelic football and hurling: the old sports. The Irish sports.

Pat has been involved in the GAA for as long as he can remember. No family of his own. 'Married to the GAA.' He laughs. 'The biggest family in the world.' Always been an organiser too. 'To me, the bigger the problem, the greater the challenge. I'm a tough taskmaster. Tough on myself. I have to do it well. Here is the Association projecting itself, not just in Ireland but in the rest of the world.' On radio, on TV – for the first time in Turkey and Israel this year – and on the Internet. The word is spreading. One person describes it as the 'Riverdance Effect'.

'Maybe when I start to slow down I might regret not having a family who can take up where I left off in the Association,' says Pat. 'But, then, people keep telling me, "One of you's enough for any day of the week."'

12.00. With the Gardai, stewards and gatemen all in place, time to open up the turnstiles. Already the streets around Croke Park are filling up. Kids and old ladies peek out of the windows of terraced houses lining the route. There are worse parts of northside Dublin, places where the Celtic Tiger has yet to bestow its gifts from Brussels and the promise of gentrification. There are better parts too. But it's tidy enough, and there's a relaxed air. Cork and Kilkenny fans peer out together over the canal bridge at the new stand going up. One says he likes the new-look Croke Park. Another thinks they should have started from scratch at a greenfield site. Arsenal, Eden Park, Mumbai: it's the same debate the world over.

By the time the builders have finished, Croke Park'll be one of the best in Europe. Just under 80,000 it'll hold. Could have been more but the authorities wouldn't let them keep any standing on Hill 16.

In the match programme the Croke Park Area Residents Alliance wishes all fans 'a pleasant day' and reminds them, 'We are here 365 days of the year and the area is a nice one in which we live.' Their appeal concludes, 'Gaelic games followers have a reputation for good behaviour. Be proud of that tradition by keeping it alive.'

Des McMahon passes by. Des is the Croke Park architect, immediately recognisable by his shock of white hair.

'Des, how's it going?'

As always, Des appears to be caught between dashing hither and thither. Nervous energy, you might call it, but always solicitous. He promises I'll have a grand time, better even than the All-Ireland Football Final he took me to a few years earlier.

'Like any art form there's an emotional dimension to hurling. But you'll see this afternoon that there's also a totally different relationship between the fans and the players. One of our great poets, P. J. Kavanagh, summed it up when he described the difference between the parochial and the provincial. He loved the first, detested the second. Hurling is parochial, and that's its strength.'

Did I know, says Pat later, that Des was a footballer, for County Tyrone. Not a bad one either, by all accounts.

In the GAA, football or hurling, you play, in the main, for the place you come from. None of this mercenary transfer nonsense you get in the professional game. Play for the parish, play for the county. Slog it out on the training field all winter, four nights a week once the season starts. Play your heart out from May to September. But never get too big for your boots, because on Monday morning (or Tuesday if it's a final) you're back at work, out on the streets, wherever, surrounded by people just waiting to tell you to your face how well or badly you played at the weekend. Three of the Cork lads are from the one village. Win today and they won't have to buy a drink for weeks. Lose and . . . well, it doesn't bear thinking about. But the point is, they don't have to put themselves through all this. Being amateurs, they could give up the game at any moment. All right, so they won't. But they could, and that makes all the difference.

I'm delighted to see Des because these are interesting times for stadium watchers in Dublin. The Football Association of Ireland, which governs soccer in the Republic, is talking boldly about a brand-new 45,000-seat stadium somewhere on the western outskirts, just like the Gelredome in Arnhem, the one with a retractable roof and the pitch that slides in and out of the building on a giant slab of concrete. Clever stuff – the bigger the boys, the bigger the toys and all that – until you begin to wonder why the FAI would want all the bother and the extra expense. Concerts, of course. Concerts and boxing, tennis, indoor athletics. Whatever events the FAI's partners, IMG, can bring to a city with no large indoor arena of its own.

The idea has plenty of merit, since the Irish soccer team doesn't play that many big internationals per season and the local club scene is still nowhere near attractive enough to deter thousands of Irish soccer fans from crossing the sea every weekend for the likes of Celtic Park, Anfield and Old Trafford. So any new stadium would need more than just a few soccer games to pay for itself.

Des tells me that the Irish telecommunications company Eircom has just pledged £11 million for the naming rights of this new stadium, which is not a bad start. Only another £54 million or so to go. And the small matter of planning permission.

In the meantime, soccer internationals are played just south of the docks at Lansdowne Road, home of the Irish Rugby Football Union (and where Michael Cusack used to help organise athletics meetings in the 1870s). But Lansdowne Road is nowadays too underdeveloped and small for international soccer or rugby, hemmed in as it is by nice middle-class homes and roads and railway lines. Certainly no match for the likes of Scotland's revamped Murrayfield, or England's monstrously enlarged Twickenham, or Wales's awesome new Millennium Stadium, which also sports a retractable roof and a burning, earning desire to get in on the concert trade. Remember the days when stadiums used to be about sport?

Des agrees that Dublin cannot possibly sustain or justify three large-scale modern stadiums; Croke Park, a new FAI stadium and a new rugby stadium. Which is why, he says, the government has commissioned a feasibility study for an altogether different solution, a new national stadium for soccer, rugby and maybe even athletics. The consultants are to publish their findings in a few weeks. But even before these are known, it appears that the government has already offered the FAI a substantial financial incentive to ditch its own plans and fall in with the national stadium idea. This incentive money could then be spent on upgrading Ireland's smaller soccer grounds.

That idea has plenty of merit too. But the most obvious idea of all is also the least likely. Now that Croke Park is well on its way to becoming one of the best venues in Europe, why not put the soccer and rugby on there as well? To explain why not would be to invite a long lecture on Irish history. Suffice it to say, instead, that in the old days, if you ever played soccer – the maligned, imported game of the Brits, the 'foreign game', as it was known – you'd be banned for life from the GAA. That rule was dropped in 1971 and nowadays relations are more relaxed. In fact, one or two players have managed to excel at both codes.

But even if the soccer authorities did want to hire Croke Park, which they don't, the GAA wouldn't let them. As an amateur association it already does more than nicely from the big games, from executive box sales, from debentures, from the TV, radio, sponsorship and the like, leaving it more than able to finance the rebuilding of Croke Park and still have enough to put something back into grass-roots Gaelic sports. (They're even putting money into plantations of ash trees, for making hurleys.) Croke Park has a pretty full calendar of its own too, maybe eighty games a season, albeit squeezed into a short period between May and September. True, the GAA might have few objections to the rugby lads sharing the place during the winter. Rugby, you see, is different. Whereas Irish soccer is split betweeen Dublin and Belfast – the Republic of Ireland representing the twenty-six counties, Northern Ireland the remaining six – the IRFU, like the GAA, covers all thirty-two counties, north and south. So they've that much in common. And there are only 20,000 or so rugby players in the entire country, so there's hardly the same threat.

Soccer, on the other hand, now, that is different. Since Irish TV started showing English and Scottish games, and the doughty Jack Charlton led Ireland to successive World Cups and European Championships during the 1980s, a ding-dong battle has raged between soccer and the GAA for the hearts and minds, hands and feet, of the nation's youth. Often it's looked as if the old-fashioned, insular GAA would lose out. Over 200 countries play soccer. Only one plays Gaelic football and hurling at a high level. Worse, kids watch television. They need heroes. And the likes of Manchester United (with Roy Keane and Denis Irwin both from Cork), Liverpool, Arsenal and Aston Villa have each had plenty of Irish heroes to be going along with over recent years. Paul McGrath was one of mine. The finest defender that ever was.

But the GAA started to fight back, as it always has in times of trouble. Working hard at parish level. Investing in youth. A series of cracking All-Ireland Finals during the Nineties helped too, as has the re-emergence of teams like Offaly, Clare and Wexford, to challenge the longstanding giants of Cork, Kilkenny and Tipperary. A sign of that resurgence is the new Cusack Stand, opened in 1995, the same year as Guinness became GAA sponsors. Gradually, kids started turning up to GAA summer camps wearing the Red Rebel shirts of Cork rather than the Red Devil shirts of Manchester United.

So every time I ask the question: 'Soccer at Croke Park – ever happen?' I hear variations on all the above themes. 'Too much bad blood'. 'Don't need it'. 'Don't want it'. I've talked this over with Des and dozens of others through the years. But on All-Ireland Finals day, as Croke Park is filling up, Pat Guthrie gives me the best answer yet.

'The way I look at it is very pragmatic,' he says. 'It would be like two big competing supermarkets making a space in one of their stores dedicated to selling the other one's products. Now why would they want to do that?'

12.15. On O'Connell Street you can now barely move between the Sunday morning idlers, Japanese tourists and the crowds from Cork and Kilkenny. Snooty 'Dubs' dismiss these country folk as 'culchies', or country yokels. The culchies in turn make snide remarks about the 'jackeens', their term for smart-arse, metropolitan Dubs. I ask a Cork man exactly what 'jackeen' means, but cannot make head nor tail of his reply. They speak differently down in Cork.

Red and white fills the pavement outside Gresham's. Black and amber congregates outside Madigan's Drinking Emporium. Hope hangs heavy in the mid-morning air. Ticketless fans are beginning to panic. Everyone has a sob story. Rumour has it that some touts have been asking up to £800 a ticket. 'Never known demand like it,' exasperated officials are quoted as saying in the papers. Could have filled Croke Park three times over, they reckon. Maybe more. It's the kids who lose out the most, is the general moan.

No one dares predict who'll win. Kilkenny's lot, losers last year to Offaly, have plenty of experience, but will they have the legs? Cork are the youngsters. Only centre-half-back Brian Corcoran has ever played in an All-Ireland before. They're low scorers too, and of course they never do well in the rain. Everyone knows that. So right now, for the Cats of Kilkenny, things are looking up, and up, as the skies darken menacingly over Dublin.

Stubborn git that I am. Didn't bring a coat. Not even a hat. She won't have any sympathy when I come home coughing and wheezing.

12.30. Croke Park is already maybe a quarter full as the Artane Boys Band lines up in a dimly lit concourse behind the huge, green sliding door of the Hogan Stand's old players' tunnel. (The dressing-rooms are now in the new Cusack Stand opposite.) Laughing, frowning, swallowing nervously, the boys juggle with their instruments, adjust their blue, red and gold uniforms. The youngest among them is eight, the oldest fifteen. Like the players they do all their practising in their spare time, after school. The Artane Boys Band has played at every Croke Park game since 1886. But today is that bit more special. All-Ireland Final day.

'Some of these lads'll have family watching 'em on TV in Boston and Toronto and places like that,' says one of the stewards.

Pat's timetable allows for a slippage of only six or seven seconds. On the previous Thursday evening he went out to Artane with his stopwatch. Timed every piece of music to the last second. Now he looks down at his watch, points to the drum major, Keith Kelly, and, with all the assurance of a seasoned schoolteacher, calls out 'Go!'

As the Artane Boys get into their opening number, 'Blaze Away', the Irish TV station, RTE, begins its live coverage of the day. The pictures are relayed on to a large video screen behind Hill 16. All over the world, in pubs and bars and GAA outposts, the Irish are settling down into the familiar rhythm of an All-Ireland afternoon.

Michael OhEithir, RTE's broadcaster down on the touchlines, stops for a chat. He saw his first All-Ireland Final from Hill 16 in 1948. Thinks that today, and not St Patrick's Day, ought really to be Ireland's national feast day.

'I've been down to Cork and I've been down to Kilkenny over the past few weeks and everything is geared towards today. Timmy McCarthy, he'd be a farmer on the Cork team, and big-hearted John Power, the same on the Kilkenny team. They'll have both been working as they never worked before to get the harvest done so that all attention could then focus on the hurling. Being amateur makes all the difference.'

There aren't just farmers on the teams, though. There's a UN army officer, a sales rep, a computer analyst, a dentist and an auctioneer. Hurling is big in white-collar circles too.

'If you went back forty years ago,' Michael says, 'it was mostly older men who followed the game. Now it's younger males and females, and that's a very good thing.'

A very good thing indeed. Ireland now has a higher percentage of young people than any other European country. Grab them now and the GAA'll be good for another fifty years.

As Michael trots away a vaguely familiar face looms up. 'Great to see you back,' the man chimes. Of course. It's Jack. Sat next to me at the All-Ireland football a few years back. Then, seeing I have a notebook, he says, 'But I won't disturb you. I can see you're working. Mind . . .' he leans forward to whisper, 'I've always thought it a contradiction in terms, "working journalist", if you know what I mean.'

1.10. 'By their stadiums you shall know them,' I wrote earlier. The same can be said of how sporting events are staged. So if you're one of those unfortunate, deracinated and alienated westerners who's never quite sure whether you'd rather be black – like Roddy Doyle's Jimmy Rabbitte – or maybe Jewish, or Brazilian, or perhaps southern Italian or Scottish, a couple of hours at Croke Park might well persuade you that, on balance, Irish is not a bad option either, at least on All-Ireland day. You'd probably not choose to be black in Ireland on any day, nor perhaps anything other than Irish Catholic in certain quarters. The place is no multi-cultural haven. But if you like your sport served up on a traditional plate, rather than from a melting pot, there isn't an event in the world to touch the All-Ireland.

By this I don't mean that the final reflects an ad agency view of the country; with sensitive hunks supping 'da Murphy's' in stage-set, music-filled pubs, and not being bitter. Or the folkloric Ireland of little people and blarney. Croke Park is neither. But in its pre-match build-up it does offer a quite seductive blend of ritual and romance. There's a definite touch of Superbowl stardust, with heaps of Wembley gravitas thrown in. Among the crowds there is also a Latin passion, cushioned by the good manners and informality one might encounter at a country fair. Above all, there is a lack of formality; like the crooked tie of a bridegroom at the altar or the giggle of a schoolboy playing Hamlet.

Those Artane Boys, for example, are far more loose-limbed and natural than would be tolerated at any American college game. From the old players' tunnel I look up into the Hogan Stand, over the plastic flowers in the presentation box, and see dozens of Catholic priests in their black clerical coats and Roman collars, chattering away with grey-haired and freckled men wearing Donegal tweeds and poplin ties. I see women in Pac-a-Macs extracting sandwiches from foil-wrapped bundles on their laps.

Out in the rest of the ground, where Lycra meets club shirts meets woolly cardigans meets Barbours and puffa jackets, where deerstalkers and hand-knitted bobble hats are only just outnumbered by baseball caps – any one of which I'd pay good money for at this particularly chilly moment – the Cork and Kilkenny fans are intermingled to a degree that would give the average safety officer at an English football ground apoplexy.

Down in the concourses the girls behind the counters of the cafeterias – and they are indeed labelled cafeterias – actually smile. I find myself watching them to be sure that I've not just caught them in an unguarded moment. But, no, they carry on laughing and serving. They sell 'freshly cut sandwiches', 'beefsteak-and-kidney pies', and, as a concession to the outside world, Coke, Mars bars and 'Cajun chicken baguettes'. I expect a director to leap out at any moment and say 'Cut!' so that the actors can all take their seats for the game.

So no question. This is different. This is good. After the hyped-up, plastic world of Premier League football I've been force-fed for the last seven years, this is something to savour. I only wish the hot dog that smiling girl just served me lived up to the same billing. So now I'm cold *and* hungry. The Irish experience indeed.

13.25. 'Stand aside now, people coming through.'

Pat is pointing again, watch at the ready. The Artane Boys strike up a salute.

Out from the old tunnel walk two men and a woman, side by side. They stop at the touchline and wave to the crowd as Pat introduces them to the crowd, using a microphone he picks up casually off a seat in the open VIP box. There's Joe McDonagh, president of the GAA, his wife Peggy, and the GAA's patron, Dr Dermot Clifford, the Archbishop of Cashel and Emly. Back in 1884, when the GAA was founded in Thurles, County Tipperary, the first patron was also the Archbishop of Cashel, one Dr Croke.

13.27. Next, on the button and on to the touchline, out steps the Taoiseach, Bertie Ahern, accompanied by his ADC in full army dress, then Liam Mulvihill and his wife Máire. The Artane Boys strike up another rousing salute. But the applause sounds only lukewarm.

'Is Bertie Ahern not so popular?' I ask Pat.

'No, no, he's actually very popular. It's just that he's one of our own. Here virtually every Sunday, or, if not here, at Lansdowne Road, so it's no novelty for him to be introduced. He's a big sports fan.'

The Taoiseach is also celebrating his birthday. 'Forty-eight. It's depressing, isn't it,' he tells the press later. Still, he adds, his late Ma and Da would be cheering on Cork from 'somewhere above'.

13.29. One minute early, so that his timetable won't slip if there are any injuries, Pat signals to the referee for the Minor All-Ireland Final to begin. Galway vs. Tipperary. The team haven't too many fans in the crowd, but enough family and friends to launch the game with an encouraging cheer.

'Puck off!' cries a crusty old character behind me.

'I'm sorry?'

'Puck off.' He winks. 'That's what they call the start of a hurling game.'

They don't – they call it a throw-in – but I suppose he enjoys saying it if there's a foreigner about.

To puck is actually to strike the ball with a hurley. The hurley, or *camán*, is like a hockey stick, made from ash, but flattened out and widened at the business end – the *bas* – which is sometimes crossed by one or two tin bands, to prevent the wood from splitting. Like cricket bats or tennis racquets the choice, the weight and the feel of a hurley is a highly personal affair.

'What should I expect?' I'd asked various people earlier in the day. Des McMahon called hurling 'the most dangerous, and the least malicious game there is'.

The secret, everyone says, is not to stand off or be afraid. Otherwise you can easily get smacked by the other guy's hurley. You have to get in close, shoulder to shoulder. Face up like a man. But if a hurley in the face can hurt, the small white ball used in hurling, the *sliotar* (pronounced slitter), whacked as it often is at over a hundred miles an hour, can hurt a lot. None of the Minor lads wear shinpads. Only a few wear protective helmets. They make American footballers or ice-hockey players look like prize cissies.

Late in the first half, Galway's number 13 – which might almost be his age as well – takes an almighty knock, right in front of me. I can see him screwing up his eyes from the pain, battling the urge to weep. He's cold, he's knackered. He's just a kid. He's not even started shaving yet. But then he staggers up, takes a deep breath and gets on with it. As Des said, it's a man's game. Even for the boys.

14.00. Half-time. Galway lead Tipperary 0–9 to 0–5. The first zeros show that no goals have been scored in the nets (as in soccer-style goals). Each goal earns three points. The second figures refer to the number of single points scored by shots going over the crossbar but between the uprights (as in rugby posts). The Artane Boys Band troop back on. Behind them run twenty boys and twenty girls, playing two games of hurling across the pitch. They leap about like puppies, hurleys clacking, for exactly six minutes. At most finals at most stadiums the groundstaff would be out there, pushing back all the divots, fussing away over their precious turf. At Croke Park they let the kids get on with it.

14.40. Full time. Galway's Minors have won a tight, defensive game, 0–13 to 0–10. Pat's timetable is holding up nicely, as John Culkin, the winning captain, strides up the steps to the presentation box, where Dr Clifford and Joe McDonagh greet him like proud parents. Their task is to present Culkin with the *Irish Press* Trophy, which shines in the glowering afternoon. Winning a final on live TV is test enough for an eighteen-year-old captain. But in the GAA, that's not enough. The winning captain is expected to make a speech.

Croke Park is now 90 per cent full, maybe 56–57,000 people. Plus there are millions more watching and listening on television, radio and, this year, as people keep reminding me, on the internet. Dr Clifford makes a speech. It sounds like a quaint homily about two men, but I can't make out the words. Then John Culkin takes up the microphone.

I try to imagine an eighteen-year-old English soccer player at Wembley, addressing a near-full stadium and the nation. I think of all the tongue-tied teenagers I know who can barely address a wall with any coherence. I remember how I quaked at having to give my barmitzvah speech at the age of thirteen, and that was to barely a hundred people, all friends and family. But they train them differently in the GAA. From an early age, captains learn how to make speeches. Not only that but they have to make at least their introductory remarks in Irish, which for most of the boys is a foreign language. I try to imagine an eighteen-year-old English soccer player at Wembley addressing the nation in French.

Gazing out over Croke Park, John Culkin, fired-up and open-faced, shows no fear. If anything, he's oh-deeing on adrenalin. His team-mates crowd around the steps to the presentation box like the excited teenagers they are, all sweaty faces and restless limbs turned towards their captain. Their captain bawls out a greeting in Irish. Croke Park applauds with proprietorial delight, like he was everyone's son or nephew.

Then in English he thanks his coaches, his teachers, his family, his team-mates. He thanks Tipperary for being such great opposition. His young voice echoes around the stadium. Three cheers for the losing team, he demands, and gets them, from all quarters of Croke Park. Whatever else life throws at young John Culkin, there will never, ever be a moment quite like this.

As he steps down to lead his team's laddish, loopy lap of honour, Pat takes up the microphone again. 'Please welcome on to the pitch,' he booms, 'the Black Mill Set Dancers from Kilkenny City and the Mill Street GAA Set Dancers from County Cork.'

14.59. Pat checks his watch, gives another signal. Off come the Set Dancers. Out from the old players' tunnel in the Hogan Stand comes, appropriately enough, a team of old players. These are the Kilkenny boys from 1974 and 1975. Another All-Ireland tradition this, to introduce to the crowd the winners from twenty-five years before. In their suits, the men appear indistinguishable from most of the other middle-aged spectators in the Hogan Stand. But after they file out to form a long line across the pitch, and are individually introduced to the crowd by another veteran broadcaster, Micheál Ó'Muircheartaigh, each one's humble posture and tremulous lower lip bears the unmistakable hallmark of a genuine winner. No amount of hype or marketing can match this communal sentiment. 'Mick Brennan!' calls out Micheál Ó'Muircheartaigh (cheer!). 'Liam O'Brien!' ('Good on you, Liam!'). 'Pat Delaney!' ('Great player!').

Ger Henderson, who is otherwise occupied as an official with the current Kilkenny team, is represented by his wife, Noreen, and for her an even warmer 'Hurrah!' goes up. It's the same for Elsie, wife of Brian Coady, also busy in the dressing-room. But it's not always for happy reasons that the wives or daughters stand in for their menfolk during these presentations.

The introductions, the waves and cascade of applause continue, along the line.

Is that a drop of rain? I wonder. No, just one or two of the older Kilkenny people around me shedding a tear or two at the sight of all these champions from their youth. Jeez, I might even be joining them if I'm not careful.

Top this, eh, Hollywood? This is *brilliant*.

15.05. As the old Kilkenny players troop off to their seats – you can scarcely imagine the thoughts going through their heads – bang on time the big screen shows a three-minute clip, the 'Path to the Final'. Now the crowd is getting pumped up. The swaggering Cork fans seem to have adopted every red and white national flag they can muster: the maple leaf of Canada, the crescent moon of Turkey, the cross of Norway. There are Stars 'n' Stripes too, and chequered flags. With each second that ticks away, the noise level rises.

A team of tracksuited teenage boys jogs past me on to the pitch, unrolling three lengths of red carpet. I say red, but one's scarlet, another's maroon, and the other's sort of pinkish, as if someone had just picked up some off cuts at the last moment. But no one cares, because the swelling roar of the crowd has finally, totally, inexorably split the heavens asunder, unleashing torrents of rain down on to Croke Park, half of which is uncovered. I glance up, then down, and see that my bench seat next to the old tunnel is way in front of the line of the Hogan Stand's roof. Within a minute or two I'm drenched.

So is Paul Hennessy, who's been pacing up and down in the tunnel close by. During the week Paul is appearing in Doyle's Irish Cabaret, a show put on mainly for tourists at the Burlington Hotel. Today he'll lead the singing of the national anthem, *Amhrán na bhFiann*. The words are something to do with ancient warriors, he tells me, but it's in Irish, which he doesn't speak. There's no money for him in this gig either. But he'll be seen around the world on TV – and on the internet, don't forget – and 'Anyhows,' as Paul says, 'some things are beyond cash.' And the GAA did give him two tickets for up in the stand, though he gave those to his sister-in-law and her boyfriend, who wanted to follow Tipperary in the Minors. So now the tenor is wet through too, suit, tie and all.

Paul is from Carlow. 'So is the ref for the Minors' final,' he says, 'so it's been a good day for Carlow.' He means it too. That's how it is in the GAA. Always remember your roots.

15.09. Pat takes up the microphone again. This time he really has to bellow to be heard. '*A Cháirde, cuirigí fáilte roimh Fhoireann Corcaigh!*' meaning 'Please welcome . . . the Cork team.' From the new Cusack Stand opposite, the Cork players bound out on to the pitch, dashing this way and that, oblivious to the downpour; leaping and stretching as if they've been trapped inside a small box for the past day. Croke Park erupts.

15.12. '*A Cháirde, cuirigí fáilte roimh Fhoireann Cill Chainnigh!*' 'Welcome to . . . the Kilkenny team.' Croke Park is now quaking. Both teams have their photographs taken by the touchlines, then break into their respective halves, frisky, pucking away, sending *sliotars* zipping at high speed across the huge expanse of turf (the size of one and half soccer pitches). The captains toss for choice of ends; towards Hill 16 or the Canal End. Either direction, it promises to be a long, wet and strength-sapping afternoon.

15.19. The Artane snare drums rrrrroll and clatter. The bass drum thumps, signalling the start of another salute. Onto the pitch, to another great roar, walks Mary McAleese, the president of Ireland, protected from the now unrelenting drizzle by a brolly-wielding lackey. She wears a long dark coat and a silver chenille scarf. Looks so relaxed she might just have popped in after dropping off the kids at a friend's. Loves the games, so they say. Goes to all the finals, All-Ireland and provincial too. 'She's a wonderful president,' says a man next to me. 'Wonderful to talk to, down-to-earth, no big airs and graces but very dignified. From Northern Ireland too.' I'd say the man was smitten. I'd say he was not alone.

Mary McAleese is introduced to the players, one by one, before they break away for 'the parade of the teams'. Another All-Ireland ritual. The players form a line behind the Artane Boys and do a complete circuit of the pitch, along the front of the Hogan Stand, turn by the half-built Canal Stand, up by the new Cusack Stand, past Hill 16 and back to where they began, like racehorses in the silver ring. The band then turns to face the Irish tricolour, flying from the roof of the odd little Nally Stand, tucked in a corner between the Hogan and Hill 16.

A bedraggled Paul Hennessy steps forward. The band strikes up the national anthem. But is he singing? Is his mike switched on? We can see his lips move on the big screen, can hear the crowd sing. But not him. Seems as if the rain has got into the wires. Whatever. The anthem is sung with only wavering gusto. There's nationalism, there's pride, but there's also a collective reserve about the Irish, as if they don't like to make too much of a fuss. Or maybe it's just the rain. (I'm told later that it's probably because the rather war-like lyrics of the anthem are actually a tad embarrassing for a supposedly modern peace-loving nation.)

As the VIPs retreat to the Hogan Stand, back come the track-suited boys to try somehow to roll back the now sodden, unwieldy carpets, as around their dripping, exposed ears the roar of the crowd grows, and grows, and swirls with a now visceral power that, to me, seems to transcend mere sporting allegiance. Individually the fans may well be urging on their teams, but rising from their bellies their cries erupt as one heaving, primeval clamour for . . . For what? For glory? For WHAT? I can't hear myself think. For honour? For WHAT? For Ireland? Ah, yes, maybe for all those things. But also . . . also because, for fuck's sake, they can. THEY CAN!

No need for high-decibel, pumped-up rock anthems like you get in the NFL or the Premier League. No need for Tina Turner or Queen. This is herald enough, this chorus of pure, unadulterated humanity. Throbbing, heady music to my ears, unencumbered by harmony or lyrics, yet with the power to make one feel both infinitesimal and all-powerful at precisely the same time.

The second Sunday in September. It's pissing down. I'm in severe danger of catching pneumonia. I should have brought a coat. And yet all I can think of is to join in with the hubbub, cry out to the weeping heavens and feel the waters cascade across my upturned forehead.

I won't even try to spell the sound that pours out of my mouth. 'Yee-aaaaargh!' doesn't begin to do justice to it.

15.35. Five minutes into the game the Artane Boys are back under cover, bedraggled, shivering and laughing, tucking into their well-deserved crisps and chocolate. They've been on the go for the best part of three hours. Pat's off somewhere. In a side room off the tunnel the tracksuited boys are puffing self-consciously on fags. Mo Mowlam's up in the stand looking bewildered by the hurling. I can also see Father Gardiner up there. Aside from his pastoral duties, he's here to assess the referee. Every bit of help appreciated. Someone tells me that the Sinn Fein leader Gerry Adams is in the Hogan Stand too, as he often is. A little boy, maybe nine or ten years old, is brought to the tunnel. He's lost his dad.

'I've lost my da,' he says, snivelling and vulnerable.

He's patted on his wet head and sat next to a nice woman from Kilkenny while someone goes off to sort it out.

'Eighty degrees in London, you said!' one of the stewards reminds me with a flick of his sopping hair. In adversity, community.

Hurling: a brief history.

Hurling could well be the oldest ball game in the world still being played at a senior level. There's strong evidence that while Romans like our friend Vicarius were crowing about their brand-new Colosseum nearly two thousand years ago, beyond the empire's clutches the early Irish were pucking around with hurleys and *sliotars*. Rather fine brass hurleys and *sliotars* too, according to some surviving examples. For centuries they played on. Long before the Brits arrived, long before cricket or soccer were codified, across the island *sliotars* were being hurled across fields and meadows. When Michael Cusack called the Irish to order in 1884, they didn't take much persuading. But they had to fight for the right. The right to be different.

On Sunday, 21 November 1920, around 3.00 p.m., a crowd of

nearly 10,000 people were gathered at Croke Park to watch a GAA football match between Dublin and Tipperary, when a British army biplane flew over and dropped a flare. That was the signal for the Black and Tans to climb over the ground walls and fire shots into the crowd, first with small arms, then with machine guns, in reprisal for the execution of fourteen British intelligence officers earlier that day. A stampede ensued. Thirteen people were killed, including the Tipperary captain, Michael Hogan. Bloody Sunday, the Irish named that day. Hogan's name lives on in the Croke Park stand. But the Gaelic Games would not die. After Independence it gradually picked up again. Guns couldn't kill it off. Nor could soccer. Nor could TV or nor will the Celtic Tiger. On the contrary, the more prosperous Ireland has become, the stronger seems to be the GAA.

Gaelic sports are among the sporting world's best-kept secrets. Like shinty or Australian Rules Football, they survive as island oddities played out at the extremities of continents. As a prim young reporter called Gertrude once wrote of the splendid 1931 All-Ireland hurling final, 'One would like the whole world to have seen it.'

Well, they are now, Gertie. And if they're anything like me, they're still totally and utterly transfixed by it all.

16.05. Half-time. Cork, 0–4, trail Kilkenny, 0–5, after a cat-and-mouse opening thirty-five minutes. Still no goals. Still no clues as to the eventual winners. Not that I, as a novice, can tell, but the word is that the game's been a real wash-out so far.

Pat's thoughts lie elsewhere, however. For the umpteenth time this afternoon, the public-address announcer reads from a prepared script. The GAA has decided that at least one, long-standing All-Ireland tradition must end today, and Pat and the team still have no idea if the message is sinking in.

The announcement starts. 'Ahem. Croke Park has been advised by the public-safety authority, in the interests of safety, *not* to go on to the pitch when the match is finished. We ask you to co-operate and *not* to go on to the pitch after the game. Please co-operate with the Gardai and the stewards. Because of these new safety arrangements the presentation will now take place at the centre of the pitch. Thank-you.'

If the fans decide to ignore the directive, the police and

stewards are under orders not to stop them too vigorously. These things take time. Not worth stirring up trouble. Been going on to the pitch for God knows how long. Trouble is, in the past it has tended to get a bit hairy out there at full-time, with maybe 20–30,000 people on the pitch. Players can get mauled or crushed. Fans get careless. Injuries are common. Public liability and all that. You can't be too careful these days, what with lawyers and litigation. So, fingers crossed for later.

The Artane Boys have meanwhile returned on to the pitch, now draped in capes like French gendarmes, followed by Paul Hennessy, still in a suit. This time his mike works a treat. We've had salutes to the VIPs and to the players. Now it's the fans' turn. First up, a song for Cork, 'The Banks of My Own Lovely Lee'. Paul's caramel voice rises above the band's opening refrain. Within a line or two the Cork fans are joining in from all over the ground.

How oft do my thoughts in their fancy take flight,
To the home of my childhood away,
To the days when each patriot's vision seem'd bright,
Ere I dream'd that those joys should decay,
When my heart was light as the wild winds that blow,
Down the Mardyke through elm tree,
Where I sported and played 'neath each green leafy shade,
On the banks of my own lovely Lee,
Where I sported and played, 'neath each green leafy shade,
On the banks of my own lovely Lee.

And then in the springtime of laughter and song,
Can I ever forget the sweet hours
With the friends of my youth as we rambled along
'Mongst the green mossy banks and wild flowers.
Then too, when the evening's sun sinking to rest,
Sheds its golden light over the sea,
The maid with her lover the wild daisies pressed
On the banks of my own lovely Lee.

And again, with real passion:

The maid with her lover the wild daisies pressed
On the banks . . . of my own . . . lovely . . . Leeeeeeee!

All around cheers and applause break out. Cork have done themselves, and their county, proud. So have the Kilkenny fans. Not a heckle or anything untoward from them. Not that you could hear, that is.

Next, it's their turn. Paul leads them through 'The Rose of Mooncoin'. Neither its tune nor its maudlin sentiments seem at all different from the Cork song, but they invite the same response. Up go the Black and Amber flags.

How sweet 'tis to roam by the sunny Suir's stream,
And to hear the doves coo 'neath the morning's sunbeam,
Where the thrush and the robin their sweet notes entwine,
On the banks of the Suir that flowers down by Mooncoin.

Flow on, lovely river, flow gently along.
By your waters so clear sounds the lark's merry song.
On your green banks I'll wander where first I did join,
With you, lovely Molly, the Rose of Mooncoin.

Oh Molly, dear Molly, it breaks my fond heart,
To know that we two for ever must part.
I'll think of you, Molly, while sun and moon shine,
On the banks of the Suir . . . that flows down by Mooncoin.

Oh yes, guffaw if you like at dear Molly and her lovelorn beau, down on the banks of the Suir. But then do me this favour, will you? Try to think of a song, just one song, that would best represent your home town or county, the place where you were born. Go on, think really hard. Does one even exist? If it does, then imagine how your fellow supporters might respond if asked to sing along with that song, at half-time, with only a tenor and a marching band as accompaniment. Then ask yourself, would the opposing supporters behave respectfully, as did the Cork and Kilkenny fans, during the singing of that song?

Hardly bears thinking about, does it? Does it? No, it does not. Call me old-fashioned, but I think that's a crying shame. We have lost so much. And half the bloody time we don't even know it.

16.15. The teams are out for the second half. So is the monsoon.

Up comes the manic roar again. Off go the Cats and the mouse Rebels. The mouse equalises. All to play for. The Cats pull ahead. One point, two points, three points, four points. 0–5 to 0–9. Croke Park is now awash with Black and Amber. The Cork boys are starting to look knackered. This time it must Kilkenny's year, surely. Experience telling. Fifteen minutes left. Rain still falling. Cork never win in the rain, everyone knows that. I've found a sheet of polythene for up top, but my arse is in a puddle.

There's now a woman sitting next to me. Don't know where she appeared from. 'C'mon, Alan,' she's crying out. 'C'mon, Joe.'

The name's Mary. From Cork, and she's not just being familiar. She really does know most of the Cork players. Maybe a majority of the 62,989 fans present in the stadium knows at least one player from either side. Friends, family, work colleagues.

'C'mon, Cork! C'mon, Cork!' repeats Mary. 'Oh, come on, Kevin!'

'Yuhhhhhhessssssssss!'

0–6 to 0–9. The Rebels have pulled one back.

But Kilkenny strike back. 0–6 to 0–10.

'C'mon, Cork!'

The *sliotar* is hurled from end to end. Follow the players, they told me. If you lose sight of the ball, watch the players. You'll soon catch up. Jeezus, but these guys are quick. No let-up. Fast and furious. They can catch the ball, puck it, run with it balanced on the *bas*, even kick it. So few rules. So few stoppages. Hurleys snap. Shoulders swing. The *sliotar* flies and the lads follow, up and down, side to side, across the sapping, soggy turf.

Sean McGrath, twenty-three, works in local radio, steps up a gear for Cork.

'C'mon, Seanie! C'mon, you Rebels.'

'Yuhhhhhhessssssssss!' 0–7 to 0–10.

Timmy McCarthy, the farmer, has also found his second wind. All on his own. A goal now would put Cork in front. 'No, Timmy,' shouts someone. 'Go for the point!' Timmy plays safe. The ball sails between the uprights but above the crossbar.

'Yuhhhhhhessssssssss!'

0–8 to 0–10.

Then, 'Shite!'

Andy Comerford, the Kilkenny stonemason, has carved a rejoinder. 0–8 to 0–11. Thirteen minutes to go. All Croke Park now baying wildly. Mass hysteria. Maybe the hurling's not up to much, but the *craic* is cracking.

Free puck to Cork. Yes! 0–9 to 0–11. Yer man McGrath again, an easy one this time. Kilkenny tiring. 0–10 to 0–11.

Mary doesn't want it to be a draw. 'Please don't let it be a draw,' she prays. You wouldn't believe how hard it had been for her to get a ticket. Only got this one at the last minute. £25 for a bench down at the front. Sitting in a puddle. If it's a draw they don't play extra time. They replay.

'I couldn't go through all this again.' Mary shakes her head.

'C'mon, Cork!'

16.51. Game over. Pat is elated. The stewards have held their ground. The pitch stays clear. For the first time ever in an All-Ireland Final, the crowd has kept off the pitch at the end.

'Today is the beginning of a new tradition at Croke Park!' Pat declares triumphantly in the tunnel.

Out come the assorted red carpets again, curled at the edges, sinking on to the sodden turf. Up in the stands the fans, delirious, exhausted, crestfallen, and now bemused, are watching a car driving on to the pitch, towing behind a small platform.

'What the . . . ?'

The platform is where the players will receive their medals, instead of up in the presentation box. Not everyone approves of this. 'They should stick to the old ways,' someone behind me complains.

'Please stay off the pitch,' repeats the PA announcer, though it looks as if no one is in the mood to disobey. Too bloody wet. Too bloody drained after that final ten minutes. Mary from Cork can barely stand. An insistent young woman, pushing a little boy in front of her and gesturing towards the celebrating players on the pitch, is trying to persuade a steward by the tunnel in her rat-a-tat-tat accent.

'Can he go to his daddy? Can he go to his daddy? Why can't he go and stand with his daddy? Please let him stand with his daddy. Please.'

The steward is pained to say no, but he must. 'It's the new rules, love. Sorry. No one goes on the pitch.'

Still she doesn't understand. 'Why can't he go and stand with his daddy? He just wants to stand with his daddy.'

But her voice is drowned out by the sound of klaxons and elation. In the centre of the pitch, up steps Mark Landers to be presented with the Liam McCarthy Trophy by GAA president Joe McDonagh. During the week Landers works for the TSB Bank. Now he gets the chance to say 'Yess!' as he lifts the trophy up towards the grey clouds. Cork have done it again. 0–13 to 0–12. All won in the last few precious minutes.

Kilkenny crushed for the second year running. Their crestfallen players can barely look up. John Power's nose is bloody. Willie O'Connor's face has swollen up like an aubergine. The Cats have their tails between their legs. Drowned by the rain. Now drowning in sorrow.

Landers now takes up the microphone. Pat had told me how some captains become tongue-tied and self-conscious at this moment. One or two write down their speeches on a slip of paper. Some victory speeches of past captains such as Anthony Daly of Clare are still remembered for their wit, power and emotion.

Landers barely hesitates as he steps up, with Pat standing by, holding an umbrella over his head. ('Who is that man who keeps popping up?' some of the viewers back home must be asking as they see Pat appear yet again in the background.) Still breathing hard from his afternoon's exertions, Landers roars out his opening. 'Welcome back to Lee-side, Liam McCarthy. We've missed you a lot!'

As the Cork fans go crazy he thrusts the trophy towards all four sides of Croke Park. When the noise has settled a little, he continues, breathlessly. 'It is indeed a great honour for me to captain this young victorious team on the last championship of the millennium.'

As is tradition, he then thanks all the team's helpers and the Cork officials. It's a long list, but you can see that he dare not miss a name. Then he continues: 'I'd like to think that this dispels the notion that Cork can't play in the rain [ecstatic laughter]. But most of all, ladies and gentlemen, we were here in 1982. We were also here in 1983. Captained by one man. He didn't have the honour of lifting the Liam McCarthy Trophy, but he did the next best thing. He brought his team to win it in 1999. Better known as JBM, we know him as Jimmy Barry-Murphy.'

All eyes turn to Jimmy, the much loved Cork coach, as Landers again lifts the trophy skywards.

'My last word, to the supporters. Thank you for travelling. Thank you for making the effort to get the tickets. For you, watching in America, Australia, England, and for you the people at home that couldn't be with us today, we're going to see you back on Patrick Street tomorrow night!'

'You bet ya we will!' comes back the response.

Three cheers for Kilkenny follow, but stuck out there in the middle of the pitch some of the impact and shared camaraderie of the moment seems lost. But only for a second or two, as if no one quite knows what to do next.

Then hugs follow back-slaps follow handshakes between the two teams – the same as is happening all around me between the two sets of supporters, before the Cork lads hare off to their fans pressing forward on Hill 16. The Artane Boys Band is playing 'The Banks of My Own Lovely Lee' again, and this time the players are joining in.

> *'The maid with her lover the wild daisies pressed*
> *On the banks of my own lovely Lee.'*

Had I fallen in the lovely Lee itself, face first, I could hardly be wetter than I am now. Yet as the noise starts to fade and the tension falls away from Croke Park with each row of seats that empties in the far stands, with each dripping steward or policeman passing by me, stamping his feet, laughing with the relief of it all, I begin to feel, at last, quite, quite calm.

I stand in the old tunnel watching the stadium empty, following the post-match interviews on a tiny TV. People go in and out, scurrying from the pitch to the concourse, ignoring the security barriers, not sure whether to hang on longer or scuttle off into the rain. To stay on, or to let the afternoon slip from their grasp? Suddenly the lights go out and it's like we're all in a cave, huddled together. Then seconds later they come back on again and there's an ironic cheer. Once we were a throng. Now we're just people. Survivors of the afternoon. Remembering only now that we all have homes to go to. It's hard to let go of the spell.

Back in the GAA reception, Pat tells me it's the wettest All-Ireland he's ever known. Hardly surprising it was not a classic. Only twenty-five scores and as many as thirty-four wides, according to the man on RTE. But, a good hard game and, as

Mark Landers reminded us, proof that Cork can win in the rain.

Pat's side of things has gone well too. Very well. The schedule worked. No one overshot their allotted times. No one got on to the pitch at the end either, which has apparently delighted Jimmy Barry-Murphy and his players.

In an hour or so, when all the VIPs have moved on, Pat will have some supper with the rest of the crew, then he'll be heading back to the Burlington Hotel for a well-deserved early night. Ah no, Pat's no killjoy, but tonight he'll be leaving the partying for others. Tomorrow morning there'll be brunch for the four teams at the hotel, Minors and Seniors, then each will return home to face their fans. A Kilkenny player tells the TV man what it's like to lose two years running. 'I don't know how much more of this we can take,' he says, only half jokingly.

Even so, there will be 10,000 people out on the streets of Kilkenny City on the following night to welcome back their bruised heroes.

And an estimated 40,000 in Cork City, making it one hell of a party on Patrick Street. Cork will then be off to Boston for an All-Stars match next month as part of their prize. Oh sweet, sweet victory.

But before that, oh yes, before that, Pat Guthrie and the Croke Park team, and the Artane Boys Band, of course, they'll be doing it all again in a fortnight, for the All-Ireland football final. Cork vs. Meath.

As eventually I take my leave, Pat sees the sodden state of my clothes and disappears into a side room. Comes back with something for me. Courtesy of the sponsors. An umbrella. 'That should get you back into town all right.'

Then I step outside on to Jones's Road, and just as I'm about to brace myself for the rain I'm half dazzled by the low sun and by the brightness of the now clear, blue skies breaking out all over the city. Suddenly it's a glorious autumnal evening, and I'm drying out before I even know it.

But I decide to hang on to the new umbrella, all the same.

9 RECONSTRUCTION

Every weekday evening, around six o'clock, the stadium builders – Jim, David, the two Tonys and Steve – would sluice away the day's dust with pints of Heineken or Kilkenny Irish bitter at the Duke of Wellington, wondering how many more evenings they would have to spend there before the job was done. The contract was supposed to have been for twenty-two months. Long enough. Nowadays you can knock up a fairly decent modern stadium in as little as eighteen months if all the conditions are right. But their contract was now into its forth-eighth month, and counting.

Above the stadium builders' heads, hunting horns and horse brasses hung from the bar fittings. On the green hessian walls were the usual Olde England country scenes, joined by a portrait of the Duke and a set of bagpipes. Two stags' heads flanked the fireplace. Pewter cannons sat on the mantelpiece.

The Duke of Wellington might have been anywhere, or at least anywhere but the British Isles. (A notice pinned on the wall for a meeting of the local Hash Harriers was the real giveaway.) A dimly lit corner of Bogota perhaps, or Lagos, or Manila, that would for ever be a pastiche of uncool Britannia. An ersatz home from home for the expatriate company reps, engineers, nurses, consular staff, foreign correspondents and all the usual global drifters.

The Duke, on the ground floor of the Mayflower Hotel, in the heart of the business district, may not have been the smartest watering hole in town. But the stadium builders agreed that it was the best one to pander to British tastes. Better certainly than Charlie Brown's, a few blocks away, or the Hare and Hounds, up in the mountains. Convenient too as a stopping-off point before Jim, David, the two Tonys and Steve trooped back to cook themselves supper in their company flats up in the north of the city. (One of the Tonys really missed his bacon.) Besides, you never knew who might pop into the Duke. This week alone a couple of

English journalists had been in, as had an Irish photographer and his mate, the odd businessman, and an even odder bloke from London asking questions about the new stadium.

One night the stadium builders had been sitting there having a quiet bevvy as usual, when the place was suddenly overrun by American secret servicemen, checking each entrance, sussing out the regulars, causing a big scene. In their wake marched another American, clearly the big cheese, demanding to know if anyone present knew a certain so-and so. They did, but he wasn't in that night. 'Hell,' cursed the Yank. 'I'd heard he was in town and was hoping to meet up. Used to play cards with him in 'Nam.' He and his minders then slipped away into the night. Just like that.

Crazy place, Beirut. Crazy times. But not crazy in the way it was during the seventeen years of Civil War, when the likes of Terry Waite and John McCarthy were disappearing in the night, when expat Brits and war-weary correspondents would gather in the Duke, or at Jackie Mann's bar across the road – before poor Jackie was taken hostage too, that is – and all routine life, such as shopping, meeting friends, collecting laundry and so on, had to be squeezed into the precious few morning hours before the fighters reclaimed the streets. 'Oh, they were very considerate,' a Lebanese woman recalled in the Duke one night. 'They usually held off until around lunchtime.'

It was now six years since the Civil War had reached its inconclusive conclusion, in 1992. As has been said so often before, if no one knew quite how it began, sure as hell no one could be exactly sure why it had finally fizzled out. Maybe it was just plain old battle fatigue. But now the fighting had ended, the sound of exploding shells and machine-gun fire had given way to the clatter of bulldozers and cranes, diggers and drills; giving continual lie to Edwin Starr's claim that war (huh!) is good for ab-so-lute-ly nothing (sayyit again). *Au contraire*, Edwin. War seems pretty damn good for the construction industry. Once the smart bombs and missiles have done their bit and the dust has settled, in rush the contractors. Go go go. Fighting from government office to office, watching their backs, checking out the enemy in the hotel bar across the road, until, *whoosh*, in comes the foreign aid. *Splat!* Down goes the ink. *Bam!* Another contract signed. A new dam, motorway, oil refinery, army base, hospital, whatever. Occasionally, very occasionally, a stadium too, just to cement good relations. Sport, the great healer. Stadiums, the ever popular sweeteners. The likes of Africa and the Middle East are full of stadiums financed as part of foreign-aid packages or arms deals; most of them built by the Chinese, the French, the Germans or the British.

A mile or so east of the Duke of Wellington, in Beirut's devastated former commercial centre, lay the largest building site on earth. The city used to be called the Paris of the Middle East. Soon it would look more like Hong Kong. The only battles now were between rival European, Middle Eastern and Far Eastern companies, fighting each other for contracts to build, restore or reclaim hundreds of hectares of shell-shocked real estate, occupying an area the size of London's West End. Replacing bombed-out concrete hulks, kidnappers' cellars and block upon block of crumbling ruins were five-star hotels, swish office blocks, a new souk, a marina, housing developments, a coastal park, roads and car parks. Skyscrapers were starting to overshadow the now exposed remains of Roman baths and centuries-old mosques. A few tourists were already ambling down smart pedestrianised streets looking up at the windows of restored Ottoman-style townhouses, occupied not so long ago by snipers and news crews. Or they could be seen in taxis, bumping along pot-holed side streets lined by weed-infested ruins – shadowy figures, grimly hanging on to domestic life just visible behind shattered balconies and cracked façades – only to turn the corner and find themselves gliding along a new underpass as if passing through Guildford town centre.

Just south of Beirut, German contractors were starting on a new airport. And halfway between there and the centre, in an area of the southern suburbs called Bir Hassan, on behalf of an Anglo-Norwegian company called Kvaerner Construction, Jim, David, the two Tonys and Steve, plus Ken the project manager and Roy the quantity surveyor, together with a team of Lebanese designers, engineers and subcontractors, and their mainly Syrian work force, were applying the finishing touches to Beirut's newest pride and joy. This was the Cité Sportive, a 48,000-seat stadium and an adjoining 3,500-capacity indoor arena: symbols, both, of the rapidly recovering nation; proof, both, to foreign investors that Lebanon's Confessional factions could work together for the common good if only they were given the chance.

Kvaerner's British crew were all agreed, it had not been an easy contract, by any standards. In Beirut, nothing is simple. Deputy project manager David Williams, one of the new boys (having arrived only five months earlier), said, 'I don't think any of us have ever worked in such a politically intense place.'

As a former student of Middle Eastern history, I should have known that this would be the case; that in order to understand why a building as relatively straightforward as a stadium was taking so long to complete would demand a search far beneath the usual piles of blueprints, contracts and routine sports headlines. And so it was to prove. Beyond the happy-hour humour at the Duke of Wellington there clearly lay a twisted trail of murky horrors and tangled relationships; between Kvaerner and their Lebanese clients, between Muslims and Christians, Lebanese and Syrians, Arabs and Israelis, Palestinians and everyone else. Yet, on reflection, how possibly could it have been otherwise? If, as I have claimed, by their stadiums you shall know them, why should I have expected this stadium story – in Beirut of all places – to have been just another quirky tale of expats in hard hats?

My first wake-up call came during the drive to the stadium on my first morning. Khalil, the taxi driver, was reminiscing about the Civil War. Six years old when the shooting began, he had been 'a fighter' for fifteen of his thirty years. Did I want to see his wounds? He showed me them anyway. The day the war ended, he said, he hurled down his gun and asked himself out loud, 'What the fuck was I fighting for?'

He was a Sunni Muslim, Khalil explained. His mother was a Christian. His sister married a Christian. 'Before, we all lived together, so why we fight? Because . . .' he counted off on his fingers as he swerved unnervingly through the roadworks and choking traffic, ' . . . because of fucking Iranians, fucking Syrians, fucking Americans, fucking Palestinians, fucking Israelis.' (Having missed out on his entire childhood schooling, he said he'd learnt most of his English from Sylvester Stallone movies. It showed.)

Of all the troublemakers in his peaceful land – the land once of milk and honey – the only ones he would fight now would be the Israelis. 'Over one hundred women and children they kill at Qana,' he snarled, still seething more than two years after the Israelis had shelled the UN base there, in southern Lebanon.

'I don't hate Jewish ["joosh", he said] people,' he went on, unprompted.' 'I hate Jewish army. It all lies about Jewish killed by Germans. The whole of Europe should be afraid of Israel.'

And then there I was, outside the stadium, shaking only very slightly. As Khalil sped off, his cheery waves seemed to say, 'Hey, welcome to the minefield!'

So anyway . . . the stadium.

There had been an older stadium on the site of the new one, dating back to the mid Fifties. Named the Camille Chamoun Cité Sportive (or Sports City) after Lebanon's then president, it was apparently a typical concrete, open bowl, seating 25,000 spectators. The second Pan Arab Games had been staged there in 1957, at a time when, just post-Suez, Lebanon looked as if it might become America's favourite client state in the region. Its capital, Beirut, meanwhile, was developing a reputation as the playground of the Arab world, famous for its exotic nightlife and the breezy delights of the Corniche, the elegant promenade lining the sea front. For the 1957 Games, a small indoor arena called the Salpoly (Salle Polyvalente, meaning multi-purpose hall) was built on the north side of the stadium. Otherwise, there were few other buildings in the Bir Hassan area, with virtually none between the stadium and where the Summerland beach resort was now to be found, a kilometre or so to the west across a sandy plain. During the 1960s and 1970s all that changed, as Beirut's sprawling suburbs spread southwards and, across the road from the Cité Sportive to the east, the refugee camps of Sabra and Chatila started filling up with new influxes of Palestinians, displaced mainly by the 1967 Arab–Israeli war and, a few years later, by a power struggle in neighbouring Jordan.

After the Civil War kicked off in 1975, not all sporting activity ceased in Beirut, however. The fighters were footballers too, and in order to play each other some Muslims and Christians did risk crossing the Green Line (which divided the city's two communities). But no sport took place in the Cité Sportive. The stadium was taken over by the Palestinians for use as a military base and arms dump. Dozens of homeless families occupied the Salpoly. Meanwhile, into Sabra and Chatila poured yet more hopeless streams of humanity, many of whom were among the 300,000 Lebanese Shi-ite refugees fleeing the border area nearest to Israel. Before long, the southern suburbs – in reality, most of them hardly more than unplanned shanties – became hotbeds of factional infighting, feeding upon a deep seam of poverty, anarchy and despair.

In 1982 the Israelis bombed various targets in Beirut in preparation for their June invasion. The Cité Sportive was all but flattened. Three months later, across the road, Israeli troops stood by while Christian Phalangists entered Sabra and Chatila and systematically slaughtered at least 2,750 Palestinians and a few hundred Lebanese. Many of the dead were buried in a mass grave dug in a nearby golf course. The death toll might have been higher, but as a group of Palestinian women and children were being herded at gunpoint into a bomb crater inside the ruined stadium – where they were told they would be buried alive – a nearby explosion sent everyone, Phalangists included, running for cover. The intended victims managed to flee in the confusion.

This is of course only one, superficial account of one minute part of the extended nightmare that was the Civil War. But in any case, all the world has since heard of Sabra and Chatila. That there happens to have been a stadium next door is barely relevant. Place is one thing. Context another.

But to see where it all happened . . . To hear the venom in people's voices . . . To be implicated in such misery, if only by association, as a westerner, as an apolitical sports writer, as a . . .

So as I went out and about and met more people like Khalil, I kept shtum. I mean, quiet. One of the Tonys at the stadium said that the secret of working happily overseas was to avoid all conversations about religion or politics. 'You soon learn to keep out of it. Not to get involved.'

Maybe. But I had only a week in Beirut, and I had eyes and ears . . .

But anyway, I was saying. When the Civil War ended in 1992 – with most of Lebanon now swarming with Syrian troops, and the southern part of the country still occupied by Israeli and Israeli-backed Christian forces – the Arab nations decided to offer to Beirut the filip of staging the next Pan Arab Games, due to be held in 1996. At a subsequent meeting in Cairo in 1993 the Arab sports ministers also magnanimously offered to underwrite the entire costs of rebuilding the Cité Sportive.

Generous though this gesture was, in truth it left precious little time for Lebanon's Council for Development and Reconstruction (CDR) to plan for the Games adequately. To be ready with a new stadium and arena within only three years, starting virtually from scratch, would have tested the organisational powers of any urban authority, let alone one that had just reformed itself after seventeen years of internecine strife and Israeli bombardment, and that had so many other pressing matters of reconstruction and reconciliation to consider. Then there was the site of the Cité Sportive to consider.

Perhaps with more time to reflect, the CDR might well have decided to start afresh elsewhere, at a larger site with fewer inherent obstacles. But now there was no time. There were also too many emotional ties to Bir Hassan. Thus plans for an extensive new sports complex were drawn up by a Beirut design agency called Laceco-bea, which at the time had no experience at all of stadium or arena design and therefore depended on a French agency for much of the technical detail. The total costs were then estimated at $120 million, making this the country's largest public-sector building project so far. (Much of the rest of the city was to be redeveloped using private funding.)

But it was not so much the prestige of the stadium contract that elicited eighteen bids from Britain, France and other Arab countries. It was the chance to gain an early foothold in Lebanon in order to grab further, more lucrative work once the serious rebuilding process began elsewhere in the country. Few of the bidders would have expected to have made much profit on the Cité Sportive deal. Some may have even budgeted for it as a loss leader.

Eventually, after a few months of deliberation and hard bargaining, the British company Trafalgar House (later taken over by Kvaerner) won the race for the contract, after reducing their bid to $112 million. In signing the deal they became the first European company to work in Lebanon after the war.

Theirs was a baptism, almost literally, of fire. The ground on which the ruins of the old stadium stood was littered with unexploded bombs, some sunk up to ten metres below ground level. Two had to be detonated on site. To complicate matters further, two hundred families living in tents on the remains of the pitch had to be rehoused. Several houses around the perimeter, erected during the Civil War, had to be demolished and their occupiers compensated. Also cleared was a temporary school and a vegetable market. More buildings on one other corner of the site should have been removed too, but followers of Hezbollah rioted in protest. Overall, 4,000 cubic metres of spoil and rubble needed to be cleared before actual construction could begin, in September 1994.

By that time, for all the grand pledges made by the Arab nations in 1993, only Kuwait, who donated $6 million, and Saudi Arabia, $20 million, had actually stumped up, leaving the CDR to find the rest. The original plans were thus slimmed down considerably by omitting the proposed hotel, a swimming pool and a tennis centre, and by leaving the new stadium without a roof. These moderations reduced the costs to a more sensible $49.5 million, of which $34 million was for the stadium element.

Relationships between the British contractors and their Lebanese counterparts were seldom easy. Kvaerner had to sack two local subcontractors for poor performances, which in the circumstances was a brave step to take given the company's desire to establish a good name in Lebanon. The construction team also struggled with the design, and with the clients' refusal to adapt it. By March 1996, with only four months to go before the Pan Arab games, it was clear that the project was way behind schedule. It was at that point that more British personnel were flown out to help speed up the process.

Among the new arrivals was the younger of the two Tonys, Tony Dorsett, who, to my delight, turned out to be the son of a former Aston Villa footballer, Dickie Dorsett (the 'Brownhills Bomber', as he was known). As a Villa fan, this discovery seemed to offer a comforting reminder of my own Englishness in this city of labelled, laboured identities.

With his silvery hair and a neatly trimmed moustache, Tony had his dad's dashing looks and trim build. He was just about to celebrate his fiftieth birthday. Why didn't I come to his party, he said, at the Duke of Wellington, naturally.

A joiner by trade, Tony was now the senior supervisor on the stadium, after several years working on various projects in Saudi Arabia, Oman (another stadium) and a chemical plant in Egypt. His stint in Beirut was supposed to have lasted only six months. It was now approaching three full years. But it had nearly ended within days.

'I arrived in Beirut with a few others in April 1996; a Thursday evening, it was,' Tony recounted in his mild Black Country drawl. 'We came down to the site on the Friday morning, and I remember we were being shown around, sometime around mid-morning, when we heard these dull thuds, two or three of them, followed by plumes of smoke. The local guys were running up to the top of the terraces, pointing to the south-west of the stadium, where we could see four Israeli helicopter gunships hovering, with one above them obviously doing the spotting. They were just letting fire with missiles into Sabra, about a kilometre away. This went on for half an hour. Everyone came back to the office to find out what was going on and it was then we heard that the Israelis had launched a new offensive.'

They called it 'Grapes of Wrath'.

'I wasn't too scared really,' Tony went on, 'so we came back to work the next day, a Saturday morning, and exactly the same thing happened. About eleven o'clock the Israelis were back again, only this time they started hitting targets to the north, by aircraft, and at the same an Israeli gunboat appeared on the coast, cruising up and down.' When its guns started opening fire, the Syrian workers at the stadium made their excuses and left.

The following day, holed up in his apartment with the other Kvaerner men, an enormous explosion sent Tony diving for the floor. 'We gave it a few minutes then made our way to the balcony, where we could see an anti-aircraft gun emplacement had been placed on the block behind us and was opening up at these F-15s flying over. Never hit them, even though all along the Corniche they'd brought up other anti-aircraft guns. On the Monday we arrived back at the site to find that the Lebanese army had placed more anti-aircraft guns just to the south of the stadium, and one other right by our site office, which had all of us pretty concerned because we thought that if it stayed there the Israelis would have a go at the stadium. They'd destroyed it before, in 1982, and maybe this would be an excuse for them to have another go.'

Eventually Kvaerner's managers persuaded the Lebanese army to move the nearest anti-aircraft gun. But the bombing continued, one bomb being dropped rather too close for comfort on Sabra. At that point it was decided to evacuate the Kvaerner men to Byblos, a town north of Beirut on the coast.

'About ten of us from the company jumped into cars with our Lebanese drivers. Had quite a scary ride through the northern suburbs, through Jounieh [the playground of Beirut, home of night clubs, casinos and strip joints], where the Israelis were bombing the power station, until Byblos, where all was quiet. We stayed there a few days, and then flew back to UK the next week.

'A few stayed here throughout. The construction manager, some of the commercial guys. Some other British guys from Tarmac, working on another project, were based in offices near Sabra, and the Israelis took out the building right next door to them. The Hezbollah HQ, I think it was. Sitting there in their office they looked out and the building next door just disappeared. But the stadium was untouched and, fair do's to the Lebanese, they continued working right through the period we were away.'

Tony returned a fortnight later, and the fact that certain Kvaerner staff had stayed on throughout the sixteen-day Israeli assault was reported approvingly in the local media, much to the company's satisfaction. But the Syrian workers did not reappear for two months, and with power supplies also erratic because of the Israeli assault, and materials in short supply anyway, the Pan Arab Games were put back a year. Nevertheless, rival companies within Beirut's gossip-ridden construction community were soon suggesting that Israel's action had got Kvaerner off the hook by buying them extra time.

In the meantime, amid growing criticism of the project's costs and its relevance to the country's needs, in March 1997 the CDR decided to allocate more funds to the Cité Sportive, so that after the Pan Arab Games work would continue for a further sixteen months, bringing the final costs to $74.5 million. Rumour had it that $10 million or so of this extra budget was to satisfy the Lebanese president's demands that at least one section of roof be built, to provide shade over the VIP section.

No one suggested publicly that the excessively complicated Lebanese design itself might have been responsible for the delays, or that specifications for certain elements of the contract were far more lavish than was strictly necessary. Italian marble wash basins, for example, in the public loos?

These frustrations aside, expats and locals alike were nevertheless all swept up in the emotional tide that coursed through the city as the stage was finally set for the Pan Arab Games in July 1997. That the stadium was more or less ready was relief enough, but in a wider context it seemed little short of miraculous that the Games were able to take place at all in Beirut, so soon after the Civil War and the latest Israeli assault.

The first row emerged a week or so before the Games, when the speaker of the Lebanese House of Parliament suggested that the new stadium be renamed after the president, then Elias Hrawi. He and the then Muslim prime minister, Rafik Hariri, were accused of trying to write Camille Chamoun out of Lebanese history. Later in the week an embarrassed Hariri would have to order the removal of banners put up by his own supporters urging that the stadium be named instead after him.

The second controversy erupted only a few days before the opening ceremony, when Kuwait and Saudi Arabia, the only two countries to have kept their pledges to fund the new stadium, refused to countenance the participation of Iraqi athletes at the Games. If a single Iraqi athlete was present, threatened the Kuwaitis, their own delegation at the opening ceremony would hold up photographs of those people still missing since the Iraqi invasion in 1990. Torn between reconciliation with Saddam Hussain and appeasing their closer and wealthier allies in the Gulf, the hosts had no choice. Three coach loads of Iraqi athletes were turned back from the border with Syria, but not before the Iraqis had slaughtered five sheep by the roadside in honour of those who had reported sympathetically on their plight.

Back in Beirut, the opening night of the Pan Arab Games threatened to descend into a riot as it transpired that an estimated 150,000 tickets had been handed out, even though only 48,000 seats were available. Once those seats, plus all the aisles and every other standing area, were filled to capacity, thousands of irate ticket holders grew restless outside. Before long, scuffles broke out. Stones were hurled at a portrait of the president. Beirut's *Daily Star* reported that a security guard issued a warning, 'Our fellow countrymen, either move back or we will spray you with water.' His words went unheeded. High-pressure hoses were turned on the crowds. Shots were fired into the air. As an exhibition of Lebanon's new-found spirit of peaceful coexistence, it did not impress.

Inside the packed stadium, the International Olympic Committee's president, Juan Samaranch, emerged from the sweltering guest rooms, where the air conditioning had failed, to find the Lebanese prime minister helping up one of his political opponents, whose seat had embarrassingly collapsed. The bullet-proof screens, the VIPs may or may not have noticed, were only up on three sides of the dignitaries' box. When the fourth side had been installed a few days earlier it had fallen out and smashed into pieces.

Thereafter, at least, all went smoothly. President Hrawi kept to his word on the naming of the stadium and announced, 'From the Camille Chamoun Sports City, I declare the Pan Arab Games open.' Prime Minister Hariri declared that the opening ceremony marked the victory of construction over destruction, of peace over war. 'Every stone built in this place is a victory for the martyrs who died during the war. Israel transformed this place into a graveyard. But it has become a place of unity, peace and Arab solidarity.' (Iraq's absence was not mentioned.)

On the pitch, hundreds of soldiers carrying white boxes formed the outline of a map of Lebanon, while the southern section of the country, depicted in black, was moved apart in symbolic recognition of Israel's continued presence in the border area. This tableau was followed by various parades, fireworks and a laser display.

That the ticket distribution had been a fiasco was unfortunate, though indicative of the organisers' inexperience. That serious violence had been averted was a huge relief. But most people seemed to agree that things would improve, *inshallah*. God willing. The country still had much to learn, but learn it would. As Robert Fisk wrote in his seminal account of the Civil War, 'The Lebanese believed in happiness with the fervour of missionaries. If they believed hard enough in something, then it would come true.'

In one other respect, however, the Lebanese public showed that it was no different from any other nation. Once the Pan Arab Games began, only the football tournament drew any substantial crowds. Indeed, by the third day of the athletics there were barely 2,000 spectators inside the Cité Sportive. Later on there were even fewer. Steve Mizen, Kvaerner's mechanical and electrical engineer, remembered leaving his office under one of the stands to catch the men's 200 metre final one afternoon, only to find he was among a tiny handful of people watching. Steve was also there to witness the start of the Marathon, when one runner left the stadium after the first lap around the track, only to collide with a car in the street outside. The organisers had neglected to close the roads. Another runner's progress was held up by a bus.

A further embarrassment was the postponement of the

women's 110 metre hurdles. Apparently the hurdles were locked away in a room for safekeeping, but no one was able to find the key. The Kvaerner people had warned their Lebanese colleagues time after time that they should adopt a simple master-key system. But would they listen? Instead, there were now different keys for every single door in the stadium. As a result the Games organisers could have created a new weight-lifting event. 'To add to the women's open 77 kg plus, the men's 105 kg plus, for the truly mighty, ladies and gentlemen, please welcome the all-comers Stadium Key Ring weight.'

Another real test for the organisers came during the semi-final of the football tournament, when 5,000 policemen were on duty to keep apart rival Lebanese and Syrian supporters. According to the *Daily Star*, the Syrian fans (most of whom would have been either members of the Syrian army, or migrant workers) chanted, 'With blood and with our soul, we will redeem you, Assad.' And to show their intent, after the Lebanese team equalised from their second penalty of the evening, the outraged Syrians started tearing out seats and hurling them on to the track. Two thousand seats were damaged, even though Syria eventually won. Further damage was incurred during the final, which this time the Syrians lost 1–0, to Jordan.

Ironically, once the Games were over, it would be Syrian workers who replaced many of the broken seats.

But, better broken seats than broken heads, and considering that few major international events go ahead without at least some unfortunate gaffes, Lebanon had done pretty well in the circumstances.

After the medals were handed out – six golds to Lebanon, several more to Algeria, several times more to Egypt – work resumed on the final phase of the stadium and Salpoly. This should have taken no more than sixteen months. But David Williams arrived nine months later to find the schedules lagging seriously behind and relationships more strained than ever.

David, aged fifty-one and a civil engineer turned project manager, was one of Trafalgar House's and now Kvaerner's trustiest operators, with long experience in the West Indies, the Yemen, East, West and South Africa. He had first received a call from Kvaerner's MD one Monday morning while back 'in UK' (as British expats like to call home). By Wednesday he was in Beirut.

Not everyone was pleased to see him.

'I got back to my apartment one day to find a message that the local internal security people wanted to see me,' David recalled with wry amusement. It was immediately apparent that someone within the local Kvaerner staff wanted him off the scene. He was too close to HQ. Had a direct line to the MD. So David rang a few influential friends and they advised him to bypass the regular security officers and go straight to the colonel, the man at the top. This he did, only to hear the top man laugh off the whole business and offer David some coffee instead.

Unlike most of the other expat stadium builders, David had opted to live on his own in Beirut. Yes, he was divorced (as were several of his colleagues). All that working overseas hadn't helped, obviously. But he had a new partner 'in UK', two daughters, and houses in Barbados and Reigate. Besides, living abroad was in his blood; born in Venezuela to parents in the oil business, he'd been to boarding school in Jamaica and university in the UK. 'You have to learn to be self-sufficient. But it's a strange existence and I still find cooking for myself a drag. You also have to keep building up new relationships in each new posting. But that's good because you find friendships you might never have made otherwise.'

Enemies too.

'Some nights I know for sure that I'm being followed, and that usually someone from within our own Lebanese staff has set it up. To find out where I drink, see if they can find something they can use against me. So I have to behave.' Which David would have done anyway, you could tell. He had the calm demeanour of an experienced army officer, laced with the watchful smile of a bank manager. He was also, significantly, the seventh deputy project manager to have worked on the contract since it had begun four years earlier. Most of his predecessors had either fallen foul of the local Lebanese manager or had given up trying to mix subterfuge with construction.

Which is why Kvaerner needed all the toughness and diplomacy David could now muster. After four years of investing truck loads of sweat, patience and spare cash, his bosses were damned if they were going to pull out of Lebanon once the Cité Sportive was completed. True, they would not undertake to build any more stadiums – no profit, too much hassle – but one or two water, fuel or port projects in the area looked promising, thought

David. A delicately balanced game was thus emerging. Kvaerner had the keys to the stadium, and wanted rid of it as soon as the CDR paid up. (They were already well behind with the payments, leaving Kvaerner to underwrite most of the costs.) For their part, the Lebanese held two trump cards: the chequebook, and the possible lure of other contracts.

But the real frustration about Beirut, agreed all the Kvaerner crew, concerned the actual construction itself, and the perception that the locals had refused to listen to suggestions or advice from the British or indeed from any other foreign adviser. Already, said David, the Saudi-supplied pitch was deteriorating, because there was no one experienced enough to maintain it. So too was the German synthetic track. And where was the 'end user', the organisation that was supposed to run the stadium? With, supposedly, only weeks to go before the finishing touches were applied, still no one from the government committee responsible had come forward with a management team. There was a serious worry that once they had finished work – and been paid of course – Kvaerner would just have to pack up and, as it were, leave a key under the mat. For whoever.

This is not generally the way these things are arranged. Normally, a stadium management team is trained and chomping at the bit as the construction is ending, with a whole schedule of events waiting to be staged so that the stadium can start earning its keep from day one. Not in Beirut. Apart from the promise of staging the Asian Nations Cup in October 2000, two years away, there had been just a handful of football games staged since the Pan Arab Games, and no one had come in to clean up the mess afterwards. Kvaerner had to do that, even though it was not their responsibility.

Then there was the design. 'They got it out of an exercise book,' complained David. The Lebanese wanted a symbol, an edifice, even though they could have built a much more functional, modern stadium for a lower outlay. It was the same with the Salpoly.

Only the other day the president of the local basketball federation had seemed over the moon as he approached the near-completed arena. But he needed only one look inside to realise that with 3,500 seats it was too small for international events. It was also discovered that by keeping the steelwork from the original roof – the steelwork that had so miraculously survived the Israeli bombardment – the height between the court and the scoreboard was 2.5 metres shorter than the minimum allowable under international codes.

'I can't do anything with it!' the basketball president was reported to have exclaimed.

David sighed as he recalled this. 'Sometimes I do think I'll go mad here. The guys here were very jaded when I arrived. It's been quite an uphill struggle getting them back on their feet and interested in finishing the job.'

Yet whatever his reservations, David shared his colleague's huge respect for the Lebanese. They were excellent engineers, insisted Ken Gilder, the overall project manager. Friendly, hospitable people, said Roy Jones, the quantity surveyor. Everyone agreed that it was hardly their fault that seventeen years of Civil War had drained the nation of its leading professionals and left the younger generation almost wholly without experience. Beirut was also a paradise compared with some of the godforsaken desert postings all of them had experienced.

Jim Law, the obligatory Scottish engineer on the job, told me of a favourite expat saying: 'The two best jobs you'll ever have are the last one and the next one.' But like most of the lads he agreed that, work issues aside, Beirut was actually brilliant. Ironically, the streets were safe at night. There was a decent social life – starting with the weekly expat gathering at the Duke – good places to eat and drink, and on the whole the locals were all pretty decent. And they were. Beirut, rather like Belfast, was brimming with friendly, accommodating, fun-loving people. You could not help but wonder how they could have fought each other so bitterly and for so long. Was it simply because they hated being told what to do?

'But, let's be honest,' added Ken Gilder: 'not listening to experts is not only a Lebanese trait. There are plenty of people like that back in UK.'

In any case, I was the stadium expert. What did *I* think? A guided tour of the complex was arranged, courtesy of Tony the elder.

Tony Pettit was a short, balding, chirpy man whose muscle-bound chest, tanned, tattooed arms and spreading midriff spoke of years of hard work, travel and good nosh. He was two weeks short of his sixty-fifth birthday. After stints in Sierra Leone, Nigeria,

Oman, Dubai, Cairo and Karachi, Beirut would be his last overseas job, he insisted. After this he would retire with his wife to Worthing.

Under a relentless, late-morning sun, Tony showed me the surprisingly neat crater where an Israeli shell had landed just by the Salpoly during the 1996 offensive, and recalled the shock of coming under fire so unexpectedly. On the seaward side of the stadium we could see construction continuing on a new four-lane highway linking the airport with the city centre. This would at least save visiting dignitaries from having to view the awful deprivation of Sabra as seen from the old road into town. On the far side of the new highway a bus station, public park and a supermarket were being built by the French.

The Salpoly itself, just to the north of the stadium, was a genuinely impressive, modern building, with the proportions of an angular Greek temple, decked in sun-bleached stone and with white tubular steel columns. It might almost have been a library in some switched-on city in the south of France. Inside, conversely, it felt like a giant sauna. The air-conditioning units had all been delivered, but vital components were still missing. Nor were there any seats. After ordering 3,500 of them, the Lebanese had decided to let spectators sit on the concrete steps instead. Still, that left plenty of spare seats to replace those damaged by the Syrians inside the stadium.

From the Salpoly Tony led me down into the blissfully cool, concrete chambers underneath the stadium. A lack of space around the site had forced the designers to incorporate vast underground car parks, a fearfully expensive option but an inevitable consequence of the CDR's insistence on staying in Bir Hassan. Even the Lebanese engineers thought they should have started from scratch elsewhere, said Tony. Arsenal, Eden Park, Mumbai and now Beirut. Different cities, same old story.

In one of the caverns below ground Tony showed me the plant room, large enough to house a fleet of double-decker buses. With no one coming forward to manage the complex, Tony's fear was that rats, cockroaches and squatters would soon find their way down into this subterranean world.

He wasn't able to show me the presidential suites because Ishmael, one of his Lebanese workers, couldn't find the right key, though he must have tried about a hundred before I persuaded him that, really, it was not that important. 'We told them they should just have a master key,' said Tony, shaking his heavily perspiring head. The air in the corridors below the main stand was stifling and still. I was shown marble features and stately rooms. A 100 metre warm-up track and a small prayer room too. No fewer than twenty-seven different dressing-rooms for athletes. But nowhere did the air conditioning function. Still waiting for parts.

Tony then took me to see the press room and café. Neither had kitchen areas nor even water supplies laid on. Again, Kvaerner had tried to warn the designers. Then we walked around the sparse but generously proportioned concourses, shaded by the stands above and lit by arched, classical-style openings and portholes. Inside the toilets the Carrera marble sinks seemed laughably extravagant. But then Tony ushered me into another toilet block. I immediately recoiled from the stench, steeled myself, then re-entered. It was as if someone had recently staged a 'dirty protest'. Soiled paper and litter were everywhere. Toilet bowls were blocked and fetid. I had to leave.

Tony explained that the toilets had been left like that after the most recent football match staged at the stadium, several weeks earlier. Kvaerner had no brief to clean the stadium, but nor, it seemed, had anyone else. After years of anarchy, it seemed, Lebanese sports fans had simply forgotten the responsibilities of citizenship.

Once inside the open bowl of the stadium, I could see what the Kvaerner men had meant about its old-fashioned design. It was not unattractive. Its single tier of blue seats created an oasis of order in the midst of the dust and rubble of the surrounding cityscape. Had such a stadium been built, say, in Italy during the 1960s, it might have merited one or two favourable articles in architectural journals. But it was obvious that too much of the expenditure had gone on unnecessary features and fittings below stairs.

High up in the television camera gantry, suspended from the cantilevered roof over the main stand area, a gang of men worked on the steel. None of them wore a hard hat or safety harness. We then walked over to the floodlights on the opposite, uncovered side of the bowl. Tony pointed out how the steel latticework legs of the light pylons extended right down to street level, offering the perfect invitation for kids to climb up and watch matches for free. But as he was talking I adjusted my gaze momentarily and saw, across the road, some kids in Sabra – proverbial urchins dressed in rags – playing a wild game of football on a patch of dusty red earth, just 100 metres away. The shadow of the pylon fell across their pitch, putting them literally as well as metaphorically in the shade of this looming symbol of peace.

As I gazed from the stadium heights down on to those kids, and across the dense mass of Sabra, with its bombed-out roofs, teetering breeze-block homes and rooftop thickets of TV aerials and wires, the nature of my own work seemed suddenly more futile and superficial than ever. I have always harboured a dim sense of its marginal importance. My stock line has always been that the reason sport is so powerful is that we all fundamentally accept that it is not in the slightest bit important. At that particular moment, it had never seemed less important.

Hatless and speechless, I stood under the mid-day sun, my eyes blinking from the stadium to Sabra and back again. 'Not your story,' insisted one voice in my head. Another cried, 'Don't turn away. That's where the real story lies.'

But did I dare cross the road? In a day or two it would be the sixteenth anniversary of the 1982 massacre. Memorial events were planned. Yet, a few days earlier the Irish photographer and his reporter friend from the Duke of Wellington had been stopped in Sabra and questioned by Palestinian militiamen. On discovering that the pair were Irish, the men toasted the IRA and allowed them free passage. If stopped myself, what would I say? In my best Dublin accent, that I had just come from the All-Ireland hurling final at Croke Park and was writing a book about stadiums?

I think not. So the following day a young Lebanese journalist called Reem from the *Daily Star* agreed to accompany me to Sabra, to act as a guide and translator. I was both grateful and nervous. She was petite, polite and businesslike. To her I was just another western reporter.

Not all the inhabitants, she told me as we drove into Sabra, were Palestinians. Some were gypsies, some were itinerant Syrian workers (the ones with darker skins, apparently). Many were just displaced Lebanese. Virtually all seemed desperately poor.

Sabra, Chatila and their ilk are called 'camps', I had been told earlier, because any concession to the notion of permanence would be a betrayal of the Palestinians' status as refugees, a status which had yet to be settled, as promised, by the 1993 Oslo peace agreement. I could understand this as an intellectual construct, but not as an emotional response. Poverty is poverty, despair is despair, and although instead of tents and fields there were shops and housing blocks in this camp, narrow streets and markets – much like any other impoverished district in an impoverished third-world city – I still found it hard to accept that $75 million was being spent on a smart but poorly designed new stadium with marble washbasins while so much patently needed to be done to alleviate human suffering across the road. Sport is not always the great healer. Sometimes it's the great distraction. Circuses before bread.

Within barely two hundred metres of the new stadium's imposing, stone-clad eastern walls, kids were scavenging on a hillock of fly-infested, stinking refuse dumped between a line of breeze-block houses and open-fronted shops. Here and there dashes of colour were provided by Palestinian flags, rusting Coca-Cola signs and pictures of the Ayatollah Khomeini. At the end of the road lay the clearing of dusty, reddish earth I had seen from the stadium the day before, where another wild game of football was continuing with yelps and cries. Still the shadow of one of the stadium's floodlight pylons cut across their pitch, like the dappled lines of a watchtower.

People in Sabra referred to the Cité Sportive by its Arabic name, *al medina ryadiye*. Only one man liked it. He had a metal workshop, and thought it made the neighbourhood look smarter. Another man, older and with parched, leathery skin, railed against the world. While the government was taking out loans to build the stadium, he cried out, 'Our children are sick. No one cares. Don't ask what the Lebanese government is doing for us, ask what UNRWA [the UN's Relief and Works Agency] is doing. Answer? They're not doing anything.'

A Lebanese man then told me that I should really go to the poorer parts of Sabra and Chatila. This section we were in, the one nearest the stadium and the old road to the airport, was probably the richest part of the camp.

Reem then spotted someone she had interviewed recently. With grey hair, shuffling feet and chillingly lifeless eyes, the man could barely lift up his face or say more than a few words. Reem explained that he was one of only a handful of survivors of the 1982 massacre still living in the camp. He was now aged twenty-one, and completely alone in the world. His family had all been murdered. I judged it best not to ask him about the stadium.

Those I did question all felt the same. The stadium was Lebanese business. They were just guests in a foreign country, even if, like one Palestinian man, their stay was now into its fiftieth year. Another, much younger Palestinian, whose arms were covered in sores, said in a matter-of-fact tone, 'We are used to money being spent on other things. Nobody puts any money into the Palestinians. We are just sitting on the sidelines.' Palestinians, even ones with university degrees, were forbidden from all the best jobs and professions. Few of them had passports. Any Lebanese person who employed them risked prosecution. Yet the Syrians came in their thousands and worked for peanuts. Everyone hated the Syrians, he said (maybe even more than the Israelis at times). Their troops filled the country as part of the peace agreement. There were Syrians working at the stadium, at the airport, in the city centre, all over Beirut, for five or six dollars a day – way below what a Lebanese worker would expect – spending a bit on themselves and sending the rest back home, tax-free. They could come and go as they pleased. As far as most Palestinians were concerned, said the youth, the stadium on their doorstep added only fractionally to their despair. But he thought he might go to a game there, and felt no anger towards the Lebanese. 'They have to build up their own country, so why not a stadium.'

On the drive back from Sabra I could barely speak or think straight. Coming to Beirut to write about something as superficial as a stadium seemed like going to Pristina to do restaurant reviews, or to Chechnya to research rare butterflies. Sick with myself and with my work, in turmoil over my alien status in an Arab country, I listened as Reem talked about her years spent in the United States, during the Civil War. Without prompting – she knew nothing about me, suspected less – she related how she had studied and mixed with Jewish students at an American university. 'I am not anti-Semitic,' she insisted. But the behaviour of the more extreme Jewish students had shocked her. They had blocked speakers coming to the Arab Society. They had even complained about there being a cross on the campus Christmas tree. 'You can't win with them,' she said in exasperation. 'It's always "poor me, poor me". But it wasn't us who killed the Jews in the Holocaust. We lived with them quite happily in Beirut.' There was still an old

Jewish cemetery even – guarded, ironically, by a Muslim family who had been made homeless by the Israeli invasion.

The world should not blame the Christian Phalangists for the massacre at Sabra and Chatila, said Reem. It was the Israelis' fault for bringing the killers in. She asked if I had ever met any Israelis, because she hadn't, and she wanted to ask them if they felt proud of what they had done.

I struggled for a response. 'Well, I . . . I mean, yes, I have . . . but, no, I . . . I mean, well, I . . .'

She dropped me off on the Rue Hamra, just around the corner from the Duke. Had she sussed why I was so flustered? Or did she just think me a particularly foolish and naïve foreign sportswriter?

Finally, I arranged to meet Mohamed.

Mohamed is a football correspondent. He could hardly have been more enthusiastic when I e-mailed him from London to ask if we could meet in Beirut. 'Blimey!!!!!!' he wrote back. 'Is this for real????'

Partly, he said, when we met up for felafel and humus in a café on Rue Hamra, this was because he'd heard me speak on the BBC World Service. But I guessed it was much more to do with the fact that I was someone he could talk to about his abiding passion for Manchester United. 'What a team, what a club!' he had enthused, filling cyberspace with his ejaculations. 'Gold Trafford. Keano & Co!!!' He signed himself 'A Red in Beirut'. (Oh Lord, is there no escape from Red Devildom?)

So after a while I changed the subject from Manchester United and asked him, as you do, about the Civil War. Mohamed's eyes lit up as if I had just mentioned Ryan Giggs.

'I was once shot by a sniper in my right shoulder, in 1989, when the city was under seige from the Syrians. I was trying to drive to some friends in Jounieh. The sniper fired twice, one across the car, once in my shoulder. I have no idea who it was or which side. I was just very lucky.'

He then repeated almost word for word something I had heard earlier in the week from another educated and westernised Beiruti. 'You know, Simon,' said Mohamed, 'Beirut is getting boring. The war was very exciting. Really! Just imagine driving your car and a bombshell lands just next to you. Kalashnikov rounds on the pavement. It was a strange life, yes, but now it's boring, routine. I miss the war.'

Mohamed knew nothing of my background. With a surname like mine, why would he think me anything other than a typical Brit? So I said nothing while he talked about international politics, and how he read the Israeli newspapers on the Internet. He was still bitter about the shelling of Qana.

'You know,' he said, leaning forward confidentially, 'I think the Jews and the Germans are very alike.'

For the first time in decades I blushed. I might even have spluttered in my confusion and disbelief. So, cravenly, I switched the subject again to ask him about the new stadium. Safe ground. No-man's land. Neutral territory.

For Mohamed, the new stadium was of immense significance. 'It is a symbol of peace,' he said with genuine enthusiasm. 'It shows the world that Lebanon is now a peaceful nation. No, no, it is not a waste of money at all. It is very important for the future of the region. When it stages the Asian Nations Cup in October 2000, eleven nations will be here. A big boost. Foreigners will come. Thankfully we are qualified automatically. Otherwise . . .' He laughed. Lebanon was then ranked 107 out of 191 nations in the FIFA football rankings.

But surely, I asked, in a city so ravaged by war, were there not many more deserving projects?

'A lot of distressed people don't approve of the new stadium,' he conceded, 'despite the fact that tickets are very cheap, three to five dollars upwards maybe. But it is the same all over the Arab world. Someone rides a horse next to someone driving a Mercedes 600. It's really shocking. But, tell me, what is all the fuss with David Beckham? Hey, guys! Give him a break!'

Mohamed left me with this thought. Everyone, he said, kept telling the Lebanese to put aside their religious and political differences for the sake of sport. But, he wanted to know, where did this leave God? Behind football? Yet if God ranked after football in the order of human priorities, why fight over him in the first place?

Back at the Duke of Wellington I was surprised to come across a short, lean, tough-looking dude in snakeskin cowboy boots, propping up the bar with a distinctly unBritish nonchalance. I thought he might be the American secret serviceman, returned to look for his old card partner from 'Nam. But he was Gordon, from Milwaukee. Just another man from the sports facilities industry, passing through. Gordon had spent the last week or so laying the new basketball court in the Salpoly, and the thirteen years previous to that laying basketball courts right across the USA. He couldn't recall how many. 'High schools, NBA arenas, colleges, everyone of 'em in Canadian maple.' The Salpoly had been only his second job overseas. The other, ironically, had been not far away, across the border in Israel.

'Oh really!' I exclaimed, nearly adding, 'Whereabouts in Israel?' But I stopped myself just in time and said nothing. Nothing of my friends and relatives in Israel. Nothing of what I had just seen and heard in Sabra.

In any case, Gordon's work in Beirut was now done and he was just counting the hours. He said that as far he was concerned, the only thing that mattered was that in his pocket, which he kept tapping to emphasise the point, he had that most precious of items: a return ticket.

And so had I. So had I.

In my thoughts, though, I have been back to Beirut many, many times since.

Postscript: One year after my visit I contacted Kvaerner to see how things had progressed. Had they negotiated any further contracts in Lebanon? So far, they had not. A downturn in the Lebanese economy, I was told, had forced a reduction in public spending. Was the stadium finished? It was, although the building work had dragged on into its fifty-eighth month, to June 1999. But at least the facilities were being used, albeit sporadically. Apart from the inevitable concert by our old friend Pavarotti – no objections from the neighbours in Beirut, unlike Auckland – various football matches had been staged, including a friendly match between a Beirut XI and a Spanish team, to raise money after the Israelis had once again targeted the country's main electrical supply. The Harlem Globetrotters put on a show at the Salpoly. Meanwhile, a newly elected government had at last appointed a management team to operate the stadium, though no one had yet actually gone in to maintain or clean up the place.

Of the stadium builders, Jim was now working on a project in Ireland. The two Tonys were in Cairo (Tony Pettit having decided not to retire quite yet). Steve remained in Beirut, working for another company on a university building. David Williams and a few colleagues from the business side were still in Beirut, chasing up millions of dollars in unpaid and disputed fees.

The Duke of Wellington, though still popular, was less busy than in the past. And the youth with the grey hair and the dead eyes was, as far as I could ascertain, still in Sabra, hoping for the miracle that might yet restore to him his soul.

Mohamed and I continue to exchange jokey little e-mails about Villa and Manchester United. I have yet to tell him that I'm Jewish, or explain why I didn't tell him (or Khalil or anyone else) when we met. But I guess now that Mohamed has received a copy of this book, he knows. I doubt it'll make any difference to him. I hope not anyway.

10
CIUDAD DE LOS ESTADIOS, 3

Wednesday, 21 October. A city on the edge.
While the people of Beirut had grown weary of killing each other, the people of Buenos Aires, the *porteños*, seemed increasingly afraid of the city killing them. *'Buenos Aires me mata!'* started out as the title of a newspaper column. Now, I was told, it was an expression in common usage. 'Buenos Aires kills me.'

This was the third day of my quest to see as many of the city's football grounds as I could possibly manage in the space of six days, and so far my travels with Mariano had gone surprisingly well, if at times they had thrown up one or two unnerving signs, and left me, after only two days, drained to the point I could feel my bones rattling. Otherwise, I had yet to come into contact with *la bronca*, the endemic rage that supposedly afflicts so many *porteños*; a rage fuelled by the traffic, by the noise, by crime, by the impossibility of making do without two jobs and by the corruption of politicians and policemen. In a studied sort of way I was even getting on with my host, Enrique, the Pipo Pescador of television, radio and theatrical fame, whose *departamento*, whose beautiful *departamento*, was my home for the week, along with Greta, his slobbering bulldog, and Helena, his Paraguayan maid. The night before, Enrique had cooked a meal for me, his ex-wife, his daughter and some friends, after which we participated in a charming cultural exchange. He showed me his collection of exquisite Japanese prints. In return I introduced him to the pleasures of duty-free Laphroig Scottish whisky. Later he played on his grand piano and sang tangos and some of his own compositions, while we sat attentively and cried out '*bravo!*' like characters in a stage play.

So the city was a long way from killing me yet, or from

deterring me from my quest. I was nevertheless learning a number of depressing facts about Buenos Aires. For example, that for every *porteño* there are eight rats, and that, according to journalist Miranda France, every two hours someone in Buenos Aires dies in a faulty lift. Enrique's beautiful *departamento* was accessed by a lift.

I was also learning more about the roots of Argentina's oft-discussed melancholia. During the early part of the twentieth century, the period when most of the football clubs in the city were being formed, Argentina had stood on the threshold of becoming a great nation. In 1900 it was the sixth-richest country in the world. Yet somehow, through a long process of indolence, corruption, maladministration and just plain incompetence, Argentina had contrived to fritter away or neglect its many advantages – its wealth, its resources, its vast areas of underpopulated, rich agricultural land, its emerging sense of nationhood – almost like a spoilt child chucking out soft toys from its pram and then screaming when no one returned them. The country, it has been said, could have evolved like Canada or Australia and become a powerhouse of the Americas. Twice Europe had handed Argentina a golden opportunity to achieve just that status, during 1914–18 and 1939–45, instead of which the nation had succumbed to a baffling malaise. V. S. Naipaul called Argentina's failure 'one of the mysteries of our time'.

Some people blamed geography, the fact that Buenos Aires is essentially a European capital so far from Paris and Madrid, trapped between a wide ocean and the loneliness of the *pampas*. I heard others blame football. If football had not been so damned popular, and so divisive, maybe the masses could have concentrated on rather more important matters. As I noted earlier, there were said to be more stadiums in Buenos Aires than libraries. And now general lawlessness in the city was turning these stadiums into battlegrounds. Every week another outrage took place. Football, commented one newspaper editor, had become Argentina's 'deadly pastime'. Highly organised and often drug-fuelled hooligan gangs called *barra bravas* (literally, tough gangs) terrorised opposition fans, players, even their own club officials. For years rumours persisted that to avoid recriminations, clubs had been buying off these hooligans with free tickets and subsidised travel to away matches. What I hadn't realised was the death toll.

According to one report, sixty-six fans had died in football-related violence in the period between the 1978 World Cup and May 1998. On several recent occasions the league programme had been suspended for weeks at a time while the authorities attempted to halt the violence. A senior judge had been appointed to oversee stricter controls.

So far the most tangible results of this clampdown had been a ban on banners and *bombos* (the drums taken into grounds), and a raising of perimeter fences. So far, the treatment was not working. In fact the week after my visit the entire fixture lists of the five lower divisions were suspended indefinitely.

Wednesday, 21 October. 09.30. The information superhighway. I have often been told that mine is the best job in the world, usually by men who adore football but like to be sure of paying their mortgages. To earn one's keep, however erratically, by visiting and writing about stadiums – how can that be bettered? Ah yes, I always counter, but think of the sacrifices. I may get to see a lot of stadiums, but rarely do I get a chance to see the sights. Art galleries, theatres, unmissable markets and famous landmarks are simply blurs in the window of my bus or taxi as I dash here and there, from stadium to stadium, criss-crossing city centres, dipping into libraries and newspaper offices, travelling out to parts of cities that few locals, let alone tourists, would ever think of visiting. Many are the lonely bus stops and deserted railway platforms I have endured with only a crumpled paperback for company in some godforsaken outpost at the end of the line.

But I know damn well that an urban man with urban tastes cannot truly complain. For though I am drawn towards the bright lights as much as anyone, I find myself savouring the dingy back streets too. The museum may have its attractions, but there is history in the stockyards and the railway yards and the back-of-beyond yards too. The one cannot exist without the others. And if one wishes to visit stadiums, it is usually to the others one must venture. The hinterlands come with the territory, as it were.

Thus this morning found Mariano steering me through the centre of Buenos Aires for the first time during my visit, along what is purported to be the widest avenue in the world, the Avenida 9 de Julio, but is in reality a series of parallel, manic highways with buildings on either, distant side and an unusually phallic obelisk at one of its main intersections. For a brief while our ride through the rush-hour mayhem of the city's spine thrilled me with its stops and starts, near misses and last-second lane changes, and I probably emitted rather more expletives than Mariano would have liked. But I was not commenting on the ride. Rather, I was lamenting our self-denying ordinance not to take time out and just stroll around the city centre for a while.

Yet there was also, I freely admit, a certain satisfaction in whizzing through obvious tourist areas, of being someone with somewhere to go, someone with a mission. Besides, I had the best job in the world, and a duty to follow the road to the wrong side of the tracks, in fact to Avellaneda, the dense metropolis separated from the Capital Federal by the noxious Riachuelo (so polluted, it is said, that instead of trying to clean it up the authorities would be better off selling its contents to chemical companies).

Avellaneda – pronounced 'Avejyaneda' – merited just one mention in all the guidebooks I consulted, and even then only in passing. The place was, I saw as we headed down from the bridge over the river and on into its congested streets, rather as Queens is to Manhattan, or Croydon to London: an appendage with no distinct character of its own, yet on a scale large enough to claim some independence. (No, Croydon marketing people, don't send me any bumph. I'll only bin it.)

But if its attractions were few for the tourist, for the stadium buff Avellaneda was, as our American friends would put it, a 'must see'. Two major clubs are based there, Club Atlético Independiente, and Racing, but more, their quite considerable stadiums are bizarrely, though handily enough, located within a proverbial goal kick of each other. Not quite as close as Dundee's Dens Park is to Dundee United's Tannadice, but closer, say, than Liverpool's Anfield is to Everton's Goodison Park. Two hundred and fifty metres would be my guess, which is actually more like three or four pretty hefty goal kicks, depending on who is doing the kicking.

In contrast with the previous day, the weather was now clear and bright. Mariano and I were feeling good. We had fought our way through the world's widest avenue and were chatting about job titles; the differences, in his world, between pyschoanalysts and psychiatrists, between therapists and counsellors. The nearest I had ever come to a professional-sounding title for my own work, I told him, had been 'stadiologist', a neologism proffered by a bibliographer called Peter Seddon and one I much preferred to 'stadium expert' (a.k.a. 'smartarse'), which is how I am routinely tagged in articles or radio interviews, or 'groundhopper', which implies a hobbyist with a rail pass and a vacuum flask.

And then Mariano remembered I had asked him the evening before to come up with a nickname for me. An *apodo*, like *El Turco* or *Don Pepe*. So now he asked, what did I think of the nickname '*El Canchólogo*'?

What did I think? Mmm. What did I think? I had been hoping for something with a little more dash, a little more romance, but as I mulled it over for a few blocks I soon decided that *El Canchólogo* suited me perfectly. It meant, literally, 'the groundologist'. Not so pleasing in English, but kind of romantic in Spanish, and less formal than 'stadiologist'. Besides, most of the stadiums we had visited in Buenos Aires were really *canchas*, or grounds, rather than stadiums anyway.

On the other hand, what did *El Canchólogo* say about me as a person? 'I do have other sides to me, you know,' I told Mariano. 'I don't just collect grounds.' I said this because something I had heard shortly before my departure to Buenos Aires had been really bugging me. At a public meeting on the future of libraries – an area I have campaigned on in the past – a white-haired old woman with a stick stood up and declaimed in a tone both strident and weary, 'All I seem to hear these days is information, information, information. I'm fed up with information. What we really need to seek is knowledge.'

This simple truism, so bluntly expressed, had struck a raw nerve. Mariano listened patiently as he drove, while I quoted something else I was once told, in my early days as a journalist. Keir Radnedge of *World Soccer* magazine said, 'A journalist is only as good as his filing system.' It was the best and worst piece of advice I had ever been given, as my burgeoning archive on stadiums around the world now bears witness. It occupies several heaving filing cabinets and more time to keep up than I can possibly bear. Just in the few months since I started writing this book the pile of cuttings and notes waiting to be filed has reached the depressing height of eight inches and rising. In this context, believe me, size does matter. Even more dispiriting, I know that it will take at least one mind-numbing week to file away the several hundred sheets so far amassed. And then the process will start afresh. Like sweeping up leaves in the autumn, as soon as one pile is cleared, another takes its place the following day. Except that, these days, such is the volume of stadium news, winter never comes.

If I were to sweep the whole lot – every file, every cutting, every brochure and report – into a skip and call a halt to the tyranny, the awful tyranny of accumulating information, what would I be left with? Freedom from information, but still the same knowledge? Or would I be able to call this knowledge wisdom?

Maybe I didn't want to be *El Canchólogo* after all.

Mariano had no answer, and nor was I expecting one. But during our drive to Avellaneda he listened, and listened, until eventually I laughed away my clumsy self-analysis by recalling one last quote, from the American writer Ralph Waldo Emerson. Emerson said, and I paraphrase, 'Don't give me quotes. Tell me what you know!'

What follows, therefore, is just that. I know stadiums, even if I don't know why I do, or to what end, and I knew that there were five on our list to visit for the day. Until the schedule was honoured, nothing else mattered.

Mariano and I did agree on one thing, however. We resolved not to work through the day, as we had done the day before, without stopping for lunch. For as we knew our mums would say, not eating properly would only make us bad-tempered. Being good Jewish boys, we had at least absorbed some wisdom.

Wednesday, 21 October. 10.30. Stadium No. 10. Independiente. I liked the Estadio Almirante Cordero instantly, for reasons which I have chosen to summarise, in the interests of informational ease, as follows:

1. Just by the main entrance, where stood a small statue of the Madonna – '*La Madre*' – an official who resembled Harpo Marx greeted us with a cheery smile. You can tell a lot about a football club from the behaviour of the man on the gate.

2. Independiente's colours are red and white, colours which, when applied to a stadium's fixtures and fittings, are generally warmer and more sympathetic when juxtaposed with concrete and

turf, than are, say, blue and white. It's the difference between Kodachrome and Ektachrome, if that makes sense. (It is also, in my view, one of the reasons why clubs such as Liverpool, Arsenal and Manchester United gain more popularity among outsiders than those who play in cooler colours. Incidentally, like Manchester United, Independiente are known as the Red Devils, and their stadium as *la Caldera del Diablo*, the Devil's cauldron.

3. The Estadio Almirante Cordero was surprisingly large, with four very different stands and terraces reaching into every corner of the site's boundaries. The capacity was recorded as 57,098, of which 12,803 were seated, and of which, I reckoned, about half had the benefit of half decent sightlines.

4. The whole stadium complex, including an open-air swimming pool, school and kindergarten, was superficially neat and orderly, but with plenty of poignant grot to add some grit. Most poignant of all was the street frontage of the main stand, facing the Racing stadium. It had all the ugliness of an unfinished car park. Yet inside were immaculate toilets, one of which had a mirror on the wall. Mariano was amazed. He had never seen a mirror in a stadium toilet before, or at least not an unbroken one. (Ask any stadium manager and he'll tell you that it is in the ladies' toilets where the mirrors get smashed first, and also where the crudest graffiti is to be found. Alas, Ana Maria's soulful efforts at Vélez had been the exception.)

5. Behind one goal, backing on to an area of rough grassland (where it looked as if railway sidings had once beeen), lay an immense open terrace whose stepped expanse, had it been in Britain, would have been divided up by strictly delineated aisles and row upon row of crush barriers, set out at precisely calculated distances. Here there were no aisles and just two barriers; lonely, laughably inadequate sentinels in a sea of concrete supposed to hold 17,635 visiting supporters. Mariano had stood on this awesome bank on several occasions and, not surprisingly for a man of his years (forty) and demeanour, hated the *avalanchas*, or crowd surges, which its design patently encouraged. Worse, after matches, he told me, visiting supporters filing down on to the street alongside the ground were regularly pelted with stones by Independiente fans gathered in the corner terrace above the exit.

On the whole, therefore, I was glad to be viewing the stadium in its benign state of emptiness. In an empty stadium one can wander about in a state of mental abstraction and think only pleasant thoughts of the world.

6. Stacked up against a wall under the terrace, we discovered, was a pile of rusting seats, and, in among them and the gathering weeds, numerous Coca-Cola signs. Back in the stadium we saw why. There were brand-new Pepsi signs everywhere.

7. On the corner of the terrace furthest from the street a railway line passed by so close we could see what newspapers the passengers were reading as they trundled past.

8. One section of seats, marked *Vitalicios,* was reserved for life members of the club, who no longer have to pay for admission. The majority of stadiums in Buenos Aires possess such sections (though a desperate shortage of cash has led most clubs to phase out the favour in recent years). But not like this one, with red, ornately fashioned metal, tip-up seats complete with arm rests and curved backs, like cabriole armchairs. Another seated section was for women and children only. A third one specifically prohibited entry to minors. At Independiente you had to know your place.

9. As at Vélez, the moats were full of dank, algae-infested water and floating litter, but at Independiente there might have been an added ingredient. Unusually, the moats were situated on the stand side of the perimeter fences, rendering them perfectly placed to double as urinals. A sign on the fence overlooking the malodorous moat warned – redundantly, I felt – 'Danger. Don't jump'.

10. Last but not, as they say, least, according to a brass plaque on a side wall the cantilevered roofs which covered the rear sections of two sides of the pitch dated back to the stadium's inauguration in 1928. Now, for stadium buffs this was definitely information worthy of note. Cantilevered, or column-free, roofs were a major advance for stadium designers when they first appeared in the 1920s (mainly in continental Europe, though not at any British football ground until the late 1950s). They freed the spectator from having to peer around columns, and they looked pretty neat too. The roofs at Independiente, painted white and so simple and elegant in form, were not only very early examples, they were also reputedly part of the first reinforced concrete structures to have been erected at any South American stadium, and were thus revered as historic monuments. I liked to think that this discovery counted as both information and knowledge.

As Mariano and I departed – or rather, as Mariano dragged me away, because I was, I confess, quite smitten – the man who looked like Harpo Marx rushed out with a gift. It was a red Independiente shirt with the name of the striker Ruggieri (Gabriel Hernán Cela Ruggieri, to give him his full name) on the back. Did I tell you that Independiente had chosen red as their colours as a homage to Nottingham Forest, who visited Buenos Aires in 1905? Whatever, the shirt is now in the proud possession of my late brother's daughter, my niece, who is beyond doubt the only girl in Birmingham to own such a shirt, and who, like most of her generation, seems quite unfazed by wearing synthetic garments next to the skin. (I mention the shirt only because there was a recent row in Buenos Aires when the coach, I think of River Plate, scolded his players for swapping shirts with members of the opposition at the end of matches. Did they not understand how sacred these shirts were? To which the coach of Independiente replied that he couldn't understand what the fuss was about. Anyone could buy one of their shirts for thirty pesos, and they were most welcome to do so. I only hope for my niece's sake that surplus supplies don't reach Birmingham. Exclusivity is important when one is twelve years old.)

In addition to the shirt the Independiente man gave me a glossy brochure about the club. This might not seem like much. Such brochures are common at European and American clubs. But in Latin America they are a mark of rare sophistication. On one page was an article entitled *'Un nuevo estadio para el siglo XXI'*. By the year 2000, it said, Independiente would be playing in a brand-new stadium to be built somewhere out near the motorway leading to La Plata. This new wonder, based upon a stadium already built in Ecuador, would hold no fewer than 107,200 spectators.

Now that the year 2000 is upon us, I hesitate to enquire whether work has actually started on the new stadium, knowing that, if it has, the wonderfully eccentric Estadio Almirante Cordero would be no more. But I see that the club's website mentions nothing of a new stadium, and somehow, knowing of the parlous state of most Argentinian clubs' finances, I doubt that anything concrete, reinforced or otherwise, has or will develop, at least not for some time. As they say in Buenos Aires, *'espera sentado'*. Take a seat while you wait.

On the other hand, Independiente are the club of the

Argentinian Football Association's president, the all-powerful Julio Grondona, who also happens to be a mover and shaker in FIFA circles. His brother Hector is now the Independiente president. In other words, nothing can be ruled out.

One other fact I learnt from the glossy brochure concerned the origins of the club's name. Around the turn of the century, employees working at an Avellaneda department store called 'The City of London' decided to form a team. Since not all the staff could get a game, a chap in the shoe department decided to form his own, breakaway team. Independiente were thus born on 1 January 1905. I was unable to find out anything about Almirante Cordero, other than the fact that the street which runs alongside Independiente's stadium is named after him. Branching off this street were three short cul-de-sacs lined by single-storey houses. At the end of these cul-de-sacs stood the imposing but troubled home of Racing, the Estadio Juan Domingo Perón. Yes, him again.

Wednesday, 21 October. 12.00. Stadium No. 11. Racing.

The plight of Racing Club de Avellaneda – 'Rassing Cloob de Avejyaneda' – is one of the longest-running sagas in Argentinian football. In essence, after years of gross mismanagement by a succession of unpopular presidents, in 1998 the club – once one of the great clubs of world football – went spectacularly bankrupt, owing something in the region of $60–80 million. Throughout the years of decline, support dipped alarmingly, to as little as 15,000 at one point. The number of *socios*, or members, always a barometer of a club's health and wealth, fell almost as dramatically, to just over 20,000 (compared with, say, the 51,000 claimed by Independiente).

Here, at Racing, was a club – an institution, no less – which seemed to encapsulate so many of the ills of modern-day Argentina. But the rot bore a deeper resonance. For Racing had once been the darling club of the Peronist movement. And now, as Mariano remarked, 'The club is just like Peronism itself: a mess, with no sense of direction.'

How different it had once been. Formed in 1903, the club was named, on the suggestion of one of the founders, who was of French descent, after a Paris motoring journal. (A rugby club called the Racing Club de France took a similar fancy to the title, as did a football club in Brussels, and who can blame them?)

Between 1913 and 1919 Racing won seven championships in succession, before, in the 1940s, their cause was famously taken up by General Perón, or at least by his government. According to Mariano, in order to win favour among the working classes during his early political career, Perón first professed his support for Boca Juniors, the club in the dock area of Buenos Aires. But later, as president, he could ill afford to show a preference one way or another, so he affected to espouse neutrality. In reality, however, his government seemed to bend over backwards to help Racing, who, in the process, won a trio of championships in 1949, 1950 and 1951.

The agent of this quite unsporting policy of favouritism was Perón's finance minister, Ramón Cereijo, who at least made no secret of his affiliations. (Mariano said that for a while Racing were derided by their envious rivals as Sportivo Cereijo.) True, several Argentinian clubs, such as River Plate, Vélez and Boca, also benefited from government loans to build new stadiums during the 1930s and 1940s. But Racing appeared to benefit the most. Hence the opening of the club's lavish new Estadio Juan Domingo Perón in September 1950, an event attended by both Perón and Evita. As a matter of honour its capacity was, of course, stated as 100,000.

The design is typical of the era. Like the Maracana Stadium in Rio de Janeiro, which opened ten weeks earlier, it forms a perfect circle, which looks fine from the air but results in lousy sightlines, since so many spectators on the sides are miles from the touchlines. Also like the Maracana its lower tier consists of a ring of virtually flat terracing, where the sightlines are at their poorest. Deep moats surround the pitch, intruding into the terraces to form semicircular abutments on both sides of the pitch (so that the turf has the shape of the London Underground logo). Unlike the Maracana there was no roof at first, but then weren't all the spectators in Perón's shade anyway?

Despite the lack of cover, and although River and Boca fans would probably disagree, the General's new monument was probably the most advanced and complete stadium yet seen in Argentina. It was also instantly identifiable by a slender, tapering concrete tower, attached to one side of the bowl and resembling a giant submarine periscope. Stadium towers were all the rage during the Thirties and Forties, and this one, I had always thought from photographs, is, in its minimalist form, one of the finest of the era (along with those at Florence, Montevideo and Helsinki). I was certainly determined to climb to the viewing gallery at its summit.

But as we approached the Racing stadium's dusty concrete exterior under the searing glare of the mid-day sun, our prospects for entry to any part of the complex, let alone the tower, did not look promising. All the gates were locked, and other than a sinister-looking armed guard in wraparound sunglasses, no one else was around. Outside, a deathly quiet filled the narrow side streets, lined by terraced houses and warehouses. On the pavement opposite, a filthy man cooked chorizo on a filthy grill, despite the apparent lack of any passing trade. Mariano feared for the safety of his dad's battered old Toyota. I, selfishly, feared for the completion of our schedule.

So we walked right around the block, found no other entrances, and went back to persuade the guard of our friendly intent. Though not in the mood for small talk, eventually he relented, though – bah! – he absolutely refused to let us go up the tower and, worse, didn't appear to be remotely susceptible to a bribe.

The stadium's fully enclosed, shadowy interior quite took me back, more so because of its tone. Whereas Independiente's red and white had thrown out a warm, welcoming hue, Racing's colours of light blue and white – the same as the national team's – created a cooler, almost sparse impression. On the upper tier was a ring of blue and white seats arranged in stripes. All the walls, terrace steps and concrete barriers were painted in a shade of matt, air-force blue. Or was it battleship grey? Whichever, the effect was chilling. Maybe I was reading too much into the Peronist link, but to me this seemed like a stadium with a distinctly military air. That tower, too, peering down on us . . . Was there someone up there, following our movements?

We felt even more uncomfortable when we reached the upper tier. With our every step Mariano and I could feel the concrete beneath our feet move, ever so slightly. With a full, animated crowd in attendance, practising the art of what structural experts call 'synchronised excitation', the tier must have vibrated as unnervingly as those wooden bleachers at Ferrocarril. Then Mariano told me more of the stadium's recent history.

Apparently, one of the factors behind Racing's decline had

been the closure of the stadium for three years between 1982 and 1985, when, wouldn't you know it, structural faults were discovered in the upper tier. Deficiencies such as these are actually common in South America – the Maracana suffered similarly – largely as a consequence of shoddy work when the stadiums were first constructed, followed by sloppy maintenance thereafter. But while Racing were forced to play at other stadiums, horror of horrors, they were relegated for the first time in their history. They soon returned to the first division, but the upper tier was passed for use again only in 1997, by which time a group of wealthy Racing fans had loaned the club sufficient funds to add a lightweight roof around the bowl. So now Racing fans had a roof over their heads, the consequence of which was that they were now faced with the very real possibility of losing their entire stadium and maybe even the debt-ridden club itself. No wonder the floor was shaking.

Racing's *sede* (or club headquarters) was a short drive away in a modernist block on the main thoroughfare running through the busy centre of Avellaneda. By the entrance, in a recess at street level, were two shiny bronze busts of Mr and Mrs Perón, both half-smiling in the direction of passers-by. Remarkably, neither bust was protected behind glass or a barrier, and yet there wasn't a hint of graffiti anywhere around them. Such, still, was the Peróns' hold upon the masses that not even their bitterest opponents dared to sully their presence.

Inside, the *sede* had been treated to a bit of post-modern tarting up, lending it the air of an arts club, in real contrast to the austerity of the stadium. But upstairs creaking institutionalism hung on. The entire length of the lobby was filled by a groaning trophy cabinet, which I confess I did admire, if only for its evocation of past glories and future uncertainties. One cup on display was a replica of the World Club Championship trophy, won infamously by Racing in 1967 after three bruising encounters against Celtic. I was twelve at the time, and can still recall the fuzzy black-and-white images of Celtic's goalkeeper, Ronnie Simpson, being knocked out by a missile catapulted from the crowd behind the goal before the match had even started. That was in the stadium we had just visited. How we British fulminated against those hot-headed Latins! First Rattin at Wembley in 1966. Now Ronnie Simpson at Racing in 1967. But Dame Fortune did not let the matter rest. Since 1967 Racing had won not a single championship.

Dora, in Racing's press office, agreed to speak to us, but it was clear she was in a difficult position. We sat in her echoing office, surrounded by metal shelves full of dusty, leather-bound volumes. On her desk was a grimy telephone and a posy of plastic flowers. We could have been in Bucharest, circa 1970.

After declaring itself bankrupt, Dora explained, the club was being run by a state judge and a new syndicate. Rumours were thick on the ground. There had even been a motion in parliament proposing that Racing be declared part of the national heritage. Debtors were meanwhile anxiously awaiting news of what, if anything, they might salvage from the wreckage of the previous administration. No doubt her own pay cheques were lost somewhere in the bureaucratic mire too.

Dora was sure she had a history of the club somewhere, in this drawer, no, in that drawer, no, in a polythene bag by her desk. Definitely in there somewhere. Oh yes, there it was. Success! But this was her only copy and the photocopier was broken. Of course. So I gave her my business card and she promised to forward more information. Even as she took the card Mariano and I knew full well that it would be stuck in a drawer and forgotten.

As we left the Racing *sede* I noticed a youth brazenly sporting a red shirt entering the building. I thought him either stupid or daring, going in there wearing an Independiente shirt. But as we turned to look again I saw that the shirt was in fact that of the other Red Devils. The English ones. Manchester United.

'Jesus!' I cried out to Mariano. 'Is nowhere on this planet safe?'

Wednesday, 21 October. 14.00. Stadium No. 12. Boca Juniors.
Back on the road, Mariano and I were discussing a phenomenon described by behaviourists as 'the culture of faking it'. This, they say, is most clearly manifest at times of mass grieving or hysteria, such as occurred in Britain at the time of Princess Diana's death. It is not a denial of genuine sorrow or hurt, but, rather, recognition of the process by which individuals who are not so deeply affected by an event may nevertheless fake or exaggerate emotion in order to maintain social acceptability. The phenomenon has been

increasingly associated with football. A game is lost, and with it, apparently, all hope. Fans weep openly in the stadium (to the particular delight of television directors). To react phlegmatically or with a simple huff is no longer enough. To be a true supporter one has to suffer, or, at least, to be seen to suffer.

Much as I love my own team, Aston Villa, their deficiencies have not caused me to throw any real tantrums since my teenage years. I can get over a defeat now in less than an hour or three. I can hardly bring myself even to hate our rivals, Birmingham City. I may actively dislike City, but I'm sure that is more because they play in blue and white – to which I have an aesthetic aversion – rather than the fact that, as some Villa fans might say, they are an uncultured bunch of cheapskate no-hopers who have not been good enough to play in the same division as Villa for as long as anyone can remember (which in my case, with a head stuffed full of stadium information, is not that long at all). If this confession opens me to accusations of indifference or fecklessness, then so be it. I, for one, refuse to fake it.

But I could see that Mariano, a fan of River Plate, seemed to be genuinely uncomfortable as we neared the home of Boca Juniors. One of his academic friends, Klaus Gallo, had told me that Argentinian football supporters are fundamentalists rather than fanatics. But I still sort of assumed that that description would not apply to middle-class, liberal, university educated *porteños*.

'Oh, come on,' I pleaded with Mariano. 'I know Boca are River's big rivals and all that, but, really, we're only going to visit their stadium. It's not as if you'll be forced to swear false allegiance or undergo any interrogation.'

But he was having none of it. 'No, really,' he insisted as, down by the docks, we were confronted by a sign saying WELCOME TO THE REPUBLIC OF LA BOCA. 'I feel like a spy going into enemy territory. I really feel as if they will smell River on me.'

Nor, Mariano insisted, was he faking it. He told me some of the derogatory names that River fans give to Boca supporters. The most common was *los bosteros*, the dung collectors. There was also a favourite song, referring to Boca's proximity to the Riachuela. Inevitably the song sounded better in Spanish. In English it went, 'La Boca, La Boca is flooded, and all of the Bocas are covered in shit.'

I had not seen this side of Mariano before. But I was not

shocked. More, amused. He really wasn't faking it. He really did hate Boca.

In Argentina, whichever other team you might support, you have also to choose between either Boca or River. I dared not tell Mariano that on balance, even though Boca play in blue – albeit softened by yellow – I would probably have gone for Boca, if only because I thought their stadium was more interesting than River's. Not better, mind. Just more interesting. Indeed, I had wanted to visit it for some years, and often felt that my footballing education could never be quite complete without doing so.

But by the end of our visit I could understand, if not share, Mariano's antipathy, all the same.

Boca means mouth, as in mouth of the river, and Boca Juniors are one of the mouthiest clubs imaginable. They were once, of course, the club of Maradona, a man who has never shrunk from voicing his opinions. Moreover, a follower of any other club cannot possibly appreciate the sheer depth of passion that underpins Boca's immense popularity. Boca, you see, you hear, you read all over the Boca area of the Cap. Fed., and far beyond, are not just a club, but a symbol, a mouthpiece even for the poor and dispossessed of old Buenos Aires. By supporting Boca the club's fans support themselves and honour their antecedents. River Plate are the fancy dans, the rich poseurs, whereas Boca Juniors let their football do the talking and leave their fans to make the noise. Boca call their fans *el jugador número doce*, the player number twelve. There is no substitute. They sing, '*Boca, te llevo en el alma y cada dia te quiero más*.' Boca, I keep you in my soul and I love you more each day.

And because of its box-like, many-layered appearance, they call their stadium *La Bombonera* – the Chocolate Box. What better feast for the mouth could there be?

La Bombonera is by far the most dominant structure in a dockside district known otherwise as one of the birthplaces of tango, and for its two-storeyed terraced houses made of brightly coloured, corrugated iron, a tradition begun by the area's mainly Genoese immigrants a century or more ago. (Boca Juniors are still known locally as Xeneise, from the original Italian dialect.) Thus you can see, gliding slowly through the narrow, tree-lined streets, air-conditioned coaches full of American tourists just *adoring* all the bright colours – so vibrant, so Latino – before they pass by *La*

Bombonera and no doubt coo over the very foreign, illicit nature of 'soccer' and that wild man they heard about during the 1994 World Cup. What was his name? Dee-ago Mara-donar. Oh yeh! The one who took drugs and had eyes like a muskrat caught in the headlights.

'Sheesh, why, there he is!'

And there he was indeed. In the midst of a garish, star-shaped mosaic on one wall of the stadium was a bronze plaque of Diago. One of twenty-one plaques honouring heroes of La Boca and the sponsors. Maradona at the top, then Batistuta, Rattin, Gatti *et al*, joined by Quilmes beer, Nike and the like.

Truly, we had arrived at a temple of honour, no less reverential than the honours boards once found at Olympia or the Colosseum, championing the great athletes or brave gladiators, but not forgetting to mention their wealthy patrons.

Hardly surprisingly, *La Bombonera* no more resembles a chocolate box than the LA Coliseum resembles the Colosseum. But it has some colourful wrappings. As well as the bronze plaques, along its street walls are stirring murals by Benito Quinquela Martin and Rómulo Macció, depicting the history of La Boca and its world-famous Juniors. A ship full of immigrants rides the waves. On the dockside, a wise old fisherman tells a footballer tales of the old country, while other Boca Juniors frolic under a nearby lamp-post. A group of players, local arists and musicians – Tiglio, Daneri, Quinquela, Menghi, Lacamera, Diomede and Lazzari – play on fiddles, guitars, a piano and *bandoneóns* (the accordions of tango halls) led by their favourite little balladeer, who is of course Diego Maradona (again). In another mural, Boca fans appear to be auditioning for the lead in Edvard Munch's painting 'Scream', each straining their jaw muscles to breaking point in order to express just how deeply they keep Boca in their souls and how much more their love for the club grows each day.

Mariano bristled visibly as he translated one of the accompanying tributes. It read, 'To the founders, the people, the artists; to the idols, to the tango and to the football that made La Boca the destiny and a myth.'

He was not finding this easy, so I shall leave it to the club's glossy brochure to relay the following story of how the club was formed by three youths in 1905.

'The founders of Boca', the brochure's English text reads, 'are almost childs, passionated footballer of a heterogeneous social whole that lived at that time in the natural entrance to Buenos Aires, its port.' (They were actually students at a Commercial College who had learnt the rudiments of football from an Irish teacher and ex-boxer called Paddy MacCarthy. That they chose the English name Juniors was largely a fashion statement. Several other clubs did the same around that time.)

Then the lads decided that their new club would adopt the colours of the country of the next ship to enter the port. Or, as the brochure put it, 'The way chosen by those young men had the uncertainty of the unknown, the melancholy look towards the horizon that certain time attracted their parents and an unequivocal way of paying tribute to the river that attented to their birth. It was the flag of the first ship that came in La Boca port that day the one that sealed the identity of the glorious singlet. Sweden, fate said, with blue and yellow forever.'

But if the club's translator still had some room for improvement, the same could not be said of *La Bombonera*. The stadium occupies a site so constrained that its stands are laid out in what I believe is a unique configuration. On three sides of what would otherwise be a standard, fully enclosed, rectangular stadium, it happily rises up to three, steep tiers. But on the fourth side, where houses line the street running immediately behind, there is only just room for one narrow block of viewing balconies, affectionately known as *palquitos* (little boxes) hugging the touchline along the length of the pitch.

Having always had a preference for discontinuity in stadium design, I was looking forward to seeing these oddities. For me, a perfectly uniform bowl is never as appealing as one that it is incomplete or interrupted by a stand of a contrasting shape or design.

But there was another feature of *La Bombonera* I was most keen to see at first hand: a slim, art deco tower which rose up from the centre of this fourth, truncated side of the stadium, and which for years had given the stadium a further stamp of distinction.

But when we arrived, I saw at once that the tower had gone. Gone! It seemed impossible but Mariano confirmed that I was looking in the right place and that my eyes were not deceiving me. The tower was no longer there. After the disappointment of not being able to go up Racing's splendid protruberance, now this.

Truly, I was having a bad tower day.

Ivan, from Boca's press office, explained what had occurred. In December 1995 Boca members elected a new president, Mauricio Macri, a young, moustachioed and extremely wealthy businessman who had genuinely supported the club all his life. ('Macri wants to turn Boca into another Manchester United,' Mariano whispered to me in an aside, knowing that I would disapprove.) Within days of his arrival, on 28 December, Macri ordered the demolition of the tower and the original *palquitos*. There was no debate, no consultation. Thus disappeared overnight one of the great icons of Argentinian football. All the fans could do was rush to the stadium and pick up whatever bits of the concrete they could retrieve for souvenirs. (Macri was thus not that savvy. Had he been the chairman of an English club he'd have had each lump of concrete mounted on a cheap plinth and sold at an obscene profit.)

In place of the tower and the old *palquitos* Macri constructed a new side to the stadium. Still unable to complete the bowl, since that would have required the purchase and demolition of the entire street behind the stadium, Macri's architects instead cleverly squeezed in a lower tier of 1,200 seats, above which rose four levels of new private boxes; one level being glazed in, the other three being modern, open-fronted *palcos*. (Not *palquitos*, note. The fans consider them far too posh to warrant this affectionate diminutive.) Brutally plain stair towers at either end flanked the new development, but there would be no central emphasis any more. Significantly or not, on a neighbouring building behind where the tower once stood was painted a mural in yellow and blue, visible from inside the stadium. In huge letters it read, '*Se viene . . . M. Macri, Presidente '95. Super Boca.*'

Altogether *El Presidente* spent some $10 million on his new luxury facilities, plus new seats for the rest of the stadium, the removal of the moat (though not the fences) and the construction of swish new offices, whose interior array of polished wood, subtle lighting and abstract art confirmed that Macri was not entirely an egotist without style. Even Mariano had to concede that much.

In addition to his wealth, Macri, the head of one of Argentina's top five industrial conglomerates, also possessed the touch of a showman. Once the new boxes were ready, in May 1996, Ivan explained, instead of selling the leases at set prices on a first-come, first-served basis, as is the norm, Macri decided on a brilliant piece of publicity. He put every box up for auction, and invited television cameras to cover the sale live.

The gamble paid off handsomely. Every single box and *palco* was sold, some at way above their true market value. The central, most luxurious suite went for $300,000 for a ten-year lease, sold via the telephone to a bidder called Maradona.

La Bombonera was definitely a stadium to be experienced full rather than empty. After clambering up to the uppermost rows, thighs aching with every step, we could see right over the docks and city, towards the Rio de la Plata. Down below us, on one side, were training pitches, a garden with its own Madonna, a small basketball arena (*La Bombonerita*) and a 100-bed hostel for young players. On all the other sides, Boca were trapped; by a railway line, by a bus station, by narrow streets.

For all Macri's genius, Boca were thus in the tightest possible corner. After the improvements he had financed in 1996, *La Bombonera* held just under 57,400, of which some 37,000 were still standing places, crammed into just a few sections of precipitous terracing. Ivan took us to one of these areas, the famous mid-tier terrace known as *La Doce*, behind one of the goals. Decked in yellow paint, presumably (from the stench) so as not to show up the floods of urine to which it was regularly subjected, this was where the famed Number 12 fans stood. Once seats were installed on these and the other remaining terraces behind the goals – as they had to be within the next few years (though Ivan and everyone else in Buenos Aires seemed somewhat vague as to the exact deadline) – the overall capacity of *La Bombonera* would tumble to just 38,000. Yet Boca had at least 40,000 *socios*, and regularly sold out their matches.

The club thus faced two choices: to relocate, no one knew where, which few *socios* wanted, or to buy up the street behind and finish off the bowl, as had been the long-term plan when the stadium was first opened, back in 1940.

In this respect, Boca appeared to have much in common with Arsenal football club in London. The Gunners too have only 38,000 seats, and have been agonising of late as to whether they should try to expand by impinging upon the property of their neighbours, or to swallow vast costs and move altogether. And like Arsenal, Boca have come up against enormous planning obstacles in trying to buy up neighbouring houses. When I suggested that, Boca being Boca, and Macri being Macri, and the houses in question being fairly modest (if colourful), surely there would be no problem, the exhalations, shaking of heads and the swivelling of palms in response confirmed that not even Boca were masters within their own republic. I was told the club had been trying to buy up the street for the best part of thirty years. 'Very political issue,' was the general verdict.

Driving away from *La Bombonera* in the mid-afternoon haze, Mariano – his strained expression visibly melting away with every block we put between us and La Boca – could not resist telling me a story. In 1970, he said, shortly after FIFA had announced that Argentina would host the 1978 World Cup, the president of Boca, Alberto J. Armando, announced that he would build a brand-new stadium for the club, one that would be perfect for staging the World Cup final (which was otherwise destined for *El Monumental*, home of Mariano's beloved River Plate). Armando even announced the time and date this new stadium would open: 11.00 a.m. on Independence Day, 25 May 1975, for a match between Boca Juniors and Boca reserves. The curtain-raiser, he declared, would take place, '*llueva o no llueva*'. Rain or no rain. From that day on he was known as Alberto '*llueva o no llueva*' Armando.

Naturally, at 11.00 a.m. on 25 May 1975 a group of River fans made the journey to the still vacant site, where they marked the occasion with a small ceremony enlivened by generous helpings of *schadenfreude*.

Mariano was not sure if it had rained at the time or not.

Wednesday, 21 October. 15.00. Stadium Nos. 13 and 14. Huracán and Barracas Central.

I started the day pondering Argentina's penchant for melancholia. Now, in the Parque Patricios district of the Cap. Fed., I fell once again into its sombre embrace.

After Boca, Mariano and I had driven south-west, crossing the widest avenue in the world, crossing the Avenida Vélez Sarsfield, to where, in a barren *barrio*, railway sidings cut a wide gash through an industrial hinterland. This corner of Parque Patricios, once the home of artists and actors, once a teaming centre of tango clubs, dance halls and bohemian cafés, presented itself as a wilderness of abandoned hope. Juggernauts heaved past us. Cars and buses sped through, there being nothing to stop for. Certainly not pedestrians. It was as though Mariano and I, trying to dodge the traffic to reach the Estadio Tomás Adolfo Ducó, were invisible. Across the tracks behind the stadium stood a prison. Somewhere beyond, the map showed, was a Coca-Cola bottling plant. Our limbs felt heavy. The afternoon light was fading.

Writing of this, several hours later, I am now so weary that in the quiet of the night, sitting here in Enrique's *departamento*, his beautiful, silent *departamento*, I find myself struggling to find the words to describe exactly the mood of the stadium that lay before me only this afternoon. I can give you some facts, some information, but I doubt my capacity to convey the sense of bathos which hung over the home of Club Atlético Huracán.

Let me just say this. Huracán means hurricane. The club formed in 1908. They were successful in the 1920s. The great Argentinian striker Guillermo Stabile, scorer of eight goals in the 1930 World Cup, wore the all-white strip of Huracán. So too, for one season, did the locally born young prodigy Alfredo di Stefano. In 1946 he came to Huracán on loan from River Plate, during which time he scored eleven goals in twenty-four appearances, including one goal deemed to be the fastest ever scored in Argentina, after just fifteen seconds of a match against, of all clubs, River.

At the time, Huracán were using the grounds of Ferrocarril and San Lorenzo, while their new stadium was being constructed. Finally, it was ready for action in September 1947 (by which time di Stefano had moved back to River), although the official inauguration would not be until November 1949. These, of course, were the boom years of General Perón. Government loans for new stadiums were readily available. Hope and glory filled the streets of the capital.

But although numerous stadiums were built during the period – at Racing, Boca, Veléz – none, I would guess, had the dignity of the Estadio Tomás Adolfo Ducó. Driving past the stadium's street frontage on Avenida Amancio Alcorta it would have been easy to mistake the façade for that of an office or an institution; a high school, perhaps. Only the word HURACAN, in red capitals on a brown brick background, under a white plastered, neoclassical pediment, caught the eye. Looking closer, I saw that displayed on either side of the central bay were the club's logo, a white air balloon with red borders, with a simple red H in its centre. Plain windows framed in white lined the upper three storeys of the façade. The ground floor, supported on red columns, formed a shadowy arcade, leading to the turnstiles.

Immediately I thought – again – of the Arsenal Stadium in Highbury, north London. No way am I an Arsenal supporter, but I do venerate their stadium (their now-threatened stadium, in fact), and here in Buenos Aires was that same, noble rectilinear symmetry, laced with touches of pure graphic imagery. Its architects must surely have been influenced by Highbury's 1930s art deco East Stand. Huracán's main stand was perhaps more understated, but it had a similar clarity and street presence. Yet there the comparison ended. Where Arsenal's façade remains today a symbol of establishment wealth, of corporate solidity and sporting verve, that of Huracán was depressingly bathed in dust and deterioration.

One rain-swept day in August 1955, less than eight years after its opening, Huracán's stadium came close to disaster. River Plate were using the venue while building work was carried out at *El Monumental*. Their match against San Lorenzo was only three minutes old when a section of one of the original stands collapsed, sending more than one hundred fans hurtling into the void below. Miraculously, no one died. The English referee, William Elliott, stopped the game, and Huracán were forbidden from using the stadium for another year.

Now it was entirely built from concrete.

When Mariano and I arrived, a reserve game was taking place. Huracán, said Mariano, were heading for relegation. Times were hard. A few club officials and hangers-on watched the game while Mariano and I wandered around at will, up and down the sweeping end terraces, along filthy, gloomy corridors, up and down blackened stairways liberally spotted with bird droppings.

But what tore my heart most of all was Huracán's tower – another tower; indeed, the most wondrous, melancholy tower I had ever seen at a stadium.

The stadium itself formed an almost seamless bowl. Crowning the central portion of the open tier opposite the main stand and forming the base of the tower was a white pavilion, reminiscent of a 1930s lido or seaside café. This had curving flanks and slender, overhanging concrete cornices, their edges picked out playfully in red, as were the frames of the viewing galleries. On almost every white surface of the pavilion appeared the names of former Huracán heroes, among them, Guillermo Stabile. Then above the base, three parallel tapering masts formed the tower, reaching up as if in search of redemption, into the grey skies above. If these masts had once been painted white, the colour had long since worn away, to reveal bare, stained concrete below. A rusting flagpole topped each mast.

I know so little about Huracán, and yet those towers, like abandoned rockets on a museum launch pad, filled me with an unaccountable sorrow. There are few sights more mournful in sport than a once proud stadium reduced to penury and distress, and few architectural styles more likely to evoke loss and disappointment than the streamlined, smooth surety of art deco, racked by neglect and the ravages of time.

Mariano and I left immediately after our wanderings. There was no one available to talk, and we hadn't the energy to find the club's headquarters. Maybe if we had, our gloom would have lifted. Instead, we walked towards the railway sidings behind the stadium, on the other side of which, we could see, was the small ground of Barracas Central, a small club in Primera C, the fourth division. A misshapen woman in a deck chair outside her ramshackle house by the sidings saw us hesitate by a sign which warned people not to cross the lines. There were no trains in sight. Some of the rails were barely visible in the long grass.

'Cross!' she prompted us. 'Go on!'

We crossed, gingerly.

There was nothing much to see at Barracas Central – their *cancha* was broadly comparable to that of Sacachispas – but as we turned, to head back across the railway lines towards the main road, we saw the back of the Huracán stadium, on the side where the tower rose up above the sidings. I had supposed the rear elevation would be unadorned. Who, after all, would ever see it from this viewpoint, other than inmates of the prison, a few passing engine drivers and the woman in her shack?

And yet the detail on the rear of the stand was a mirror image of the club's main street frontage. Except with one difference. On this side there was hardly a window intact, or a hint of colour to be seen. Instead, the entire structure was coated in thick, brown dust, and, along its base, in graffiti and grime. Weeds sprouted from the brickwork and plaster. Litter blew about along the pavement, whipped up like a cliché by the occasional passing truck on its way to or from one of the nearby warehouses.

Here was abandoned splendour. Here was a building, once regarded with pride, now rotting unseen in a back alley (which somehow made its decay all the more poignant and cruel). Here, and it is the only word I can find to express the aching in my heart when I saw it, was pure *tristesse*. In Spanish, *tristeza*. In English, what? Sadness? No, more. Melancholy.

We drove back into town saying little. I was beginning to understand the expression,'*Buenos Aires me mata*'.

11 ROD AND RON DOWN UNDER

Frank telephones. He wants to know, have I visited the new stadium at such-and-such a place?

I have.

'So what did you think?'

I know why Frank is calling, which is why I won't tell you his real name. 'Frank' is a stadium architect, and obviously he did not design the new stadium at such-and-such a place. He'd have liked to, but a rival architectural practice won the contract instead. So instantly I know what the call is about. Frank is hoping I'll tell him how much I dislike the new stadium at such-and-such a place. How boring it is. How it fails on this count and that count, and how cheap and nasty and derivative it looks.

Honestly, architects are such bitches. Tarts, too. Unless fantastically successful and therefore able to pick and choose their commissions, architects will pretty much work for anyone, and then justify the servile relationship they have entered by assuring themselves that the client from hell who is now paying their fees – they hope – is not such a bad egg really.

So architects and freelance writers such as myself really do have a great deal in common; and, boy, when we get together do we love, love, love to gossip.

Even so, I was rendered almost speechless when, having just arrived in Sydney to visit Stadium Australia – the main venue for the 2000 Olympics, whose construction was then nearing completion – someone let slip that two of the leading stadium architectural practices in the world were merging.

'But . . .' I gasped, 'after all the things they've said about each other privately over the years . . . '

'Yeh, but . . .' came the reply. Way of the world and all that.

Architects are forever entering marriages of convenience, forming new alliances, changing their line-ups. In many ways they're like rock bands, continually re-inventing themselves in order to stir up the creative mix.

Nevertheless, that the world's largest sports architectural firm, the American HOK Sports Facilities Group, was now joining up with Lobb Sports Architecture, a London-based company that had led the Stadium Australia design team, to form a new giant called – unsurprisingly, HOK+LOBB – was, in my world at least, a bit of a . . . no, one hell of a bombshell. Indeed, it was the biggest bit of gossip I had heard for years. In stadium-design circles it was the equivalent of Nike and Adidas, or Mark McCormack and Don King, joining forces. In other words, BIG big.

The trade press would soon be calling the new conglomerate 'the dream team'. Before the merger – under the portentous title of the World Stadium Team – HOK and Lobb had already been working together on the highly controversial designs for the new Wembley Stadium, alongside that beacon of the British architectural scene, Sir Norman Foster. They had also collaborated several years earlier on the master plan for the new Croke Park in Dublin, with Des McMahon, whom we bumped into in Chapter 8.

But if the HOK and Lobb merger was headline news within the relatively narrow confines of the stadium industry, in the sporting press it went almost entirely unreported. Because, frankly, who in the sporting world gives a damn about architects? Certainly, in the past at least, not many of the sports clubs who hire them. The pioneering American architect, Louis Sullivan, famously stated in 1896 that 'form follows function'. Thereafter, British architect Richard Rogers rued the fact that in the late twentieth century, more often than not, 'form follows profit'.

And in the early 1990s the obscure writer Simon Inglis, after having visited yet another mundane new stadium – maybe even the aforementioned one at such-and-such a place – concluded that, in all too many instances of sporting architecture, 'form follows whatever the club chairman's builder pal from the Rotary Club could come up with at a cut-price'.

Indeed for many years, within British sport especially, stadium architects were looked down upon with almost as much contempt as journalists. Architects, so the boardroom (and bar room) experts had us believe, hold highfaluting ideas, use arcane jargon and invariably end up costing the client vastly inflated fees for buildings which, in the end, do not function properly. (That the clubs who chose not to use decent architects also tended to end up with poorly functioning buildings somehow never seemed to matter. Crap designs they may have been, but at least they were cheap crap.)

Since the early 1990s British attitudes have softened, partly helped by the popular reception accorded to a number of new stands and stadiums built in the wake of the 1989 Hillsborough disaster. But even in loftier architectural circles, designing for spectator sport has frequently been dismissed as a specialist area offering scant prestige. As purists might ask rhetorically, did Frank Lloyd Wright or Mies van der Rohe ever do a stadium? Or Walter Gropius or Le Corbusier? And of course they did not (though how fascinating to see the results if they had).

Occasionally a respected name has dipped his nib into the ink-well of sporting design: Tony Garnier at Lyons in the 1920s, Pier Luigi Nervi at Florence in the 1930s, and Renzo Piano at Bari, in the late 1980s. And there have been some genuinely acclaimed Olympic stadiums: for example, Jan Wils' design for Amsterdam in 1928 and my own favourite, Torben Grut's fantastical, brooding stadium of brick and wood built for the 1912 Olympics in Stockholm.

More recently, surely few people over the age of thirty would not be able to identify a photo of Frei Otto and Günter Behnisch's Olympic Stadium for Munich in 1972, with its famous translucent, tent-like structures, or Roger Taillibert's giant concrete clam of a stadium for Montreal, dominated by its ominous, sci-fi tower. (For their part, Montreal taxpayers may wish they could forget it, but alas they are still paying off the massive debt incurred by the city's ill-fated hosting of the Games in 1976.)

But the fact remains that despite being lauded by architectural critics, from a spectator's or operator's point of view, the stadiums at Munich and Montreal, and at Lyons, Florence and Bari too, display serious deficiencies. In those instances, form had not followed function. They were, instead, examples of what sceptics have called 'structural exhibitionism'.

You might ask, why all this concern with the architecture of a stadium? Surely, as long as the action is entertaining and the building is safe and reasonably comfortable, why should the aesthetics matter?

This one question has dominated my professional life, and its answer is one I find myself continually rehearsing. But the essence of my response never changes. If one accepts that sporting endeavour is as important an outlet for human expression as, say, the theatre or cinema, fine art or music, why shouldn't the buildings in which we celebrate this outlet be as grand and as inspirational as those we would expect, and demand, in those other areas of our cultural life? Indeed, one could argue that because stadiums are, in many instances, far more popular than theatres or art galleries, we should actually devote more, and not less, attention to their form. Stadiums have frequently been referred to as 'cathedrals'. Football has often been dubbed 'the opera of the people'. What better way, therefore, to raise the general public's awareness and appreciation of quality design than to offer them the very best buildings in the one area of life that seems to touch them the most? Could it even be that better stadiums might just make for better citizens?

But then maybe, as my detractors have labelled me in the past, I am a snob. Maybe I should just accept that sport, and its associated accoutrements and products, is an essentially tacky and ephemeral business, while stadium design is all too often driven by pragmatists and penny-pinchers.

Certainly, when I first started writing about stadium architecture in the early 1980s – after studying the history of architecture at university – one of the first and most uncomfortable truths I had to confront (apart from the most basic truth of all, that to be a stadium buff was to be regarded in most polite circles as nerdishly eccentric) was that some of the most popular stadiums in the world were also amongst the least attractive or innovative in architectural terms. 'Worthy but predictable' has usually won more votes than 'daring and different'. Old Trafford football ground in Manchester. The Yankee Stadium in New York. Ellis Park in Johannesburg. The list is long and is not intended to suggest that these are necessarily poor buildings. Rather, that each has derived its reputation more from the events it has staged, from its associations, than from the actual form it takes.

Equally, those stadiums whose forms have been revered – such as the Maracana in Rio, or the San Siro in Milan – have turned out to be rather poorly designed in several respects, once one analyses them not as icons but as functioning 'public assembly facilities' (to use the current jargon). Finding the balance between beauty and practicality has never been easy.

Two recently completed stadiums in Europe illustrate this dilemma further.

Ooh, you should hear what fellow professionals in the business are saying about the so-called 'state-of-the-art' Amsterdam Arena (opened in 1996) and the Stade de France (1998) in Saint-Denis, just outside Paris. Barely concealing their joy that design faults have been exposed in two such landmark projects, rival stadium architects have gone to town and back in their eagerness to point out that, of course, they would have done better.

But don't imagine for a minute that you would find me posing as 'holier than thou' in the midst of these nit-picking interchanges. Oh no, I'll bitch with the best, given half a chance. That concrete moat around the pitch at Amsterdam, for example. What a passion killer. And the external colour scheme, yuk! And don't even mention the dying turf or the dreadful acoustics. And as for that system they have at Saint-Denis for moving the lower tier of seats in and out over the athletics track. Or the concourse toilets. Did they get the tea lady to design them?

Sometimes, I accept, this *schadenfreude* can get out of hand. The Stade de France is, after all, a fine-looking edifice, and the French did win the World Cup there, so doesn't that count for more than queues for the loos? And if the Amsterdam Arena has its faults, as was always likely given that it was the first stadium in the world to feature both a retractable roof and a natural pitch, shouldn't we applaud its Dutch designers for making such a bold leap into the unknown? Goodness knows, as I write, a legion of rival designers, in the United States, in Europe and Japan, are working on refined versions of that Amsterdam original. Lobb, for example, have just seen their latest attempt unveiled in Cardiff: the 72,500-capacity Millennium Stadium, Britain's first venue with a retractable roof. Is it perfect? No, it is not, though fortunately it is a good deal better than Amsterdam. But the next one of its type will be better still. And so on.

Moreover, as any architect or engineer knows only too well, perfection is an elusive and cruel master. There are few sites without limitations (such as at Beirut) or local obstacles (Eden Park), and few clients unencumbered by political baggage (Mumbai) or by financial constraints (anywhere you care to mention). Every new building, be it a stadium, hospital, school, library or whatever, is, ultimately, a compromise.

If truth be told, these competing interests and tensions may often turn out to be far more compelling then the routine complexities of a stadium's design. Indeed, the fact that a particular stadium is completed at all is sometimes far more remarkable than its actual appearance. Like sport itself, the business of building stadiums is highly competitive, with winners and losers, frequent clashes of personality and moments of controversy, long periods of preparation and sudden bursts of activity. Then, when the final product is unveiled, there is always a sense of triumph and delight tinged with the regret that still, it could have been better. As they say in sport, 'You're only as good as your last game.' For architects, read, 'You're only as good as your last building.'

So it's a tough old world out there, catching the eye, winning contracts, satisfying every different interest group. And for an architect in the stadium world it's nowhere near good enough to know where it's at. You have to be at least one step ahead.

Which brings me back to Sydney, on one blustery week in the middle of an Australian summer. For if there are two architects in the world whose views on stadium design I will happily listen to with the utmost respect – if not necessarily always in agreement – it would have to be Rod Sheard, the erstwhile chairman of Lobb, and Ron Labinksi, a senior director of HOK. And now both were passing through Sydney, at the beginning of what they hoped would be a beautiful friendship.

Knowing the importance of the merger I didn't feel at all put out when told I wouldn't be able to interview Rod Sheard for a few days – obviously he was preoccupied – or that Ron Labinski's arrival in Sydney meant I wouldn't be able to bed down at the Lobb company flat in north Sydney, as Rod had promised when we'd last talked in London. No sweat. Instead, I happily found a cheap motel near Bondi Beach which turned out, according to locals, to be doubling as a brothel, and was run by a woman who made Basil Fawlty seem like a paragon of diplomacy. (One morning, when I must have taken a nano-second too long to glance at a bill, she remarked caustically, 'Yeh, we had a Jewish chap here last week. He questioned the bill too.')

Still, had I gone to north Sydney instead I would not have been so forcefully and enjoyably reminded of why it is that I so love stadiums.

Someone else has already written that 'All the world's a stage', so it's probably too late for me to claim that 'All the world's a stadium'. Besides, only selected parts of the world are like a stadium.

The steps of a brownstone building overlooking a pavement are like small grandstands. So are the tables of a street café, looking out over a town square, or the balconies in shopping centres, looking down on to the concourses below. 'The girls watch the boys watch the girls watch the boys watch the girls go by.'

Eye to eye. I to I.

You see, kittens and puppies and frolicking baa-baa lambs are all very well for a few minutes' light entertainment. Landscapes and sunsets are wonderfully diverting and occasionally inspirational. But of all God's creatures and natural phenomena, *homo sapiens* is infinitely the most compelling creation of all. Whether running, jumping, kicking, hitting, singing, dancing, falling over, talking, walking, or simply just standing there looking good, or prattish, we humans are fabulously interesting to look at. We just can't help ourselves. You get the picture?

You are the picture.

Now here's another. Imagine the sweep of a beach. A perfect crescent. Sparkly-lit promenade to the west, oceanic horizon to the east. Promontories at either end. An orange sun is dropping almost imperceptibly out of a salmon-streaked, violet sky. Out on the surf, bobbing, bobbling creatures dance fitfully in the foam. Eyes adjust. The creatures are men. Ten, fifteen, maybe twenty of them, on boards, surfing towards the shore in a line. Jinking, gliding, stumbling, crashing. One holds a dog. One juggles. One kneels backwards, another goes bottom first. Others stay erect, the lucky and skilful ones beaming triumphantly as they hit the warm, squishy sand, still standing on their boards, undefeated by the waves.

A nice enough picture, I hope you will agree, except that save for numbers tied to their backs, every single one of the surfers was stark bollock naked.

For this was the annual 'Nude Surfers' Night' on Bondi Beach, where I ended up purely by chance one evening, and where on the sand, on the perfect crescent of warm, squishy sand, there were around 8,000 of us, male and female, young and old, straight and gay; spectators all in one of the finest natural stadiums in the world.

Why were we all there? The women for the men? The men for the men? The men for the women? Or because the event was just too absurdly wonderful to miss? I don't have the answer. I was just a spectator. This was just a stadium, of sorts. But I definitely wasn't there for the sport. I was there for the event, and for its setting.

The following morning I went to Homebush Bay, the site of the main Olympic Games complex.

To put it politely I am no great admirer of the Olympics as an event, or, rather, of the insane pressures its past bidding procedures have placed upon candidate cities (before the most recent scandals forced a rethink at least). Nor, as a spectator, do I much enjoy the bloated Games programme and the consequent demands this places upon the designers of stadiums. All that expenditure and effort to provide a gilded, one-off stage for drug-fuelled cheats does no one a service, least of all the honest athletes, or the viewing public, who otherwise seem relatively indifferent towards attending live athletics events (though they apparently love the opening and closing ceremonies). Hold the Games, if we must, say I, in Greece every four years, as did the ancients, and be done with the whole travelling circus.

Yet in my calmer moments it would be churlish to deny that, if approached sensibly and imaginatively, the opportunity to stage the Games can yield enormous benefits in the long term (as well they should, considering the expenditure involved), if not for sport then at least for the cause of urban regeneration. Following in Barcelona's footsteps, Sydney was undoubtedly going about its urban regeneration in a wholly impressive way. To an outsider the 760-hectare site at Homebush Bay, once the home of an abattoir, a racecourse, brickworks and light industrial units, seems miles from anywhere – it is actually fifteen kilometres from the city centre – though, fair dinkum, it is in fact pretty much in the heart of the city's extensive conurbation. Some £1.3 billion worth of construction and reclamation has been commissioned, all of it, crucially, with an eye to post-Olympic usage. Strict guidelines, studiously monitored by Greenpeace, have ensured that the 2000 Games should be the most environmentally friendly ever (though inevitably not friendly enough for Greenpeace's liking). What's more, much of the work is good-looking, distinctive and lively. 'That's a reflection of the Australian spirit,' I was told, and when the sun did finally break out I believed it.

All right, so bitter controversy had shrouded the handling of advance ticket sales. There has been an uproar among residents about Bondi being taken over for weeks on end by the Olympics' beach volleyball tournament. Scandalous behaviour in IOC circles had not helped the cause much either. But at Homebush itself I found the place to be buzzing like no other Olympic complex I have ever encountered. The Aquatic Centre had just recorded its five-millionth visitor in four years of operation (this in a city of four million inhabitants). The new Sydney Showground – a round, 12,000-seat stadium scheduled to stage the Olympic baseball competition – had already held its first Royal Easter Show, attracting 1.26 million visitors (human ones, that is; I don't have figures for the livestock). That was the show's highest attendance for fifty-one years. During my visit the Showground was being set up for a rock concert.

In other parts of the Homebush site a 21,000-seat indoor arena was in mid-construction. Both the hockey centre and warm-up athletics stadium were ready, and work was just about to begin on the tennis centre, with its 10,000-seat Centre Court. Meanwhile, several of the other Olympic halls were packed with shoppers attending a sale, and the visitors' centre (in the abattoir's former administration building) was, despite the iffy weather, packed to the gills.

By August 1999 the Olympic Co-ordination Authority reckoned the site had clocked up nearly 20 million visitors, and that was still thirteen months before the Games even began. If there was widespread public cynicism about the Games and their spiralling costs, therefore, there was, at Homebush at least, a sense that the Olympics had offered a bloody good excuse to provide a new focus for the hyperactive, pleasure-seeking folk of Sydney. After all, if they're prepared to turn up in such numbers to watch a bunch of nude blokes surfing, then surely they'll turn out for anything.

At the centre of Homebush lay the main venue for the Olympics, Stadium Australia.

Now I have enough information on this single structure alone to bore you rigid with pages and pages of facts and figures, most of which in any case you can find out from the Internet or from Olympic hand-outs. But the following should be enough to irritate your friends when there's a lull in the televised coverage of the Games.

Stadium Australia is the largest Olympic stadium yet built, with a capacity of 110,000. On its opening day in 1999 it broke two records: the 104,583 spectators formed the largest crowd ever to attend a rugby league match, and between them they drank more beer than has ever been consumed at a single sporting event, thanks not only to the legendary capacities of their antipodean bladders but to the installation of a high-tech piped system capable of pouring a heady total of 85,000 pints per hour. This system is apparently called the Joy Machine.

Sydney does not need such a large athletics stadium once the Olympics have ended. Routine athletics events simply do not draw the crowds (which is a cruel joke in itself given the scope of the IOC and IAAF to make demands on athletics' behalf). In Atlanta in 1996, half of the Olympic stadium consisted of temporary seats. These were removed after the Games and the permanent half was converted into a baseball park. At Sydney, once the track is dug up, the two uncovered end stands, each holding 14,000 seats, will be demolished. The lower tiers on all four sides will then be reconfigured, the ends covered, and a final capacity of 80,000 created. Two sides of the lower tier will be retractable, so that the stadium can stage rugby and soccer, plus Australian Rules Football (known as AFL), which requires a larger, oval pitch. This last fact is significant, as will soon be revealed.

The stadium was funded by means of a BOOT (Build, Own, Operate and Transfer) contract, which means that the Stadium Australia consortium, led by the contractors Multiplex and the financiers Hambros, bore the bulk of the construction costs, in return for which it will operate the facility for thirty years, and thus, it hopes, recoup its outlay, before handing the whole building over to the New South Wales government in the year 2030.

However, when the consortium tried to raise a large chunk of the construction costs by offering for advance sale various long-term seat deals, labelled Gold and Platinum, the lacklustre response resulted in what was billed 'the biggest corporate flop in Australian history'. Fortunately for the consortium, interest in advance tickets bucked up considerably once two rugby league clubs agreed to become the new stadium's tenant teams, various rugby union internationals were signed up, and the stadium's post-Olympic design was amended to cater for AFL matches after 2001. Thus, once again, field sports had baled out an athletics stadium.

Barcelona's stadium for the 1992 Games would have become a virtual white elephant had it not been for its later use for football. Atlanta's stadium would have been insupportable without baseball, and now rugby league, rugby union and Ozzie Rules football had come to the rescue in Sydney.

So you have to hand it to athletics. Its governing bodies make all these demands upon stadium designers, for running tracks, jumps, warm-up areas and suchlike, then get other, more popular sports to foot the bill.

But enough carping. Stadium Australia is also the most environmentally friendly Olympic stadium ever built. Every single product and material used had to meet strict guidelines, even if it turned out to be more expensive. All the timber is either recycled or derived from renewable sources. In order to reduce energy costs, the design allows for natural lighting in as many public areas as possible, supplemented by solar-powered units. Rainwater collected from the roof runs off into storage tanks, where it can be tapped for pitch irrigation. Stormwater run-off is collected for toilet flushing. Wherever possible, passive ventilation is used instead of mechanical air-conditioning. Even the steel and concrete from the two end stands due to be demolished at the end of the Olympics is to be recycled. Furthermore, no private cars will be allowed on the Homebush site. Instead, every spectator will arrive by public transport, and quite right too.

Overall, therefore, if ever there was a stadium to persuade a sceptic like myself that the Olympic Games do, after all, have a useful function in at least setting design and planning trends, this was the one. I was, and still am, I freely confess, quite knocked out by Stadium Australia and by what has been achieved at the Homebush site generally.

Not just by Homebush either. Everyone had told me just how much Australians love an event. At Bondi I saw this for myself, in the flesh. But this enthusiasm, stoked by a lively, sometimes bitter intercity rivalry in Australia, had also helped to create a market for new stadiums quite unlike anywhere else in the world.

In Melbourne, for example, a few weeks earlier a representative from the architects Daryl Jackson Bligh Lobb (another of Lobb's Australian tie-ups) showed me round the 52,000-capacity Colonial Stadium then being built in the city's up-and-coming docklands area. This quite stunning design lay barely a mile across town from the epic but more conventional 100,000-capacity Melbourne Cricket Ground.

I also visited the AFL's own 75,000-capacity stadium in Melbourne, called Waverley Park – or Arctic Park to its chilly detractors – plus a number of soccer grounds and of course the much admired Melbourne Park tennis complex (next to the MCG), where the Australian Open was just about to begin, and for which I couldn't get a ticket for love nor money.

Melbourne, I was told, boasts the highest overall number of spectators attending sports events per capita of any Australian city, and therefore probably of any city in the world. But for how long? With Stadium Australia's arrival on the scene, there were now some mightily anxious stadium operators in both Sydney and Melbourne fighting to keep their events in the face of the new competition at Homebush.

(One consequence of this rivalry has been the AFL's recently developed policy of 'Best Fit' under which teams now play at whichever stadium the AFL directorate deems most suitable, thus running totally counter to the tradition of 'home' grounds. I shall say no more about this for fear of the idea catching on elsewhere.)

Back in Sydney, with my head still full of 'Best Fit' and still trying to remember who or what were the AFL, NRL, ARL, ARU, ACB, MCG and SCG – not forgetting OCA and SOCOG in charge of the Olympic facilities – I eventually met up with the HOK architect Ron Labinski at a café on the Homebush site.

Ron's white hair, cropped beard and wire-rimmed spectacles suit well his almost legendary status as the so-called 'father of modern stadium design'. Yet he seemed as overwhelmed as I was by the vibrancy and complexity of the Australian scene. Or, at least, so I thought until he explained his reasons for appearing somewhat wide-eyed.

Two weeks before, Ron explained, he had left HOK's base in Kansas City to fly, via Copenhagen, to Dublin (to check on progress at Croke Park). He had then flown to Budapest for a day's talks on a new stadium, then back to Kansas for twenty-three hours, before flying, via Denver and Los Angeles, to Auckland, from where he flew on to Christchurch with two hours to spare before being interviewed as part of the new HOK+LOBB team pitching for a new stadium contract, and then on to Wellington to see another of Lobb's projects (the new 'rucket and crigby' stadium mentioned in Chapter 5). After that it was back to Auckland (where HOK was working on the controversial redevelopment of Eden Park), then on to Brisbane (where HOK+LOBB are also bidding for a new stadium contract), and finally, via Melbourne, where he took in the new Colonial Stadium, to Sydney. The following day Ron was returning to Kansas for two days, before making a return trip to Dublin. 'That's international practice for you,' he said, shrugging.

My own schedule seemed pathetically indolent by comparison, and I'm a good fifteen years his junior, but then Ron is one of those architects who seems to relish the game as much as the art of design. Popular acclaim for the first stadium he worked on, the 79,000-seat Arrowhead Stadium in Kansas City, led him to set up the HOK Sports Facility Group as a small department within the practice of Hellmuth, Obata and Kassabaum, then the world's second-largest firm of architects. (They are now said to be the largest.) So influential did Labinski and his co-specialists become that if one looks at the personnel of three of the other most prominent stadium-design practices currently active in the United States – HNTB and Ellerbe Becket, both around the corner from HOK in Kansas, and NBBJ in Los Angeles – each appears to form part of a complex family tree, all with one link or another to Labinski, HOK or Kansas.

But the HOK Sports Facility Group remained the daddy of them all. The company has worked in one capacity or another for no fewer than twenty-nine of the NFL's thirty franchises, and twenty-two of the Major League's twenty-eight baseball clubs.

As we chatted and stared out at the rain lashing down on Homebush, what, I asked, did he think would be the reaction of his competitors to the HOK merger with Lobb?

'Oh,' he said, grinning casually, 'I hope they shit their pants.'

Ron's opposite number at Lobb possesses a similar hard edge and determination, although you would never guess it to meet him casually. Rod Sheard is a tall, affable man in his late forties, with a schoolboyish gait, a deceptively laid-back manner and a ready smile. His trademark greeting is 'Hi, matey,' delivered in a soft,

Australian accent, still discernible after more than twenty years working in London.

After the deaths of ninety-five football fans at Hillsborough, Sheffield, in 1989 – the tragedy that sparked off a stadium revolution right across Europe and, to an extent, beyond – Rod was one of several architects with whom I spent many long hours working on a series of guidelines aimed at improving standards in stadium design. Indeed, almost everything I know about sightlines I learnt from Rod and his colleague Jay Parrish. I seem to recall we did some pretty sterling research on stadium toilets, too.

That Rod was born and brought up in Brisbane has always been significant in my estimation. It meant he did not share the typical Briton's first response to anyone planning a new stadium: 'Ooh dear, not sure about that.' Also, in common with Ron Labinski, Rod had been the driving force behind Lobb's decision to specialise in sports-related work.

A personal favourite from the Lobb portfolio is the North Bank Stand at Arsenal (opened in 1993). My godson loves it too, although the quality of burgers on offer may have something to do with that. But Lobb had also greatly enhanced the reputation of sports architects as a whole by winning the Royal Institute of British Architects' Building of the Year Award in 1995 for their distinctive Alfred McAlpine Stadium in Huddersfield, the first stadium ever to be chosen for this considerable honour. (It was designed by Rod Sheard in conjunction with Jay Parrish and Derek Wilson, together with a brilliant young engineer, Stephen Morley, whose 'banana' trusses at Huddersfield were now writ large at Stadium Australia. As the ancient proverb reminds us, an arch never sleeps.)

Lobb's successes might easily have led Rod to succumb to preciousness, an affliction that seems all too rife among high-profile architects. Here, for example, is an extract from the writings of the esteemed Italian architect Vittorio Gregotti: 'For us the initial act of architecture is not construction but delimitation, the marking out of the site with a trace, an edge, a limit, the three-dimensional enclosure of the stadium is identified with a remote form, a form of appearance, in which the primary value of the principle of settlement is the same as its spatial expression, in a determination that may be archetypal but that is not regarded as definitive or immutable for that reason.'

Quite, although, having interviewed Gregotti and visited his truly original stadiums at Nîmes and Genoa, I know his designs to be far more accessible, even more legible, as it were, than his theories. Without his arrogance and erudition, his buildings would surely not be as crisply defined or as strident. I learnt a lot from talking to him, even if his words took some months to absorb fully.

The likes of Ron and Rod, on the other hand, more accustomed to dealing directly with sports-club owners, have never been able to get away with such theoretical discourse. In their world, a spade has to be expressed as a spade, a stadium as a stadium, and not, as Gregotti has described it, as 'a symbol for the capture of instantaneous action in its true form by means of the image and, at the same time, for the interpretative falsification that is made of it through the amplification of communication'.

There was one other reason why I found Rod's views on stadiums rather easier to assimilate. When eventually I caught up with him in Sydney, he straight away invited me to spend the day with himself, his Sydney-based colleague Paul Henry, and a bottle or two of chilled Chardonnay, sailing on the Lobb company's yacht around Sydney Harbour. Under the Harbour Bridge, past the Opera House, maybe up to Point Piper and back. We could talk then, and maybe over a meal later.

Well, it would have been rude to refuse.

Over the years Rod and I have argued over numerous aspects of stadium design. In fact, we have often performed a double act at conferences and seminars. Rod expounds his vision of the brave new world, then I come on, as the unreconstructed sports fan, and milk unwarranted applause from among the reactionary elements in the audience.

But before we re-entered that debate, and because I was far too busy ogling the sites around Sydney Harbour – which of course I had not yet seen, having been far too busy, ho hum, visiting stadiums around the city – I asked Rod to speak more generally on the role of the stadium and the architect.

'OK, matey,' he started in characteristic fashion. 'Well, I think the stadium is possibly the only building left where we actually relate to each other as a community. We may walk in through the doors as individuals, but once inside we react like a community, with a common purpose. In a stadium we still share this common desire to be uplifted.

'As a stadium architect, my chief role is to build dreams, and so the first step is to build the dream in the mind of the client. So many things can go wrong when it comes to planning a new stadium. So many difficulties have to be overcome. Not just money or planning issues but fans and local residents may have a stack of their own issues too. So unless the dream is clearly embedded in the mind of the client, the stadium will probably never become a reality.

'The trouble is that a lot of clients have very low expectations of what a stadium can do, of what it can deliver to their fans and the local community. So another of our jobs is to educate. To pass on our knowledge of what is happening around the world and the way trends are developing. Because, at the end of the day when they do see the final design and if they say, "Wow, that's a great design, let's build it!" I want their reaction to be based on solid knowledge and information, and not because we happened to pick the right colour for the cladding.

'As in sport, we designers work very much as a team. Like the team coach I might get to do all the press and TV interviews, but for example on Stadium Australia I am only one of about a hundred architects, engineers and technicians from around forty different countries who've been involved. These are big complex buildings and they need a lot of people's input.

'Certainly none of us is in this business as an ego trip. I mean, when you think that something like half the world's population will see television images of Stadium Australia, that our work will be put into the same sort of spotlight as the likes of Carl Lewis or Michael Jordan, and yet no one will know our name, that is extraordinary. But it's also fantastic that we will get a reaction, that stadiums are such public works. An architect could design ten office blocks in a row and nobody would bat an eyelid. But design a stadium and your work, warts and all, is out there, being seen and used by thousands, millions even, of critical punters. In that respect we are under as much scrutiny as any sportsman or sportswoman.'

Rod reckoned that stadium design is still very much in its formative stage. Melbourne's Colonial Stadium and Stadium Australia he described as early examples of what he calls 'fourth-generation' stadiums. In fact he had used the expression in so many interviews that it had now become common currency in the stadium industry. I was still not sure myself what he meant by it or whether it was just a neat bit of sales patter.

'I guess I use the word generation,' he explained, 'because it implies that stadiums are evolving as a building type, that there's a sense of the process never ending, of stadiums forever adapting to the changing needs of society. The first generation was the simple concrete bowl. Wembley, the old Wembley from 1923, was a good example of this early type. Although a magnificent physical icon, it was essentially a bowl with very little underneath it or added.'

I took his point but suggested that, surely, stadiums of that ilk were still being built today. They might appear more modern, but their facilities were hardly more advanced. Rod encouraged me not to get bogged down in the chronology, however, and to think of the typology instead.

'The second generation started to evolve once televised sport began, giving people the choice of whether to go to the stadium or stay at home and watch the event for free, in comfort. It took maybe ten or twenty years for television to have an effect on actual design, but if you look at attendance figures you see that at most of those first-generation stadiums they start to drop off pretty dramatically by the late 1950s. So the aim of the second generation was to provide more than just a concrete bowl. They had to offer decent toilets, more seats, more weather protection, executive suites and so on. Concourses were created to give people a place to buy hot food and a beverage more easily, that type of thing. To make people feel that what they were getting at the live event was still qualitatively better, more fun, than what they could get by staying at home and watching the box.

'And that lasted fine until again the next big event started to take an effect, the opening of Disneyland in 1955. Walt Disney said that all who entered Disneyland would find happiness and knowledge. He demonstrated to stadium operators in the United States that you could actually cater for an entire family within the one complex, that it didn't just have to be a place for committed sports fans, or for dads and sons alone. Each family member would find his or her own happiness and knowledge in different ways. To which Disney added superb management, absolute cleanliness, and all sorts of techniques which we now virtually take for granted. For example, that when you stand in a queue, you'll always be kept informed of how long you have to wait, and there'll always be something to distract you as you inch forward. Very little was left to chance.

'The birth of theme parks, I think, led eventually to the third generation of stadiums. These have more and more activities on the concourses, giant video screens visible from the stands, and television screens around the public areas to keep people entertained and informed, that mix again of happiness and knowledge. In our own third-generation stadiums, at Arsenal for example, we put in video-game arcades to keep kids involved and bandstands to stage live music, different types of bars and restaurants, to try and widen the appeal and, to some extent, to make the stadium a destination in itself. A place where, rather than just go to watch sport and then go home again, you could have a pleasant and varied experience.

'Most of the stadiums you see being built now are like this third generation. However, the seeds of the fourth generation were already planted, I think, in 1969. That was a key date in so many ways. Apart from the fact that it was the year I started my architecture course in Brisbane, it was the year man landed on the moon, that Concorde flew for the first time, and so did the Jumbo Jet, the Boeing 747.'

'Ah yes,' I thought. That very day I had read that four Boeing 747s could be parked side by side under each 295-metre span of the main roof trusses at Stadium Australia. Or at least they could be if there weren't all those seats and suites in the way.

'But most importantly of all,' continued Rod, '1969 was the year that the American military commissioned the first ever linking of computers, the link that eventually became the Internet. The unleashing of all that immense power – those dots and dashes, ones and zeros, offs and ons – would launch us eventually into the digital era, and twenty years later mean that, apart from changing our lives in all sorts of ways, people could start to experience sport not through the atoms of the event but through the medium of the digital revolution.'

I had heard Rod bang on about this digital revolution on many an occasion in the previous two or three years, but only now that I was finally connected up to e-mail and the Internet was I beginning to cotton on.

Rod would often explain how in the stadiums of the future – and he stressed this was the near future – each seat would be wired up to a digital network and have a small in-built screen on the armrest or attached to the seat in front, as on aeroplanes, allowing spectators to watch their own action replays. Or, via what Rod called Personal Digital Assistants, they could call up statistics or player information on the screen, or order snacks or merchandise, or even tickets for future events. A stadium smart card could be used for payments, as well as for entering the stadium in the first place. A headphone socket would also give spectators the option of listening to an in-house commentary. (Stadium Australia had been 'future proofed' to carry this technology, via fibre optics.)

Rod's vision of the future depressed me enormously whenever I heard it. The smart cards I had already come across in the Amsterdam Arena, where they are used for purchasing goods within the stadium. The stadium operators had even invented their own unit of currency, an Arena. But Rod's 'smart seats' worried me more. Instead of being part of a crowd enjoying (or enduring) a communal experience, the level of interactivity they promised would, I felt certain, turn us all into individuals again. I imagined the fractured responses of spectators after a goal or a try or a six was scored. After the initial cheer every spectator would retreat into his or her small-screen world, thus dissipating whatever atmosphere had been momentarily created. Signs of this were already evident in stadiums with video screens. Instead of a buzz after an incident, a silent hush falls as all eyes turn to the screen for the replay.

In addition, I have repeatedly rejected the assumption that spectators somehow all thirst for information; that we should want to call up statistics or replays in the middle of a game; that, using Walt's terms, happiness should have to be accompanied by knowledge, preferably with a burger and chips on the side. Whatever is wrong with pure, visceral experience on its own?

Besides, I contend that we have enough of all that techno-gadgetry in our daily lives, what with mobile phones, pagers, e-mails, voice mails and digitised females telling us to press option five on our telephones in order to go through the menu of modern-day 'communications' (when in practice the system usually serves to do the exact opposite, by avoiding all real or meaningful communication). Surely we go to stadiums to get away from all that button pressing and info-seeking?

Or perhaps the next generation of spectators will see 'all that' as quite routine and natural, whether they're in a stadium, a restaurant, or on the number 82 bus. No doubt there was a time in the 1930s when spectators thought the newfangled public-address systems were equally intrusive.

But anyway, the past few years have shown that Rod was right in the sense that the digital revolution is not only going to change our everyday lives. It may also change the way we view sport.

He cited two examples. He said the website for the 1998 Whitbread Round the World yacht race received 474.5 million hits over nine months. In January 1999 the Australian Open Tennis site had 12 million hits, per day. But what was more significant was that, before they left the port, racing yachts could now be scanned in their three-dimensional entirety on to a computer. The actual boats could then be fitted with a Global Positioning System device, which relays exact information about the boat's position and its movements to the web surfer at home. Although this does not create a true broadcast image, in the sense that there are no conventional cameras on board, it does nevertheless provide an accurate, digitised, virtual simulation of what is actually happening to the yacht.

It will not be long, reckons Rod, before the same technology can be applied to humans. To footballers, to athletes, to tennis players. Anyone. Their exact movements during a game could be duplicated via digitised simulations.

Now, you might ask, as I did, why bother when you can watch the real thing. But as Rod points out, it won't be long before the technology will be routinely used to allow viewers, or surfers, to track individual players during a game and to replay moves in greater detail. More powerfully, embedded virtual imagery is already promising sponsors and advertisers the ability to superimpose simulated logos and ads on to players' shirts, as well as on to pitches and pitch-side hoardings, so that viewers in each country might see targeted, virtual advertising quite different from what is visible by spectators at the actual event.

Imagine, said Rod, the enormous commercial and editorial powers sports clubs and stadium operators will wield once they control not only the commercial rights and images of each event but also their virtual spin-offs in every country of the world? If one thinks of sport as being the software, clubs and stadium operators will become the software developers, with the stadium itself acting as the studio and information storehouse.

'Hand in hand with these advances is the plummeting of costs of actually setting up new types of technology. We already have radio stations for specific events, like Radio Wimbledon or Radio Silverstone. And now we're seeing MUTV [Manchester United's own cable channel]. Watching live video on the Internet now, it's all a bit jittery and staccato, whereas in the next five years it will become perfect, a better picture than we get via our television sets. Add to that, interactivity [the ability to select your own camera angles and statistics], as BSkyB are now offering through one of their digital sports channels, plus maybe fifty to a hundred different channels, and you can imagine how our consumption of sport, as spectators, is going to change radically.'

Even if the future does not pan out exactly as he predicted, what Rod was saying in effect was that the so-called 'fourth generation' of stadiums has to be ready to meet the digital challenge. In other words, it has to be specifically designed to cater for two completely different audiences: the live audience and the global audience, watching or listening at home. That means stadiums fully wired up for cameras, microphones, information databases and so on.

Yet if, I asked, there is a sufficiently large audience at home, willing to pay-per-view, whether via the TV or the Internet, did Rod think that in time the live audience would become an unnecessary irrelevance?

He did not, because of course it would always be advantageous to have a crowd in attendance, if only to create an atmosphere for the players and to make for better television pictures. Banks of empty seats hardly convey public confidence in the quality of the event.

But I harboured a deeper fear. For if Rod's 'fourth-generation' stadium evolves into a form of large television studio, surely the next step would be for the spectators to become invited guests; that is, admitted free of charge (as they are for most television shows) but expected to dress in an appropriate manner and show their support in an appropriate manner. I could see the cheerleaders down on the touchlines, waiting for the producer's signal. 'Mexican Wave, start now!' Who knows, stadium operators might even try to engineer a mix of young and old guests, male and female, black and white, in order to demonstrate to the viewers that theirs is a wholesome event for all sectors of the community.

Rod thought I was overstating my anxieties in this respect, though he accepted that certain sections of certain stadiums do now operate a dress code. There are plenty more where smoking is prohibited and where swearing and jumping up and down is discouraged, and although I would never defend hooliganism I did fear where all these controls might lead spectators, from active participation to programmed response. Once that happened, heaven help us, maybe we really would need cheerleaders.

So we agreed to differ on that, and for some reason, perhaps because we had strayed from the information-superhighway theme – or was it that we'd now finished the first bottle of Chardonnay – we started to toy around with the possible uses of mini-cameras.

Rod started it. He envisaged a time when fans could go into stadiums with mini-cameras strapped to their hats. These cameras could send live pictures of a game, accompanied by the fan's commentary, via a mobile phone to the Internet. A sort of webzine pirate TV, as it were.

No, I said, the stewards would soon track him down and chuck him out. Instead, surely the best use of mini-cameras would be to attach them to the foreheads of players. The viewer at home (or in his 'smart seat' at the stadium) could then choose whose viewpoint of the game to follow; say, the goalkeeper's, the wicket-keeper's, or maybe even the referee's. Imagine the soundtrack!

Taking this one stage further, instead of simply watching a two-dimensional screen, imagine the image translated into virtual reality, experienced through a headset.

Taking that one stage further still, and remembering how the progress of racing yachts could now be simulated digitally, we then discussed the idea of wiring up each player with pads on key points of his or her body, and with the aid of a special suit receiving direct signals from the player the viewer at home could gain the complete bodily experience of actually playing. Maybe one day we could even tap into the players' thought processes, although imagining what it would be like to be inside Michael Atherton's head as Allan Donald pounded up the wicket soon brought us both shivering back to reality.

It also brought us back to the point, which was that, in Rod's opinion, stadiums clearly have to adapt and modernise if they are to compete with the joys of home viewing, virtual spectatorship or whatever the digital revolution might offer us next.

As Rod argued, the stadium had to become more than just a stadium. Consider all the pressures upon stadium operators these days, he said, and consider all the money-making, pleasure-giving opportunities now available. Consider airports, he suggested. They now make more money from shopping than they do from flying. Look at Manchester United's income. More derives from commercial sources, sponsorship and merchandising than from ticket income (which amounts to around only 35 per cent of the total). Just as United have constantly to find new ways of separating fans from their money, so it was in the leisure industry with its continual search for the latest in megaplexes and themed malls.

This brought us to the modern-day 'leisure box', the sort of tin-shed increasingly found in retail parks, providing a day or night out for the whole family, under the watchful eye of private security guards. These quick-build attractions are specifically designed to be as flexible as possible, so that if, in one corner of the shed, the bowling-alley craze or the latest laser action game suddenly goes belly-up, or if one fast-food outlet loses it edge, replacement attractions can easily be slotted into their place. It is reckoned that in the night-club corner of the shed, as on the high street, interiors and themes have to be changed, on average, every seven years.

In the United States nowadays, some stadiums were lasting for only twenty to thirty years, cast into oblivion not because they were falling down but because they had fallen out of fashion (like Melbourne's doomed Waverley Park, opened in 1970). So, I wondered, how long would Rod's 'fourth generation' of stadiums survive before they too succumbed to the next new trend?

Of course that depended on fashion too, on changing trends, he agreed. But he also felt that we were moving much closer towards an ideal, or, as he put it, back to what the Romans had once created at the Colosseum. That is, a stadium in the heart of the city, forming the hub of a whole range of enterprises. In ancient Rome, as Vicarius describes in the Prologue, those enterprises were essentially small shops and food stalls, with prostitutes thrown in for good measure. The modern ideal was similar, if without the same temptations of the flesh. (Although that too was not unknown. Most famously of all, in the Toronto Skydome, which has hotel rooms overlooking the pitch, one preoccupied couple, thinking their window was made of one-way glass, apparently kept a baseball crowd of 55,000 quite amused until someone knocked on their door to inform them, if you will, of the score.)

But back to the 'fourth generation'. As Rod was saying, there may be a pitch and seats at the core of this new generation of stadiums, but around the edges there would increasingly be found shops, offices, restaurants, casinos, museums, visitor attractions, and yes, hotels, so that spectators could theoretically spend a whole weekend without ever leaving the vicinity, as in Las Vegas.

The current debate in the stadium-design world revolved around a host of technological and engineering issues such as retractable roofs, retractable pitches, movable tiers, various types of turf technology and fibre optics. But Rod believed that there were still other areas that had yet to be addressed, such as whole tiers of seating being designed so that their profile could be changed according to need; fitted with seats for one event, and then realigned to form café-like terraces for another. In time, with ever more interchangeable structures, the distinction between outdoor 'stadiums' and indoor 'arenas' would disappear altogether. This was called 'venue convergence' and was aimed at offering operators the maximum flexibility and therefore the maximum profit. 'Follow the trail of where the big money is,' emphasised Rod, 'be it with the Disney Corporation, Bill Gates, Rupert Murdoch, Ted Turner, Canal Plus, whoever, and you will begin to see what the main influences will be on the stadiums of the next fifty years.'

Melbourne's Colonial Stadium, which Rod considered to be the world's first 'fourth-generation' stadium, forms one such pointer to the future. Only a short walk from the city centre and with 2,500 parking spaces (many of them under the actual pitch), it forms the hub of a whole new docklands district, complete with its own residential, business and commercial area. There was a 200-seat theatre in the stadium complex, a cinema, and silver-service dining facilities for up to 6,500 people. Spend per head, both inside and outside the stadium, was now as important, if not more important, than ticket income. He said that current estimates reckoned that for every dollar a spectator spent inside one of the new Australian venues, ten were spent outside, providing a huge benefit to the surrounding economy.

Moreover, if the Colonial Stadium was designed to be plugged into the urban matrix, it was also directly linked to an adjoining digital broadcast centre belonging to Rupert Murdoch's Channel Seven. Because the stadium roof can close completely over the pitch and its undersurface has been acoustically treated, in effect the television company has on its doorstep a vast studio, wired up for sound, light and action. There can thus be complete synergy between sport, the stadium and the media.

This then leads the way for stadiums to host events which do not necessarily require an audience. Some might be staged for broadcast only – say, a table-tennis tournament, of interest mainly in China – via the Internet. Others may be for participants only. (Oh yes, never forget that human urge to participate. After all, all over the world athletes regularly perform in virtually empty stadiums.) Rod mentioned two such potential activities: paper-plane competitions and indoor windsurfing. Don't laugh. Such events have already been staged in European stadiums. Maybe you can think of some of your own twenty-first-century stadium activities; mini-golf, or mini-cricket, or even maxi volleyball. Or how about Brazilian-style funk-balls, in which gangs of dancers fight each other in mass, orchestrated brawls to a raucous soundtrack laid on by DJs? Or robot wars. How about that on a grand scale inside a stadium the size of Wembley!

There are, said Rod, hundreds of registered sports around the world, only a fraction of which we ever get to see on our screens today. Maybe some of the lesser-known ones will eventually find their way into our stadiums of the future. We had to remember that all sports had to start somewhere. Not all evolved gradually, like football or cricket. Some were invented out of nothing, such as basketball (the brainchild of a YMCA College professor in Springfield, Massachusetts, in 1891).

Rod's point was that, as an architect who loves stadiums, he had to do everything he could to ensure their survival and popularity. A designer of houses could be pretty sure that mankind would always need somewhere to live. We could be fairly sure too of man's continuing patronage of bars, restaurants and shops. But stadiums? The world seemed to have got by pretty well without them between the fall of the Roman Empire and their revival in the late nineteenth century. Maybe it could do so again.

'The bottom line,' he emphasised, 'is that if this building type is to survive at all in its present form or even close to its present form, it has got to be a place that people enjoy going to. It may not be good enough in the future just to say Arsenal are playing Manchester United, or the Yankees are playing the Dodgers, and assume that a large crowd is bound to turn up.

'I agree that there will always be something special about going to a sports event, for the atmosphere and for that sense of being part of something special. But in the digital age it has to go beyond that. It has got to keep pace with what is happening in other types of building and with other developments in technology and entertainment.'

By this stage of our discussion, Rod and I were back on dry land, in the Lobb company flat looking down on the twinkling lights of the Harbour Bridge and the floodlit curves of the Opera House. In a short while the city would have a third building known and recognised throughout the world, Stadium Australia. And now its architect had one last point to make. In essence, Rod concluded, what we had really been discussing was the transition of the stadium from the analogue to the digital; from the uncontrolled terraces of old to the all-seated, number-controlled environment of today.

Now that was either a brilliant insight or a dubious analogy. But by then both of us agreed that we had had enough of stadium talk for the day, so we opened up another bottle of wine and instead I told Rod about the nude surfing. Within a minute or two I could tell he was already wondering, now how would that look in a stadium of the future?

12 NO PLACE LIKE DOME

To: Judge Roy Hofheinz [creator of the Houston Astrodome]
From: Simon Inglis, December 1999

Dear Judge Hofheinz,

Forgive me for disturbing you in your truly Celestial Suite. Is it any better than the one you created down here at the Sheraton Astrodome Hotel? Are you still partying as always? How about all your other adversaries from Houston? Any of them make it through the pearly gates?

Anyway, as the minutes tick away at the tail end of the twentieth century, I fear I may be the bearer of some sad tidings. It's about the Astrodome, the building you created, and, oh jeez, I hardly know how to write the words.

So perhaps I should first explain why I am writing this letter. You see, Judge, like you I have this thing about stadiums, and about the magical power of the spectacle, and whatever else my views on Astroturf in particular, I fully recognise that when the Astrodome itself opened in 1965 it was by far the most advanced and innovative stadium of its era. No, I'll go further. It was to the twentieth century what St Paul's Cathedral and the Taj Mahal were to the seventeenth century, and what the Crystal Palace was to the nineteenth. A building that rejoiced in the possibilities of the age and didn't give a damn for what had gone before. The Astrodome changed everything, though of course you hardly need me to remind you of that.

Maybe I should explain further. You see, Houston was, by chance, the first place in the United States that I ever visited. This was back in 1980, a couple of years before you 'bought the farm' (as I believe they say rather crudely in your former neck of the woods). I was twenty-four, starting off on a five-month meander through Texas, Central America and South America. I'd only just qualified as a history teacher, but fancied trying my hand at freelance writing instead, though what that entailed I hardly knew. I think I just liked the sound of the words 'freelance writer'. In those days I was not intent on visiting stadiums. If a game happened to be on when I passed through somewhere, then yes, fine. But I didn't go looking for them. Really, I just wanted to see a bit of the world and reckoned that since everyone else in those days headed east, I would go west and follow the Gringo trail, starting in Houston, where a distant cousin lived (just off Westheimer, near the Galleria mall in fact, not far from one of many plots of land you bought in the 1940s and then sold later at a handsome profit).

I know that by the age of twenty-four you were already a man of some considerable standing; the youngest county judge in the history of the United States, no less, and a go-getting firebrand with a reputation for fine oratory and stirring up the Texas fat cats. This was after you had already made a name for yourself as a teenage radio announcer and a promoter of dances. I loved all those stories of you booking Louis Armstrong before he became a big name and of driving around downtown in your yellow-painted Model T. Was it true that you deliberately broke down on Main Street during the rush hour and just left your car there, holding up all the traffic, so that everyone would see the posters on the windows, publicising your next big event? I can hardly imagine downtown Houston buzzing like it used to. It seems so ghostly now, with everyone scurrying about unseen, along air-conditioned tunnels and walkways under streets and between buildings. They say that the new ballpark . . . but hold on, I'm getting ahead of myself.

Once you decided to practise law, do you remember how your long-time buddy LBJ said that if only he could prepare and deliver his speeches as well as you he could become the president? Others reckoned that you could have made it to the White House yourself if only you had learnt to play the game and not upset so many folk. They called you the Great Huckster, but I know they didn't always mean it as a criticism, and nor did you take it that way. You even called your amazing family retreat in Galveston Bay 'the Huckster House'. What a fantastically kitsch place that was. Gives me a headache to just to look at the photos.

Still, you sure did blaze a trail once you became mayor of

Houston, in 1952, at the age of forty; standing up for minorities, bringing down segregation barriers, supporting the public-school system, setting up programmes for juvenile delinquents. But in the end you couldn't beat the bigots or get your own way with the Houston oligarchy and so you went on to make your millions (and lose plenty of them too) from radio, TV, property and, eventually, the Astrodome. Few people, not even Bob Smith, whose money made it all possible, would deny that you were the brains behind the stadium, not forgetting the Astrohall next door, and the Astroworld amusement park and all those hotels – such as the Astrodome Sheraton – you built in that corner of Houston that would thereafter be known as the Astrodomain. Between the Astrodome and the astronauts from NASA, Houston rocketed from an oil-rich provincial cowtown to global fame within just a few years. Did you know it is now the fourth-biggest city in the United States?

Actually, of all the many cities I've visited on my trail around the stadiums of the world, Houston is among my least favourite, even though, for various reasons, I've been back four times since. Sorry, Judge, but there are too many freeways and not enough streetlife for my liking. 'Great place to live, lousy place to visit,' as one Houstonian told me. A guy called Joel Garreau, who wrote a book about Edge Cities – cities such as Houston with a neglected downtown and a string of major urban centres spread around the place with seemingly neither rhyme nor reason – said that going to Houston and not hiring a car is like going to Venice and not hiring a boat. It was, he said, to miss the whole point. Well, I plead guilty to that, which is why I seem to have spent a lot of time in Houston waiting for and riding buses with the poor, and a whole heap of dollars more on yellow taxis. I suppose I don't know when I'm beaten. I remember one time going to the Astrodome and then walking the three or four miles back to downtown, past the legendary Shamrock Hotel (which, as you know, started the city's expansion south in 1949), past Rice University and the Texas Medical Centre, passing hardly a single pedestrian and finding barely a decent sidewalk along the entire route, though I did pass by some pretty seedy-looking joints offering 'totally nude girls'. (Incidentally, I note that the sports editor of the *Houston Post* credited Glenn McCarthy, the man behind the Shamrock, with being the first person in town to consider a covered stadium, ten years before you got round to discussing the idea with Buckminster Fuller in the late 1950s. Did you and McCarthy ever discuss the idea?)

Anyway, hearing of my trek from the Astrodome to downtown, the locals reacted as if I were some kind of deranged hobo. They made me feel that walking as a means of getting from A to B was practically an unAmerican activity, or at least unTexan, whereas I thought they were the crazy ones. I mean, those dudes thought nothing of driving a few hundred yards to their office, then at lunchtime getting back in their cars to drive miles to a jogging track on top of a shopping mall.

But I'm not writing to tell you what I think of Houston, because I know that, like Rhett Butler, frankly, you won't give a damn. I know also that you thought Houston the best-planned city in the world, because the voters would never accept the old-fashioned notion of restrictive zoning, and therefore there didn't seem to be any planning at all. So what can I say? I'm a European child of the ghetto, through and through, and if ever I'm more than 300 metres from a corner shop I get panic attacks.

Why go to Houston, then? Well, Judge, the first time I was just *en route*, though being a sports fan of course I went to the Summit arena for a basketball game, saw Michael Jackson in the audience, and witnessed my first ever Mexican Wave. And of course I also went to the Astrodome, which in those days every visitor did. Who would not want to see the world's first indoor stadium, the largest air-conditioned building in the world, the first ever to feature artificial grass – Astroturf, what a brilliant name! – and the stadium which really kicked off a whole new era of stadium design across the United States. I mean, you didn't have to be a stadium expert to acknowledge that the Astrodome was far, far ahead of its time. It made even the newly built Dodgers Stadium in Los Angeles and the Shea Stadium in New York look relatively basic. Hey, who'd have even heard of Shea Stadium had it not been for the Beatles?

That first visit, in 1980, was four years after you had had to sell off your interest in the whole Astrodomain to recoup your massive debts, so I need hardly remind you that by then the Eighth Wonder of the World, as Billy Graham called the Dome, was already looking somewhat tired around the edges. No one cared for it quite like you did. Those bright colours you were so proud of in 1965 were starting to lose their gloss, and as for your private quarters up in the gods . . . well, to a Limey, to anyone with only a modicum of taste, they just seemed so OTT. Over The Top, or in your case, given your penchant for Barnum and Bailey imagery, over the circus top. Remember how Bob Hope called the style 'early Farouk' when he came to call? What a card he was, eh? Or was he just trying to be polite? All that mock-classical statuary, the Italian marble-inlaid desk, the chandeliers, the crushed-velvet drapes, your gold telephone. Then there was the Medieval Chapel, the bowling alley, the Presidential Suite and the Tipsy Tavern (where beer – heh heh, I loved this – was served in metal pitchers, so that the barman could slide them down the bar and then activate a magnet to catch the pitcher just before it toppled over the end). Some likened the riot of colours and themes to Nero's Palace; but I thought your Astrodome quarters were, to borrow an Americanism, 'totally unique'. At least, I hoped they were.

Certainly to a young Englishman they seemed to sum up all that was both gross and wonderful about Texas during the 1960s. You had your reasons, though. You always said that if you'd done out your offices in the modern style of the day no one would have remembered them. 'Be different!' you used to tell schoolkids in Houston. And, boy, Judge, were you different.

And the funny thing is that although had we met I would probably have found your cigar-toting swagger repugnant, like most sports fans I've always had this love–hate relationship with powerful club owners. On the one hand I like to kid myself that my club belongs to me and all the other fans. Yet I depend on money men and big shots like you to deliver the dream. It's hard for us fans to accept the truth, that professional sport is really just an arm of showbiz. Harder still, as one of many fans who has never enjoyed watching games in a domed stadium, to admit that without people like you, who relentlessly push the frontiers of spectator provision, stadium design might never have progressed the way it has. So I suppose that I both admire you and abhor what you did in equal measure. Sorry, Judge, but I know you always preferred honesty.

But whatever I think, fact is that the concept of the round, multipurpose stadium that you and your design team fathered has in any case become discredited in recent years. Virtually all those domes and soulless concrete lookalike bowls that followed the

Astrodome – in New Orleans, Seattle, Minneapolis, Pontiac, Atlanta, Pittsburgh and elsewhere – are now either rubble or awaiting the wreckers' ball. Times change. Fashions change. The name 'dome' stuck, however, even if a lot of the so-called domes were not really that at all, but stadiums with air-supported fabric roofs. And virtually everyone calls artificial grass Astroturf these days, despite the fact that much of it is manufactured under different names by companies other than the original inventors, Monsanto. So one way or another you left behind quite a legacy.

And think of all your other innovations at the Astrodome that have since become *de rigueur*: carpeted skyboxes with CCTVs relaying the action; padded, tip-up seats with arms and generous leg room; themed restaurant and bar areas (the Skyblazer Restaurant, the Countdown Cafeteria, the Domeskellar); stadium tours; branded merchandise; uniformed ushers; movable seating tiers (to allow baseball, football, concerts, conventions and exhibitions to be staged); the very idea of the stadium forming the hub of a giant entertainment and leisure complex. Judge, stadium developers are still trying to achieve that blend now, and they'd kill for the kind of figures you achieved. During the Astrodome's first twenty years you staged 2,750 sporting events and attracted 74 million visitors – 5.3 million for guided tours alone – resulting in some $1 billion being pumped into the local economy. No wonder they were so pig sick with envy in Dallas, and in all those other cities where they tried to repeat what you did and failed, at huge cost to the taxpayers. You were right, Judge. After the Astrodome, no other dome paid for itself.

Now, I know all this is familiar to you, but just for old time's sake, let me recall some of the early years, when Houston was described as 'a goin' and blowin' kinda town' and you and your partners had just won Houston a slot in Major League baseball with a team called the Colt 45s (a name chosen after a newspaper competition). In particular I love that photo of you and some of the Colt 45 players all wearing ten-gallon hats in the Pepsi-Cola building in New York, showing off the model of this outrageous Dome you were proposing to build. How those urbane Manhattanites must have smirked behind your ramrod Texan backs and muttered, 'It'll never stand up.' Well, can you blame them? It was the largest clear-span building ever conceived, a good 200 feet larger in span than anything ever attempted before.

And that other famous photo of the ground-breaking ceremony for the Dome, when seven of the original shareholders 'speechified' (as was reported in *Newsweek*), before you each fired your Colt 45s into the ground. Bam! Beats ribbon-cutting or silver shovels any day.

For a while the $31.6 million Astrodome, said one reporter, was not just news. It was the only news. Changing the club's name from the Colt 45s to the Astros – your idea, so I believe – was a masterstroke in that respect. Some thought it a silly name. But, again, no one forgot it.

And then, after months of the nation's press and media watching your every move, came the Dome's inaugural night, in April 1965, and there you were, four hours before the doors opened, driving around the concourses in a golf cart, making sure that every toilet was spotless. As it said on the brochure, 'Astrodome – more than a stadium. It's a way of treating people.'

The reaction of the people was exactly as you had hoped. They were just blown away. Even hardened news reporters struggled for superlatives. Said Buddy Diliberto in the *New Orleans Times*, 'When the first astronaut [Uncle Sam's] climbs out of his capsule and sets foot on the moon, five, ten or twenty years from now, he won't be any more awed by the sight than you'll be the first time you step inside the Astrodome. The place is unbelievable. Just unbelievable.'

The man from the *Baltimore News American* wrote, 'Not even Jules Verne or Walt Disney in their most fantastic moments of genius ever conceived anything quite like this unbelievable palace of baseball luxury.'

One of the best endorsements came from the much respected former Dodgers manager and Hall of Famer, Branch Rickey, just eight months before he died. Rickey said that the minute you opened the doors of the Astrodome, every other stadium in the world became obsolete. And he was right.

Inevitably reporters from the bigger cities were more critical, no doubt because they realised Houston had stolen a march on them. The *New York Times* complained that the viewing distances were too long, and that the players appeared like mosquitoes. The *LA Times* columnist Jim Murray wrote scathingly of the Dome, 'Like most of Texas it owes its existence to a lot of hot air. It's a monument to the unliveability of East Texas.'

Hot air! Well, of course hot air played its part, which is why you made the place fully covered with air-con in the first place. Remember how the crowds at the earlier Colt 45 stadium, and the older Buffs Stadium before that, had to endure the discomfort of sitting out in Houston's notoriously damp, sweaty, mosquito-plagued climate? Ushers used to go around the stands with insect spray between innings, and it was not unknown for dozens of fans to seek first-aid treatment for heatstroke. When it wasn't stifling, cold rains would send hundreds of fans scuttling for home. You had to be tough to be a baseball fan in Houston before the Dome.

Anyway, those guys in LA were probably just mad because they'd spent all their money on a Dodgers Stadium that wasn't anything special, while by your first evening you'd already taken $3 million in advance-ticket sales. Mind, you needed every cent. Talk about a gas guzzler! Just keeping the lights on and the air conditioning going cost you $30,000 a month, and that was on top of the $750,000 annual rent you had to pay to Harris County.

Amazing to think that the official name on that opening night was still the Harris County Domed Stadium. And that there were supposed to be seats for 42,217, though somehow 47,876 managed to get in. They saw the first ball being pitched by Texas Governor John Connally (who'd been in the car with JFK in Dallas two years earlier). But you weren't at the opening ceremony, were you, Judge? You were waiting frantically in the wings for the arrival of your old friend LBJ and his wife, Lady Bird, after they had been delayed by a hoax bomb threat.

That the President came at all was such a personal endorsement of your effort, busy as he was sending all those US marines and B-57s into Vietnam at the time, and worrying over civil-rights marches in Alabama. Was it true that you had to lay on nine special telephone lines in your suite, just for LBJ's use?

Mickey Mantle of the New York Yankees scored the first home run, before the Astros won 2–1 in a twelve-inning game. But the baseball was incidental. The Dome was up and running, after seven or eight years of planning, of battles over finance, of votes over bond issues, and of months of speculation that the roof structure would collapse the minute the supporting towers were removed. Remember some of the crazy notions going around then? One was that if the air conditioning was turned off it would start to rain inside the Dome. Another was that the air conditioning would be turned into blow-mode to stop visiting teams scoring home-runs.

But even the sceptics weren't able to predict the real problem the roof would present, were they, Judge, with its 4,596 translucent Lucite panels (the same material as used in B-17 gunner turrets). To everyone's horror, during daytime practice sessions before the first Major League fixture the players lost the flight of the ball against the pattern of the roof and, according to *Time* magazine, ended up staggering around 'like asphyxiated cockroaches'.

'It was like looking at a million suns,' said a bemused Bob Lillis, the Astros shortstop. Some of the players took to wearing sunglasses.

So you hurriedly called your experts together – boy, did you have an army of them at your beck and call – and they decided to paint some of the panels with a special coating. And although that helped the players, it slowly but surely starved the original Bermuda grass of light, so that by the end of that first season you had to spray the dying turf with green paint to cover up your embarrassment. 'Any mistake you can correct with $20,000 worth of paint is no big thing,' you told the press, but surely, Judge, you must have been worried sick. Hell, you can admit that now.

How you managed to track down Monsanto's experimental synthetic turf then being tried out at Brown University in Rhode Island is a whole saga in itself, but Tal Smith, who you'll recall was a key man in your team at the time (and is now the Astros president), told me one story which typified your approach. Tal said that after finally deciding to go with this new and completely unproven product, you ended up in a late-night bargaining session with Monsanto in your private quarters at the Dome. Monsanto were asking for $3 million to fit out the Dome with the new turf, to which you replied, 'Well, that's interesting, because that's exactly what I was thinking of charging you for the marketing rights and the exposure.' So you and Monsanto agreed a trade-off. They would adopt the trade name Astroturf, and you would get the installation for nothing. Never missed a trick, did you, Judge?

How ironic, nevertheless, that the whole Astroturf revolution started because of one unforeseen design flaw in the Dome. On the other hand, some say that you had always anticipated a synthetic surface being necessary in the long run. Whatever, Astroturf's timely arrival certainly saved the Dome in more ways than one. Apart from safeguarding baseball and then later football, with the Houston Oilers, its hard-wearing qualities and easy removal allowed far more events to take place in the Dome than would ever have been possible had the original grass survived. But, Judge, did anyone ever tell you that apparently Monsanto only managed to turn Astroturf into a profitable product, not after fitting out so many stadiums with the stuff, but from selling small samples of it as door mats? Now that is something, don't you think? (It has found other uses too. During the recent trial of President Clinton – don't ask – it was reported that he lined the back of his pick-up with Astroturf.)

Did you also know that artificial turf is now more or less on its way out in the United States? It had a damned fine run, but wherever possible stadium owners are now going back to grass. I'm not sorry about that. I always hated the stuff, as do most fans and players. But all the same, it was one of the most significant developments in twentieth-century sport and, again, it was all down to the Dome.

But if few people ever truly liked Astroturf, everyone just went crazy for that original electronic scoreboard of yours at the Dome. You sure did love gadgetry, eh, Judge? Is it true that you had a car telephone as early as the 1940s? I know that even then your various houses were stuffed full of televisions, and intercoms and suchlike, and that when you owned the radio stations (remember WILD in Alabama?) you pioneered the use of tape recorders, and had built one of the first mobile studios, which was unknown even in New York in those days.

But that scoreboard was just something else, for 1965 at least. As with everything in the Dome, it came complete with a page full of statistics. It was the world's largest animated display, costing $2 million (at a time when $2 million was still big bucks). It had 1,200 miles of wiring and 50,000 lights. But it was the sheer wit and inventiveness of the animations that quite literally lit up a ball game and often really pissed off umpires and visiting teams with its satire and sound effects. Do you recall how, during a lull in games, you would ring down to the operator from your suite and get him to put on the display that went 'Chaaaarge!' Or when an opposition pitcher was stood down, the scoreboard showed a cartoon figure taking a bath, accompanied to the tune of 'April

Showers'. Best of all, when the Astros hit a home-run a forty-second spectacular would follow. First, the Dome's roof appeared to lift off as a baseball soared skywards to a target. Then two cowboys would appear having a noisy gunfight, only to be interrupted by a bull pounding across the scoreboard, with an American flag flying from one horn, and a Texan Lone Star flag from the other. Yi hi! Now that was, to borrow Larry McMurty's phrase, 'echt-Texas' at its best.

Well, Judge, you must realise that nowadays, what with all our fancy computerised animations and Playstations – hell, you'd just love those – your original scoreboard would be thought of as downright primitive. Like Stone Age etchings. But I tell you, when I was last at the Dome and saw a film of that original display, it had all the freshness and purity of an early Disney cartoon. I confess, I felt quite emotional seeing it go off again, just as I had back in 1980.

What you don't know, Judge, is that, sorry to say, the scoreboard got ripped out in 1988, when your successors made a whole load of changes to the Dome, and ended up spending more on taking away all the asbestos behind it than the board had cost in the first place. There's now a huge matrix board – still the largest in the USA, naturally – and two video screens, which relay much better pictures, but I have to say, Judge, without any of the style or verve of the original. The Astro's current art director, Logan Goodson, told me that when he watched games at the Dome as a small boy, the scoreboard had a personality all of its own. He said, 'It was almost like the building was watching the game with you. It reacted to the plays as if it was speaking directly to you. Taking it down in '88 was like cutting out the building's tongue.'

Nowadays the only place you can get a glimpse of what the board was like is in your old apartment, the one you modestly called the Celestial Suite, on the top floor of the Sheraton Astrodome Hotel, which you'll be pleased to hear still exists and has in fact been recently renovated. And yes, Judge, rest assured that is still the most expensive suite in the world. A nice young man showed me round and I think he said it would cost $5,000 a night, though mostly it was hired out for parties. Many of the original features and fittings put in by you and your first wife, Dene, are still there, just as they were when the likes of Elvis Presley stayed. I won't waste your time recalling the various rooms – the Marble

Library, the Bird Cage dining room, the Tarzan Room or the P. T. Barnum and Lady Chatterley suites – as the names pretty much speak for themselves, but I will just mention the Mini-Dome, which I believe you used as your own private bar. My guide showed me the spot on the dance floor-cum-mini-baseball-diamond where you can stand under the Mini-Dome and, on second base, hear the same echo effect as in the real Dome (which you can still see through the windows). Apparently when the suite is booked the mini-scoreboard still lights up whenever the Astros score a home-run across the road.

Someone else I met at the Dome recently was one of the original usherettes, still working there after thirty-seven years. You won't remember her name. You had, what was it, 2,000 staff on duty for every ball game; stewards, ushers, cleaners, elevator operators, you name it, they were there, all with their own uniform and title. Virginia Layton joined up in 1962, when the Colt 45s started playing in that temporary stadium (now re-erected in Mexico, I believe) you built next to the site where the Dome was being constructed. She was twenty-three at the time and had just started teaching English at Fonville Middle School when she became an original Triggerette – as you called the usherettes in those days – in order to supplement her income and be part of the sport she loved. She remembered how you sent all the staff off to charm school to learn how to deal with the public, how to stand, how to get the hair and make-up just right. For stadium staff in those days that was pretty radical stuff. Virginia's now close to sixty, but I tell you, Judge, she's a credit to the Dome and to the State of Texas. Slim, sweet-natured and turned out real neat, just how you'd approve. I couldn't believe she'd never married, but she said she spent so many evenings and weekends at the Dome that it just wouldn't be fair to a husband. I guess she was, like so many of the staff there, married to the Dome. You come across that a lot at stadiums. People just sort of fall in love with the place. I can understand that, and I know you can. You and your wife even lived in the Dome for a while.

With a glint in her eye, Virginia told me that as a Triggerette she wore 'a straight skirt with blue stitching down the side, with a boxy-type little short-sleeved jacket, a baseball cap – either orange or blue – orange patent shoes, and an orange decal on my shirt which said Colt 45s'.

Three years later in the Dome she was transformed into a

Spacette. In fact, Judge, she still has her original Spacette uniform back home as a keepsake, which I know will touch you because you took so much care in working with the designers on every detail, right down to the buttons. Virginia described the uniform to me as a gold lamé skirt, with little blue Western boots trimmed in gold and a dinky little pillbox hat. Later on the style changed to yellow go-go boots with hot pants, worn under wraparound yellow and orange skirts. How did we look in the Seventies, eh, Judge! I expected her to say those uniforms were embarrassing, but, no, she said they were 'real cute'.

She also said you insisted that all the ushers were female, although a few guys were always on hand in case there was any trouble. But there never really was. The Dome just wasn't that sort of a place. There were male staff down on the turf, however, dressed in orange spacesuits and white helmets. Was it you who decided to call them Earthmen? One of their jobs was to vacuum the Astroturf in between innings. They made quite a show of it, as I recall, though they must have been boiling inside those suits.

But it wasn't just the staff who dressed up. 'In the early years,' Virginia reminisced, 'everyone dressed up to come to the Astrodome. It was not as casual as today. Men wore shirts and ties and blazers and what-have-you. A lot of women wore hats, most were in dresses, and in winter they wore furs, because this was *the* place to come. People would walk into the Dome and their mouths would drop and they'd say, "Oh my God, look at this!" People were spellbound. The colour and the size of the place were just overwhelming.'

Virginia reeled off a list of all the famous people and events she had seen. There was Lyndon Johnson and Lady Bird, of course, and all the astronauts from nearby NASA, who used to parade around before being presented with their gold life passes for the Dome. She also recalled the concerts by Elvis, the Rolling Stones (three times), the Beach Boys, Frank Sinatra, Andy Williams, and the night Bob Hope hosted a show featuring Raquel Welch, Bobby Sherman, Cary Grant and Glen Campbell, in aid of three Apollo astronauts who were killed in a fire on the launch pad. One of that poor trio was Gus Grissom, a gold life pass holder. Strangely enough the worst attended concert at the Dome was the first one, starring Judy Garland and the Supremes. Diana Ross is still packin' 'em in, by the way, Judge. So are the Stones. You know, I would bet that those boys have been to more stadiums than I have.

What else? Well, checking through my long, long list, there was Billy Graham's Crusade for Christ, which as you'll recall filled the Dome to the rafters. (Maybe because a few years earlier Graham called Houston the most corrupt city in the nation and folk wanted to prove how wrong he was.) Close to your heart were the regular circuses put on by the Ringling Bros and Barnum & Bailey (which of course you later bought a slice of, because you loved the circus more than anything, certainly more than baseball or football). Evil Knievel did his first indoor jump in the Dome in 1971, and there were all kinds of weird events involving motorcycles and tiny little racing cars, and the movie première of Robert Altman's *Brewster McCloud*, which he filmed inside the Dome. (Judge, I still haven't seen that film, can you believe that?)

Sportswise, in addition to the occasional oddity such as polo, athletics and lacrosse, the University of Houston and Tulsa played the world's first indoor American football game in 1965. Real Madrid and West Ham played the world's first indoor soccer match in 1968, and in that same year the University of Houston beat UCLA 71–69 in front of a world-record crowd for a basketball game of 52,693. Another world record was the 37,321 who saw Muhammad Ali beat Ernie Terrell, in 1967. In fact, just about the only world record I have not been able to verify is the possibility that the Astrodome has garnered more statistics about itself than any other stadium on the planet.

Virginia also remembered the huge fuss over the bloodless bullfights you put on, and that famous night when Billy Jean King and Bobby Riggs played out the 'Battle of the Sexes' in 1973. Billy Jean sure showed Bobby who was boss, and went home $100,000 richer.

Virginia never liked the Auto Thrill and Destruction Derbies, because of the type of custom they attracted. I didn't ask her either about the night when Karel Soucek, billed as the 'Last of the Niagra Daredevils', attempted to drop from the roof in a barrel, into a small tank of water. He missed, and therefore sadly lived up to his billing.

Finally, I need hardly add, there was the annual 'Go-Texan' Houston Livestock and Rodeo Show, that riot of Wild West cowboy capers which you always loved, and which became, once it switched to the Dome, the biggest event of its kind in the world, drawing something like 1.8 million visitors over the course of twenty days (more than baseball). Those Livestock people and their 13,000 volunteers grew to become one of the most powerful lobbying organisations in Houston.

But hellfire, Judge, you know all this and I reckon you must sense by now that I'm stalling. So I guess it's time to quit bullshitting and come to the point.

Earlier on I mentioned how your successors tore out the old scoreboard in 1988. Well, Judge, I'm afraid they did more than that. Shortly after you passed on in '82, Houston went through some real bad times. Oil prices slumped. Unemployment rose. At the Dome the roof was beginning to leak so bad that fans used to bring in umbrellas, and the seats got all worn and torn. So did the Astroturf, even though they'd put down a replacement surface in 1978. Staff even started to see rats scooting around the place.

But the real crunch came when your old sparring partner Bud Adams threatened to take the Oilers away to Jacksonville if Harris County didn't spend some serious money on upgrading the Dome. He said there were too few seats between the end zones. The skyboxes were just too sky-high for comfort, and by the mid Eighties, with just under 48,000 seats for football, the Dome was the smallest of the twenty-eight NFL stadiums. Bud also made a big noise about the rent the Oilers were paying. He said that if the Dome was the eighth wonder of the world, the rent was the ninth.

So Bud fought and scratched and in 1987 he managed to persuade Harris County to issue $60 million in bonds to pay for an upgrade. That was when they tore out the scoreboard, added another level of sixty-five private suites closer to the action, laid down concrete on the arena floor, bought new Astroturf pitches, one for baseball, one for football, and squeezed in an extra 10,000 seats. Something had to give, though, and sorry, Judge, but your private quarters were cleared away. Typsy Tavern, bowling alley, the lot. Apparently a lot of your stuff went into storage, though your Italian marble inlaid desk was put on display in the Dome museum, where I have to tell you it looks like a duck out of water.

If that wasn't sacrilege enough, they stuck up four huge stair towers around the outside of the Dome to service all those extra seats, thus ruining for ever the clean, uncluttered lines of the bowl. A lot of people got angry about that, and quite rightly too, though if that was the price of keeping the Oilers in town, what could be done?

But that wasn't all. Bud carried on hollering about the rent and by the mid 1990s he was demanding either equal status with the Astros – which Harris County refused – or more public money to . . . wait for it, build a completely new stadium! Can you believe that, Judge? Not content with having helped to bring about the destruction of many of the Dome's finest, best-loved features, he now wanted out altogether. As you can imagine, that made Oilers fans crazy as hell. But Bud wouldn't budge and in 1996 – I hope you're sitting down when you read this – he went and took the Oilers off to Tennessee. Imagine that! A Houstonian, robbing his own people of pro-football action.

But it gets worse, Judge. You see, the annual Bluebonnet Bowl had already gone from the Dome, in 1985. They took the game back to the Rice Stadium. Then the University of Houston Cougars football team left the Dome for the Robertston Stadium. They said it felt more like home, being back on campus.

This left just the Astros and the Houston Livestock and Rodeo Show as the Dome's only regular, major tenants.

Well, I guess you know what's coming next. Once the Oilers had departed, the new owner of the Astros, Drayton McLane, started saying that he wanted a new stadium too. Frightened of losing the Astros as well as the Oilers, what could the city do but, after months of debates and referendums, agree to put up yet more bonds to finance a new ballpark. Some critics call this kind of dealing a form of legalised blackmail. They say that it's wrong for wealthy club owners to threaten to take away their teams unless the public pay for stadiums designed for private gain. In fact, there are whole books on this very subject, full of densely argued economic data. But the bottom line is the same as ever. In stadiums as in life, if you want to have a party, someone has to pick up the tab. Still, why should either of us care about that, eh, Judge? You're in your Celestial Suite and I don't pay US taxes.

So, going back to this new ballpark they're building in Houston, you may be interested to know that it has been designed by a firm of architects based in Kansas who I don't think were into sport when you were around. They're called HOK, and they worked on the design with the Houston engineers Walter P. Moore Associates, who did so much brilliant work for you back in the early days at the Dome. The new ballpark is now finished, at a cost of $265 million, and is called Enron Field (for which Enron paid $100 million naming rights). Now, where's the romance in that? Anyway, Enron Field has 42,000 seats and a retractable roof (not because the climate got any better in Houston but so that they can grow natural turf inside). And can you guess where this modern marvel is sited? Downtown, on the site of the old Union Station. It's a crazy old world, is it not, Judge? In your day everyone was shoving stadiums out on to the prairies, where they could park tens of thousands of automobiles and keep the traffic out on the freeways, where it belonged.

Yet now, cities all over the US are bringing baseball back to the downtown areas in the hope that this might trigger an economic and social revival. Lots of Wrigleyvilles all over the nation, that's what is wanted. I can see why. I've met several Houstonians who say they haven't been downtown for ten or fifteen years. No need. No desire. So maybe the ballpark might just change their minds. Otherwise, in another twenty to thirty years you can bet your sweet bippy what'll happen. The whole process will go into reverse and it'll be 'Hey, let's get these darned stadiums out of our cities, just like they used to be.'

As for the retractable roof, well, Judge, they're all the rage these days. Big great ugly things they are in many cases. But whether they're needed or not, every city wants one, just like they used to want a dome. It'll certainly be interesting to see how often they play with the hood off. Could we see the return of insect sprays in Houston for the seventh-inning stretch?

Anyway, Judge, I know all this is maybe a huge shock to you, so I'll finish my tale quickly before coming to my final point.

After the Oilers quit town for Tennessee a group of local businessmen led by Bob McNair worked their socks off to try to get an expansion place being offered by the NFL, so as to bring pro football back to Houston. In the end the one place up for grabs was between LA and Houston, with the main battle being to see who could deliver the best stadium. So Harris County and the architects did all kinds of studies at the Astrodome to see if they could turn it into a modern football stadium. But, I'm sorry, Judge, they found that it would still have cost too much, with too few seats ending up in prime locations.

Result? Yessiree, they're going to build a new, $310 million football stadium for 69,500 people, with, of course, a retractable roof and a natural turf pitch. HOK are the architects on this one too. Shoot, they get everywhere, those Kansas boys.

And where is this second new Houston stadium going to be built? Why, Judge, since you ask, it's going to be built right next door to the Astrodome, as it happens, opening, they hope, in 2002. They haven't decided on a name for the new team yet, but you can be pretty sure the stadium name will go to the highest bidder. It's the modern way.

OK, so now what's going to happen to your dear, thirty-five-year-old Dome? The Astros don't want it. (They played their last game there in 1999, going down 7–5 to the Braves in the NL play-offs.) The new football franchise doesn't want it. None of the college teams want it. So who does want it?

Well, Judge, at the time of writing, sorry to say, no one seems quite sure. When I first heard of what was happening my big fear was that they would tear the place down and turn it into a car park for the new stadium. You know Houston better than most, Judge. Build 'em up, knock 'em down. No sentiment there. Why, they've even torn down the Shamrock, which was about as close to a piece of history as Houston ever got before the Astrodome.

That's why I went back to Houston a few months ago to talk to a few people and tell them exactly what I think, as someone who believes that the Astrodome deserves better than to be flattened. After all, the United States has plenty of car parks, but there's only one Astrodome.

It seems, thank heavens, that the threat of demolition is only slight, so that is a huge relief. If nothing else, they tell me, there's still $70 million owing on the place, left over from the last refit. Instead, they've had a few approaches from interested parties. A major studio and entertainments group is looking at it as a possible performance centre. Or it could be preserved for use by the Houston Livestock and Rodeo people, to supplement their main show, which will transfer to the new football stadium. Seems like it could otherwise end up as either a hotel, or for retail, or even as an indoor arena for ice hockey and basketball, with an accompanying museum.

If any of these options means saving the Astrodome, then so be it. After all, plenty of buildings change use throughout the course of their lives. Here in London we've opened a Dome of our own, for a big Millennium 'experience', and after a year that'll also be converted into something else altogether.

But being a bit of a maverick myself, I believe that the Astrodome deserves an entirely different fate, and that is the real reason I am writing to you now, because I happen to think that you might be quite tickled by the idea.

This is what I told the Dome people when I was last there. I said please, please don't pull down the Astrodome. Don't turn it into something undignified either. Instead, I suggested, pull down those stair towers, so we can at least see the Dome in its original glory. Then, build a tall fence around the whole damn building, to keep out vandals. Seal all the gates except one, and have this gate lead up to a steel cage, from where the interior of the Dome could be viewed by members of the public, maybe for a dollar a time. Next, dig up half the concrete floor until you get back to the earth, but leave the other half of the Astroturf pitch in place. Set up some time-lapse cameras on the inside, and on the outside. Then turn off all the lights. Turn off all the power, except those feeds to the steel cage and to the cameras.

By this stage of my 'speechifying', Judge, as you can imagine, the guys at the Dome were starting to give me some suspicious looks, as if I were completely mad.

'And what do we do then?' they asked, open-mouthed, maybe thinking about calling security.

And I said, 'Nothing. You do nothing.'

'Nothing? Why would we want to do nothing?' (Spoken like true Texans.)

'Because,' I said, 'if you do nothing, eventually the Dome will fall down.'

I could see that they were not, how shall I put it, 'comfortable' with this idea.

OK, I conceded, it might take some time for the building to fall down. A lot of time, in fact. But, in the end, fall down it will. Maybe not in twenty years. But maybe in fifty years you'd start to see some serious structural faults occurring. And in maybe a hundred years sections of the roof might start to fall in. Meanwhile, wild grass would start growing up on the exposed half of the pitch, providing a poignant contrast with the fading Astroturf. But all in all the elements, and time, would do most of the work.

Well, you can imagine, Judge, they were now ready to call a

doctor to have me certified. But I held my ground. I said, gentlemen, the Astrodome is one of the greatest American buildings of all time. Once it symbolised the future. Once it demonstrated the genius and power and optimism (and sense of fun) of a whole generation of Americans, at a pivotal point in your country's history, and just because it may now be surplus to requirements does not in any way invalidate the original vision which made it possible.

I was not just talking about the building's merits as a testbed for new technology. The Finnish architect Alvar Aalto once said that you could not truly judge the merit of a new building until it was at least thirty years old. So now the Astrodome is thirty-five years old, I think it's time we stood back and took another, objective look at its magnificent drum and its elegantly shaped domed roof, and acknowledge that in fact the Astrodome is also a breathtakingly beautiful and superbly proportioned piece of modern architecture.

In short, I declared in triumphant conclusion, the Astrodome would make a damned fine ruin. Maybe the best ruin the United States of America will ever have.

Well, you can imagine, the guys at the Dome smiled politely, shook my hand and said the idea was an interesting one. But once I'd left the room I knew what they'd be saying, especially the one who seemed very twitchy throughout the meeting and kept crunching mints loudly.

But, Judge, I want you to know that whatever ridicule I may bring down on myself as a result of this suggestion, I meant what I said, and if only I had your powers of oratory, then maybe I could persuade enough people that this crazy notion of mine actually makes perfect sense.

If the Astrodome truly was the Colosseum of the twentieth century, as I know you believed it was (and I agree), and if it truly was the eighth wonder of the world, then why not allow it the same fate as the Colosseum and all other great wonders, the pyramids of Egypt, the Hanging Gardens of Babylon, the statue of Zeus at Olympia, the Colossus at Rhodes? What greater honour could our generation bestow upon the Astrodome than to allow it to die with dignity? And, besides, think of all the tourists it would attract over the course of the next few centuries.

So what do you think, Judge? Good idea or what? Of course

there's no way of you letting me know, me not being into spiritualism and all that, but, somehow, I sort of think that your answer would be yes.

Anyway, that's enough from me. I have to get on with some stuff I'm writing about the new Wembley Stadium in London. Do you know, Judge, they're saying that it'll be the greatest stadium ever built. Now, where have I heard that before?

13
CIUDAD DE LOS ESTADIOS, 4

Thursday, 22 October. 08.30. Breakfast at Enrique's.
Totally nude girls. Typsy Taverns. Triggerettes in hotpants. Phew, some dream that was last night. So where was I? Oh yes, I was just saying to Mariano that if this quest of mine, of ours, to see as many Buenos Aires football grounds as possible in six days had gone horribly wrong – perhaps if I had been rebuffed, or mugged *en route*, or if Mariano and I hadn't hit it off so well – maybe the setbacks would have nudged me closer towards that final, fateful moment, which I know will come, but am not sure when, of letting go. Of letting go, once and for all, of this stadium obsession of mine. Just letting go.

Adios, El Canchólogo. It was nice knowing you. Bye-bye, filing cabinets. Oh yes, and farewell to that accursed pile of cuttings. There it lies, my mountain of paper, abandoned, crumbling into dust, like, like a magnificent ruin on a Texan prairie.

I had thought, I said to Mariano as we drank coffee before setting off, that this trip might serve as some kind of aversion therapy. But, no, I had checked, and it wouldn't have worked in any circumstances.

According to the experts, aversion therapy, which in any case is largely discredited, depends on administering some form of 'painful stimulus' in order to wean the subject from his or her 'undesired emotional response' – say, an addiction to cigarettes or 'fetishistic objects'. (Oddly enough, the books don't mention stadiums in the latter category.) But I had not received an electric shock every time I entered a stadium in Buenos Aires. I had not received any shocks at all. In fact most people had been so friendly and welcoming, or at least unfriendly but interesting, that, far from putting me off stadiums, my obsession had merely been fed.

Like a crazed cat let loose in a wool shop, I was having a good time. We both were. No one to tell us what to do. No penalties for fuck-ups. Reaching into parts of Buenos Aires where no tourists, let alone many *porteños*, ever dare to roam. We could do anything we liked. Idle away hours in bars. Creep furtively into strip clubs. Stroll in the city's parks. Go to the beach.

But we didn't do any of these things, Mariano and I. We were having fun with my quest. With our quest. With our adventure.

All right, maybe I was still seeking some sober justification for what seemed otherwise a fairly vacuous form of pursuit. It was not as if I were doing the trip to research a travel guide. Not even a stadium guide. Not even for a dare.

Maybe I had become the man in the joke who goes to his doctor and says. 'Doctor, all my friends think I'm weird because I like sausages.'

'But that's ridiculous,' replies the doctor. 'There's no harm in liking sausages. Why, I like sausages too.'

'You do?' exclaims the man. 'That's great! You must come to my house and see my collection.'

'You know, Mariano,' I went on, 'that expertise is rather like a rash. It creeps up on you, until one day you get a telephone call and a reporter or a researcher asks, could you comment on this or that in relation to your chosen subject, and if you do it well, and within the time allotted, preferably ending on a pithy note, full of conviction, your name goes down in a contacts book, or on a database, and you are thus formally enrolled as "an expert". And then you're hooked. Marked for life. Trapped.'

On one day, I told Mariano, I once managed eleven radio interviews in just under two hours. Sometimes I get calls from the strangest of sources; for example, from an agency wanting to track down a perfectly circular stadium for a television commercial, or from a location manager needing to shoot a scene in an old-fashioned stadium dressing-room. On occasions I get calls from complete strangers wanting me to furnish them with a quiz answer.

There are experts on everything these days. At the last estimate in 1998, the department which covers the BBC's daily news programmes had over 32,000 names and organisations on its collective contacts list. One of them, I know for certain, is an expert on the BBC. Apparently my name comes up, along with thirty others, if you type in the word 'stadium', but, oddly, it does not appear at all amongst those listed under the word 'stadia'.

God, I was tired.

This morning over coffee I confessed to Mariano: 'I am getting bored with stadiums, you know. Not with the stadiums themselves, so much as the study of them. Sometimes I feel like an actor in a soap opera who stayed on in a bit part too long. I've become typecast. I'm losing my range of vocabulary. I've learnt some jargon, but lost a whole language in the process. Sometimes I feel as if I am just a bore in polite society, and on other occasions that I am just too polite in boring society. You wouldn't believe how dull some of the stadium hobbyists are. I've heard of one groundhopper who will not tick off a ground from his list until he has seen at least one goal scored there. If it's nil–nil after ninety minutes he has to go back. Even if the ground's in the far north and he lives in the far south, or wherever.'

Mariano smiled and suggested we make a move. His silence as we went down to the car seemed to say, 'There are worse things in life.' No doubt he heard much worse in his consulting room. He understood, as do those who reject aversion therapy, that it is not the act of visiting stadiums (or the need to see goals being scored in them) that forms the root of the poor groundhopper's problem. It is the void in his life that he chooses to fill with such nonsense; the unforced setting of targets, the compilation of travel plans, the contrivance of arbitrary rules.

That settled, Mariano and I set off once again with our maps and lists for another day and another five stadiums on our schedule.

Thursday, 22 October. 09.30. Stadium No. 15. Atlanta.

We were driving by the famous Chacarita cemetery in Buenos Aires, resting place of the revered *tanguista* Carlos Gardel and also of Juan Perón, who was eventually ousted by a bloody coup in 1955, only to die after a brief return to power in 1974. Ironically his first wife, Evita, despite her humble origins, lies in the much posher cemetery of Recoleta.

A few blocks from the Chacarita graveyard, in the predominantly Jewish *barrio* of Villa Crespo, is the ground of Atlanta, once a regular contender in the top-flight, now just middling in the second division. The club's honorary architect, Gonzalo, happened to be there when we arrived, and he told us the story behind one of Argentinian football's bitterest rivalries. This was an even better start to the day than I had expected.

Atlanta, said Gonzalo, had started out in 1905 as a nomadic club, hence their nickname, *los bohemios*, the bohemians. Eventually, in 1922, they settled at a ground with the address 400 Calle Humboldt, Villa Crespo. Eleven years later, another local club, Chacarita Juniors, known as *los funebreros* (the grave-diggers), started renting the field next door to Atlanta, at 300 Humboldt.

Familiarity soon bred contempt. The two sets of fans bated each other continually, until finally, in 1943, Atlanta's members managed to raise sufficient cash to buy both their own field and that of Chacarita's. Thus erupted an even fiercer and quite vitriolic rivalry which continues until today.

Turned out on to the streets by their neighbours, in 1945 Chacarita set up a new ground seven kilometres east, in the adjoining municipality of San Martin. After the homely bustle of Villa Crespo, San Martin must have seemed as bereft of life as the Chacarita Cemetery itself. Less so, in fact, since no tourists ever bother with San Martin and there are fewer trees. Meanwhile, to exacerbate relationships further, Atlanta did not actually build on Chacarita's old field until 1960. It just lay unused, other than for training. How the hurt must have festered, particularly when Chacarita had to return to Humboldt to face Atlanta.

In fact, during the week of my visit, the sporting press was full of doom-laden predictions of violent confrontation when the old rivals were due to meet for a Primera B Nacional clash in a few weeks' time. Moreover, Chacarita's *barra bravas* were amongst the most notorious in the whole country.

The new stadium Atlanta eventually built on part of Chacarita's old pitch in the early 1960s followed a now quite familiar format, essentially consisting of three sides of wooden bleachers and a fourth side filled by an uncovered, concrete main stand. Under the stand was a gymnasium, filled, when we were there, with excited, clamorous schoolchildren.

I was still enchanted and appalled in equal measure by all these wooden bleachers I was seeing in Buenos Aires. Much of Atlanta's wood, said Gonzalo, came from Boca Juniors in the early 1960s.

He described it as 'quebracho' – a form of hard wood – although it felt distinctly pliable when we walked up and down it, being careful not to let our feet slip through the wide gaps that appeared here and there between some of the more warped planks. After the year 2000, said Gonzalo, all the wood would have to be replaced by concrete. He reckoned this would cost $3.5 million. I asked how Atlanta would afford this. Average gates were down to 4,000 (though still good for the second division). A few years earlier the club had been declared bankrupt.

The architect shrugged. 'God will provide.' Another man who had joined us muttered something about Japanese sponsors.

Atlanta's real hope lay in persuading the Argentinian Football Association to put back the deadline. Most second-division clubs depended heavily on wooden terracing, said Gonzalo, but whereas Primera A clubs were allocated $1.2 million from television revenues every season, Primera B clubs received only $90,000. Just maintaining the existing wood was a constant headache. His real job as an architect was for the city council, in flood control. No one paid him to work at Atlanta. He did it for love. Every year it was his name on the ground's safety certificate. For an honorary official it was big responsibility.

As we spoke I couldn't help but notice an *asado*, or barbecue, being lit by groundstaff on the scrubby earth beneath one of the banks of bleachers. 'Ahem,' I interjected. Wouldn't this tend to, er . . . burn the wood above?

Not at all, Gonzalo insisted blithely. Quebracho does not catch light easily, and Atlanta always make sure there are firemen on duty during games. Besides, the *asado* is one of the great traditions of Argentinian life. (Indeed, no lunch break at a football ground is complete without one.)

I then asked if there were still any Jewish links with the club.

There were, Gonzalo said, though not officially. He pointed out that the central section of the main stand was dedicated to one Leon Kolbowski. The last two presidents had also been Jewish, but that was only by chance. Visiting fans chanted insults such as 'Yiddos!' (as they do at Tottenham Hotspur in London, also a club with a strong Jewish association). But then Chacarita, despite moving out of town so many years before, had their fair share of Jewish fans too, so a lot of the chants meant little. 'That's football,' Gonzalo concluded.

As we returned to the car I decided to take a photograph of Atlanta's now crumbling clubhouse, a few yards down from the ground. It had clearly been abandoned some time before. You could even see in the background remains of an old stand and ticket booths, presumably left over from Chacarita's old ground.

An old lady walking her dog berated us. 'Why are you photographing that? Don't! It's ugly! It's not the same any more. In the old days it was beautiful. Nice and clean. The club was full of members, but the committee stole all the money.' Maybe she was a Chacarita supporter.

I told Mariano of a chant I had heard at Tottenham a year or two earlier. It had been sung by fans of my own team, Aston Villa, about Tottenham's German striker, Jurgen Klinsmann. At the time, surrounded by supposed allies, I had not known whether to cringe, to berate my fellow supporters, or to admire their inventiveness. Sung to the tune of a well-known song from the musical *Mary Poppins*, it went: 'Chim chimeree, chim chimeree, chim chim cheroo, Klinsmann was a Nazi and now he's a Jew.'

Mariano told me of a chant he had heard at matches involving Atlanta. In English it went something like this: 'Fucking Jews, we are going to kill you.'

'Ah well,' we sighed, returning to Mariano's battered old brown Toyota. 'That's football.'

Thursday, 22 October. 11.30. Stadium No. 16. Chacarita Juniors. By the time we had driven out to the fraying edges of the metropolis, to the humble suburbs of San Martin, Chacarita's groundstaff had fired up an *asado* under their own bleachers and opened up some wine. Smoke drifted up between the planks, through more gaps wide enough to insert one's foot. The smell of roasting meat wafted across the pitch.

All four sides of Chacarita's ground were made of narrow bleachers on steel supports, so that at pitch level the stands took on an unnerving transparency, as if the whole affair had been knocked up the week before and would move on to another field the week after, like one of the itinerant wooden Roman amphitheatres of ancient times. Only the hacienda-style ticket booths, dressing-rooms and *intendente*'s house – with its Madonna in a niche and an early Christmas greeting pinned on to the door –

suggested any permanence. All around the ground the *barrio* appeared to consist of block after block of one-storey houses, laid out on a regular grid plan. From the top of the bleachers we could see for miles in all directions, across a flat terrain that only a few decades ago had no doubt been wide open *pampas*. But this was no sleepy suburb. A gaggle of swaggering men and youths appeared from nowhere, watching Mariano and me like hawks. In the distance a helicopter hovered above some houses. 'Sons of bitches!' cried the youths, shaking their fists up to the overcast skies. In the helicopter, we saw, were uniformed police, searching for someone on the ground.

One of the lads, with long, lank black hair and the feline features of a South American Indian, approached Mariano.

'Give me some money,' he demanded.

Mariano, knowing the score, gave him two dollars.

'Give me more.'

Mariano gave him another two dollars.

'Now give me some cigarettes.'

Mariano gave him some cigarettes.

The youth then offered Mariano some *chorizo*. Mariano declined.

Business over, one of the older men started bragging. He had been one of fifteen *barra bravas* from Chacarita – hired hands, mercenaries, dedicated to causing a stir – who claimed to have travelled to the recent World Cup in France courtesy of the Argentinian Football Association (which of course denied all such nonsense). In Mexico, in 1986, he and others had stolen banners from English fans in a set-to elevated to legendary status within hooligan circles. They still had the banners stored away, said the Chacarita man. Trophies of war.

I felt as if we were in some wild Andean outpost, a million miles from the Villa Crespo and from all the usual assurances of the city. One of the club officials ambled out from the dressing-rooms and agreed that the club did still feel as if it were in exile. Older fans would never forget what Atlanta did in 1943. Half the club's support still came from what he called the Capital. The rest were locals from San Martin.

No one was sure what the future held for the club. In 1968 Chacarita had won the Championship. (Mariano remembered it well. As a small boy he had cried because they took it from River.)

Now they were challenging for promotion back to the top division. Yet to look at their ground it seemed hardly adequate to sustain any serious professional outfit. I could not believe that it held 30,000, as the official insisted. How did the flimsy wood support all those feet? (I realised, I was beginning to develop a bleacher fixation.)

Chacarita's man told us that there were currently three options: to renovate the ground, by replacing the wood with concrete, to build a new ground, or to ground share with another second-division club, called Tigre. 'Tigre are gay!' one of the youths grunted, making as if he were vomiting at the very mention of the name.

Back on the street outside the ground we were relieved to find the car still in one piece. We were glad to get away ourselves in one piece.

(The following Sunday there would be yet another outbreak of serious crowd violence at Chacarita. According to one newspaper report, fans of the visiting club, All Boys, started attacking the local fans, officials and the press. The police waded in with CS gas and rubber bullets. Chacarita's president, a union leader, tried to calm the situation by appealing over the public-address system for his own fans not to respond to provocation, but in the process managed only to worsen the situation. Before police reinforcements were able to restore order, total anarchy reigned for half an hour, during which time, bizarrely, the referee signalled for the game to start in order to meet the television schedules. Later, with blood on his shirt, the All Boys president denied that his *barra bravas* had started it all.

Just another afternoon in Argentinian football.

I suppose I should have been shocked, yet the first question that came to mind when I read the report was how on earth did the wood stand up to all that aggro?)

Thursday, 22 October. Afternoon. Stadiums Nos. 16, 17, 18.
Too much now. I was starting to suffer from information overload, and I guess that by now you must feel the same.

Lots of stadiums. Lots of wooden bleachers. Time to speed up. Though Mariano and I were determined to plough on, ticking off the names on our schedules, after our unsettling excursion to

Chacarita we were talking less about football and more about music, and films, and what it was like to be a Jew in modern Argentina. Sometimes, he said, it was fine. Buenos Aires was, after all, home to the largest Jewish community in Latin America, and the fourth largest in the world. Jews were the third-largest ethnic group in the city after the Italians and Spanish. As Jorge Luis Borges said, 'Our entire country is imported. Everyone here is really from somewhere else.'

Sometimes things were not so good. Four years earlier eighty-six people had been killed by a bomb at a Jewish cultural centre. But, then, said Mariano, life in the city was hard for a lot of people. How else would he have been able to make a living as a pyschoanalyst?

By now we were back in the suburbs of the Cap. Fed., a few miles between Atlanta and Vélez Sarsfield, and more than ready for lunch in the splendidly dingy surrounds of the café under the main stand of the Estadio Islas Malvinas (or Falkland Islands Stadium). The stadium, the *cancha*, more like, was the home of the second-division club All Boys, one of a dozen or so Argentinian clubs (such as River Plate, Boca Juniors and Newell's Old Boys) whose nationalistic passions had never been roused quite enough to persuade them to abandon their obviously English nomenclature.

But if any of the All Boys old boys in the café realised that I was British, as I studied the fading team photographs on the walls, none seemed to care enough to take his eyes off the mountainous, steaming portions of pasta being served. Creaking fans circled above us. Plastic flowers sat on the Formica-top tables. A companionable clatter filled the café. While Mariano ordered our lunch, a grey-haired woman shuffled out from the Secretaría across the corridor (which itself formed the players' tunnel) and handed me a single sheet of typewritten paper. This explained that the ground had opened in 1963 and now held 9,400. It had been named after the Malvinas on 2 April 1982, the day of the Argentinian invasion of the islands. All Boys had been with their boys in battle all the way.

Nineteen eighty-two. Was it really that long ago? What had I been doing during the war? asked Mariano. As it happened, finishing off a book. My first, and what I assumed would be my last book on . . . football grounds.

After lunch and a chat with a genial *socio* called Tony, we ambled out into the ground and saw that it was decked in white and black paint, in a poor state of repair, and had a narrow terrace so close to the back of one goal net that you could imagine fans whispering all kinds of lewd insults to visiting goalkeepers from behind the safety of the perimeter fence.

'Hey, keeper, who's your wife with today?'

'Hey, fat-arse, why so nervous with crosses?'

Overlooking the opposite end was a tall building. A school for the deaf, I later discovered, which was just as well, for on the pitch rusting scaffolding was being assembled in readiness for a rock concert. We asked one of the roadies who would be playing. *Los Piojos*, he said, showing us his T-shirt.

Los Piojos, Mariano explained, meant literally 'the lice'. In Buenos Aires, he said, allegiances to bands (and once also to *tanguistas*) were often as passionate as they were to football clubs. *Los Piojos* he described as one of the country's leading urban grunge bands with a solid following among working-class kids. All Boys (which may well have also described the band's following) were expecting to make $8–9,000 from the gig, money which would go towards replacing their wooden bleachers with concrete terracing.

A mile or so away, Argentinos Juniors were clearly midway through that very same process. Or at least they had started. Their ground was now boarded up completely, though through gaps in the fence we could see what appeared to be a half-built concrete stadium. Nothing unusual there. Argentinian clubs often take years to raise the capital to complete their ground works. Argentinos Juniors, the club where Diego Maradona started as a teenage prodigy in 1976, had apparently started work on their reconstruction eighteen months earlier, and were now sharing at Ferrocarril. Indefinitely, I would have thought, judging by the slow progress being made and the weeds growing up around the new sections of concrete. Outside the club's *sede* (or HQ) across the railway line, part of the Complejo Polideportivo las Malvinas, a sinister-looking guard told us that no one was there from the club to speak to us. Mariano felt it best not to describe me as a British journalist. You just never knew. So this time we chose not to persist.

'Normally,' said Mariano, 'I wouldn't even dream of speaking to a guy like that.' In Buenos Aires, with its long memories of the dictatorship, 'guys like that' did not look menacing in sunglasses purely as a pose. Instead of CVs they carried notches on their guns and scars on their face.

So we moved on hastily to the nearby *cancha* of the Primera C (or fourth division) club, Comunicaciones, set in the grounds of a huge sports club and private high school. A teacher called Enzo sent one of the pupils to show us around, but I needed only one look at the basic ground to see that there was nothing there to detain us. The kid was a sweetie, though. He'd never heard of Manchester United.

Comunicaciones, I assumed, were the club of the post and telegraph company (as is the case with other similarly named clubs in Latin America), and true enough, their nickname was *El Cartero*, the postman. But the club's origins were apparently not quite that simple, so when Enzo said it was a long story we made our excuses and headed back into town for our last engagement of the day. It was now burning-hot. We were downing whole bottles of mineral water in huge gulps.

I had arranged to meet with someone from the Argentinian Football Association to find out more about the deadlines and criteria supposedly being set for stadium improvements. The AFA was like an old gentlemen's club, grand but ghostly, with white leather armchairs and poor lighting. After we had met with my contact in a back office and heard that, confusingly, there were in fact no set deadlines for either making stadiums all-seater or bleacher-free – though the inference was that no one was actually making that public in case the clubs grew complacent – Mariano and I nipped into the association's one-room library. There, half a dozen men sat around a large table, poring over old books and magazines like rabbinical students, watched by a portly, unsmiling librarian. I wanted to read some of the Sacachispas columns written in the late 1940s by Borocotó in the weekly magazine *El Gráfico*, the ones we had been told about earlier in the week. Overhearing our request, one of the old readers approached us. With barely a prompt he launched into a monologue, standing over us like a schoolmaster.

The Evita championships for young boys, he insisted, had not been political. They were social. We had to understand that. He remembered them well because he had been part of the organising committee, nearly half a century earlier. The rules of the competition were aimed at strengthening family ties, he emphasised. They were not political. The Peróns were trying to do good.

After he had finished, Mariano and I spent a happy half-hour ogling covers from old bound editions of *El Gráfico*, both of us glad to be sitting down in the quiet, both becoming inordinately nostalgic about logo-free team strips and inky pages. Then we found a café a few doors down from AFA, where, to Mariano's delight, a group of well-known football referees sat nattering over coffee. Mariano could hardly believe the week he was having. First Pipo Pescador, the television legend of his youth (in whose beautiful *departamento* I was staying), then Cesar Aira, the writer we encountered in that café on the corner of Eva Perón and Carabobo, and now the referees. Best of all, did I not realise the identity of the hectoring old man in the library? Of course I did not.

He was, said Mariano, as if he could hardly believe it himself, none other than Horacio Aielo, one of . . . no, *the* doyen of Argentinian television football commentators. Their equivalent, I guessed, of Kenneth 'they think it's all over' Wolstenholme. Aielo had provided some of the most memorable commentaries of Mariano's youth. Most of all he recalled Aielo's catchphrase. In the early days of football coverage on television, said Mariano, the broadcasters had been keen to draw in audiences other than committed male football fans. So, in his honeyed, rich tones, Aielo would identify a player and then add something like, 'And there he is, to the left of your screen, madam.'

Millions of Argentinian housewives and grandmothers heard Aielo speak to them directly, and were totally charmed. As now was Mariano, and so too was I, by association.

What memories filled our heads as we drove back to Enrique's flat that evening; snatched moments from our own personal histories, of being allowed to stay up late to watch games on black-and-white television sets, of old football strips, of crying when games were lost, of simple mundanities. Mariano mourned the disappearance of his Sacachispas boots, I of my orange Slazenger laceless ball. Where did all that stuff go? Where did all the years go? Would I end up one day in a library lecturing a couple of innocent bystanders about stadiums of old?

'We were trying to do good, you know, making people sit

down at the stadiums and behave. It wasn't political. It was social. You have to understand that.'

Enrique was out when I returned. I fell into the silence of his *departamento* like a desert traveller into an oasis, wanting no more than simple repose and a complete absence of stimulus. No more characters. No more *canchas*. Just a beer from the fridge and a bed. A bed which lay through the door on the right of your screen, madam.

Friday, 23 October. Stadiums Nos. 20 and 21. Tigre and Platense. Too tired for detail now. Best job in the world. Sorest shoulders in Christendom. Tonight Mariano and his wife took me out to a traditional *parrilla* or grill restaurant, where I consumed vast quantities of red meat and red wine and probably bored the pants off their friends because I was aching to talk about something, anything, other than fucking stadiums. And if there is one thing that Argentinians care more about than football it must be red meat. The old *gauchos* could live on nothing but for days. My host Enrique, a small man of exceptionally delicate tastes, told me the other day that he was having to cut down on steaks. I was startled that he even touched them. Now, he said, on doctor's orders, he could only manage maybe one or two a week. A week! I had probably cut down to one or two a year, and I worship faithfully at the altar of meat in all its gories. But, then, in Britain, as we say in restaurants in the wake of the BSE crisis, 'Oh, go on then. Let's go mad and have the T-bone.'

Mariano and I scheduled only two visits for the morning, so that in the afternoon I could go back to River to collect my press ticket for Sunday's Superderby. While I waited for the ticket a hack from Cordoba thrust a tape recorder in my face, and without saying hello, fired questions at me. As an English football writer,

1. What did I think of Argentinian football?
2. What did I think would be the likely outcome of the River vs. Boca match on Sunday?
3. What did I think of President Menem's visit to London that week?

Of course I thought of some brilliant answers, albeit not until a few hours later.

In the morning we drove north, the furthest distance so far

covered, through the comfortable commuter suburb of San Isidro – with its Californian-style high street lined with boutiques, Blockbusters and McDonald's, running parallel with the banks of the Rio de la Plata – to Tigre, or, rather, to the neighbouring suburb of Victoria, where Club Atletico Tigre are based. Their *cancha* did not appear to have a name. Just an address, wouldn't you know it, on the Avenida Presidente Teniente-General Juan Domingo Perón. This man's title was growing longer with every mention.

The sky was so deliciously clear, the riverside air so fresh and the ground so visually appealing that I shot reels of films. Looking at the photographs now I can see pigeons and sea gulls settling on the ground's curving concrete end terrace, on which, ironically, the initials CAT were painted in huge white letters on a blue and red background. A section of the terrace was dedicated in 1981 to a former groundsman, José Noain. In other photographs I can see a modest, French-style concrete stand, dating from 1962, with a vaulted cantilevered roof. Its *Palco de Honor* was dedicated to Mario Piotti, a former president who built the concrete terrace in 1957. Again, that transition from wood to concrete bore such a deep significance, marking as it did the passage from the temporary to the permanent.

Tigre had come to this site in 1936, said an old Tigre *socio* called Mario, who wandered over to chat. Before then they had played on a field situated on the riverside in Tigre. This ground had been quixotically named *La Cancha del Lechero Ahogado,* the Ground of the Drowned Milkman.

Legend had it that once, during their early days at this Ground of the Drowned Milkman, angry Tigre fans had hurled a referee into the river midway through a game. As to whether the poor man had also been a milkman, Mario was uncertain. But he was fairly sure that he hadn't drowned. Instead, he thought, the ground's unusual name was more likely to have referred to the regular floodings that occurred in the area, and to the proximity of the *cancha* to various dairy farms. Whatever, I instantly voted *La Cancha del Lechero Ahogado* as the worthiest winner of the 'Best Name for a Ground' category that I have ever heard, outdoing even Clapton FC's Spotted Dog Ground in London and an old baseball park in Nashville known for some reason as Sulphur Dell.

For forty-one years Tigre were a fixture in the first division.

Nowadays they were all too comfortably ensconced in the second division, with only 2,500 *socios*, and gates of 4–5,000. But Mario assured us that the club were in a comparatively healthy state. Their debt amounted only to $700,000.

But the photographs of Tigre I like the most, looking at them now, the ones which persuade me that, if ever I were to live in Buenos Aires, Tigre would be my sort of club, are those I took of one side of the ground, the one filled, inevitably, by bleachers. A section of these had rotted away completely, revealing a rusting skeleton of steel supports and, behind, an exposed high brick wall painted in white, dividing the ground from the surrounding houses. Tucked under the steel framework and partially covered by the rest of the surviving bleachers lay the dressing-rooms. To get from these on to the pitch the players had to walk along a narrow path through a lovingly cultivated garden, dappled under the striped shade of the wooden planks above. Vines clung to the steelwork and to the back wall. Chairs were set out around an *asado*.

Stadiums have often been likened to gardens and parks: oases of green in the midst of concrete urban jungles. But at Tigre, amid the pristine, low-rise and tree-lined residential streets of Victoria, this corner of verdure and dilapidation seemed to offer the ultimate enchantment. I was, I might even say, in my idea of stadium heaven. In the Ground of the Besotted Groundologer. And I think what really thrilled me most was that luxuriant plants called Elephants' Ears were being encouraged to grow up and up, from the garden below, up through gaps between the bleachers until their leaves emerged in a lush trail of green across the wooden terraces. Some plants had crept higher, popping out through a hoarding at the back of the terrace, on which was advertised the Easy Home Center of Tigre. Two fluffy tufts of greenery adorned the E of Easy. If this represented neglect, it was most artfully done.

Alas, the terrace would hardly survive for long. Soon, though no one seemed sure exactly when, Tigre would be replacing all their spindly, sun-parched wooden bleachers with concrete steps. It was the modern way. It was the mark of progress. But it would kill the garden, and in the process encapsulate all that I dread about stadium modernisation: the eradication of enchantment, the imposition of uniformity, the severance of sport from its natural roots. We may not be stardust, we may not be golden, but why shouldn't we get ourselves back to the garden?

Of course I also knew that the bleachers were unsafe. Mariano and I tried one or two of the bendier ones and had to jump off in fright like giggling schoolgirls. And yet we were still charmed.

Then, as we stood in the shade of the ground's modest entrance hall, which led a short distance from the street directly on to the pitch, a middle-aged woman in a housecoat and slippers approached us, thinking that Mariano and I worked for the club.

Could we tell her when the next home match was? It was not for her, she explained, but for her son. He got so frightened when matches were on. They lived in one of the houses opposite. One afternoon some hooligans had lobbed a chunk of concrete through his bedroom window, showering his bed with glass.

Mariano and I were appalled. The poor little boy. In this apparent haven of tranquillity too. How old was her son, asked Mariano (who has two children of his own).

She told us her son was thirty-four.

Oh. Still, it must have been a shock. Had this happened recently?

Oh yes, she said. About five years ago.

And now, it seemed, every week or so she came to the ground to find out when the next home match was to be played.

Mariano consulted a fixture list on a noticeboard, told her the dates, and for his care and concern received a theatrical '*Ciao*!' and a matronly kiss. I got a peck too, just for listening.

Half an hour later Mariano and I were standing on the new concrete terraces of the first division club, Platense. Their stadium, opened in 1979, was safe, functional and neat. We did not stay long.

Monday, 25 October. Stadiums Nos. 22, 23, 24 and 25.

And so, at last, to our bitter-sweet final day. If this were not a book about stadiums I would happily tell you more of my weekend adventures in Buenos Aires.

Of how on Saturday afternoon I was sprayed with mustard by some Bolivians in the city centre, before being hustled away by *World Soccer*'s veteran Buenos Aires correspondent Eric Weil, who knew a mugger's trick when he saw one. Thanks, Eric.

Of how Enrique hired a chauffeur-driven car on Saturday night and took me along the neon-bathed Avenida Corrientes – where limousines, crowds and theatre queues created a throng like I imagined filled Broadway during the 1930s – and then on to the artists' quarter of San Telmo, to see the tattered banners of the British invasion forces, famously repelled in 1806, now hanging in the Iglesia y Convento de Santo Domingo. It mattered not one jot to Enrique that a society wedding was taking place in the church at the time. To the bemusement of the guests he just marched me up to the back of the choir, then he marched me back again. And then we ended up at an old tango bar run by a friend of his, where we were given the best seats in the house and served endless glasses of champagne. At one point in the middle of the evening's stunning entertainment – of upright sex masquerading as dance, of haunting melodies, and a Japanese *bandoneonista* giving it his all – the compère came on stage and, without warning, announced to the audience that in their midst, in their honoured midst, was a great entertainer and songwriter, and would they please give a warm welcome to . . . Pipo Pescador!

Brimming with unashamed delight, Enrique stood up to bow theatrically and to milk the generous applause, but also to make sure that I could now see proof of just how famous he really was. I of course applauded him wildly, and only partly because he clearly craved the limelight so desperately. He had, after all, been a wonderfully generous host and his *departamento* really was beautiful.

And then, to my drunken consternation, I heard the compère continue, reading from a slip of paper, '. . . *y su amigo, el escritor y periodista de la BBC, señor Simon Eengleez.*'

So now I too had to rise to my feet – unsteadily, I might add – and face members of the audience clapping politely all around me while asking friends out of the corner of their mouths, 'Who the hell is he?'

Nor will I say much about Sunday's Superderby between River Plate and Boca Juniors at *El Monumental*, where I joined nearly 80,000 fanatics for a 0–0 draw which was so tiresome that, despite the constant noise and vibration of the stadium, I found it embarrassingly hard to stay awake.

In fact, so tired had I become that by Monday morning, when Mariano arrived in his beaten-up old Toyota – no doubt pretty saddlesore himself – I could scarcely bring myself to pick up the maps, schedules and my now mustard-stained camera bag. Having tasted some of the joys of the city at the weekend, if Mariano had dared suggest it I could happily have spent our final day together ambling around the city centre. But he didn't, and nor did I, because in truth we were still in thrall to our list and all those still unvisited yellow blobs on Mario's now mightily crumpled map.

It was Monday morning, and back to work.

Although my body ached for our quest to be done, nor could I bear the thought of it ending. Mariano, I suspect, felt the same. A mood of wistful resignation took hold of us both. Tonight we would part, and each return to our own realities. To our lives beyond the list.

Before the weekend, in one of our several 'let's be sensible' reviews of the schedule, Mariano had suggested that we drop off the list several smaller clubs whose *canchas* we now suspected would be hardly more than enclosed fields. These included Lamadrid (near Vélez), which we had somehow missed earlier, Lugano (which we couldn't spot on the map anyway), Los Andes, Colegiales, Claypole, Liniers and Almagro. I remember my lower lip quivering momentarily during these brutal culls, but knew Mariano was right. Sometimes even a hardened *canchólogo* has to know when to stop.

In any case, we were still left with eight remaining stadiums, *canchas*, whatever, on our list for the final day, and we also had to allow time to catch my flight home in the early evening. If we made six out of the eight we'd be lucky. Lucky or reckless.

Our first stop was Lanus, another wonderfully eccentric first-division stadium out in the suburbs, where building work on one stand was in an advanced state. In the car park an old floodlight pylon lay on its side, like a beached whale, making us both, close to, gasp at its enormity.

Oscar emerged to show us around. A round-faced, smiling man, his pride in the club was self-evident as he told us stories from the past. In 1956 Lanus had been dubbed the Globetrotters, because they played like a basketball team. Yet, oddly, the stadium had never been given a name, despite having been opened in 1920. Maybe, said Oscar, when the rebuilding was completed (by which time the capacity would rise to 46,000) they would name the stadium after one of the *socios*. Lanus, it transpired, were big on self-help. When redevelopment began a few years ago, 400 *socios* each donated $200 worth of steel and cement to the club, in return for which they received a signed memorial from the president. Then the club helped the municipality to set up a community bingo game, from which 1 per cent of profits went to the stadium, another 1 per cent to local hospitals, and a third 1 per cent to local firemen. We saw a poster addressed to the Lanus *socios*. It read: 'We have built this stadium together, with order and cleanliness. You have to be involved in this effort. This is your club and your place.'

We also saw how clean the water in the moats looked. Oscar asked us into his office for a drink – he seemed so proud that a visiting journalist should have come to Lanus – and in the heat we were sorely tempted, and felt rotten for being in such a hurry. But time was moving on.

Next came Banfield, in the midst of a discreet, middle-class neighbourhood, where, maddeningly, we found all the stadium gates to be locked. Mariano and I were now starting to get twitchy, looking at our watches. He was saying we wouldn't make it to Quilmes, the home of the city's main brewery, miles away in the deep south of the metropolis. I wanted to stomp my feet and bawl out loud until he relented. Quilmes were one of the great old clubs of Argentinian football. I felt sure their ground would be steeped in history. It was one of the priority stadiums on our list. ''S not fair!' cried a childish voice inside my head.

'All right,' I eventually conceded, trying to stay calm. 'If we can't get into Banfield, how about carrying on up the railway line to Temperley, or cutting off east for a couple of miles to Los Andes? Or maybe we could still make Quilmes if we went now and forgot Dock Sud and Arsenal later.'

Arsenal? Yes, Arsenal. I'll explain later.

Mariano wasn't sure. Quilmes was a hell of a drive, and it was now roasting-hot.

I thought we were about to have our first tiff, when right on cue a man opened the door of the Banfield stadium and cheerily invited us in. He was the *intendente*, the caretaker, a tanned, white-haired and handsome man called Ricardo. If he'd known we were coming he'd have prepared an *asado* for us. Suddenly everyone was being so welcoming on the very day we had no time to indulge.

The all-concrete, 38,000-capacity Estadio Florencio Sola was developed from 1940 onwards, and was now a real mix of open terraces and quirky appurtenances, including an end terrace flanked by viewing towers that had been designed for the press but were clearly in totally the wrong place, which explained why the press no longer used them. Every available wall, facing surface and fitting was painted in green and white. In the immaculate, shrub-lined courtyard, where two lads were tucking into roast chicken and Gatorade, was a relief of a musician called Horacio Alfredo de Angelis. My, what big hands he had.

But Banfield's most illustrious supporter was undoubtedly Eduardo Duhalde, Argentina's vice-president and the Justicialist (or Peronist) Party's candidate tipped for power when Carlos Menem finally stood down in 1999. One piece of pro-Duhalde graffito filled an entire side of the stadium's boundary wall. (In the end Duhalde lost the election. Some said Menem had deliberately sabotaged his campaign, so that he, Menem, could have another crack at the presidency in the subsequent election.)

Menem, Mariano told me as we sped off to the next stadium – not, I now had to accept, Quilmes – was a lifelong River Plate fan, which apparently was not always an asset. In fact, the man was popularly regarded as a bit of a *mufa*, a jinx. Whenever he turned up to watch River, they seemed to lose. The same with the national team (such as for the opening match of the 1990 World Cup, against Cameroon), and even the tennis ace Gabriela Sabatini.

We were getting a little lost and agitated ourselves now; temperature rising and the car engine hotting up . . . heading down side streets, trying to cross the railway line so that we could drive back towards Avellaneda . . . finding our path diverted by 'no left turn' signs or one-way streets. Schoolchildren idled across zebra crossings. Traffic lights turned against us. It was now past mid-day and the minutes were ticking away. If Mariano had stopped there and then and just said '*Basta!* Enough. Let's just stop now before we have an accident or the engine blows,' I would not have blamed him. But then, in a bleak industrial estate near to the docks we saw a long stretch of open road ahead of us and were just getting cooled down in the flowing air when suddenly a hulking great juggernaut pulled out in front and blocked our way completely. Completely! As if the driver had been waiting for our approach.

This was just too much. What could we do but steam silently

in our seats, drumming our fingers against the Toyota's red-hot windowsills while we watched the juggernaut driver attempt an absurdly difficult reversing manoeuvre into the narrow gateway of a warehouse.

Minutes ticked away. Sweat trickled down our foreheads.

We imagined we had become desperadoes in our own road movie, one of those straight-to-video ones from the Seventies, starring Pipo Pescador as the evil trucker who had escaped from gaol a few days earlier, and who was now intent on preventing us, in our dust-covered Pontiac Firebird, from reaching a stash of gold medallions said to have been buried under the pitch of the old San Lorenzo football stadium many moons ago by Alicia and her gang of cut-throats. Coming soon to a cinema nowhere near you: *The Adventures of El Turco and El Canchólogo*.

Still, without success, the juggernaut driver tried to line up his rear end between the warehouse gates.

I told Mariano the only honourable thing for him to do now was to shout 'Duck!' then put his foot down and drive straight under the side of the truck. OK, we'd lose the Toyota's roof and would have to limp to the final three grounds, losing oil, attracting stares along the way, before struggling on to the airport, where the car would finally die on the runway as I sprinted across the melting tarmac to leap on board (with the gold medallions in an old suitcase, of course) just as the aircraft's steps were pulled away. I would then sink into my seat, as planned, next to Goldie Hawn and, as the plane taxied away, see Mariano wave me off with a nonchalant grin as, one by one, the Toyota wheels collapsed, sending hubcaps spinning away in all directions. The credits would then roll as a Ry Cooder slide-guitar kicked in.

But then the juggernaut finally made room for us and we were back on the trail, back in the real world, hysterical, wide-eyed and, oh Jesus, not again, lost in an infinitely depressing wasteland around the docks in a *barrio* called Sarandi. We stopped to ask a kid if he knew the way to the Arsenal Stadium. I couldn't believe I was saying the name like that, there, then.

'Stadium!' he chortled. 'You mean *cancha*.'

'Yeh, yeh, smart arse. Whatever.'

We found the *cancha*, parked the car in a deserted street, prayed for its safety and, inside the clubhouse, found a rotund *intendente* called Nestor.

Arsenal, he explained, were formed in 1957. He was one of the founders. So was Julio Grondona, a son of Sarandi, who was now a senior vice-president of FIFA and president of the Argentinian Football Association. They chose the name simply because they liked it and because Arsenal had been such a great team. When the original Arsenal had won the English premiership the year before, Arsenal of Sarandi had sent a congratulatory telegram. They were still awaiting a reply. I promised I would drum one up on my return to London, and cajoled Nestor into posing for a photograph by a sign showing the club's name. Poor Nestor could barely look towards the camera. The sun was now blinding.

At the time of our visit, Arsenal were second in the second division, behind Banfield. Yet their *cancha* – a collection of flimsy bleachers with a concrete clubhouse – had no name, was in an awful state of disrepair, and had no floodlights. Nestor was a taxi driver, but spent most of his time at the club. This was a tough, working-class area, he told us, in case we hadn't noticed. We had. The fans came from the tower blocks we could see across the canal and the marshes. When he heard we were planning to go to the ground of San Telmo later, he urged caution. 'Don't be seen with your cameras around there,' he warned. 'Very bad place.'

A few miles up the dock road, opposite where grain silos were being pummelled into oblivion by demolition crews, we came to stadium number 25, home of third-division Dock Sud – Southern Dock – another small, barely developed ground forming part of a sports complex. 'We're like a family here,' said a man called Natalio, greeting us with a huge Alsatian straining on a leash. Natalio was of Croatian stock. All Dock Sud's *socios* were immigrants from places like Croatia, Poland and Belarus. That's why they called their modest, dockside ground the Estadio de los Inmigrantes. 'But we're not all poor here,' said Natalio. Not like San Telmo, up the road. They were really tough there, he warned. We shouldn't go, if we had any sense.

In the street outside a man stopped to beg for some coins. He said he needed his fare to get to Quilmes. 'You and me both!' I thought to myself. But too late now. The time had passed. Our movie was near the end.

As we headed tentatively up the road to San Telmo, we found ourselves unexpectedly driving on an overpass which we saw led to the bridge across the Riachuelo and back into the Cap. Fed.

Down to our left, we saw, in an enclave of narrow streets on an isolated peninsular, was a small football ground.

Number 26 on our list. The *cancha* of San Telmo.

Mariano and I exchanged glances, toyed with the idea of looking for a turn-off, thought of the warnings we had been given, thought of the consequences of taking the wrong turn-off, thought of the plot of *Bonfire of the Vanities* and then, seeing the city-centre skyline before us, silhouetted against a cloudless blue sky, we said out loud, almost in unison, 'Fuck it!'

'Fuck it!' we shouted.

Fuck it indeed. Enough was enough. *Basta*! Our quest was over.

Mariano put down his foot and yelped out of his window in sheer elation at the waters below. I banged my fist on the car roof and suddenly felt a huge wave of relief surge through my over-heated body.

Buenos Aires had never looked more beautiful. The river had never smelt so sweet, or the air felt more cool.

Twenty-five grounds from our masterlist of thirty-six, in six days. We had hoped for more, but somehow it felt right not to hit the target. To have done that would have seemed as if we had been trying too hard. So twenty-five it was. More than enough.

From Excursionistas to Los Inmigrantes. We had laughed. We had cried. We had toiled and sweated, and in the process we had found friendship. If I had gone through the week feeling constantly unsure as to why I was undertaking the quest, I harboured no such doubts now.

Never mind the twenty-five stadiums. Mariano and I had had a ball.

At the airport we embraced, and embraced again. And then we embraced for one last time. Tomorrow Mariano would be back in his consulting room. Pipo Pescador was off to Spain with a touring company. And in a day or two I would be back at my desk, wondering if I could face visiting another stadium ever again.

And of course, wouldn't you know it, Goldie Hawn missed the flight.

La Ciudad de los Estadios. Postscript.

Truth be told, it had not been my intention to write so much about my time in Buenos Aires. But after I told my wife all about the trip and about the city and about my time with Mariano she said to me, holding my hands and looking me right in the eye, 'Simon, be honest. You haven't been visiting stadiums at all, have you.'

'What do you mean?' I countered. 'Not visiting stadiums! We got to twenty-five of them in six days.'

She said, 'No, no, no. Forget the stadiums. Don't you see what you've been through? It's obvious. You've been in therapy all week.'

In therapy? Me? Now it was my turn to say 'No, no, no.' All right, I gabbled, so Mariano happens to have been a psychoanalyst. But that didn't mean anything. We just happened to get on well. I mean, I . . . I don't go in for therapy, at least not for myself. Why would I need therapy? The idea was absurd. I just write about stadiums.

Honestly!

But over the ensuing days I started to think of all the hours, as we drove hundreds of miles around the city, that Mariano had listened to me chuntering away, going on and on about the nature of my work, my obsession, and my cries for freedom, for freedom from information. And I realised that my wife was absolutely right. And, more than that, maybe the therapy had worked. A little.

All right. Maybe a lot.

So now that I'm done, I just want to say thank you again to the friends who led me into my week's therapy. Thanks to you I can now move on. *Gracias*, dear Mario, for the wonderful map of Buenos Aires you bought for me, all those years ago, the map that started it all and which stretched from one side of the bed to the other and which is now gracefully retired, yellow blobs and all, to my filing cabinet.

Gracias, too, to Buenos Aires, the world's finest *ciudad de los estadios*. Truly, you did not let me down. You were everything I had hoped for, and I will go back to see more of you. I promise.

And *gracias*, Enrique, for being Pipo Pescador, the weaver of dreams and the guardian of childhood fancies.

But most of all, *gracias*, Mariano. *La pasamos de primera*. We had the bestest of times, did we not? For that one week, I swear, we really did have the best jobs in the world.

14
THIRTY THOUSAND FEET

We were flying over Europe on the way back from somewhere. I honestly don't remember where. I do recall, though, that it was an exceptionally clear day, with few clouds around and gorgeous sunlight reflecting off the smooth metallic surface of the aeroplane's wings.

I had been gazing out of the window for some time, taking in the view, enjoying the Alps and the forests and rivers below. Always the spectator. I can't understand people who, when they have the opportunity, don't look out of aeroplane windows when the light is so perfect. For thousands of years man has yearned to fly, and yet now that our generation has been blessed with this extraordinary facility most people still seem to find their newspapers or books more interesting than the awesome sights to be seen beyond the window. More interesting than looking down on our own planet? I don't think so.

Anyway, at one point my wife yawned as she unwound from her sleeping position and asked if I knew where we were. So I looked again out of the window, looked down at the ground miles below, and after a few seconds of adjusting my eyes I said to her, 'We're just passing over Frankfurt.'

At that very moment the pilot's voice sounded out over the cabin speakers and said something like, 'Ladies and gentlemen, we are now cruising at an altitude of 30,000 feet and if you look out of the right-hand side of the aircraft you can see that we are now flying over Frankfurt.'

'Hey, how on earth did you know that?' asked my wife, wearily, though she already knew the answer, of course.

Even from the air, even from an altitude of 30,000 feet I could not only pick out the shape of a stadium down below, but, what's more, I could identify it. Even from thirty bloody thousand feet up in the air.

Now I ask you. What would you have said to yourself if you had been in my shoes at that moment? How would you have reacted? Especially as this was not the first time this had happened, if not flying over Frankfurt then certainly over La Coruna in Spain, another time over Oldham in England, and once over Phoenix, in Arizona.

So what would you have said?

If you had any sense you would not have said to yourself, 'Gosh, aren't I clever. I should go on *Mastermind*.' If you had any sense at all you'd have thought, 'Right, that's it. Enough. It really is time to move on.'

Time to move on. If you were at all *muy listo*, that is exactly what you should have said.

Did I mention, though, that there may be plans to rebuild the stadium in Frankfurt?